Secondary Education in Modern India

(1800 – 2022)

Dr V.B. Shastry

DEDICATION

This book is dedicated to all the Secondary School Teachers who gave their to- day for the bright tomorrow of the posterity.

I dedicate it to my revered father Late Vedula Ramamurty, B.A.,B. Ed. (1904-1951), who had served as a secondary school teacher from 1925 to 1951 in the districts of Rayagada and Koraput at a time when these districts totally lacked facilities of communication, health and education. A spirit of adventure and deep devotion to the cause of education inspired these pioneer teachers to work under the most inhospitable conditions in such an extremely backward area.

The book is also dedicated to my loving mother late Mahalaxmi Devi (1914 to 2007), who was a witness to the steady expansion of secondary education from two high schools in late 1920s to more than 260 high schools by 2007, in the undivided Koraput district as her husband, two sons, one daughter-in-law and two daughters had worked as secondary school teachers in this region.

– Dr. V.B. Shastry

TABLE OF CONTENTS

ACKNOWLEDGEMENT

I convey my respectful gratitude to Professor Baidyanath Rath, M.A. (Patna), D.Ed.(Patna), M.A.(London) the Principal, Radhanath Training College, Cuttack who, as my teacher, instilled in me a deep abiding love for History of Education.

I am grateful to the authorities of the Directorates of Secondary Education and Higher Education, Board of Secondary Education, Orissa, Council of Higher Secondary Education, Orissa for supplying data relating to their organizations.

I am thankful to my two grandsons-Mr. Aditya Menon and Mr. Naman Shastry, who provided me peace and happiness while silently signaling that my time is running out. I thank Cdr. T. Ranjith Sundaran for helping me in a variety of ways. I convey my thanks to Mrs. Tanushree Shastry and Mrs. Kumkum Menon for their constant support and encouragement. Thanks are conveyed to Dr. V.B. Shastry for his endeavour in getting the book see the light of the day.

I convey my thanks to my learned colleagues Mr. Braja Kishore Patnaik, Dr. Bharati Mohapatra, Dr. Meenaketan Pathy, Dr. Rama Chandra Padhi, Dr. Radha Kant Rath, Dr. Bala Krushna Prahraj, Dr. Kishori Das and Dr. Digaraj Brahma, for their constant goading and continuing help in completing this work.

I convey my gratitude to Sri Nirakar Chand, M.A, Dr. Bharati Nath and Sri Aniruddha Rout for all their help. I am also thankful to my friends, Mr. M. S.. N. Murthy, M.A. and Mr. Balunkeswar Mishra for the unforgettable help and encouragement.

– Dr. V.B. Shastry

ABOUT THE AUTHOR

Dr. V. B. Shastry (b.1938) has wide teaching experience in the field of education right from the K.G. level to the post-doctoral level. He is an M.A. in History (first class 2nd rank), M.Ed. (Goldmedalist). Ph.D (History of Education) from the Utkal University. He obtained the Diploma in Educational Administration from the Birmingham University (U.K.) on a Commonwealth Fellowship. He has guided 14 Ph.D.s and a D.Litt. in Education; two Ph.D.s in Home Science; and a Ph.D in English. He has more than 200 publications to his credit. He was formerly the Director, Centre for Adult, Continuing Education and Extension Programmes; Director, UGC Academic Staff College; and Director, Population Education Centre of the Utkal University. He was the Principal of two Institutes of Advanced Studies in Education, Berhampur and Cuttack. He is presently residing at N-1-61/A, POIRC Village, Bhubaneswar-751 015. and can be contacted through Tel. +91-674-2558024.

PREFACE

This is the story of secondary education in India right from its faint faltering beginnings in the early decades of the 19th century up to the first decade of the 21" century, as it steadily unfolded itself successively readjusting itself to the changing demands of the time-spirit or zeitgeist. It is the story of the social reflections in secondary education. The British came to India; conquered it; ruled it for almost two centuries; and finally left its shores for good in 1947. The confrontation of East and the West was evident in the early decades of the colonial rules; and the compromise after 1947. The imported imposed instructional system implanted during the colonial times seems to be robustly thriving during the six decades after independence (1947 to 2007). English continues to be the official language of India along with Hindi; and is the medium of instruction in all spheres of professional, technical and higher education. It is the medium of instruction in all the public schools, central schools, etc. The enigmatic love-hate relationship baffles the academic analysts. The colonial legacy looms large on the educational horizon with minor marginal cosmetic changes Independent India failed to evolve a nationalistic ethnic educational ethos. The top educational administrators of post-independent India had thoroughly been indoctrinated and brainwashed to appreciate the western educational system and denigrate the Indian cultural approach during their long stint in the colonial climate; and they were afraid to effect radical changes and to explore innovative educational alternatives relevant for a renascent nation that had solemnly decided to travel on the path of democracy, secularism, and egalitarianism to usher in development at a rapid pace. Democracy and planned economy demand a paradigm shift in education; and that challenge was never faced with real seriousness. The lack of a missionary real to reform and restructure the irrelevant educational hegemony of the past has generated cascading social problems.

The creation of States on the linguistic basis created problems of territorial readjustment. New districts were created and some old ones vanished. New place names replaced the old. Introduction of the decimal system in currency, weights and messures and distances compelled the rewriting of text-books especially in mathematics, geography, etc. The old date-bases required to be realigned, re-adjusted and re-written. Attempts have been made to present the old currency statements in rupees, annas and pies in the new decimal system, so that the present generation can comprehend the past.

Some historical documents have refreshing relevance even for the present times. The hierarchically articulated educational system and the grant-in-aid system continue to hold their sway because they are useful administrative strategies. The grant-in-aid system continues to be the bed-rock of financing education. The extra-ordinary emphasis accorded to elementary education by the Hunter Commission of 1882 is being implemented with real rigour only after 1990. The Calcutta University (Sadler)) Commission of 1917 had very categorically recommended the rolling back of the Intermediate classes to the secondary school; and it is under active implementation in the post-NPE, 1986 years. Revisiting history sharpens our intellectual insights

All the noteworthy educational policy documents of India have been critically examined with reference to secondary education. The operational realities have been stated with reference to the Orissa state, and it is needless to state that comprehensive documentation of each and every state is well nigh impossible. It is an exemplar study, and it can be replicated with reference to the other states of India. Attempts have been made to demonstrate how a holistic picture of a state can be portrayed on the basis of the data dispersed in twenty-seven parts viz.,

Madras Presidency, Bengal Presidency (later Bihar & Orissa Province), the Central Provinces and of the twenty four feudatory states ruled by their respective native chiefs. It is based mainly on government records and so may read like a neutrally-tinted court chronicle.

The author is wholly responsible for the opinions and comments. He is also responsible for linguistic mistakes, if any. Portrayal of a holistic state-picture with the backdrop of all India developments in the field of secondary education may inspire researchers to attempt such studies of other States of India.

– Dr. V.B. Shastry

CHAPTER-1

SECONDARY EDUCATION SUBSTANCE & SYSTEMS

HIGHLIGHTS

- Importance of Historical Insights
- Criticality of Secondary Education
- Meaning of Secondary Education
- Secondary Education in U.K., U.S.A., U.S.S.R., France, Germany, China andJapan.
- Aims
- Secondary Education in India

Present day educational problems, policies, programmes, perspectives and predicaments have their roots buried in the forgotten antiquity. The present can be understood through careful, critical objective study of the past. Sir Winston Churchill had aptly remarked, "The further back you can look, the further forward you can see". Incisive historical introspection can assist in having ideational clarity and inspire us to forge ahead avoiding the mistakes of the foregone days. Educationists of the earlier times have left behind a rich legacy of their experiences which have high relevance even to-day. The study of the happenings of secondary education would stimulate a sense of professional pride and commitment among the teachers. The educational administrators stand to benefit as it would acquaint them with profound pedagogic thoughts of past practitioners and equip them with intellectual insights to take the right decisions with greater ease on the basis of historical precedents. The past of our present secondary education is highly interesting.

Secondary education is second to none of the other stages of education. Its profound and pervasive influence and importance is universally acknowledged. Lyndon B. Johnson, the President of the United State of America from 1963 to 1969, had very forcefully highlighted its importance and stated, "The secondary school is the keystone of American Education, for millions of our young people it lies on the threshold of higher learning, for millions more it is the pathway to adult life. It is terminal for many and is preparatory education for a few". It holds the golden master-key for upward mobility in every sphere of life. The secondary school years of the youth are rightly considered as constituting the *make or break* period of life[1]. The focused educational experiences of the secondary schools shape the character, personality and outlook of the adolescents to a very great extent.

---

1   UNESCO Institute of Education, *Youth and the Changing Secondary School'* IBE, Hamburg, 1961, p. 27.

According to the UNESCO, "education, provided to the adolescents of the age group 14 years to 19 years is the secondary education"[2]. Secondary educations succeeds elementary education and precedes higher or tertiary education and is sandwiched between these two stages of education. It builds upon the academic foundations laid at the stage of basic education, "... after theelementary tools of learning have been acquired and which can lead on to further general education"[3]. It's duration, depth and direction depend upon the quality of the two stages of education between which it is positioned. The quality of academic preparation provided at the primary stageand the emerging educational needs of a new world order engulfed in the explosion of knowledge determine its aims, objectives, processes, curricular offerings and procedures of evaluation. The Hadow Report entitled *'Education of the Adolescents'(1926)* had the right psychological perspective when it stated that *secondary education is education for the adolescents* as elementary education is education *for the children* and higher education is education^ *the adults*. It is the "Education of the young people... it covers the intermediate stage between dependent childhood and independent adulthood"[4]. It is the end of the road for the majority and entrance to the echelons of higher education for the few privileged, intellectually or socio-economically.

The roots of secondary education that developed in Europe and England can be traced back to the twelfth century. It started as a trickle in India in the first five decades of the nineteenth century. It was an imported imposed instructional system totally alien to the academic tradition of India. Very often Macaulay, Bentinck, Hardinge and their tribe are castigated in the most vitriolic and violent language for imposing English educational system. Historical data completely confirms that

---

2   UNESCO, *World Survey of Education, III: Secondary Education*, Paris, UNISCO, 1961.

3   Ibid, p. 67

4   Hadow Report or "Report of the Consultative Committee of the Board of Education", London, 1926.

it is Indians themselves who willingly welcomed the new system of secondary education for a variety of reasons. Secondary education planted by the British in India really developed by leaps and bounds only after it attained independence. Secondary education is prolonged basic education and it assures a safer and more secure life for those who have it. According to Emile Durkheim "the origins of different types of secondary schools lie in the arts faculties of medieval universities. These faculties were set up to prepare entrance to other faculties, particularly law and theology"[5]. The education of the adolescents is a matter of prime national concern. *Education for All* has borne fruits; and its cascading compulsion is secondary education. Quantitative expansion has adversely affected the quality. Rupert Maclean opines, "However, as access to secondary education has expanded, its overall quality has often been in decline as resources have been stretched thin and system has become more inefficient"[6].

In most of the countries, it commences at about the age of twelve years and may continue up to the age of 19. Professor R. H. Dave had summed up the emerging trend thus, "During the past few decades a large number of developed countries have already extended the age of free and compulsory education. A developing nationlike Venezuela has extended compulsory education up to class IX. The pace of change will, of course, vary from country to country and region to region, but the overall trend indicates massive expansion and eventual universalisation of secondary education is abundantly clear"[7]. During the six decades of independence from 1947 to 2007, India has exponentially extended the network of secondary schools and in 2006 the Hon'ble Minister of Education announced in the Parliament that Government of India

---

5   Emile Durkheim, Moral Education, Paris Quoted by Cecika Braslavskes in the Editorial of Prospects,. XXXI, March 2001, p. 5.

6   Rupert Murdoch, "Overview: Secondary Education at the Crossroads". Prospects, XXXI, UNESCO, p. 39

7   R. N. Dave, "Secondary Education in the 21st Century", COBSE, New Delhi. Prospects, XXXI, UNESCO, p. 39

is seriously seized with the problem of universalisation of secondary education. There is no international uniformity of duration, aims, approaches, content and other facets of secondary education. It eludes precise definition. According to Prof. S. N. Saraf, "It is not even clear where the stage of secondary education begins, whether it is after the first five years of primary school or after the VIIth or VIIIth standard"[8]. In this connection, the pertinent and poignant observation of Prof. Buell needs to be deeply reflected upon. He says, "If the characteristics and needs of early adolescents are to be considered seriously, the junior high school, which includes grades 7, 8 and 9 should be provided for pupils at this age level. If there are not enough pupils to organize a junior high school with these three grades, then a six year secondary school should be provided."[9]

The secondary schools have different names in different countries. In U. K. there are *'public schools'* for the privileged; *'grammar schools'* for the intellectually gifted and industrious children who could successfully passthe "11 + Examination"; and *'secondary modern schools'* for the under-privileged.

The hidden caste-system of the English society is fully reflected in its secondary education system. The democratic ethos, the egalitarian philosophy and the developments abroad have constrained the English to come forth with the concept of a *"Comprehensive Secondary School'*. The old order persists and the comprehensive schools are expanding. The duration of the secondary education is of seven years from 12+ to 18+ years of age.

Grammar Schools of U. K. provide secondary education to the bright children who pass the 11+ examination. They are schools which admit

---

8   S. N. Saraf, Secondary Education in the Rural Areas in N.C.E.RTs. Fourth year Book of Education, New Delhi, NCERT, 1973, p. 227.

9   Clayton E. Buell., "What Grades in the Junior High School ? Reprinted in "The changing secondary school curricular tT edited by William M. Alexander, Holt, Rinehart and Winston, N. Y. 1967, pp. 56 to 59.

students on the basis of ability. They are selective in their admissions. In Greek *'grammatike techne'* means the 'art of letters'. These schools were promoting the study of Greek and Latin aspreparation for admission to colleges and universities. It is a preparatory school for higher learning. They maintain high standards of scholarship. They are all independent institutions free from governmental control.

Public Schools are of the rich, by the rich and for the rich. They cater to the needs of the aristocracy. The heads of these schools are members of the Headmasters' Conference, in case of boys' schools; and of Governing Bodies Association, in case of girls' schools. These schools are regulated by the Board of Governors of their own school; and none else can interfere in their functioning. Personality development and promotion of qualities of leadership are the two major commitments of these schools. It is the students who mainly maintain discipline in these schools; and needless to say that, they do uphold and maintain the highest standards in this respect.

Secondary Modern Schools are non-selective schools established in England and Wales by the Education Act of 1944. They are open for all; and access to secondary education for the common man is provided by these schools. A *Comprehensive School* is, "one which is intended to cater all types of secondary education for all the children in a given area", as per the instructions contained in Circular No.144 dated the 16th June, 1947 of the Ministry of Education. In 1965, the Department of Education and Science directed the Local Education Authorities to introduce the system of 'Comprehensive Schools' in place of the selective and specialized secondary schools like the 'grammar', 'technical','secondary modern' etc. But the Government can only advise and goad; it cannot compel. This comprehensive approach to secondary education eliminates labeling at too early an age and is more in tune with the democratic spirit of the times. In it there is built-in flexibility so that children can switch-over from one stream to the other. The hidden educational apartheid perpetuated by public schools and grammar schools is expected to slowly vanish. It purports to provide a healthy educational environment for the all-round development of all the children. India needs to learn much from this comprehensive approach to secondary education of U. K.

Sir Geoffrey Crowther, the eminent economist, was the Chairman of the Minister of Education's Central Advisory Council. This Council reviewed the educational provision available for the children in the age group 15 to 18. The Crowther Report entitled "15 to 18" was published in 1959. It recommended the raising of school leaving age (ROSLA). It strongly advocate *"education in depth"* and specialization to be commenced at the secondary stage. It laid emphasis on the understanding of the scientific methodology by the students of the humanities and arts subjects. TheNewsom Report entitled *"Half our future"* was published in 1963. It exhorted that *'exacting standards'* should be expected in the last stage of secondary education.

In the United State of America there are *Junior High Schools* which facilitate transition from the elementary school to the *Senior High Schools*. The Junior High School provides four years education after eight years of elementary education, and has grades 8, 9, 10 & 11. There are also *five-year High Schools* with grades 8, 9, 10, 11 & 12. There *are Junior Colleges* also known as *Community Colleges* which provide secondary education of a wide range for two years. There are *'2-Year Junior College/*and *'Branch Junior Colleges'* attached to colleges. Flexibility, experimentation, and continuous reorganization are the basic characteristics of the American secondary school system. They constantly monitor the developments taking place all over the world, and reform their system so that it is globally competitive.

The "Cardinal Principles of Secondary Education" have deeply influenced the objectives of secondary education of U.S.A in the post-war years. They are:

    i.   Safeguarding and promoting health.

   ii.   Increasing the proficiency in fundamental processes more effectively.

   iii.   Building right attitudes towards home responsibilities.
   iv.   Developing an effective programme of vocational guidance.
    v.   Providing civic education so that the individual may well act his part as a member ofthe neighborhood, city, state and nation and understand international problems.
   vi.   Training in the worthy use of leisure.
  vii.   Developing ethical character through wise selection of content and methods of instruction, social contacts and opportunities for developing a sense of personal responsibility, spirit of service and principles of democracy."[10]

"The Commission on Life Adjustment Education"[11] added the following objectives to the Cardinal Principles:

- "Education for enabling one to understand the basic rules of learning.
- Education for developing the spirit of appreciation of beauty.
- Education for understanding the significance and method of science.
- Education for moral development and development of mental health."

In France, it is of 7 to 8 years duration. The first four years of secondary education is imparted in *Colleges* and the last three years in the *Ibycees'*. At the end of the course the *baccalaureate diploma* is awarded.

In Germany the lower secondary school is called the *'Realschule'*. It is of 6 yearsduration and classes V to X belong to this school. The *'Gymnasium''* is realschule plus grades XI & XII. It is the higher secondary school of Germany.

---

10   National Association of Education, Cardinal Principles of Secondary Education, Bulletin No. 35, U. S. Bureau of Education, Washington D. C. 1918.

11   U. S. Govt. Report on Life Adjustment Education, Washington D C. 1947.

The objectives of Japanese secondary education are to provide, "...basic knowledge and vocational skills necessary in a society, an attitude of respect for labour, and the ability to select one's own future career"[12]. Here lies the secret of Japan's astounding success in every sphere of technical advancement. The lower secondary school called *Chugakko* are of three years duration and provide education to children of the age group 12+ to 14+ or 15+. The upper secondary schooling is of three years duration for children of the age group 14+ or 15+ to 16+ or 17+ years of age. It is known as *'Kotagakkd"*. The course can be completed through *day* or *evening* or *correspondence courses*. These are 'general' and 'specialised' secondary schools.

Russia i.e. U. S. S. R. has different types of secondary schools. *Incomplete secondary schools provide* education to the age group 11+ to 15+ or 16+ from grade IV to grade VIII. *General and Polytechnical schools* provide secondary education from 15+ or 16+ to 17+ or 18+ years of three years duration. *Technical and Special Secondary* Schools provide technical or special education of 3 or 4 years duration. *Vocational Secondary Schools* provide vocational or technical education, the duration of which varies from one year to three years. *Evening and shift secondary schools* provide secondary education during the spare time especially to workers. *Correspondence Secondary Education* is for those who cannot attend institutional courses.

Russia is wedded to the socialistic philosophy. It aims and approaches to secondary education are expectedly and naturally different. The aims are expected to be fulfilled by the end of secondary education. The secondary school leavers are expected to:

- Understand one's own identity.
- Help the school.
- Be bold and principled to perform the social duties.

---

12 K. G. Larson & M. R. Karpas, Effective Secondary School Discipline, Prentice Hall Inc, Boston 1963, p. 19.

- Assist the society in times of disasters, calamities and other situations of emergency.
- Deeply love the country.
- Remember with gratitude the sacrifices of the national martyrs.
- Have deep love and concern for all children all over the world.
- Be disciplined, courteous and diligent.
- Imbibe an abiding love for work.
- Respect and love national property.
- Love nature.

Russia believes in a classless society. It subscribes to the pedagogic principles thatlearning should be through understanding, thatconceptual clarity is essentialand that abstract concepts should be completely comprehended; and that construction of theoretical knowledge must begin at this stage. Its approach to secondary education is comprehensive; and has high technical and professional orientation.

In China, *Junior Secondary Schools* provide three to four years of instruction after five or six years of elementary education. There are *Comprehensive Nine-year schools* which provide both the elementary and junior secondary education. The *Senior Secondary Schools* provide schooling of four years after nine years of education in the elementary and junior secondary schools. Vocational and professional education is incorporated and in-built into the secondary education.

India had a rich, legacy of education. Radhakumud Mookerji's classic *Ancient Indian Education* is the richest authoritative source relating to immemorial Indian education. It mentions only the higher education and the preceding preparatory education. The Islamic approach was analogous to the earlier educational system. The *madrasas* provided primary education; *makatabs* higher elementary education and the *Jamias* higher education. It is the British colonial administration that established an articulated and graded educational system. The "High Schools" prepared students for the Junior Scholarship and Senior Scholarship examinations equivalent to the secondary school and higher secondary school levels up to 1858. The scholarship examinations both senior and junior were abolished with the establishment of the Universities of Calcutta, Madras and Bombay in 1857.

In India, secondary education is of two years duration provided in classes IX and X of a "High School" after 8 years of elementary education. A two-year higher secondary course is provided in "Higher Secondary Schools" or "Junior Colleges".

Secondary education builds upon the academic intellectual achievement provided in the elementary schools. It reinforces the learning skills and lays the firm foundations for professional proficiency and occupational expertise. It is considered as 'a stage of consolidation'. Higher thinking processes are nurtured at this stage.

Secondary education was viewed as a sub-system serving the needs of the higher education system. The examination at the end of the high school was conducted by the universities. The Hunter Commission (1882) advocated an independent terminal Secondary School Leaving Course which was implemented only in the Madras Presidency. Modern secondary education is more than 175 years old. It presents a fascinating story. The past of our present secondary education is presented on the basis of carefully researched data.

Secondary education tries to prepare students fit to enter higher education, and"is very sensitive to the requirements real or fancied, of colleges"[13]. It is a major national concern. It "has evolved from being the limited preserve of a few into a vast system serving the many".[14]

Classes VI and VII were considered to be *junior secondary classes* from 1855 to 1966. The Indian Education Commission (1964-66) in its scheme of a Ten-year School has put forth the idea of eight years of elementary schooling followed by two years of secondary education enriched by a 2-year higher secondary course leading to the first degree

---

13   S. N. Mukherjee, Secondary Education in India, 1972, Orient Longman, P. Cover Flap-introduction. Ibid. p. I

of three year's duration. This is commonly known as the "10+2+3" system of education. Psychological needs and developmental tasks of children and early adolescents differ and differ greatly. Clubbing these two groups in *an 8 years elementary school* is a philosophical mistake and a pedagogical blunder. Classes VI, VII and VIII could have become the junior secondary school classes, IX and X could have constituted the secondary classes, and classes XI and XII constituting the higher secondary classes. These classes for the adolescents could have been amalgamated, so that the limited resources of the school could have been used optimally and wasteful duplication avoided. Fragmenting the adolescent population into three divisions is not academically sound and cannot be explained away on the grounds of administrative convenience. The concept of *'basic education'* may extend up to the higher secondary classes, but the *concept of primary education should be limited to education of the children.*

Vocationalisation of secondary education is a grand failure in India. The technical, industrial, agricultural high schools along with the Post-Basic schools have died. The secondary schools have lost classes VI, VII and VIII to elementary education. Class XI was abolished due to the introduction of the Ten-year schooling. The secondary school is left with only two classes—classes IX and X in the high schools. Classes XI & XII have co-existed as the organic preparatory course for the first degree in the college system for the last 150 years and these classes are in no mood to forsake their age-old halo of higher education. The 'old six-year high school' with classes VI, VII, VIII, IX, X, & XI has died.

The comprehensive secondary schools should be big enough to optimally utilize the resources of the school. But it should not be too big to become over crowded. Prof. Buell feels, "these schools are best in some systems".

India is on the threshold of 'Secondary Education for All'. Secondary educationhas come to be generally considered as the basic education. As India is wedded to the democratic way of life the increasing popular demand can never be ignored and access to this stage of education has to be augmented - willingly or unwillingly. It is a democratic demand that must be met.

There is evident quality-divide between rural and urban India; and this divide must be eliminated. Rural India too has a claim for quality secondary education. The holding capacity of the secondary schools in rural areas, slums, and those for the Scheduled Tribes and Castes is low. The mind-boggling drop-out rates need to be arrested if future social tensions have to be pre-empted. Gender disparities at the secondary school level are deeply disturbing. Women are half the fortune of this nation. India can ill afford to suffer from gender paralysis in education.

The management of secondary education is in a poor state. The whims of the politicians and the wisdom of the generalist bureaucrats have precedence over the opinion of educationists of eminence with expertise, erudition and long experience who have steadily been marginalized. Regular teachers are not employed and contractual para-teachers manage the academic show. The Delor's report remarks. "Good schools require good teachers". This has not been understood. For curricular revisions the governments awaits the promptings of the NCERT No curriculum framework (1988 or 2000 or 2005) has been implemented with thoroughness and sincerity. "Computers and ICT" are still a slogan for most of the secondary schools. Secondary education is haunted by financial crunches. Teacher Training Institutes are grossly under staffed and under-equipped; and consequently the quality of teacher education is degenerating. Community support is not forthcoming. The only prayer for the secondary school teachers, students and administrators seems to be, "Amidst this encircling gloom, lead thou me on, lead kindly light." Provocatively it is said, perhaps it might be time to 'abolish' secondary education altogether as a model, and to set up instead a new type of education system for young people, which would be better suited to their need for more years of basic education to impart the key skills required in the twenty-first century[14]. Gandhiji offered a relevant viable alternative — the Basic Education — and we dumped it in the dustbin. Secondary education has emerged as an unavoidable education bereft of definite objectives, a desirable curriculum and devoted teachers. We are facing an uncertain future on the basis of the colonial legacy which we do not have the courage to depart from. It is time to pause and ponder whether to have or havenot the present structure, substance and education.standards of this single-track secondary

---

14   UNESCO, Prospects, XXXI, p. 5

CHAPTER-2

OLD ORDER CHANGES (1835-1854)

HIGHLIGHTS

- Earliest Beginnings
- India Bill, 1813
- Hindoo College, 1816
- General Committee of Public Instruction, 1823
- Macaulay's Minutes, 1835
- Pooree Free Academy
- Pioneering Secondary Schools
- Early Evolution of Educational Administration

SECTION I

EARLIEST BEGINNINGS

A brief account of the earliest beginnings of Western Education in India would provide the necessary backdrop to the understanding of educational developments during the British rule. The officials of the East India Company have referred to the existence of the following four types of native education, viz: *instructions provided by scholarly Brahmins to their disciples; the seats of Sanskrit learning known as "Tols"; centers of Islamic learning known as Maktabs and Madrisas; and large number of village schools where indigenous education was imparted.* The indigenous schools were numerous throughout India. A detailed description of indigenous education in Bengal can be gleaned in the exhaustive and excellent reports of Mr. William Adam. He had described the indigenous education of "Orissa Proper" in Section III of his Report of 1835. These schools provided "elementary education to the trading classes and to the children of the petty landholders and well-to-do families among the cultivators."[15] They were supported by the villagers themselves and received no governmental assistance.

East India Company seized power from the rulers of Delhi. It continued to perform exactly the same functions as its predecessors. The endowments bestowed by the erstwhile Mughal rulers on educational institution were respected and continued. Its earliest educational efforts were to establish colleges of Sanskrit and Mohammedan learning of the old types. The *Calcutta Madrissa* was established in 1781 by Warren Hastings (1732 to 1818), the first Governor-General of Bengal (1774-85).

---

15   C. D. Maclean, Manual of Administration of the Madras Presidency, 1885

It is the first educational institution in India established by the East India Company. In 1792, the *Sanskrit College* was founded at Benaras (now Varanasi) by Jonathan Duncan and it was categorically stated that, "the discipline of the college was to be conformable in all respects to *Dharma Shastra* in the chapter on education. The scholars were to be examined four times a year in the presence of the Resident, in all such parts of knowledge as are not held too sacred to be discussed in the presence of any but Brahmins.

The Charter of the East India Company was placed before the British Parliament for its renewal in 1813. Mr. R. P. Smith, who had worked as Advocate-General at Calcutta under the East India Company prior to his return to England, had become a member of the British parliament. He proposed that "a lakh of rupees should beappropriated to the revival and promotion of theliterature and the encouragement of the learned natives of India and for the introduction and promotion of a knowledge of the sciences among the inhabitants of the British territorial acquisition." It was passed and formed part of the India Bill, 1813. This provision of India Bill, 1813 was interpreted, both in England and in India, to apply chiefly to the revival and encouragement of Hindu and Mohammedan literature. The grant was understood to be intended primarily, though not exclusively, for that object. The fund was not utilized for ten years.

When Lord Moira (later Lord Hastings) was the Governor-General of Bengal (1813-23), education received a fillip for the first time. Lady Hastings established a school at Barrackpore Park. She also compiled treatises for the use of scholars. Missionaries like Mr. May, Mr. Carey and his colleagues established a large number of vernacular schools in the neighborhood of Calcutta. These schools received encouragement not only from the public but also from the government. He penned a Minute on Judicial Administration of the Bengal Presidency on 2nd October, 1815. In it he made incidental reference to the sad state of indigenous education in India and emphasized the need for improving it. He wrote:

"The humble but valuable class of village school masters claims the first place in this discussion. These men teach the first rudiments of reading, writing and arithmetic for a trifling stipend which is within reach of any man's means, and the instruction which they are capable of imparting suffices for the village zameendar, the village accountant and the village shop-keeper"[16].

He strongly advocated the advancement of elementary education among the Hindus and Muhammedans. He categorically stated that native higher education was almost dead, where there no longer remain any embers capable of being fanned into life. According to Lord Moira, native higher education was dead and what it required was a neat burial. The Sanskrit College at Banaras was referred to as University of Benaras by Lord Moira. He was deeply dissatisfied and dismally disgusted with its academic performance. He forwarded his considered opinion about this institution to the Court of Directors of the East India Company in London and stated that any money set apart for the advancement of education would be much more expediently applied in the improvement of schools, than in gift to seminaries of higher degree. Indian intellectuals like Raja Rammohan Roy could sense the changing course of winds and stoutly demanded new education suited to the emerging needs of the changing times.

The 18th century was coming to a close. The dawn of 19th century constrained Indian intellectuals of high standing to think of a new education better suited to the demands of the new century. Mr. David Hare (1775-1842), the watchmaker, was the propelling force; and Raja Rammohan Roy (1772-1833) was the vocal spokesperson. Raja Rammohan Roy was a social reformer and a scholar of eminence. He had worked for the abolition of *Sati* (burning of the living wife with her dead husband on the same pyre), child marriage and *Purdah* (hiding of women behind the screens). He had founded the Bramho Samaj. Due

---

16   H. Sharp, Selections from Educational Records Vol I, Calcutta, Govt Press, p. 24.

to the sustained and sincere efforts of David Hare and Raja Rammohan Roy, the Calcutta Hindoo College was established at Calcutta in 1816. Lord Moira was its first Patron. The studies in this college included the works of Locke, Adam Smith, Shakespeare, Milton, etc. The Hindoo College accorded importance to Bengali, the mother tongue of millions of Bangalees, in preferences to Sanskrit, the classical language, which had dominated the educational scenario for centuries. It also taught modern Western thought and English and put into practice Hare's mission of "*'uncompromising modernism'*". This paradigm shift in the medium of instruction from classical languages to modern Indian and European languages "was the first serious blow aimed at Oriental classical learning"[17]

The Hindoo College, Calcutta was the first window to Western thought and literature for the Indians. Mr. Chaplin, Commissioner of the Deccan, noticed that the Peshwa was distributing large sums of money every year among highly scholarly Brahmins of repute. Mr. Chaplin proposed to the Peshwa to continue his noble endeavour of encouraging erudition among the natives, and further proposed that a part of the grant be spent in supporting a college. The Peshwa readily agreed and the Poona College was established in 1821.

The *General Committee of Public Instruction* was constituted on 17th July, 1823 by the acting Governor General Mr. Adam. The Committee was to function under the superintendence of the Persian Secretary to Government. It was directed to place an annual report before the Governor-General. The Local Committees were directed to correspond through the General Committee of Public Instruction henceforth. The first General Committee of Public Instruction was constituted on 31st July, 1823. It had a President and nine members. It had a whole-time Secretary. This Committee had full powers over all government educational institutions. The private institutions were out of its

---

17 H. V. Hampton, Biographical Studies in Modern Indian Education, London, 1947 Oxford University Press, p. 73.

purview. It existed from 31st July, 1823 to 9th January,1842. On 10th January, 1842, the

Council of 'Education replaced the erstwhile General Committee of Public Instruction. It had a President and its *ex-officio* Secretary was the Deputy Secretary to Government of India and Bengal in the Persian Department.

A whole-time Inspector of Schools and Colleges was appointed on 20th June, 1844. The first Director of Public Instruction of the Bengal Presidency was Mr. William Gordon Young, who took over charge on 26th January, 1855. The Council of Education was abolished with effect from that date. The Calcutta University was established on 24th January, 1857.

There were deep differences among the administrators and high intellectuals as regards the manner in which the amount of rupees of one lakh, which was earmarked for education in the India Bill of 1813, should be spent. The forceful debate that raged from 1823 to 1835 as regards the best mode of educating the Indians through the indigenous education of the country or the imported and the imposed Western system of education is generally known as the Aglicist-Orientalist Debate.

In the terms of reference of the General Committee of Public Instruction dated the 17th July, 1823, it was requested to suggest measures for the better education of the people in useful knowledge, and the arts and sciences of Europe and the improvement of public morals. At this very juncture, a Despatch was received from the East India Company to augment the existing Calcutta Madrisa and the Benaras Hindu College: and to establish a Hindu college at Calcutta on the lines of the one at Benares. Mr James Mill, a historian and high officer of the India Office, London rebutted the suggestion made in the Despatch. He wrote, "in professing to establish seminaries for the purpose of teaching mere Hindoo or mere Mohammedan literature, the Government bound itself to teach a great deal of what was frivolous, not a litde of what was purely mischievous and a small remainder indeed in which utility was in any way concerned. The great end of the Government should be not to teach Hindoo or Mohammedan learning, but useful learning"[18].

Still, the Orientalists held their sway and the Imperial Government was not prepared to take any risk to antagonize any of the two major communities. So, most of the funds were spent on Oriental education up to 1833, with a few exceptions. The mode, the medium and the scope were altogether Oriental in their approach.

In the meanwhile, there was mounting demand and pronounced pressure to provide more of Western education. The General Committee on Public Instruction was divided in its opinion. The Orientalists led by Mr. H. T. Prinsep, advocated theallocation of all funds to the promotion of indigenousknowledge; and the Anglicists led by Thomas Babington Macaulay supported western education. Macaulay's Minute of 1835 totally tilted the scales in favour of western education. Macaulay is a greatly misunderstood and grossly maligned genius, who played a critical role, though unwittingly; in shaping the educational, legal and cultural oudook of India. The details of his life are rarely noticed in India. Hence, this brief biographical sketch of Thomas Babington Macaulay, Baron Macaulay of Rothley. He was born on 25th October, 1800 in the village of Rothley Temple of Leicestershire of England. He died on 28th December, 1859 at London. He lived for 59 years 2 months and 4 days. He was a profound scholar of literature and history. He was a forceful writer and an outstanding orator. He studied in the University of Cambridge. He was a Member of the Supreme Council of India from 1834 to 1838. He vehemently advocated the equality of Europeans and Indians before law. He is the author of the Criminal Procedure Code of India and also the controversial Minute on Education. He was a Member of the British Parliament (1830 to 1834 and 1838 to 1843). He was a conservative in outlook, He had tremendous literary skills which can still be seen in his books *Critical and Historical Essays;* (1843), *Lays*

---

18   C. D. Maclean, op. cit. p. 563

of Ancient Rome (1842) and *History of England* (1688 to 1702) in 5 volumes. His footprints reverberate in India, even today (2007).

In his Minute of 1835, he wrote: *"We have to educate a people who cannot at present be educated by means of their mother tongue. We must teach them some foreign language*[19]*"*. Macaluay was convinced that English alone can bind the British Empire in India and provide the cementing force to the linguistically divided sub-continent. Lord William Bentinck assented to Macaulay's Minute and wrote "i" *give my entire concurrence to the sentiments expressed in the Minutes.*[20]*"* However, his successor in office, Lord Auckland, had great apprehension regarding the introduction of English education and desired a slow and steady approach. The Asiatic Societies in Calcutta and London deeply resented Bentinck's Resolution. The important Resolution of 1835 had its immediate impact. The publication of the oriental texts was stopped forthwith. Government withdrew its support to Calcutta Madrisa and Sanskrit College of Benaras. The Asiatic Society severely condemned these steps as "destructive, unjust, unpopular and impolite"[21]. H. T. Prinsep, the forceful advocate of Orientalists education, bitterly criticized the policy advocated by Macaulay and accorded official sanction by Lord William Bentinck. In policy advocated by Macaulay and accorded official sanction by Lord William Bentinck. In his Minute, he stated that, "the government's policy of promoting English education in India was inconsistent with past and with recent professions of the government, as proclaiming a principle unfair and illiberal in itself and calculated to set against us those without whose cooperation we can do nothing to promote science and literature"[22].

Prinsep's pleadings had no impact. The General Committee on Public Instruction steadily proceeded to promote English education. The days

---

19   H. sharp, op. tit. Macaulay's Minute.
20   *Ibid.* [7]C. D.
21   Maclean, *op. tit.* p. 563-565.
22   *Ibid.*

of the Orientalists had become history. Indians themselves clamored for more and more of English education, a syndrome visible even in 2007. Macaulay and Bentinck advocated; but it is the Indians who willingly accepted English education due to a variety of motives. The inexorable march of Western education and the continued neglect of Indian languages and thought can safely be dated from 1835. At such a critical momentous time of history of Indian education, the Pooree Free Academy was established at Puri. It was the first secondary school as per the definition of secondary education at that point of time.

Note: (1) The East India Company ruled India from 1757 to 1858. Warren Hastings was the Governor-General of Bengal from 1774 to 1785. He was succeed by Lord CornwalUs (1786-1793), Sir John Shore (1793-98), Lord Welssesley (1795-1805), Lord Minto (1807-1813), Lord Hastings (1813-1823), Lord Amherst (1823-1828), Lord William Bentinck was the Governor-general from 1828-1833.

EAST INDIA COMPANY RULE

SI. No.	Name of the Governor General of Bengal	Period	
		From	To
1.	Warren Hastings	1774	1785
2.	Lord Cornwallis	1786	1793
3.	Sit John Shore	1793	1798
4.	Lord Wellesley	1798	1805
5.	Lord Minto	1807	1813
6.	Lord Hastings	1813	1823
7.	Lord Amherst	1823	1828
8.	Lord William Bentinck	1828	1833

Note: (2) In 1833, the Governor-General of Bengal was declared as the Governor-General of India. Lord William Bentinck was the first Governor-General of India from (1833-1835). In 1858, the Crown took over the administration of India from the East India Company.

The Governor-General of India became also the Viceroy from 1858 onwards. Lord Canning was the first Viceroy of India (1858-1862).

SI. No.	Name of the Governor General of India	Period	
		From	To
1.	Lord William Bentinck	1833	1835
2.	Lord Auckland	1836	1842
3.	Lord Ellenborough	1842	1844
4.	Lord Hardinge (earlier Sir Henry)	1844	1848
5.	Lord Dalhousie	1848	1856
6.	Lord Canning	1856	1858

CROWN RULE

SI. No.	Name of the Governor General and Viceroys	Period	
		From	To
1.	Lord Canning	1858	1862
2.	Lord Elgin	1862	1863
3.	Lord John Lawrence	1864	1869
4.	Lord Mayo	1869	1872
5.	Lord Northbrook	1872	1876
6.	Lord Lytton	1876	1880
7.	Lord Ripon	1880	1884
8.	Lord Dufferin	1884	1888
9.	Lord Lansdowne	1888	1894
10.	Lord Elgin	1894	1899
11.	Lord Curzon	1899	1905
12.	Lord Minto	1905	1910
13.	Lord Hardinge	1910	1916
14.	Lord Chelmsford	1916	1921
15.	Lord Reading	1921	1925
16.	Lord Irwin	1926	1931
17.	Lord Willingdon	1931	1936

SI. No.	Name of the Governor General and Viceroys	Period	
		From	To
18.	Lord Linlithgow	1936	1943
19.	Lord Wavell	1943	1947
20.	Lord Mountbatten	March,1947 to August 1948	
21.	Sri C. Raja Gopalachari	1948	1950

Note: (3) Calcutta (now Kolkata) was the capital of India up to 1912, the capital was shifted to Delhi in 1912.

SECTION II

POOREE (PURI) FREE ACADEMY
(1835-1840)

The year 1835 A. D. is a major landmark in the history of education of India in general and of Orissa in particular. It had ushered in a new era in Indian education. The great Anglicist-Orientalist controversy came to an end. Lord Bentinck's Resolution dated 7th March, 1835 stated in definite terms the educational policy of the British in India. It stated: "His Lordship in Council is of opinion that the great object of the British Government ought to be the promotion of European literature and science among the natives of India; and all the funds appropriated for the purpose of education would best be employed on English education alone". The Resolution further stated, "it is not the intention to abolish any college or school of native learning" and that, "no portion of the funds should hereafter be employed for the printing of oriental works", and that, "all the funds which these reforms will leave.... be henceforth employed in imparting the native population a knowledge of English literature and science through the medium of English language..."[23]

The year 1835 heralded the new epoch of English education in Orissa. In November, 1835, a Second Class Anglo Vernacular School was opened at Pooree (Puri). This marked the faint beginning of a new educational system that would slowly expand in the years to come and stamp out the existing indigenous educational system. The definite

---

23 'Resolution dated the 7th March, 1835 of Government of India, in H. Sharp's "Selectionsfrom Educational 'Records". Vol. I (Govt, of India Printing Press. Calcutta, 1920) p. 130-131.

educational policy as outlined in the Resolution and the opening of the Anglo Vernacular school at Puri together made the year 1835, a year of new directions. The English officials had a very low opinion regarding the education and civilization of Indians, in general. As foreigners with a radically different cultural background and out-look, this was nothing by natural. The state of education in the post-Mughal period was in a chaotic condition due to lack of patronage from kings, who in their turn were not secure. The political situation was in a turmoil and this had its deleterious effect on education. Henry Rickets states that, "At the conquest we found the Ooreas in a state of degradation and to our shame be it recorded that our policy was to perpetuate it. If schools be established and properly attended, the Ooreas will soon shed that degradation which is usual consequence of misrule".[24]

Mr. Henry Rickets, the Commissioner of the Orissa Division, was exhorting the Government of Bengal to open schools in Orissa. But Mr. William Wilkinson, the Collector of Puri, was a practical enthusiast in the field of education. Instead of being content with imploring the higher authorities to open schools, he collected donations and subscriptions for the purpose. On 17th June 1835, he wrote to Mr. Grant, Apothecary-General at Calcutta that they at Puri had already collected Rs. 1005 as donation and Rs. 867.00 as subscription. Mr Wilkinson hopefully remarked "Our school will be in the town of Pooree, and all or nearly all our scholars will be Hindus, as there are scarcely any Mahamadans in the district."[25] He hoped to start the school by Ist October, 1835 after the rainy season was over, and further because he expected the school building to be ready by that time. Money and buildings could be procured by Mr. Wilkinson; he could not procure a master at Puri, and those of Calcutta were reluctant to travel such a long distance of fifteen days journey in those days. Mr. Ganganarayan Bose was appointed the master; and after much hesitation and some correspondence regarding

---

24   Henry Rickets: *Communication dated the 7th December, 1837'from the Commissioner, Orissa Division to the Sudder Board of Revenue.*

25   *General Committee of Public Instruction: Correspondence,* Vol. 40 pp. 1-4 [n]

the sanction in his favour a conveyance allowance of Rs. 100, he joined the school on 10th November, 1835. By March, 1836 there were only 25 students in the school of whom 12 had been admitted in the last quarter of 1835. Mr. Bose while explaining the low enrolment commented on the apathy of the local inhabitants towards English education in these words: "The inhabitants of the town chiefly consist of priests of the temple of Jagannath, to whom a knowledge of the *Shaster* is more profitable than the English language."[26]

The new school was called the Pooree Free Academy. It was housed in a building which was centrally situated and was spacious and airy. It was the largest available building. The only disadvantage was its low roof Previously this building was used to house the cutcherry and residence of the Sudder Aumeen.

Puri Free Academy was designed to provide secondary education. But a sudden vertical take-off is not possible in matters of education. Necessarily it had to do the requisite spade-work relating to primary education. Mr. Bose frankly avers to this in his return and states that, "the school having only just opened and almost all the students having entered entirely ignorant of the alphabet, none are sufficientiy advanced in reading and writing to commence any particular branch of study."[27]

The school had initially four classes. "The students of the 4th class were of thelowest class. There were 8 students in this class. They were not yet at acquainted with compound letters and could only read words with three syllables. The next higher class was the 3rd class in which there were only 4 students. They could read simple passages and words of five syllables and could spell them with tolerable correctness. The students were regular in their attendance and absented themselves only on adequate grounds." The teachers were quite satisfied with their conduct and industry. The 2nd class had 6 students "who were neither impeccable in their conduct nor intent in their books. But they could

---

26   *Report of the G. C. P. I.* 1836-37 pp. 17-18
27   *Ibid.* pp. 17-18

read short lessons, spell the most difficult words with great accuracy and were just learning to write". There were 7 students in the 1st class, the top most class of the school. Their ages varied from 7 to 15 years. They had finished the first spelling book. They could write, spell and translate and they were well behaved."[28]

Mr. C. R. Payne was the Secretary of the Local Committee. Mr. Ganganarain Bose, was a good teacher and put the school on a firm footing. But his health was failing and he had frequent attacks of fever. The Secretary of the Local Committee was constrained to recommend his transfer on health grounds. The ill-health of Mr. Bose made him pessimistic and his report for the 3rd quarter was not assuring.

Mr. W S. R. Davies took the charge of the school early in 1837. At the time of his appointment, he neither knew Oriya nor Bengali, but soon made himself familiar with both these languages. He was the first headmaster of the school. In 1839, he was absorbed in the General Executive Service and so became the Secretary of the Local Committee in place of Mr. Payne. Mr. W E. Capon was appointed to succeed Mr. Davies. But he never reached Puri. Next, Mr. Henry Walpole was posted as the Headmaster.[29] In 1839, there were two masters including the Headmaster and a Pandit. There were 43 students on the rolls. By 1840, the financial situation of the school was very good and it could meet from its own funds the expenditure of the English School. A Branch Oriya school was functioning. The College i.e. the upper classes of the school had three Departments: (1) English and Vernacular, (2) Sanskrit and (3) Mahomedan. There were no students in the last department. Corporal punishment was forbidden in the school. Right from the days of Mr Bose, there was a constant complaint of the lack of Oriya text-books. When Mr Walpole joined the school he was totally ignorant of the native languages. Therefore, the appointment of a Pandit became

---

28   *Ibid.*
29   Report of the General Committee of Public Instruction, 1837-38

imperative.[30] Mr. Walpole resigned abruptly. One Mr. A. A. O'Brien, a dismissed assistant overseer, took over as Headmaster. But he was found to be a drunkard and so was dismissed.

On 27th August, 1840 the Local Committee and the subscribers to the Puri school met at a meeting and unanimously passed a resolution abolishing the English and Sanskrit departments. From 1835 to 1840, the school had been struggling under the most trying circumstances. Teachers could not be had of, parents were not sympathetic and students were not enthusiastic.[31]

Thus the first experiment in English education in Orissa ended in failure. The school died, but the Experience gained at Puri was utilized with profit at Cuttack in the later years. This educational system did not appeal to the people and so it died. The experiment at Puri school goes to prove that no educational system can ever succeed unless the people are genuinely interested in it and there is an adequate supply of good teachers.

---

30   Report of the General Committee of Public Instruction. 1839-40
31   Report of the General Committee of Puhlic Instruction,! 840-41

PIONEERING SECONDARY SCHOOLS (1841-1854)

The era of direct government management of education began from 1855. In accordance with the terms of the Despatch No.49 dated 19th July, 1854 from the Honourable Court of Directors and Letter No. 166 from the Secretary to the Government of India in the Home Department, the Lieutenant Governor of Bengal dissolved the Council of Education with effect from 27th January, 1855.

Mr. William Gordon Young was appointed as the first Director of Public Instruction of the Bengal Presidency on 26th January,1 855. The responsibility in respect of the educational institutions managed by the Council of Education devolved on the D. P. I. The Secretary of the Council was directed to report to the D. P. I. and be guided by his instructions. The Inspectorates came into simultaneous existence with the Directorate in 1855. The Inspector of Schools, South West Division was in charge of the schools of Orissa.

From 1841 to 1853 there was only one secondary school in Orissa. It was the Cuttack School. In 1853, two more secondary schools were started at Puri and Balasore. On the eve of the publication of the Wood's Despatch of 1854, thesewere the pioneering three secondary schools, whose brief history has been sketched.

THE CUTTACK SCHOOL

On 18th March, 1841, the Cuttack School started functioning with the joining of Mr. John D'Souza as its first teacher. Sri Ragabananda joined the school as its Assistant Pundit of the school on 1st April,1841. Sri Biswambar Bidyabhusan joined as the Head Pundit of the school on 19th August, 1841. The school had a peon, a durwan, a bearer and a sweeper. Mr J. K. Rogers joined as the Headmaster of the school on 4th January,1843.[32]

The General Committee of Public Instruction was superseded in 1842-43. In its place the General Council of Public Instruction was constituted. For every school there was a Local Committee which managed the school.[33] The Local Committee of the Cuttack School was composed of the following persons:

1. Mr. A. J. M. Mills (President),Commissioner of Revenue
2. Mr. J. Stainforth, Special Commissioner
3. Mr. H. B. Brownlow, Judge
4. Mr. G. G. Mackintosh, Officiating Collector
5. Mr. E. T. Trevor, Assistant and exercising the powers of a Joint Magistrate and Deputy Collector
6. Moulvi Golam Rasool, Principal Sudder Aumeen
7. Baboo Tarakant Bideasagar, Sudder Aumeen
8. Moulvi Mohomud Fazal, Law Officer
9. Baboo Kasinath Rai Choudhary, Zamindar[34]

During 1843-44, Mr. C. Cardew became a member of the Local Committee having succeeded Mr. J. Stainforth as Special Commissioner.[35] During 1845-46, Mr. J. W Templer became a member of the Local Committee in place of Mr C. Cardew. M. S. Gillmore Esq., Collector, E. G. Bedwell Esq., Civil Assistant Surgeon, Mr. T B.members of the Local Committee, eight were officials and one was a non-official member. The President

---

32 General Report, on Public Instruction in the Bengal Presidency 1842-43, (Bengal Mily OrphanPress), p. 141.
33 *Ibid,* p. 4
34 Loc. Cit
35 General Report on Public Instruction in the Bengal Presidency, 1843-43. p. 144

of the Local Committee was the Commissioner of Revenue of the Orissa Division. Almost all the important officers of the Revenue and Law Departments were associated with the Local Committee of the school. Of the four native members, two were Hindus and two were Muslims.

Mr. J. K. Rogers was the Headmaster of the School from 4th January, 1843 to July, 1846 on a monthly salary of Rs. 150.00. Mr Rogers had worked as a supernumerary teacher of the Hindu College, Calcutta from 24th May 1841 to 20th December, 1841 on a salary of Rs. 60.00 per month. Then he worked as Headmaster of the Azimghur Government School from December,1841 to January 1843, on a salary of Rs. 100.00 per month. Mr. Rogers had considerable experience before he joined the Cuttack School. He had started his career in the Hindu College, Calcutta and he must have carried with him some of the institional practices and traditions of that old institution. Mr. Edward Fell succeeded Mr. Rogers, who was transferred to Chittagang as Headmaster on 16th September, 1846 and continued to be the Headmaster up to 1853. During his tenure of office, the Cuttack School became the Cuttack Zilla School in 1851. He was the first Headmaster of the Cuttack Zilla School. Mr. Charles Bramlow was the Headmaster from 1853 to 1856.[36]

Mr. Nobin Saringy, an ex-student of the Cuttack school, was appointed as the second master in place of Mr John D'Souza during 1848-49. Mr. Saringy tendered his resignation with effect from 9th August, 1850, and one Mr. J. T Cooper, a student of this School succeed him, on 21st September, 1850 on a monthly pay of Rs. 60.00[37] During 1845-46, Sri Oomachurn Chatterjee joined the as third master. On 1st June, 1846 Sri Kalimohan Ghosal joined in place of Mr Chatterjee as the third master on a pay of Rs. 30.00 per month.[38] Sri Ochoot Sahoo, was appointed the 4th master during

---

36   General Report on Public Instruction in the Bengal Presidency, 1842-43. p. [141]

37   General Report on Public Instruction in the Bengal Presidency, 1845-46,1846-47,1847-48,1848-49, 1850-51, 1851-52, 1852-53, 1853-54

38   General Report on Public Instruction in the Bengal Presidency, 1849-49 p. 8

1852 on a monthly pay of Rs. 20.00[39] Sri Biswambhar Bidyabhusan, the Head Pandit resigned on 24th February, 1850. Sri Rudreswara Panda was appointed the Pandit in place of Sri Bidyabhusan on 3rd April, 1851.[40] Mr. Nobin Saringy rejoined the School on22[nd] October, 1852.[41]

There were 35 paying and 36 non-paying students during 1842-43. However, the amount paid was nil. What the paying students were paying is not clear from the records. All the students were studying English and Oriya. Sixty of the students were Hindus, 9 were Christians, and only two were Muslims. The daily average attendance during the period 30th April, 1842 to 30th April, 1843 was 62[42]The number of scholars did not increase appreciably during 1843-44 and the reasons attributed were that the natives did not appreciate the benefits of English education, and that only natives connected with the different offices who were sufficiently enlightened to perceive the advantages of English education, sent their children to this school. The existence of a Missionary School formerly and its proselytizing activities had also deterred the common people from sending their children to this English School. This new school was far below in matters of discipline and many parents were unwilling to send their children on that account[43]

To prevent irregularity of attendance, the system of giving daily tickets and "a handsome prize to the holder of the largest number of tickets at the Annual Examination, provided he conducted himself well", was introduced during 1842-43. In the extreme cases, and where reward or reprimand had no effect, expulsion was stated to be the proper measure to be adopted, "in order that the pernicious example may be removed.'[44]

---

39   General Report on Public Instruction in the Bengal Presidency,1846-47

40   General Report on Public Instruction in the Bengal Presidency,1852-53

41   General Report on Public Instruction in the Bengal Presidency, 1850-51

42   General Report on Public Instruction in the Bengal Presidency,1851-52

43   General Report on Public Instruction in the Bengal Presidency, 1842-43, p. 142

44   General Report on Public Instruction in the Bengal Presidency, 1843-44, p. 144

In 1843-44, seventy nine scholars were studying of which 75 presented themselves at the annual examination. The students were divided into four classes, the two junior classes consisting of 55 boys, being subdivided into sections. "The majority of the boys were the sons of Bengalees who had settled down in the province, but a few of the indigenous Oorya population also attended. They were represented to be respectful and obedient, and very assiduous in the prosecution of their studies. The attendance was 62. None of the students were sufficiently advanced to compete for a Junior Scholarship."[45]

During 1846-47, the paying-system was introduced whereby each scholar was expected to pay fees. As a consequence, the roll strength of the school decreased;Simon Peters and Nobin Saringy, were awarded scholarships.

The Committee commended Sri Nobin Saringy, a student of this school during 1846, when he was transferred to Hooghly College where he held a Senior Scholarship for two years "for his ability, zeal and patience... in the performance of his studies". It was a common experience of the Cuttack School that adequate number of scholars were not available to compete for the scholarships. This was because, "majority of the students, whose parents were in moderate circumstances, after having attained the standard required, were leaving the institution, stating as reason, that inducements offered to them to proceed to Hooghly were not sufficiently advantageous; they, therefore, readily accepted situations of 8 to 10 rupees a month, in and about Cuttack, in preference to those of double the emoluments out of Orissa."

During 1847-48, there were 78 students on the rolls. "The Committee testify to the increased appreciation of the institution on the part of the inhabitants."[46] "Some few are the sons of wealthy persons; but the

---

45   General Report on Public Instruction in the Bengal Presidency, 1842-43
       p. 144
46   General Report on Public Instruction in the Bengal Presidency,! 843-44,
       pp. 111-114

remainder being principally the children of natives holding offices under Government and others of the middle classes of native society."[47] In spite of the best of its efforts, "the increase in the number of students has been so small". The results were unsatisfactory due to irregular attendance which was considered to be the prime cause for the low achievement and bad results.[35]

The average age of the first class (i.e. the top most class of the School), consisting of 14 students was 17 years. The second class was composed of 7 students, whose average age was 12V£ years. The third class consisted of 20 students, whose average age was IOV2 years. The fourth class, which consisted of 40 "very promising lads" was divided into three sections, their ages varying from 7 to 11 years, with an average age of nine.

Nobokisto Roy, Dinonath Mukherjee, Murray Xavier and Dwarakanath Mukherjee of the first class; Rajaninath Bannerji, J. W D. Costa of the second class; Phillip Thomas, Gourisankar Bose, Madhusudan Mitter and Goluckchunder Bose of the third class; and Chitun Prasad Sain, An'am, J. Rennel, Hemachandra Roy, and Sadananda Rout of the fourth class won prizes during the year 1846-47.

The products of the Cuttack School had obtained employment by 1849. In the report for 1850-51, it has been stated that, "The Committee have the satisfaction torecord that four scholars educated in the institution under theircharge have obtained Government employment during the year. One of these formerly held a junior scholarship at the Hooghly College, and is now employed as a Darogah (Sub-Inspector of Police) in which capacity he discharges his duties to the satisfaction of the magistrates. Another has been appointed Pundit of the Pooree Vernacular School, which appointment appears to the Committee to be a very advantageous one, as tending to improve the system of education in the Vernacular School, and to more generally known the advantages

---

47   General Report on Public Instruction in the Bengal Presidency, 1847-48, p. 8

derivable from the liberal education...".[48] In consequence, there was a steady increase in the roll strength of the Cuttack School. The roll strength of the school stood at 135 during 1853-54.[49]

To start with, the school was housed in a rented building for which a monthly rent of Rs. 25.00 was paid. However, the school-house was later constructed at an expenditure of Rs. 4310. Out of this, the Government had paid only Rs. 2,000.00 and an amount of Rs. 2,310.00 was defrayed through subscription. This in itself was a good indication of the increasing interest of the public towards the English education. The school moved to its won premises with effect from 16th April, 1843.[50]

It was constructed under the superintendence of the Executive Officer. It was, "a good substantial building, well-ventilated, in a central situation, consisting of four rooms, 36 X 22 feet each, and two others 22 X 22 feet each, about 18 feet high, flat-roofed, with a thatched verandah all round 11 feet wide. It was about 1 *Vz* miles from most of the European houses (now known as the Cantonment area), and was in a large compound in which the Collector's and the Magistrate's Cutcheries were situated." This is where the Ravenshaw Collegiate School stands today. It was partially destroyed by fire during 1846-47 and the Executive Engineer was requested to repair it.

The monthly salary of the Headmaster was Rs. 150.00, that of the second master Rs. 60.00; of the third master Rs. 30,00; and of the fourth master Rs. 20.00; of the Head Pundit Rs. 20.00; and of the assistant Pundit Rs. 10.00. The durwan, peon and the bearer were paid @ Rs. 4.00 per month and the sweeper @ Rs. 2.00 per month.

The salaries of the English teachers amounted to Rs. 2,350.96 ; that of the vernacular teachers Rs. 360.00; and of the establishment Rs. 168.00.

---

48   *Ibid,*
49   General Report on Public Instruction in the Bengal Presidency,1848-49, p.8
50   General Report on Public Instruction in the Bengal Presidency,
      1847-48 p. 8

The totalexpenditure on account of salaries was Rs. 2,878.96 as against an estimated annual expenditure of Rs. 3,084.00. The annual provision for purchase of books was Rs. 300.00, out of which an amount of Rs. 75-50 was expended.[51] The following were the actual charges on various heads during 1849-50.

Rs.

1.	Salary of English teachers	2,793.87
2.	Salary of Vernacular teachers	240.00
3.	Salary of Establishment	168.00
4.	Book Allowance	300.00
5.	Contingencies	44.06
6.	Stationery	60.08

The total expenditure for the year was   3,606.01

The resources of annual income consisted of the Government assignment from additional grants dated the 16th December, 1840 amounting to Rs. 3,996.00 per annum. The establishment and expenses were also fixed by the Government in its Resolution of the same date.

The following was the expenditure on account of the Cuttack School from October, 1852 to 31st March, 1854.

Rs.

1.	Salaries	5,211.77
2.	Contingencies	101.68
3.	Books for Library	272.50
4.	Books for prizes	91.87
5.	Stationery	18.65

Total expenditure for the period   5,696.47

Total allotment for the period   5,994.00

---

51 *Ibid*

During 1846-47, the paying system was introduced, whereby each scholar was expected to pay fees. It is interesting to note that "the schooling fees varied from four annas to one rupee eight annas according to the supposed means of the parents or guardians as ascertained by Headmaster." The Secretary of the Council who visited the school on 24th December,! 850 recommended a uniform scale of fees.[52] Themonthly feescollected from the school varied from Rs. 68.50 in November, 1852 to Rs. 90.00 in January, 1854.

The Cuttack School was inspected for the first time during 1845-46. The report was generally favourable. However, the practice of dividing the classes into different sections was not appreciated as the uniformity of progress was hampered.

Up to 1851, the Cuttack School was imparting instruction up to the junior scholarship standard. In 1851, it became a Zilla School. It was the first high school of the State. It was called **Cuttack Zilla School.**

ORIYA TEXT BOOKS

The preparation of Oriya text books received the special attention of the Local Committee. Pundit Biswambhar Bidyabhusan completed an Oriya Grammar Book consisting of twenty four 12 m.o. pages. Its price was 6 annas (i.e Rs. 0.38). He translated Harle's Arithmetic into Oriya. Government purchased 500 copies of this book for use in the Vernacular Schools.[53] Mr. Sutton prepared a Vocabulary Book of 200 pages. This was priced at Rs. 3.00. Mr. Sutton completed the Vernacular Reader and a second edition of the Oriya Primer was brought out.

THE POOREE (PURI) ZILLA SCHOOL

It was established on the 1st November, 1853. The Local Committee of the School consisted of the Collector, the Assistant Collector, the

---

52 General Report on Public Instruction in the Bengal Presidency,! 842-43, p. 143

53 *Ibid.*

Deputy Collector, the Civil Surgeon, the Sub-Assistant Surgeon and the Munsif. Baboo Russicklal Sen, was its first Headmaster. He joined the school on 1st November, 1853 on a pay of Rs. 150.00 per month. Babu Bistochunder Mukherjee was the second master with effect from 22nd November,1853 and Sri Dinonath Mukherjee joined as the third master on 29th November 1853.

The total roll strength of the Puri School was 82 during 1853-54, of which 81 were Hindus and 1 was a Muslim. All the students were fee-paying students. All of them were studying English and Bengali and Oriya. An amount of Rs. 86.19 was collected towards school fees during the period 1st November 1853 to 30th April 1854. The total expenditure on account of the school was Rs. 1,666.90 for thisperiod. The studies of the Puri School were analogous to thatof the Cuttack School. However, History of Orissa was taught in the two upper classes and Neetikotha was in the lower classes, which was not done at Cuttack. Prof. Kerr thus remarks in his inspection report: "Pooree is the seat of a celebrated Hindu Temple. Consequently, the Brahmin and merchant class people were not interested in English education."[54]

BALASORE SCHOOL

In 1846, the inhabitants of Balasore made an application for the establishment of an English School, which was forwarded by the Commissioner of the Orissa Division. This request was turned down by the Council of Education as "the education fund did not afford the means of complying with their request." The Balasore School was established on 1st November,1853 and started functioning from 8th November,1853. The Collector, the Joint Magistrate, the Civil Surgeon, the Assistant Salt Agent, the Deputy Collector and a Zamindar were the members of the Local Committee. Babu Biswanath Sen joined on 21st October, 1853 as Headmaster on a pay of Rs. 150.00 per month, and

---

54 General Report on Public Instruction in the Bengal Presidency,1851-52, p. 120

Shib Charan Shome as Second Master on a monthly salary of Rs. 50.00, on 24th October, 1853. Both of them assumed their offices before the school started functioning. Babu Bhubanananda Raha, joined as the third master on a pay of Rs. 30.00 per month on 17th November, 1853. There were three servants on a monthly pay of Rs. 4.00 each.

There were 82 students on rolls during 1853-54. Of these 4 were Muhammadans, 4 were Christians, and the rest 74 were Hindus. Prof. Kerr's report states the roll strength of the school to be 54. The Bengalis were 28, the Oriyas were 18, Muhammadans 4, East Indian Christians 2, and Native Christians 2. All the students were fee-paying students. All of them were studying Bengali. There was no provision for instruction in Oriya.

No fees were collected from the students during November, 1853 as the classes were incompletely organized. An amount of Rs. 173-8-0 was collected towards school fees from December 1853 to April, 1854. The total expenditure on account of this school from November, 1853 to 30th April, 1854 was Rs. 1588.80. The members of the Local Committee were chiefly engaged in matters relating to the completion ofthe school-building, the fixing of age for admission of the boys and the rates of fees to be collected.[55]

It is interesting to note here that though there was no provision for the teaching of Oriya in this school and all the students studied Bengali. "A donation of five rupees had been made by Mr H. V. Bayley, Judge of Dacca, to be given as prize for an Ooriah essay", and it was not competed for.[56]

---

55 General Report on Public Instruction in the Bengal Presidency,1846-47,p. x
56 General Report on Public Instruction in the Bengal Presidency, September 1852 to January, 1855. pp. 188-191.

CHAPTER-3

EMERGENCE OF A SYSTEMOF EDUCATION (1854–1881)

HIGHLIGHTS

- Wood's Despatch, 1854
- Profiles of Pioneering Secondary Schools
- Middle Schools
- Secondary Education in South Orissa
  - Onslow Institute, Chatrapur
  - Berhampur Zilla School
  - Taluk Schools
- Hunter Commission (1882)
- Developments after 1882

SECTION I

MODERN SYSTEM OF EDUCATION TAKES SHAPE

WOOD'S DESPATCH (1854)

The Despatch No. 49, dated the 19th July 1854, from the Court of Directors of the East India Company to the Governor-General of India in Council,[57] has been described as the "Magna Charta of English Education in India".[58] This Despatch is commonly known as the Wood's Despatch of 1854. It is a landmark in the history of education of India and ushered in the era of reforms. The East India Company had laid, though faint, firm foundations of a well articulated educational infrastructure for the country. The Despatch contains the complete exposition 'of the wishes and intentions of the Honourable Court of Directors', and 'it lays down very clearly the principle by which the instruction of the natives of this country is to be carried on'.[59]"The major recommendations of the Wood's Despatch relate to:

1. Machinery for managing the Department;
2. Establishment of the Universities; and
3. Grant-in-aid."

---

57 Despatch No. 49, dated the 19th July, 1854 from the "Selections from the Educational Records",Vol. II, p. 364

58 Minute by the Marquis of Dalhousie, Governor-General of India dated 30th December,1854 - Selections from the Educational Records, Vol. II, p. 394

59 *Ibid*

The establishment of the machinery for the management of the department led to 'the creation of a properly articulated system of education from the primary to the University'. As a result, the Departments of Public Instruction were created in the Provinces. Lord Dalhousie had commented that it was, "far wider and more comprehensive than the Local or Supreme Government could ever have ventured to suggest."[60] In 2007, after more than a century and half's progress, the proposals of the Despatch seem to be limited in scope and lacking in vision. But it was stated that the envisaged improvements of the Despatch were, "best calculated to secure the ultimate benefit of the people committed to our charge."[61] The Despatch emphatically declared that "the education which we desire to see extended in India is that which has for its objects the diffusion of the improved arts, science, philosophy and literature of Europe; in short of European knowledge."[62]

The educational systems of India received a new orientation after Wood's Despatch of 1854. The Education Departments were organized and the major responsibility of these Departments was school education. The establishment of the Universities totally altered the objectives of secondary education. Secondary education was viewed more as a preparation for the University and less as a well rounded course for preparing youngsters to enter the serious business of life. According to the Despatch, the objectives of the schools should be, "not to train highly a few youths, but to provide more opportunities than now exist for the acquisition of such an improved education as will make those who possess it more useful members of society in every conditionof life"[63]. Theclear-cut objectives of the secondary education had not specificallybeen visualized up till this time due to the confused educational scene. The higher education had not developed

---

60   *Ibid*
61   J. A. Richey, "Selection from Educational Records", Vol. II p. 366.
62   *Ibid,* p. 366, item 7.
63   *Ibid,* Part II,p. 376.

and universities were non-existent. The schools encompassed the entire intellectual horizon and they aimed very high. The schools were *"the"* institutions of higher learning and also of specialization, as a result of which many a youth left the schools with education as an unfinished business. With the emergence of the colleges and the anticipated establishment of the Universities, it became imperative to spell out the objectives of school education. The social aims of school education had been given greater importance and the individual aims were yet to be stated. This clear-cut formulation of objectives made the burden of the schools lighter and freed them from the intellectual mess they were in. School education was to concern itself solely with the general preparation for citizenship and the colleges were to look after specialization.

The East India Company's days were drawing near and the Mutiny of 1857 sealed its fate. The Government of India was transferred to the Crown, and the Governor-General became also the Viceroy of India. The last great act of the East India Company was the Despatch itself which continued to provide broad guidance to the educational policies that were framed in the subsequent three decades.

The Despatch reaffirmed the Policy of 1835 relating to English Education and the diffusion of European knowledge was the major aim. Macaulay's logic prevailed again and the faint murmurs of the Orientalists were silenced for ever under the Juggernautic wheels of Western education. A daring and dangerous experiment had been launched in the field of education. Education was seen as an instrument of social change and acculturisation. How far the subsequent developments had been influenced by the Wood's Despatch may be the proper study of socio-cultural history.

That the indigenous educational system was slowly and steadily gagged to death and that the development of modern Indian languages was definitely hampered can easily be stated. Even today, Indian education has not been able to become a means of mass instruction partly due to the hampered growth of the Indian languages. The Downward Filteration Theory was bid goodbye and it became "the sacred duty of government to diffuse knowledge amongst the people." The Despatch emphasized the need for providing. "Education suited to every station of life." The spread of education was a committed goal and secondary education was fortunate enough to get adequate importance and attention in the following years.

The Despatch accurately gauged the immensity of the problems relating to education in these words:

"When we consider the vast population of British India, and the sums which are now expended upon educational efforts, which, however successful in themselves, have reached but an insignificant number of those who are of a proper age to receive school instruction. We cannot but be impressed with the almost insuperable difficulties which would attend such an extension of the present system of education by means of colleges and schools entirely supported at the cost of the government as might be hoped to supply, in any reasonable time, so gigantic a deficiency and to provide adequate means for setting on foot such a system as we have described and desire to see established."[64]

The 'gigantic deficiency' in the field of education has to be met and 'the consideration of the impossibility of the government alone doing all that must be done' impelled the government to come forth with the grant-in-aid system. Therefore, it was resolved to adopt in India the system of grant-in-aid. "Drawing support from the local sources" and "fostering a spirit of reliance upon local exertions and combination for local purposes, which is of itself of no mean importance to the well-being of a nation" — were the two main objectives of introducing the grant-in-aid system. It was confidendy anticipated of drawing support from the local resources in addition to the contribution from the State. State aid supplemented by local resources was to be the future pattern

---

64   *Ibid*, p. 376

of educational finance. Private patrons, voluntary subscribers or the trustees of endowments were to undertake the general superintendence of the schools and were to be answerable for their performance. The procedure of financing school education was quite sound theoretically. It had in it the seeds of community control of education and ultimate democratization of education. But these healthy seeds never grew well in the poverty-stricken soil of India.

The principle of grant-in-aid practically became the bed-rock of educational financing. The developments in England around this time had greatly influenced the Indian educational scene. The New-Casde Report of 1860 recommended, "searching examination by competent authority of every child, in every school to which grants are to be paid." This was the beginning of payment by results in England and which soon, as is only natural, spread in a contagious way to the Indian education system. The later development of secondary education in India was primarily the outcome of the operation of these two principles of grant-in-aid and payment by results.

This new system of financing education undoubtedly contributed to the quantitative growth of education, but it adversely affected the qualitative development of education. Mr. F. Watkins righdy pointed out in his report that "from the very nature of examination, which is entirely formal and mechanical, only mechanical results can be expected." The schools contributed to a colonial ethos, and were bastions of conservatism and operated mechanically. The spirit of creativity was nipped in the bud.

The grant-in-aid rules became operative in Orissa from 1867 A.D. But the results were not immediate and spectacular. The position of the various secondary schools in the post-Despatch years is a story of mixed results.

There were four Zillah Schools including the one at Sambalpur in 1856. There were no middle schools. The government vernaculars shown in the annual returns, were simply primary schools of the Western type and are to be distinguished from the *Chatsalis* (the indigenous village schools). The first aided Anglo-Vernacular School was started at Bhadrak during 1858-59. We come across the term "Middle class Schools' - English and Vernacular — for the first time in the Report for 1863-64. There were two Anglo-Vernacular Schools in South Orissa by 1855. The Berhampur Zillah School was established during 1856. The Sambalpur Zillah School was converted into an Anglo-Vernacular School during 1859. By 1881, there were six high Schools in North Orissa, one in South Orissa and none in the 24 Feudatory State of Orissa. The development of the high schools has been dealt first; followed by that of the middle schools in Orissa.

Cuttack Zillah School

The Cuttack High School was renamed as Ravenshaw Collegiate School in 1875 after Mr. T. E. Ravenshaw, the Commissioner of Orissa Division, who had great love forthe Oriya people and did his best to improve their lot. Thus the Ravenshaw Collegiate School of to-day came into existence.

Mr. Edward Fell was the Headmaster of the Cuttack Zillah School from 1851-1853, Mr. Charles Bramlow worked from 1853 to 1856, Baboo Jadunath Mukherjee from 1856 to 1863, Baboo Peary Mohan Chartterjee from 1864-1867, Sri Chandi Churn Bandopadhyaya from 1867 to 1876. The names of the Headmasters who worked from 1877 to 1883 are not available from the various records.[65]

There were 118 pupils on the rolls of the School on 1st April, 1855, of these 12 were Christians, 13 Mohamedans, and the rest 93 were Hindus. The proportion of the Christian and Mohomedan students indicates that the minorities were taking due advantage of English education and that they were not lagging behind. All the 118 students were fee-paying students. Two students were studying Oriya only and the rest

---

65   Ravenshaw Collegiate Centenary Souvenir Issue, 1954

116 students were studying both English and Oriya.[66] The number of students at the end of the session 1856-57 was 109, in 1857-58 it was 101; in 1858-59 it was 103; n 1860-61 it was 175; in 1863-64 it was 207; in 1866-67 it was 171, in 1868-69 it was 203; in 1869-70 it was 200 and in 1870-71, 178 and 179 in 1871-72. Of the 178 students studying in the school section in 1870-71, "two... belonged to higher classes of society, whilst 144 belonged to the middle, and 23 to the lower classes. Twenty were residents of Bengal temporarily settle in Orissa, seventy-three were the children of Bengali settlers and forty-eight of Uriyas; whilst thirteen belonged to the Mohammadan, and fifteen to Christian families."[67] This socio-economic break-up of students provides us with the information as to the actual beneficiaries of education. The abrupt fall in the enrolment during 1866-67 was due to the unprecedented famine of 1866. The average age of the students of the first class was 15.8 years; of the second class was in between 12 to 15 years; of the third class 11.8 years; of the fourth class A' section 11 years, and of the 'B' section was 10 years.[68]

The Calcutta University was established on 24th January, 1857. The schools at Cuttack, Puri and Balasore were affiliated to it and were preparing candidates for the Entrance Examination of this University. The Entrance Examination of the University roughly corresponded to the erstwhile Junior Scholarship Examination standard,requiring "besides the proficiency in the usual studiesof the First Class of a Zillah School, a knowledge of Vegetable Physiology, of Mechanics and Natural Philosophy." The Zillah Schools were overstraining themselves to prepare candidates for the Entrance Examination and the schools at Puri and Balasore did not have the necessary staff to provide this

---

66 General Report on the Public Instruction in the Lower Provinces of the Bengal Presidency, 27th January to 30th April, 1855. Thos. Jones, Calcutta Gazette Office, 1856, p. 117

67 General Report on the Public Instruction in Bengal, 1870-71, p. 123.

68 General Report on the Public Instruction in the Lower Provinces of the Bengal Presidency, 1856-57, pp. 108 to 111

additional instruction. Consequently, the Cuttack School was the only first Grade Zillah School; the other two at Puri and Balasore were designated as second grade Zillah Schools in 1857.

The Cuttack Zillah School was one of the most advanced and best conducted schools of the Division. It was expected that several students would pass the University Entrance Examination. "But unfortunately the students lost the reward of the whole year's labour by using unfair means to pass that examination, and thus had brought discredit on the school. Careful inquiries were held by the Inspector and members of the Local Committee, but the mode in which the deceit was effected could not be known".[69] So it was decided not to hold the Entrance Examination at Cuttack. But the Local Committee tried to remove this restriction and succeeded in their efforts at the eleventh hour during 1859-60.[70] In 1859, Sri Hemachandra Ray passed the Entrance Examination in the First Division from this School; and four others in the Second Division. Table 3.1.1 indicates the results of the school at the Entrance Examination from 1859 to 1881.

TABLE 3.1.1

Entrance Examination Results of the Cuttack School[71] 1859-1881

SI. No.	Year	Number of Passes			Total Passes
		1st Division	IInd Division	IIIrd Division	
01	1859	1	4		5
02	1860		3		3
03	1861		2		2
04	1862		3		3

---

69   General Report on the Public Instruction in the Lower Provinces of the Bengal Presidency, 1858-59,p. 108

70   General Report on the Public Instruction in the Lower Provinces of the Bengal Presidency,l859-60,p. 105.

71   Ravenshaw Collegiate Centenary Souvenir Issue, 1954, Appendix B, pp. iii to vi

SI. No.	Year	Number of Passes			Total Passes
		1st Division	IInd Division	IIIrd Division	
05	1863	1	2		3
06	1864		5		5
07	1865	1	3		4
08	1866		1	2	3
09	1867		3	1	4
10	1868		4	3	7
11	1869	3	3	1	7
12	1870		6	2	8
13	1871		5	2	7
14	1872	1	3	2	6
15	1873	1	4	1	6
16	1874		1	8	9
17	1875		1	1	2
18	1876	2	7	3	12
19	1877		3	4	7
20	1878	1	6	2	9
21	1879		3	4	7
22	1880		7	2	9
23	1881		2	2	4

From 1868 onwards, the school provided "steady help and inspiration... for the development of other schools in other parts of the Division." As a result the period from 1868-1900 was one "when the school began to stabilize as one of the best schools in the whole of Bengal and remained a model school".[72] Those who passed out from the Cuttack Zillah School became teachers in different other schools.

On Monday, the 20th January, 1868, the High School with First Arts classes was started at Cuttack with four students who had passed

---

72   B. N. Rath "A Short History of the R. C. School, Cuttack" in the Ravenshaw Collegiate SchoolCentenary Issue, 1954, p. 3

from the Cuttack Zilla School. Subsequently, two more students from Balasore, including Radhanath Rai joined the First year Arts class.[73] Here it is necessary to clarify the meaning of the term 'High School' as it was understood at that time. A 'High School' was one which had instruction up to the First Arts standard (i.e. to-day's Higher Secondary Courses). The 'Higher Class School' was one which prepared students for the EntranceExamination of the University. In modern Indian educational terminology, we shall call the 'High School of 1868' a Junior College or Higher Secondary School and 'the Higher Class School' the High School. During 1868-69 there were 16 students reading in the First Arts Standard. Of these 6 were second year students and 10 were first year students.

A Law Class was opened in 1868-69. So, by 1868-69 this school consisted of three departments: (1) College Department, (2) Law Classes, and (3) Zilla School.

Balasore Zillah School

The Balasore School started functioning on 8th November, 1853. Sri Biswanath Singh was the Headmaster from 1853 to 1857. Sri Shibcharan Shome and Sri Poorna Chandra Shome officiated as Headmasters for temporary periods in 1857. Sri Dwaraknath Chakravarty joined as the regular Headmaster of the school in 1857 and continued up to 1859. Shri Shibcharan Shome, and Sri Poornachandra Shome again officiated for temporary periods during 1859. Sri Shibcharan Shome, the assistant master of the school was promoted and posted as Headmaster of the school in 1859 and he continued as such up to 1863. He was succeeded by Sri Gangadhar Acharya who worked as Headmaster from 1864 to 1869. Sri Srinath Sen was the Headmaster of the School from 1869 to 1874 and Sri Kunjabehari Pal from 1874 to 1878. Shri Trailoykyanath

---

73   Utkal Dipika, January 25, 1868

Ghose officiated as Headmaster during 1878. Shri Durgadas Dutta was the Headmaster from 1879 to 1881.[74]

The first educational architects who laid the foundation of the school were the Headmaster Sri Biswanath Singh, who was appointed on the 21st October, 1853, Sri Shibcharan Shome, the 2nd master, Sri Bhubanmohan Raha, the 3rd master and the members of the Local Committee of Public Instruction of whom Mr. V. H. Schalch, officiating Magistrate and Collector and Salt Agent was the first President and Mr B. H. Perkins, Civil Surgeon, was the first Secretary. The only non-official member was Sri Padmolochan Mondal, a Zamindar of Balasore, who had made available a house, pending the construction of the school building. The school was managed by the Secretary and was under the Council of Education, Calcutta till the post of Director of Public Instruction and the Divisional Inspectors of School were created.[19]

The internal management of the school was entrusted to the Headmaster. The members of the Visiting Committee were appointed by the Lt. Governor of Bengal. Each of the members of the Visiting Committee visited the school and inspected the working of the school every month according to the programme drawn up by the Secretary. They used to hold the Annual Examination of the School in the month of December, assign marks to the boys and recommend the names of prize-winners for each class. One of the prize winners of 1857-58 was Radhanath Rai, a student of the First Class during 1857-58.[75] Raja Shyamananda Dev, Sri Brundabana Chandra Mondal and Phakirmohan Senapati served as non-official members of the Visiting Committee for a long time. In 1873, the Local Committee of Public Instruction was replaced by a District Education Committee. The Headmaster of the Balasore Zilla

---

74 Balasore Zilla School Centenary Souvenir Issue, 1953, Appendix A pp. I to ii.

75 General Report on the Public Instruction in the Lower Provinces of the Bengal Presidency, from 30th September 1852 to 27th January 1855, pp. 188-191

School became the Secretary of this Committee. The District Education Committee was abolished in 1888.

As teachers cannot be had of locally due to the educational backwardness of Orissa, all the teachers were recruited by way of transfer from such far off places like Gouhati in Assam, Chittagang and Rangpur now in Bangladesh, Maldah and Bankura now in West Bengal, which then formed part of the Bengal Presidency. One cannot but admire the teachers of those days for their spirit of service and adventure that stimulated them to undertake tedious, long and risky road journeys, the only means of communication in those days. Sri Bholanath Das, Sri Hariprasad Das, and Pandit Sadasiva Nanda were the first men of Balasore to be appointed as masters of the school between 1870-73.

As the Balasore School did not have the necessary staff to cope with the stiff requirements of the Entrance Examination, it was overstraining itself and the lower classes had been neglected due to the increased attention that was given to the upper classes. During 1857-58, this school was designated a 'second grade' Zilla School.[76]

The School opened with three classes, i.e. 1st year 2nd year and 3rd year. The 4th and 5th years were added during 1854-55 and the 6th year during 1858. Subsequendy, two more classes were opened — the 7th year and 8th year classes.

As Orissa was a revenue division of Bengal Presidency; and due to Balasore's proximity to Bengali speaking tracts, the Bengali language predominated up to 1859. All the students of the Balasore Zilla School used to take up Bengali as the M. I. L. However, due to high failure rate in Bengali, the students switched over to Oriya M.I. L. in which it is said, "that no one has yet failed." [77]

---

76   General Report on the Public Instruction in the Lower Provinces of the Bengal Presidency, 1857-58,P

77   General Report on the Public Instruction in the Lower Provinces of the Bengal Presidency, 1857-58,pp. 102-105

The Balasore Zilla School was opened in a house generously lent by Sri Padmolochan Mondal, a wealthy landlord of Balasore. This old house in the heart of the town is now used as a market; and still stands as a mute witness of the institution. "The school house at Balasore is the worst school building of the entire division" wrote the Inspector of Schools during 1862-63. The work of erecting the school building was taken up soon after its establishment. It was built pardy from the Government grant and pardy from the donations of the landlords and the Rajas. The total expenditure incurred was Rs. 85,993.00. It was finally completed in 1870 and was formally opened on 30th April, 1870, on the prize giving day. This building wad demolished in 1930 and a new building was constructed.

From December, 1853 school fee was collected at the rate of half a rupee per students. It was raised to one rupee in the year 1857-58. A graduated school fee for different classes was introduced later, ranging from half a rupee for the 1st year class to two and half rupees for the seventh year class.[78] This was revised and enhanced in 1887-88.

The roll strength as well as the results of the Balasore Zilla School in the Entrance Examination from 1854 to 1881 has been depicted in Table No. 3.1.2

TABLE 3.1.2

Roll Strength and Entrance Examination Results of the Balasore Zilla School from 1854 to 1881

SI. No.	Year	Roll Strength of the School	No. of candidates sent up	Passes				
				1st	2nd	3rd	Total	%
01.	1854	82	......	...	.....	....	......	......
02.	1855	88	......	.....	.....	....	......	......
03.	1856	81	......	...	.....	....	......	......
04.	1857	82	....	....	.....	....	......	......

---

78   General Report on the Public Instruction in the Lower Provinces of the Bengal Presidency, 1862-63-p. 80

SI. No.	Year	Roll Strength of the School	No. of candidates sent up	Passes				
				1st	2nd	3rd	Total	%
05.	1858	68	....	....	...	.....	.....	.....
06.	1859	65	.....	.....	....	.....	.....	.....
07.	1860	50	1	....	1	....	1	100
08.	1861	52	....	.....	....			
09.	1862	56	.....	.....	.....	.....	.....	.....
10.	1863	73	3	1	2	....	3	100
11.	1864	98	.....	.....	....	.....	.....	....
12.	1865	105	4	1	1	2	4	100
13.	1866	91	.....	.....	....	....	....	....
14.	1867	93	2	1	1		2	100
15.	1868	78	5	...	2	1	3	60
16.	1869	107	5	.....	1	3	4	80
17.	1870	129	5	.....	3	1	4	80
18.	1871	118	2	....	....	1	1	50
19.	1872	118	5	1	....	2	3	60
20.	1873	113	4	2	....	1	3	75
21.	1874	136	2	....	1	1	2	100
22.	1875	137	6	1	....	1	2	33
23.	1876	144	8	....	....	....	....	0
24.	1877	149	9	...	....	3	3	33
25.	1878	140	7	....	3	1	4	57
26.	1879	155	10	....	4	1	5	50
27.	1880	145	9	....	7	1	8	89
28.	1881	168	9	....	2	5	7	78

The sudden decrease in roll strength of the school during the period 1866 to 1868 was due to the great Orissa Famine of 1866. From 1869 onwards there was a steady increase in the roll strength of the school. The Entrance Examination results were very good up to 1870; but then there was a steady decline in the percentage of passes.[79] The

---

79   Ibid p. 81

school prospered during this period under the fostering care of such eminent persons like Sri Padmolochan Mandal, Bhuyan Abdus Sobhan Khan; of eminent visitors like the Lieutenant Governor of Bengal, Commissioner T. E. Ravenshaw, and Phakirmohan Senapati and due to the unflagging zeal of headmasters like Biswanath Singh, Srinath Sen and Trailoykanath Ghose.

Puri Zillah School

During 1849-59, Mr. Forbes, District Magistrate and Collector of Puri, recommended the establishment of an English school at Puri in view of the growing demand for English education. The success of the Cuttack School and the appointment of the matriculates of this school to lucrative posts under the Government, inspired the people of Puri to demand for such a school.[80] "The school was originally a vernacular one, the inhabitants of Puri having subscribed to pay an extra teacher to enable those boys who wished to learn English, Geography, History and Arithmetic".[81] Babu Dinonath Mookerjee was in charge of this Vernacular School.

The Local Committee of Public Instruction was superintending and managing the school. The L. C. P. I. was composed of Collector, Magistrate, and Salt-Agent as the President, and the Assistant Magistrate, Civil Surgeon, Sub-assistant Surgeon, Deputy Collector and Munsif were the members. Mr E. Drummond, C. S. Collector was the first President and Mr. E. B. Thring, Civil Surgeon was the Secretary of the Local Committee.[27]

On 1st November, 1853, the Puri School was established. Sri Rasiklal Sen was the Headmaster of the School from 1853 to 1856; Sri Chandramohan Tagore from 1856 to 1859; Sri Kali Churn Chatterjee from 1859 to 1866; Sri Kunjabehari Chakravarti from 1867 to 1869; Sri

---

80 Balasore Zilla School Centenary Souvenir Issue, 1953, Appendix C. p. xxiv to xxv

81 Puri Zilla School Centenary Souvenir Issue, 1977, p. 2,

Gurudas Chatterjee from 1870 to 1871; Sri Ramdas Chakravarti from 1872 to 1878; Sri Kshirod Chander Ray Choudhary during 1879, Sri Sagar Chandra Chakravarti during 1880; and Sri Sashdhara Ray from 1881 to 1889.[82]Sri Bistocharan Mookerjee and Sri Dinanath Mookerjee were the first assistant teachers of the school. A Pundit was appointed during 1857-58.[29]

The school had 82 students on rolls on 30th April, 1854. Of the students, one was a Muslim and the rest 81 were Hindus. All the students were fee-paying students. Four students were studying only Bengali and Oriya; the rest 78 were studying English. "The attendance of the school had been tolerably good". There were four classes; the fourth class had two sections A and B. The average age of the students of thefirst class was 15 years. The ages of thestudents ofSecond Class ranged from 10 to 16 years and that of the Third Class from 10 to 17 years.

The roll strength of the school was 82 during 1854 and it increased to 89 by 1857. During 1858, there was a sudden fall in enrolment as "several boys whose boarding and schooling were paid by the late Deputy Collector Baboo Neelmony Burm, were obliged to leave Puri on his death."[83] The roll strength increased to 107 during 1870-71.

In 1859, five candidates were sent up for the Entrance Examination for the first time and one candidate passed in the second division. In 1860, one candidate passed the Entrance Examination in the second division and the results continued at the rate of one in each year during 1862 and 1863. There were no passes during 1867. The results of the school from 1868 to 1881 have been depicted in Table No. 3.1.3.[84]

---

82   General Report on the Public Instruction in the Lower Provinces of the Bengal Presidency, 30[th]Sept., 1852 to 27th Jan. 1855 p. 184

83   Op. cit p. 182

84   Op cit. p. (a)

TABLE 3.1.3

Entrance Examination Results of the Puri Zillah School 1868-1881

SI. No.	Year	Number of Passes			Total Passes
		1st Division	IInd Division	IIIrd Division	
01	1868	.....	1	....	1
02	1869	1	....	...	1
03	1870	1	1	1	3
04	1871	...	...	1	1
05	1872	....	....	2	2
06	1873	...	...	....	....
07	1874	...	...	....	...
08	1875	...	3	1	4
09	1876	....	2	3	5
10	1877	..	....	2	2
11	1878	...	2	1	3
12	1879	....	....	2	2
13	1880	...	2	3	5
14	1881	...	3	1	4

During 1857-58, the Puri School was designated a second-grade Zillah School. In the report for 1859-60, the disastrous impact of the University Examination on the academic life of the school is described as follows:

"The Headmasters of the Zillah Schools have the natural wish, that their schools should attain, as soon as possible, the prescribed standard. If the instructive staff is large enough, this is easily effected, as the classes are all steadily progressing; but where this is not the case, as for instance in Balasore and Pooree, the other classes are comparatively neglected to push on the pupils of the first and the passing of one or two pupils is no proof whatever that the school has really gained the prescribed standard."[85]

---

85   General Report on the Public Instruction in the Lower Provinces of the Bengal Presidency, 1857-58,p. 104

The academic progress was suffering due to the irregular attendance of the students. The Report states, "At first sight the attendance will appear unsatisfactory, but when the peculiar circumstances attached to the town are borne in mind, it may be accounted for. In this town, the great seat of Hindoo Worship, there are so many holidays, that it can hardly be expected that the school should be closed on every one of these occasions. On this account the school was opened on many of these holidays, especially when the holidays allowed to the school were regulated by the old rules, which were not at all adapted to local circumstances, but the attendance on such occasions, was invariably very thin."[86]

Even after a decade's existence the Puri School could not become popular and the Pandahs of Puri, the leading members of the native society, were avoiding the school and did not send their children to this school. As per the Report, "the temple interest appears too powerful for them to make any adequate head against it."[87]

St. Joseph's High School, Balasore

The Jesuit Missionary School at Balasore was known as the St. Joseph's High School. It was established in 1873. The school was not succeeding as it should because "an element of race antipathy and jealousy, between the teachers and the pupils had been introduced, which the Committee seemed inclined to foster rather than discountenance."[88] It had 104 pupils on rolls during 1873-74, out of which 51 wereHindus, 22 Muhammadans and 31 Christians. It charged less fees than the Zillah School and so many students were attracted to it.

---

86   General Report on the Public Instruction in the Lower Provinces of the Bengal Presidency, 1857-58,p. 315

87   Puri Zilla School Centenary Souvenir, 1977, Appendix p. 1.

88   General Report on the Public Instruction in the Lower Provinces of the Bengal Presidency, 1859-60,p. 73

The Sayeed Seminary, Cuttack

The Cuttack Urdu School was founded during 1874-75 to safeguard and promote the Muslim interests. In 1913, it was upgraded and became a high school. Sri Akshya Kumar Roy was the first headmaster. The school was named after Moulvi Mohammed Sayeed Saheb. The school could be established due to his dedicated selfless efforts. He commanded great respect at Cuttack. He had a highly secular oudook while tirelessly trying to uplift the muslim community. At his request the saint-poet Madhusudan Rao penned a patriotic Oriya prayer; and it was the daily prayer of the Sayeed Seminar for decades together.

The Lakhannath High School, Balasore

The Zamindar of Lakhannath was the first to start a private unaided high school at Lakhannath in 1875. It was also the first rural high school of Orissa. At that time there were no high schools at all in north Balasore. Therefore, many students flocked to this school. However, the instruction imparted in the school was not up to the mark and the Inspectors were dissatisfied.

The Peary Mohan Academy, Cuttack

Sri Peary Mohan Acharya founded the Cuttack Academy in 1873. It was a private unaided institution. It had 12 students on rolls when it was started. Pandit Gobind Rath assisted the founder greatly in this venture. Babu Kailash Chandra Ghosh became the President and Babu Nimai Charan Neogi, the Vice-President of the Managing Committee which was constituted on 31st March,1875. It was started at Darghabazar of Cuttack. It became a High School in 1879. Sri Bipin Chandra Pal, the great revolutionary, was its first Headmaster.[36] It was a bold venture of the times. Peary Mohan Acharya was a Brahmo and the P. M. Academy had strong Brahmo leaning in its earlier days. On 3rd December,1887, it was named the Peary Mohan Academy after its founder

Stewart School, Cuttack

In 1881, this Protestant European School was founded due to the unremitting zeal of Mr. Stewart, the Civil Surgeon of Cuttack. Today this is known as the Cuttack Stewart School. It is a flourishing institution of high standards and bears the holy memory of its founder. Mr. Steward will go down in the history of Orissa as one of the greatest benefactors and patrons of education. He donated his palatial building to this school. Now, the Christ Collegiate School is held in this building. The Stewart School is located in the building used by him as residence and donated to the school. Mr. P. Smith was its first Headmaster. He was succeeded by Miss Bundy. At his behest a Medical School was established at Cuttack.[89] It has become the S. C. B. Medical College now.

Sambalpur Zilla School

Sambalpur School was started during 1856-57. to induce the parents to send their children to the School, it was resolved in a meeting dated the 15th January, 1857 that "none but those educated should be employed in offices under Government."[90]Babu Ughore Chandra Mookerjee was its first Headmaster. There were four classes - the second, the third, the fourth and the fifth classes. The first class was in abeyance. In April, 1859, the School was converted into an Anglo-Vernacular School (i.e. an M. E. School). Thus the first attempts at establishing a Zillah School at Sambalpur failed.

MIDDLE SCHOOL IN NORTH ORISSA*

An aided Anglo-Vernacular school was started at Bhadrak during 1857-58. The school owed its establishment to the exertions of Babu Sreenath Ghosh, Deputy Collector of Bhadrak. An amount of Rs. 30.00

---

89   General Report on the Public Instruction in the Lower Provinces of the Bengal Presidency, 1859-60,p. 334

90   General Report on the Public Instruction in the Lower Provinces of the Bengal Presidency, 1863-64,p. 160

per month was sanctioned asGovernment aid.[91] It had 40 students on its rollsduring 1859-60[92]. Its roll strength decreased to 29 in 1860-61. It was considered to be a 'moderate' class school. The cost to Government per each boy was Rs. 1-0-7.[93]

There was an Aided Anglo-Vernacular School at Sree Krishnapur and another at Jajpur which were established in 1863. The Sreekrishnapur School was considered to be a moderate one and got a monthly grant of Rs. 25.00. The Jajpur School had 52 Scholars; but was considered to be 'indifferen't. It got Rs. 25.00 per month as Government grant.[94]

A Church Mission Anglo-Vernacular School was opened at Cuttack during 1863-64.[95] It had 145 students on rolls and got a Government grant of Rs. 150.00 per month.

There was an aided Anglo-Vernacular School for Bengalees at Cuttack which was established in 1863. An aided Anglo-Vernacular School was started at Kendrapara during 1863-64. The Kendrapara School had 33 students and got Rs. 25.00 as grant-in-aid.[96] In 1881, Madhusudan Rao established Town Victoria M. E. School at Cuttack. Now it is Bhakta Madhu Vidyapeeth.

---

91   General Report on the Public Instruction in Bengal, 1873-74, p. 42

92   Centenary Souvenir of the Peary Mohan Academy, 1975, pp. 130-132

93   Prafulk Kumar Patra, Odisare Baptist Mission ro Karya, Mission Press, Cuttack 1943, pp. 152-159.

94   General Report on the Public Instruction in the Lower Provinces of the Bengal Presidency, 1856-57,p. 119.
     * Note: North Orissa means the three districts of Cuttack, Puri, Balasore, and Angul and Kondhamalof present Orissa. Sambalpur was in north Orissa up to 1861 when it was transferred to theCentral Provinces and retransferred to Bengal in 1905. North Orissa was under Bengal Presidencyup to 1912 and in Bihar & Orissa up to 1936

95   General Report on the Public Instruction in the Lower Provinces of the Bengal Presidency,l 857-58,p. Ill

96   General Report on the Public Instruction in the Lower Provinces of the Bengal Presidency,l 859-60,p. 71

By 1872-73, there were 2 M. E. Schools and 11 M. V. Schools in the Balasore district; 9 M. E Schools and 11 M. V. Schools in Cuttack district; one M. E School and 13 M. V Schools in the Puri district. In all there were 12 M. E. Schools and 35 M. V. Schools in Orissa districts during 1873-74.[97]

The General Report on the Public Instruction in Bengal, 1872-73 states: "In some middle schools, English is taught, and in others the whole of the instruction is in the vernacular. Middle schools were consequently classed as English schools or vernacular schools, accordingly as English is or is not taught in them. The standardaimed at is the middle English Schools is that laid down in the course for minor scholarships, representing a stage of progress from two to three years short of that reached in the higher schools. In the same way the Vernacular scholarship course defines the standard aimed at by the middle vernacular schools. It is the same standard as the standard of middle English schools in all subjects except English."[98]

In 1862, an M. E. School was established at Bargarh, then in Central Provinces. It became the George High School, Bargarh in 1920.

In 1868, an M. E. school was established at Dhenkanal. It was the first of its kind in the feudatory states of Orissa. It was established by Sri Bhagirath Mahendra, Raja Saheb of Dhenkanal. One M. E. School was established at Bhawanipatna in 1871 by Raja Udit Pratap Deo, ruler of the Korond (Kalahandi) state.

There were 10 M. V. Schools in the 24 feudatory states of Orissa. The ruling chiefs of these states hardly evinced any interest towards the education of the people.

Cuttack and Balasore districts were more advanced in English education than Puri district. The M. E. Schools were increasingly favoured in the

---

97   General Report on the Public Instruction in the Lower Provinces of the Bengal Presidency,1861-62,Appendix A, p. 18

98   *Ibid* Appendix A. p. 18

Cuttack district. M. V. Schools were highly popular in Puri and Balasore districts.

The M. E. Schools and M. V Schools were easily convertible one into the other, by addition or abolition of English as a subject. The M. E. Schools became popular because they served as stepping stones to high schools. By 1881, there was a general demand for high schools and the Inspector of Schools was constrained to recommend the upgradation of some of the advanced M. E. Schools to High Schools.[99]

An important side feature worth noting is that all the M. E Schools were private managed, whereas the M. V. Schools were maintained and aided by the Government. This indicates the popularity of the M. E. Schools at that time. The M. V. Schools were frequented by those who had not the benefit of Pathsalas.

By 1881-82, there were 23 Middle English Schools and 35 Middle Vernacular Schools in Orissa. Of the M. E. Schools 19 were aided and 4 were private schools. In case of the M. V Schools only one was private and the rest 34 were Government Aided Schools.[100]

SECONDARY EDUCATION IN SOUTH ORISSA*

The Oriya speaking tracts of Ganjam and Koraput were part of the Northen Circars and these passed into British administration when the Northern Circars were ceded to the British by Salabat Jung, Nizam of Hyderbad, on 14th May,1759. The British actually occupied the Northen Circars on 12th August, 1765. It was ratified by the Mughal Emperor on that date. The British took possession of the Ganjam district on 12th November, 1766. In 1778, Jeypore estate was constituted as the Vizagpatam Agency. Ganjam for a pretty long time was the citadel of Oriya literature and great poets like Upendra Bhanja, Kabisurya Baladeb

---

99 General Report on the Public Instruction in the Lower Provinces of the Bengal Presidency,l 863-64,p. 165

100 General Report on the Public Instruction in the Lower Provinces of the Bengal Presidencyl 866-67,p. 218

Rath and Gopal Krishna Patnaik were born here. However, the Britishers considered the Oriya people as educationally backward. The medium of instruction in the schools of Ganjam was Oriya as Ganjam, Ganjam Agency and Koraput were considered to be Oriya-speaking tracts.

Western culture could not influence the Ganjam District in the Madras Presidency till 1854, though the district was under the direct British administration. The first Anglo-Vernacular School in the district of Ganjam came into being in1855.

The Onslow Institute, Chatrapur

Mr. Arthur Pooly Onslow was the Collector of Ganjam from 29th July, 1849 to 24th January, 1854. On 3rd January 1854 he lost his wife, Rosa Robertia, on the eve of his returning to his native land. After his retirement, he bequeathed in a deed of trust a house, which was then the Collector's residence, and some landed property in and about Chatrapur, to be held by the trustees, the Bishop and Archdeacon of Madras, on certain trusts, the principal of them being the establishing at the station of Chatrapur or within a convenient distance thereof, a school for the education of such of the Christians and native population as might resort thereto and keeping the same on foot forever.

The School was established in 1855. It is presently known as the Onslow Institute, Chatrapur. It was housed in a temporary erection. The number of scholars was 65. Mr. H. Margenout, a young man of respectable character, who had been educated at Bishop's College, Calcutta, was appointed the Headmaster. M. W Knox, the acting Collector of Ganjam, and the Rev. J. Griffiths were appointed as the firstco-trustees of the School on 10th April, 1854.

The School was submitted to Government inspection in 1856, with the view of obtaining Government aid. The Madras Government sanctioned a grant of Rs. 40.00 per month for the Headmaster, and another Rs. 40.00 a month towards the salaries of the other assistant teachers and Rs. 1000.00 for the construction of school building.[101] Mr. H. Margenout worked up to 1857 as Headmaster. He was succeeded by Mr. D. Venkaty who worked as Headmaster from 1857 to 1858. Mr. Ch. Appa Naidu was the Headmaster from 1859 to 1861; Mr. W G Browne from 1861 to 1862, and again Sri Ch. Appa Naidu from 1863 to 1865. Mr. A. Appiah, Mr. Narayana Murty and Mr. S. Narayana Rao were the Headmasters from 1866 to 1867. Mr. W H. Synch was Headmaster up to 1888.[102]

Berhampur Zilla School

In 1856, the Government of Madras established the Zilla School at Berhampur. Later, there was a proposal that it be shifted to Chhatrapur. But this never happened. Mr. Margenout and Mr. Venkaty of the Onslow Institute joined this new school as teachers. Inspector McDonald had recommended the establishment of the Zillah School at Berhampur which was a populous town of 30,000 souls.[103] By 1860, the Berhampur Zillah School became a full-fledged high school. Seventy seven Scholars were studying in this institution in 1857 and this number rose to 235 in 1860. Three students of this school passed the Matriculation Examination of the Madras University in 1860.[104] During 1869, this school was upgraded and an Intermediate College was established. It was abolished in 1871. It was soon re-established and continued up to 1887, when the Government decided to abolish it. The Collector, Ganjam and the people of Berhampur vehemently protested against this. The Maharajah of Khallikote volunteered to finance the College. The College was then known as the Native College. On 1st July,1894, it

---

101 General Report on the Public Instruction in the Lower Provinces of the Bengal Presidencyl 872-73,p. 323

102 *Ibid* pp. 5-6

  *** Note:** South Orissa means the Ganjam District, Ganjam Agency and the present Koraput district which was under the Madras Presidency up to 1936.

103 Report on Public Instruction in Bengal, 1881-82, p. 29.

104 Report on Public Instruction in Bengal 1881-82, p. 29

was named the Khallikote College. Today it is one of the two premier post-graduate Colleges of Orissa. The high school department was known as the Khallikote Collegiate School. The Berhampur Zillah School was handed over to the local management in accordance with the recommendations of the Hunter Commission (1882).

The Taluk Schools

During 1855-56, three Taluk Schools (equivalent to the middle schools of North Orissa) were established at Ganjam, Russelkonda (present Bhanjanagar) and Purushottampur. A sum of Rs. 80.00 was sanctioned for the establishment of a Taluk School at Parlakhemundi by the Court of Wards. By 1860, the number of Taluk Schools had risen to six and the total number of scholars studying in these institutions was 132. By 1867-68, there were 22 Government Schools with 1,176 scholars, and 7 private schools and one Mission M. E. School. In addition the Zilla School, there were two M. E. Schools at Berhampur - the Mission M. E. School and the Town M. E. School. The Mission M. E. School later became the Queen of Missions High School, Berhampur and the Town M. E. School became the Town High School, Berhampur.

In 1857, a primary school was established at Paralakhemundi. It became an M. E. School in 1878 and a High School in 1884. It was recognized as a first grade High School.

In 1884, the Oriya school at Bhanjanagar (then Russekonda) was handed over to the Local Board on the condition that the Government would pay the net cost to the Local Board.

The Anglo-Vernacular and Vernacular schools were classified under the same head. The erstwhile differences were ignored. It was realized that at least one school should exist in every district of India. It was realized then, as it is now, that the quality of instruction primarily depends upon the quality of school masters. The non-availability of qualified and competent teachers was the greatest barriers in the expansion on of education. The number of qualified and efficient teachers was limited because the definition connoted only teachers with mastery over English and Western knowledge. In consequence, the indigenous scholars with deep erudition in classical languages and Oriental learning, were ignored and their services were never utilized for the betterment of education.

SECTION II

LOSS OF PRIMACY (1882-1901)

The year 1882 is highly significant in the history of education in India. Lord Ripon, who had become the Viceroy of India in 1880, initiated an era of development and progress. Edmund Burke had castigated the British administration in India and hadridiculed it as 'magisterial administration'. Indians were not associated with the administration due to the climate of suspicion that was generated by the First Movement for Freedom of 1857. The British did not bother to consult the Indians; and Indians, in their turn, developed cynical apathy towards the imperial administration. To remedy the situation, Lord Ripon sought to elicit the co-operation of the Indians through the various institutions of local self-government, which he had introduced. The recommendations of the Indian Education Commission of 1882 opened new avenues for Indians to associate themselves with the spread and management of education.

INDIAN EDUCATION (HUNTER) COMMISSION (1882)

The first Indian Education Commission was appointed on February 3, 1882 with Mr. W W. Hunter as its President. Mr. Hunter had officiated as the Inspector of Schools, South West Division of Bengal during 1867 and Orissa was under his jurisdiction. He had written an exhaustive history of Orissa in two volumes which serves as a benchmark survey even today. Mr. B. L. Rice, the Director of Public Instruction, Mysore was appointed the Secretary of the Commission. Mr. D. M. Barbour, Revd. W R. Blackett, Mr. A. W. Croft, Mr. K. Deighton, Mr. J. T. Fowler, Mr. A. P. Howell, Mr. H. P. Jacob, Mr. W Lee Warner, Rev. W Miller,

Mr. C. Pearson, Mr. G. E. Ward, Revd. A. Jean, and Mr. C. A. R. Browning were the British members of the Commission. The Indian members were Sir Syed Ahmed Khan, Mr. Anand Mohan Bose, Mr. P. Rangananda Mudaliar, Mr. Bhudev Mookherjee, Maharaja Jatindra Mohan Tagore, Mr. Kasinath Trimbuk Telang, and Mr. Haji Ghulam. Of the 20 members of the Commission 7 were Indians.

In accordance with the terms of reference, the Commission devoted itself to an examination of "the manner in which effect has been given to the principles of the Despatch of 1854," and "the present state of elementary education throughout the Empire and the means by which this can everywhere be extended and improved." The report of the Commission ran into 700 foolscap pages. Though the Commission devoted itself to primary education, it did make certain salient recommendations relating to secondary education.

According to the Commission, provision of primary education was of paramount importance and so it was considered to be the duty of the Government to provide it. Secondary education was not that important and so the Government was under no obligation to provide it. The people should exert to educate themselves. The Commission, therefore, recommended that, "secondary educationshould as far as possible, be provided on the grant-in-aid basis," and that "government should withdraw, as early as possible, from the direct management of secondary schools."[105]

As regards the secondary schools already under Government management, the Commission recommended that the goal of Government effort should be to transfer gradually all Government secondary schools to a suitable non-governmental agency, "without lowering the standard or diminishing the supply of education and without endangering the permanence of the institution transferred."[106] However, "the withdrawal of direct departmental agency should

---

105 Centenary Souvenir of the Onslow Institute, Chhatrapur, 1963, pp. 10-11
106 *Ibid* p. 47

not take place in favour of missionary bodies and that departmental institutions of the higher order should not be transferred to missionary management."[107] It exhorted the Government to promote the private initiative and enterprise in the field of education. It stated that, "it must not be forgotten that the private effort which it is mainly intended to evoke is that of the people themselves. Natives of India must constitute the most important of all agencies, if educational means are ever to be co-extensive with educational wants."[108] However, the Government may establish secondary schools "in places where they may be required in the interests of the people, and where the people themselves may not be advanced or wealthy enough to establish such schools for themselves with a grant-in-aid."[109]

The Commission considered the issue relating to the medium of instruction at the secondary stage and made an ambiguous statement. In consequence of this recommendation, the development of the Indian languages was greatly hampered. English held its complete sway over high school education and its dominance grew in the years following the Commission's Report. It stated:

"We do not put forward any definite recommendation... It is a question in the decisionof which much must depend on local circumstances and hence the freest scope in dealingwith it should be left to the managers of the schools, whatsoever be the view which theDepartment in any Province may be disposed to adopt."[110]

By 1882, there was only one Training College for Teachers at Saidpet of Madras in India. Training facilities did not exist on a large scale. Under the circumstances, the Commission could not categorically state that the

---

107 Report on Public Instruction in the Madras Presidency, 1856-57
108 Report on Public Instruction in the Madras Presidency, 1860-61
109 J. P. Naik & Syed Nurullah: A Students' History of Education in India, Macmillan Co. of IndiaLtd., 1974, p. 239
110 S. N. Mukherjee: Secondary Education in India, Orient Longmans, April, 1972. p. 70

training was essential for secondary school teachers. A heated debate was on as regards the necessity or otherwise of training for secondary school teachers. Therefore, the Indian Education Commission, 1882 recommended that, "an examination in the principles and practices of teaching be instituted, success in which should thereafter be a condition of permanent employment as a teacher in any secondary school, Government or aided," and that "graduates wishing to attend a course of instruction in a normal school in the principles and practices of teaching be required to undergo a shorter course of training than others."[111]

The most important recommendation of the Commission was with regard to the need for the institution of a School Leaving Course of a practical and modern character free from the domination of the University matriculation examination. Alternative S. L. C. Examinations were instituted; but they did not find favour with the people. It stated,

"We, therefore, recommended that in the upper classes of high schools there be two divisions; one leading to the Entrance Examination of the Universities, the other of a more practical character intended to fit youths for commercial or non-literary pursuits."[112]

Some other recommendations of the Commission relating to secondary educationwere as follows:

- "That the middle English Schools should be amalgamated with the High Schools as Classes VI & VII were lower secondary classes.
- That the scales of pay of teachers of aided schools should be equal to that of the Government schools.
- That experienced teachers of the private schools should be associated with educational administration and school inspection, and to effect this the restrictions relating to

---

111 Government of India Resolution dated the 11th March, 1904
112 A. N. Basu, Education in Modern India, p. 64

- minimum age of entry to government service be done away with.
- That co-operation of teachers should be sought in all examination matters. They should be remunerated for examination work.
- That teacher should not be expected to teach for more than three hours at a stretch.
- Teachers should have the absolute powers relating to class-promotions.
- That scholarship-holding student should also pay school fees. Scholarships should be instituted for every class.
- That school-library should be improved through the appointment of fixed grants for the purpose. Specific grants should be made for furniture and equipment."

These recommendations provided the broad guidelines for the development of secondary education in India. Of course, the different Provinces implemented the recommendations in different ways. The grant-in-aid codes were revised. The number of private aided schools increased appreciably.

PROGRESS OF SECONDARY EDUCATION IN NORTH ORISSA

According to the Census of 1891*, the total population of the Orissa Division was 40,47,352, out of which the male population was 19,82,493 and female population was 20,64,859. Of these 1,15,320 males and 5,615 female were receiving instruction. The percentage of literacy for males was 5.84, for females it was 0.27, and for the entire population it was 2.98.

By 1881-82, the number of different types of schools was as follows:

- Government High English Schools   ...   3
- Aided High English Schools   ...   2
- Government M. V. Schools   ...   13

- Aided M. V. Schools ... 34
- Aided M. E. Schools ... 19
- Unaided M. E. Schools ... 4

In all there were 75 institutions which were imparting secondary education. As regards the number of high schools, it may be clarified here that the number of full-fledged high school was 5. They were the three Zillah Schools at Cuttack, Puri and Balasore and the two aided high schools of P. M. Academy, Cuttack and the Lakhannath High School at Lakhannath in Balasore district. The Stewart School was started in 1881 and the Christ Collegiate School in 1882. the Anglo-Urdu High School, Cuttack was languishing and so was the St. Joseph's High School at Balasore. All these schools were incomplete high schools.[113]

After 1882 there was an increase in the number of secondary schools in North Orissa. But the progress was rather slow. The total increase was by 8 institutions. The following was the position of secondary schools by 1899-1900.

- Government High English Schools ... 3
- Aided High English Schools ... 7
- Unaided High English Schools ... 1
- Government M. E. Schools ... 3
- Aided and Unaided M. E. Schools ... 32
- Government M. V. Schools ... 14
- Aided M. V. Schools ... 22
- Unaided M. V. Schools ... 1

The total number of institutions imparting secondary instruction in 1899-1900 was 83. There were no Government M. E. Schools in 1881-82. By 1899-1900, there were three such schools. One Practicing Upper Primary School was upgraded to an M. E. School; and two Government M. E. Schools were opened in the Angul-Kondhamals district. The

---

113 Haridas Mukherjee & Uma Mukherjee, Origins of the National Educational Movement (1905-1910).

number of M. V. Schools decreased from 47 in 1881-82 to 37 in 1899-1900. The Vernacular education was steadily losing ground and English education was becoming increasingly popular.[114]

The development of secondary education, in particular, and of education, in general, was slow in Orissa during this period. The following extracts from Sir A. Croft's Report for 1893-94 clearly explains the reason why there were such wide differences between the progress obtained in the metropolitan districts on the one hand and the outlying tracts like Orissa on the other:

"The indigenous system of education was, from time immemorial, in extended operation in Burdwn Division, which used to supply gurus to other parts of Central Bengal before the system of departmental supervision began. Orissa was quite independent of Bengal in this respect and had its own national system of education, which was probably more far-reaching in its influence than even that of Bengal."[115]

However, the British tried, though unsuccessfully, to turn Orissa into an appendage of Bengal. They wanted to raise the same educational crops in Orissa as in Bengal and so they failed because the education was totally foreign for the Oriyas. The spirit of "general and ready acceptance of education, when offered was very much there is Orissa, but was not taken good advantage of it."[116]

In the Setdement Report of 1881 prepared by Mr. Maddox, I. C. S. there is mention of a large number of Oriya Zamindars. It is strange to note

---

114 Indian Educational Policy 1913, Superintendent, Government Printing, Calcutta, 1913. As 4, pp.16-24.
      *Note: In 1881, the total population of Orissa was 15,61,738 out of which 922,622 were males and 639,166 were females. The total population of the Feudatory states of Orissa was 12,11,001, out of which 702,753 were males and 508,248 were females. Literacy figures for Orissa & Tributary States were 7. 03% and 3. 05% respectively. (Census of Bengal, 1981, p. 97 & p. 192)
115 J. P. Naik & Syed Nurullah, op Cit.. p. 258
116 Arthur Mayhew, The Education of Tndia, p. 213.

that none of them,barring the solitary exception of the Zamindar of Lakshannath,cameforward to develop education. The Zamindars of South Orissa were much enlightened in this respect. The feudal chiefs never desired the enlightenment of the common masses, lest they might lose their hold over them.

In spite of the sincere efforts of Mr. T. E. Ravenshaw, the Brahmins of North Orissa were not interested in English education and Sanskrit education was in a decadent state. It was Mr. Harihar Dash, the Head Pandit of the Sanskrit classes attached to the Puri Zillah School who dreamt of making Puri the *Educational Capital of Orissa,* in addition to its pre-eminent position as a place of pilgrimage. Jajpur, one time centre of high Brahmanic culture, had also lost its hoary tradition of educational excellence. In short, it may be stated that the Zanindars and Brahmins, who were the most influential natives of Orissa did not evince adequate interest towards English education. It is the Karans, specially of Cuttack, who realized the importance of English education and took full advantage of it. During 1882-83, there were 8 Brahmin boys and 37 Karan boys reading in the Cuttack Zilla School. The Karans could compete with the Bengalis in matters of education and employment. The Khandayats were the most numerous according to the Census of 1891. But they were far behind in the educational race. The Khandayats had developed a subconscious hatred towards the English education due to the barbarous treatment meted out to them by the British during the Paik Rising of 1817 and the Sepoy Mutiny of 1857. The Khandayats remained aloof for a long a time, and when they woke up to the realities of the situation, it was already too late and they had been left behind in the race.*[117]

In 1896-97, there were 38 M. E. Schools in which 153 teachers were employed, of which one was an M. A.; 3 were F. A passed or old Senior Scholars; 21 had passed the Entrance or the Junior Scholarship Examination; 28 had passed the Vernacular Mastership Examination;

---

117 A. N. Basu, op. Cit, p. 62

7 had passed the Guru Training class examination; 29 had passed the M. E. Examination; 25 had passed the M. V. Examination; 3 had passed the Upper Primary Examination; 1 had passed the Lower Primary Examination; 2 had other qualifications and 33 had no certificates

* *Note:* According to the Settlement Report of 1891 of Maddox, the caste-wise break up of Orissa was as follows:

1.	Khandayats	600,000	5.	Panas	160. 000
2.	Chasha	430,000	6.	Kandaras	135,000
3.	Brahmins	400,000	7.	Karans	123,000
4.	Gopalas	350,000	8.	Kaiborto	122,000

Lower Primary Examination; 2 had other qualifications and 33 had no certificates of any qualification.[118]

During 1896-97, thetotal number of High Schools was 390, that of Middle English Schools was 927 and of the Middle Vernacular Schools was 1163 for the entire Province of Bengal.[119] During the same year, the number of High Schools was 11; that of M. E. Schools was 38, and that of M. V. Schools was 50 for the Orissa Divison.[68] The total number of scholars studying in all the secondary schools of Bengal was 2,17,054, and that of Orissa Division was 6,477.[120]

In 1896-97, there were 50 M. V. Schools with 164 teachers. The qualification of the M. V. School teachers was — Entrance passed 3, Vernacular Mastership examination passed 64; Guru-training examination passed 2; M. E. passed 2, M. V. passed 58; UP. passed 8; L. P. passed 6; no qualification 21.[121]

All the secondary schools were charging fees. The rates in schools under private management were generally lower than those charged in

---

118 Progress of Education in Bengal, 1881-82, pp. 41-47
119 Review of Education in Bengal, 1892-97, p. 4
120 *Ibid* p4
121 *Ibid.* General Statistics, p. xxviii

government schools. The average incidence of fees in a high school was Rs. 17.50; in a Middle English School it was Rs. 5.37 and Rs. 3.06 in a Middle Vernacular School during 1896-97.[122]

There were three grades of scholarships tenable in secondary schools of two years. The Middle Vernacular and Middle English, the former being tenable for four and the latter for three years in high schools. The system was a continuous one. Middle and Upper Primary Scholarships were awarded by the Inspectors. The expenditure was met from the provincial revenues. There were besides some few local scholarships paid out of endowed funds, for the benefit of students reading in secondary schools.[123] Seventy-nine candidates appeared at the Entrance Examination in 1897, out of which 38 passed from the 11 high schools of Orissa.[73] There were six M. V. Schools for girls during 1896-97. The roll strength of these schools was 398.[124]

In 1882, the native Christians of Cuttack with the assistance of London Baptist Mission established a high school which is to-day known as the **Christ CollegiateSchool.** It boldly introduced 'co-education'. It was a courageous educational experiment at that time. It speaks volumes about the foresight of Mr. George D. Souza, its illustrious first headmaster. Of the three Zillah Schools in Orissa, Cuttack School was a first grade Zillah School; the Puri Zillah School was third grade and Balasore Zillah school was second grade.[125] There were no high schools in the Angul-Kondhamal district during this period. The number of high schools and scholars reading therein during 1892-93 to 1901-02 has been shown in Table No. 3.2.1.

---

122 IM^JG^neraLStatisiks, p. xxvii
123 *Ibid.* General Statistics, p. xxviii to xxvii.
124 *Ibid.*
125 Review of Education in Bengal, 1892-93 to 1896-97, p. 93

TABLE 3.2.1

Number of High Schools and Scholars during 1892-93 to 1901-02

SI. No.	Year	Cuttack		Puri		Balasore	
		High Schools	Scholars	High Schools	Scholars	High Schools	Scholars
01.	1892-93	5	913	1	131	3	330
02.	1893-94	5	912	1	138	3	340
03.	1894-95	5	869	1	147	4	391
04.	1895-96	5	874	1	159	4	369
05.	1896-97	5	894	2	365	4	376
06.	1897-98	5	962	2	309	4	496
07.	1898-99	5	1053	2	358	4	512
08.	1899-1900	5	1108	2	358	4	541
09.	1900-1901	6	1194	2	358	4	579
10.	1901-1902	6	1328	2	386	4	584

Up to 1899-1900, all the high schools of the Cuttack district were concentrated at Cuttack. In 1900-01, a high school was opened at a Jajpur. In 1896-97, a high school was opened at Khurda in the Puri district at the instance of Mr. H. Macpherson, I. C. S. Sub-Divisional Officer, Khurda. In 1894-95, the Bhadrak High School was started at Bhadrak. High Schools began springing up in mofussil towns. The enrolment in the high schools of the Orissa Division during 1892-93 was 1,374 and it increased to 2,298 by 1901-02. to 1901-02, in the districts of Cuttack, Puri, Balasore and Angul[126]s portrayed in TableNo. 3.2.2.

---

126 *Ibid* p. 94

TABLE 3.2.2

Number of M.E. and M.V. Schools from 1892-93 to 1901-02

Sl. No.	Category of Schools	Year									
		1892-1893	1893-1894	1894-1895	1895-1896	1896-1897	1897-1898	1898-1899,	1899-1900	1900-1901	1901-1902
	Cuttack District										
01. 02.	(a) M.E. Schools	22	23	21	22	22	21	23	25	28	29
	(b) Scholars	1203	1304	1185	1282	1405	1441	1598	1591	1733	1694
	(a) M.V. Schools	13	12	13	13	15	13	12	11	09	07
	(b) Scholars	630	636	616	663	824	769	709	589	498	406
	Balasore District										
01. 02.	(a) M.E. Sschools	12	12	12	12	12	11	14	12	11	11
	(b) Scholars	721	735	752	704	817	721	905	788	715	696
	(a) M.V. Schools	16	16	16	18	18	19	18	18	19	19
	(b) Scholars	737	748	707	789	838	875	839	792	843	856

Sl. No.	Category of Schools	Year									
		1892-1893	1893-1894	1894-1895	1895-1896	1896-1897	1897-1898	1898-1899,	1899-1900	1900-1901	1901-1902
	Puri District										
0 1 . 02.	(a) M.E. Schools	05	06	06	06	04	05	08	05	06	05
	(b) Scholars	221	305	312	332	293	318	405	319	386	357
	(a) M.V. Schools	16	15	15	15	15	15	15	14	14	15
	(b) Scholars	565	561	551	524	548	517	599	559	518	535
	Angul District										
0 1 . 02.	(a) M.E. Schools										
	(b) Scholars										
	(a) M.V. Schools	02	02	02	02	02	02	02	02	02	02
	(b) Scholars	103	100	80	98	117	106	111	94	84	105

Source for (1) Cuttack District: Cuttack District Gazetteer, 1901-02, (2) Puri District: Puri district Gazetteer, Statistics 1901-02; (3) Balasore District: Balasore District Gazetteer, Statistics, 1901-02; published by the Bengal Secretariat Book Depot, Calcutta, 1905.

From Table No. 3.2.2 it is evident that in the district of Cuttack the M. V. Schools were losing ground and the M. E. Schools were becoming increasingly popular. However, in the Balasore district, a reverse trend is discernible. The situation was stagnant in the Puri and Angul-Kodhamal districts. A parallel trend is observed in case of enrolment.

The total expenditure in respect of High, M. E. and M. V. Schools was as follows during 1901-02.

Cuttack District:	
(a) High Schools	25,970.00
(b) M. E. Schools	20,393.00
(c) M. V. Schools	4,548.00
Balasore District:	
(a) High Schools	15,517.00
(b) M. E. Schools	8,281.00
(c) M. V. Schools	7,712.00
Puri District:	
(a) High Schools	9,220.00
(b) M. E. Schools	2,899.00
(c) M. V. Schools	4,062.00
Angul-Kondhamal District:	
(a) High Schools	Nil
(b) M. E. Schools	Nil
(c) M. V. Schools	1,202.00

The total expenditure on secondary education during 1901-02 in the Orissa Division was Rs. 99,804.00 [127]

---

127 *IM* p. 56

TABLE 3.2.3

Management of Secondary Schools in the Orissa Division in 1901-02

SI. No.	Type of Schools	Management				Total
		Government	District Board	Aided	Un-aided	
01	High Schools	03		08	01	12
02	M. E. Schools	01	06	38		45
03	M. V. Schools	04	08	30	01	43

The aided Schools were the most numerous and the recommendations of the Indian Education Commission, 1882, seems to have borne fruit.

SECONDARY EDUCATION IN THE SAMBALPUR DISTRICT

Sambalpur District was in the Bengal Presidency up to 1861, when it was transferred to the Central Provinces on its creation on 2nd November,1861. Again it was transferred to Bengal Province on 16th May, 1905. The total population of the Sambalpur District as per the census of 1901 was 8,29,698, out of which 13,936 were literate. The total percentage of literacy was 1.68. Total male literacy was 3.32 per cent and female literacy was 0.09 per cent. Sambalpur School was the oldest. It was a Zilla School from 1856-57 to 1859. From 1859 to 1885, it was an M. E. School. It was again raised to the status of a high school during 1885. Its roll strength was 142 in 1886. It was situated in a small building in the heart of the Sambalpur town. A Middle Vernacular school was started at Bargarh in 1868. At the end of the century there were 6 Middle Vernacular schools in the district. The number of secondary schools, scholars reading therein and the expenditure on secondary education during 1891-92 to 1902-03.[128] has been shown in Table No. 3.2.4.

---

128 Mp. 57

TABLE 3.2.4

Number of Secondary Schools, Scholars, and Expenditure in the Sambalpur District from 1891-92 to 1902-03

SI. No.	Year	Number of		Scholars in Secondary Schools	Expenditure on Secondary Education (Rupees)
		High Schools	Middle Schools		
01.	1891-92		6	538	976.00
02.	1892-93		7	577	11,191.00
03.	1893-94		7	597	10,884.00
04.	1894-95		7	554	12,281.00
05.	1895-96		8	606	11,214.00
06.	1896-97		8	697	11,779.00
07.	1897-98		8	614	10,996.00
08.	1898-99		5	644	11,772.00
09.	1899-00		5	531	11,346.00
10.	1900-01		5	218	8,088.00
11.	1901-02		6	236	11,048.00
12.	1902-03		6	241	9,175.00

Source: Central Province District Gazetteers, Sambalpur District, Ed. R. V. Russell, I.C.S., Allahabad, 1905. p.84.

SECONDARY EDUCATION IN SOUTH ORISSA

By 1881-82, there was one Government High School, six Government M. E. Schools, 3 Aided M. E. Schools and 2 unaided middle schools in the district of Ganjam. The total number of secondary schools was 12.[129] By 1899-1900, there were 3 Board High Schools, and 9 Government and aided middle schools. The Town M. E. School of Parlakhemundi became a high school in 1894. It prepared the ground for the establishment of the M. K. C. College, Parlakimedi on 9th October,1891 largely due to the initiative and patronage of the Maharaja. The Government Zillah

---

129 Mp. 60

School, Berhampur had been transferred to Board management. Thus, there were no Government schools left in Ganjam district by 1900. All the secondary schools were either managed by the District Board or were aided institutions.[130] The expansion of secondary education was unsatisfactory in South Orissa. The emphasis on 'quality' adversely affected the quantitative expansion of secondary schools in South Orissa. The Secondary School Leaving Certificate (S. S. L. C) scheme was introduced in the Madras Presidency in accordance with the recommendations of the Hunter Commission (1882).

The Curriculum of the High School was as follows:

Group A: (for Public Examination)

English, Vernacular (Oriya or Telugu) and Elementary Mathematics.

Group B: (for Class Examination)

Science, Geography, History of India and Drawing

Group C: Any *two* optional subjects for the public Examination:

History, Vernacular (Oriya or Telugu) Advanced Mathematics, Advanced Science.[131]

SECONDARY EDUCATION IN THE FEUDATORY STATES OF ORISSA

The twenty four feudatory states that were merged in Orissa in 1948 and 1949 constituted the most backward educational region. The ruling chiefs did not evince any interest for the spread of education. They were all the feudal pockets of poverty, ignorance and conservatism tempered by tyranny and exploitation. The levels of literacy of these states were naturally the lowest in the Bengal Presidency. However, the

---

130 Z£^pp. 61-62
131 *Ibid*, p. 130

rulers were constrained to establish primary, middle and high schools. Access to education was abysmally low in these states.

The Tributary States of Orissa were the following:

1. *North Mahanadi Circle* which included the States of Pallahara, Athagarh, Talcher, Athmallik, Hindol, Narasingpur, Baramba and Tigiria.
2. *South Mahanadi Circle* which included the States of Khandapara, Nayagarh, Ranpur, Daspalla and Boud States.
3. Mayurbhanj State
4. Nilgiri State
5. Keonjhar State
6. Dhenkanal State, and

The feudatory states of Patna (Bolangir), Korond (Kalahandi), Sonepur, Bamra (present Deogarh) and Rairakhol were in the Central Provinces; and the states of Bonai and Gangpur were in the Chotanagpur Division of the Bengal Presidency. They were transferred to Orissa Division on 16th October,1905. A Political Agent was appointed with headquarters at Sambalpur on the very same date to look after these states which were designated as Eastern States Agency.

Bamra High School, Deogarh (1885)

Bamra was fortunate to have an enlightened ruling chiefs who took the initiative to develop the state on many fronts. During the rule of Raja Basudeb Sudhaldeb, the Middle School at Deogarh was upgraded and became a high school. It was affiliated to the Calcutta University in 1885. It was the first high school in the states of Orissa ruled by native chiefs.

Mayurbhanj Raj High School, Baripada (1893)

The Middle English School, Baripada became a proposed high school in 1889; and a full-fledged high school in 1893 and was affiliated to the Calcutta University. It was known as Mayurbhanj Raj High School. In 1951, it was renamed Maharaja Krishna Chandra High School.

Nijgarh High School, Dhenkanal (1896)

The Middle English School established at Dhenkanal in 1868 was upgraded in 1896, and became the Nijgarh High School, Dhenkanal. It became a full-fledged high school in 1897. It is known as Brajnath Badajena High School, Dhenkanal to-day.

The roll strength of the two schools are indicated in Table No. 3.2.5.[132]

TABLE 3.2.5

Scholars in the Schools of the Feudatory States of Orissa
1892-93 to 1901-02

SI. No.	Year in	Number of students in		Total for the Tributary States of Orissa
		M.R. High School, Baripada	Nijgarh High School, Dhenkanal	
01.	1892-93	105	.....	105
02.	1893-94	112	.....	112
03.	1894-95	113	....	113
04.	1895-96	113	....	113
05.	1896-97	103	175	278
06.	1897-98	100	204	304
07.	1898-99	98	206	**304**
08.	1899-1900	112	177	289
09.	1900-1901	137	161	298
10.	1901-1902	147	166	313

Note: M.R. High School means Mayurbhanj Raj High School,Baripada from 1889 to 1951

The position relating to Middle English and Middle Vernacular Schools in the Feudatory States of Orissa is depicted in Table No. 3.2.6.

---

132 Centenary Souvenir of the Onslow Institute, Chatrapur, 1963, p. 15

TABLE 3.2.6

Middle Schools and Scholars in the Feudatory States of Orissa

1892-93 to 1901-02

SI. No.	Category of Schools	Year									
		1892-1893	1893-1894	1894-1895	1895-1896	1896-1897	1897-1898	1898-1899	1899-1900	1900-1901	1901-1902
	North Mahanadi Circle										
01.	(a) M.E. Schools	...	....	....	....	....	....	....	...	....	02
	(b) Scholars	....	......	.....	......	.....	.....	.....	.....	.....	128
02	(a) M.V. Schools	06	06	06	06	06	06	06	06	06	04
	(b) Scholars	232	254	267	309	284	311	397	419	408	282
	South Mahanadi Circle										
01.	(a) M.E. Schools	03	03	01	01	01	01	02	02	02	02
	(b) Scholars	161	167	70	61	58	58	121	101	114	123
02	(a) M.V. Schools	02	02	04	04	05	05	04	04	04	03
	(b) Scholars	49	64	164	192	253	254	165	177	158	84
	Mayurbhanj State										
01. 02	(a) M.E. Schools	02	02	02	02	03	03	03	03	03	03
	(b) Scholars	186	166	162	163	206	305	290	251	250	241
	(a) M.V. Schools	01	01	01	01	01	01	01	01	01	01

Sl. No.	Category of Schools	Year									
		1892-1893	1893-1894	1894-1895	1895-1896	1896-1897	1897-1898	1898-1899	1899-1900	1900-1901	1901-1902
	(b) Scholars	54	70	70	60	56	56	63	60	47	56
	Nilgiri State										
01. 02.	(a) M.E. Schools	01	01	01	01	01	01	01	01	01	01
	(b) Scholars	75	76	75	81	77	92	116	128	114	102
	(a) M.V. Schools	....	.....	.....	.....	.....	.....	.....	....	....	.....
	(b) Scholars	...	....	....	.....	...	....	....	....	....	....
	Keonjhar State										
01. 02.	(a) ME. Schools	....	01	01	01	01	01	01	01	01	02
	(b) Scholars	....	83	82	68	70	68	60	58	54	153
	(a) M.V. Schools	02	01	01	01	01	01	01	01	01	....
	(b) Scholars	118	45	40	52	46	54	54	54	50	....
	Dhenkanal State										
01. 02.	(a) M.E. Schools	01	01	01	01	....	....	....	....	....	....
	(b) Scholars	123	125	121	139	....	....	....	....	....	....
	(a) M.V. Schools	....	....	....	....	....	....	....	....	....	....
	(b) Scholars	....	....	....	....	....	....	....	....	....	....

In the Tributary States of the North Mahanadi Circle there were 6 Middle Vernacular Schools from 1892-93 to 1901-02. In 1901-02, two of these M. V. Schools were converted into Middle English Schools. Practically, there was no progress whatsoever in this ten-year period. At the end of the decennium, a slight tilt towards English education was noticeable. Mayurbhanj State had one high school and one M. V. School during this period. There were 2 M. E. Schools in 1892 and their number rose to 3 during 1896-97 and remained so up to 190102. Nilgiri State had a single M. E. School throughout this period. Dhenkanal State had an M. E. School by 1892. This School was upgraded to a High School during 1896-97. There was no other progress in the field of secondary education. Keonjhar State had 2 M. V. Schools in 1892-93. In 1893, one of the M. V. Schools-at Keonjhargarh was converted into an M. E. School. It was called the Gibson M. E. School. The M. V. School at Anandapur became an M. E. School during 1901-02. In the Tributary States of the South Mahanadi Circle, there were 3 M. E. and 2 M. V. Schools in 1892-93. By 1901-02, there were 2 M. E. and 3 M. V. Schools in these states.

The expenditure on account of secondary education in the Feudatory States during 1901-02 was as follows:

			Rs.
1.	State of North Mahanadi Circle	...	2,861.00
2.	States of the South Mahanadi Circle		
3.	Mayurbhanj State	...	6,044.00
4.	Nilgiri State	...	1,008.00
5.	Keonjhar State	...	1,805.00
6.	Dhenkanal State	...	3,608.00

The total expenditure on secondary education in the Feudatory State of Orissa in 1901-02 was Rs. 18,005.00.[133]

____

133

SECONDARY EDUCATION IN THE CHOTANAGPUR TRIBUTARY STATES

Bonai and Ganpur of the present Sundergarh district were the two States of the Chotanagpur Tributary States up to 1905. By 1901-02, there was one M. E. School with 7 scholars and one M. V. School with 70 scholars in the Gangpur State. Bonai State did not have even an Upper primary School by 1901-02.[to]

SECONDARY EDUCATION IN THE EASTERN STATES AGENCY

The native States of Kalahandi, Bolangir, Sonepur, Bamra and Rairakhol were underthe Eastern States Agency of the Central Provinces up to 1905, when they were transferred to Bengal. Kalahandi State had a single Middle English School at Bhawanipatna; Sonepur had two Middle English School and one Vernacular School. The Sonepur M. E School had been established in 1894-95. Bolangir State had one Middle English School and one Middle Vernacular School by 1901-02. There was a flourishing Middle English School at Deogarh in the Bamra State. It was soon to become a High School. Rairakhol State was very backward educationally. It had not a single Middle English or Middle Vernacular School. All the schools in the Eastern States Agency were inspected by the Agency Inspector of Schools, Raipur. In 1905, they were transferred to Bengal and came under the jurisdiction of the Inspector of Schools, Orissa Division.

78 *lbid.*

[79]Central Provinces District Gazetteers, Sambalpur district, Ed. R. V. Russel, I. C. S., Allahabad, 1905, p. 84

[80]Report on the Progress of Education, Madras, 1881-82, p. 56

Ibid, & Angul District Gazetteer, Statistics 1901-02

[83]Gazetteer of Orissa Feudatory States, 1901-02, 1950.

[84]*Ibid.*

[85]Chotnagpur Tributary States Gazetteer, Statistics, 1901-02, Cal. 1905. p. 20.0

CHAPTER-4

GREAT EXPECTATION IN THETIMES OF CATASTROPHES (1901-1947)

HIGHLIGHTS

- Indian Educational Policy, 1904
- Indian Education Policy, 1913
- Calcutta University Commission, 1917
- Montague-Chelmsford Reforms, 1919
- Hartog Committee, 1928
- Sapru Committee, 1934
- Zakir Husain Committee, 1937
- Abbot-Wood Report
- Post-War Reconstruction Plan
- Vernacular System, 1901
- Secondary Education in

  - North Orissa
  - South Orissa
  - Feudatory States

- Education in the Orissa Province
- Education in the Feudatory States
- Amalgamation of North and South Orissa Systems

SECTION I

The Victorian era came to an end. The turn of the century ushered in, in its wake, a series of developments. British imperialism was at its height. Lord George Nathaniel Curzon (1 859-1925), the eminent British statesman was the Governor-General and Viceroy of India from 1899 to 1905. He was the foreign Secretary of Britain from 1919 to 1924. The Department of Education and Skills of U. K. is located in the Curzon House of Curzon Street of London as the Ministry of Human Resources Development of Government of India is located inthe Shastri Bhawan, New Delhi. He was a man of strong views and thorough actions. The old days of meek and unquestioned loyalty to the Empire were fast vanishing. The national consciousness was on the rise; and the first volcanic outburst was the Swadeshi Movement of 1905. To appease the sentiments of the people, the Morley-Minto Reforms of 1909 were introduced. The partition of Bengal was undone in 1911. For administrative convenience, Bihar and Orissa wereseparated as a province in 1912; and the Capital of India was shifted from Calcuttato Delhi. The first World War of 1914-18 had thoroughly undermined the financial situation of India; and money was hardly forthcoming for developmental activities. Educational development suffered greatly. The Non-Cooperation Movement of 1919-1921 had awakened the people and forced the Government to grant further concessions. The Montague-Chelmsford Reforms (1919) came into effect in 1921. The situation after the Hunter Commission (1882) First World War wasbleak. There was economic depression. The Round Table Conferences of the 30's culminated in the Act of 1935. The Quit India Movement of 1942 came when the British Government was embroiled in the Second World War. The War came to an end in 1945 and Indian independence was not far off. India got her independence in 1947 and that closed one chapter of Indian history.

EDUCATIONAL POLICIES

In 1902, the Indian Universities Commission was appointed. In 1921, education was transferred to Indian control. According to Nurullah and Naik, the distinctive features of the period are, "(a) larger financial allocation for education, (b) more active role of State in educational matters, (c) vigorous attempts at qualitative improvement of education, (d) unprecedented expansion in almost all branches of education; and (e) thegrowth of militant nationalism among the people."[134] Dr. S. N. Mukherjee commenting upon the developments of the period says, "During this period, attempts were made to put into action Lord Curzon's plan of educational reconstruction."[135] This was a period of virulent imperialism tempered by vibrant nationalism.

INDIAN EDUCATIONAL POLICY,1904

The educational policy of the Government was clearly spelt out in the Government of India Resolution of March 11, 1904. The Resolution stated the policy relating to secondary education as under:

"Whether these schools are managed by public authority or by private persons, and whether they receive aid from public funds or not, the Government is bound in the interest of the community to see that the education provided in them is sound. It must, for example, satisfy itself in each case that a secondary school is actually wanted, that its financial stability is assured, that its managing body where there is one, is properly constituted; that it reaches the proper subject up to

---

134 J, P. Naik & Syed Nurullah: *A Student's History of Education in India,* Mackillan Co. of India Ltd.,1974, p. 239.

135 S. N. Mukherjee: *Secondary Education in India,*Orient Longmans, April,1972.p. 70

a standard; that due provision has been made for instruction, health, recreation, and discipline of the pupils; that the teachers are suitable as regards character, number and qualifications; and that the fees to be paid will not involve such competition with any existing schools as will be unfair and injurious to the interests of education. Such are the conditions upon which alone schools should be eligible to receive grant-in-aid or to send up pupils to compete for, or receive pupils in enjoyment of government scholarships; and schools complying with them will be ranked as 'recognized schools'."[136]

This policy statement had stated sound educational principles couched in the proper administrative setting. It was brief and to the point. Prof. A. N. Basu has apdy commented, "Lord Curzon was right in many of the things he said; but it was the way in which he wanted to reform that raised grave suspicion in the minds of the educated Indians. They thought that this reform move camouflaged some deep political motives."[137] The Resolution was looked upon as an instrument with which the Government desired to throttle the schemes of educational expansion.

To counteract the spirit of this Resolution, eminent Indian educationists like Bepin Chandra Pal (one time Headmaster of the P. M. Academy, Cuttack) and Satish Chandra Mukherjee came forth with the idea of National Education impartedon national lines and under national control. They wantedit to beimparted through the medium of the mother-tongue (which in turn would necessitate the preparation of text books in the Vernaculars) promoting physical and moral education; attaching special importance to a knowledge of the country; imparting scientific and technical knowledge; exacting a high degree of proficiency and enforcing strict discipline.[138]

---

136 Government of India Resolution dated the 11th March, 1904

137 A. N. Basu, *Education in Modern India*, p. 64

138 Haridas Mukherjee & Uma Mukherjee, *Origins of the National Education Monemmt (1905-1910).*

On 19th March, 1913, Gopal Krishna Gokhale introduced a Bill "for the gradual introduction of the principle of compulsion into the elementary educational system of the country," in the imperial Legislative Council which was turned down by it.

INDIAN EDUCATIONAL POLICY, 1913

A Resolution was issued by the Governor-General-in-Council on 21st February, 1913 and this was the Indian Educational Policy, 1913. The salient features of this Resolution relating to secondary education were:

19. "The importance of the secondary English education and in particular of high school education is far reaching. Secondary education of one grade or another is the basis of all professional or industrial training in India. The inferior output of secondary schools invades colleges and technical institutions and hinders the development of higher education. At the Allahabad Conference, the Directors of Public Instruction unanimously regarded the reform of Secondary English Schools as the most urgent of educational problems. The improvement of Secondary English Education has for some time occupied the attention of the Government of India and the Local Government and it is hoped in the near future to remedy many defects of the present system.

20. The admixture of private management and State control was again emphasized in the Resolution of 1904. To this policy the Government of India adhere. It is dictated not by any belief in the inherent superiority of private over State management but by preference for an established system and, above all, by the necessity of concentrating the direct energies of the State and the bulk of its available resources upon the improvement and expansion of elementary education. The policy may be summarized as the encouragement of privately managed schools under suitable bodies, maintained in efficiency by

Government inspection, recognition and control, and by the aid of Government funds.

21. Schools have sprung up into existence in destructive competition with neighbouring institutions. Physical health has been neglected and no provision has been made for suitable residential arrangements and play-fields. Fee rates have been lowered; competition and laxity in transfer have destroyed discipline; teachers have beenemployed onrates of pay insufficient to attract men capable of instructing or controlling their pupils. Above all, the grants-in-aid have from want of funds often been inadequate...

22. Subject to the necessities of variation in deference to local conditions the policy of the Government of India in regard to Secondary English Schools is—

(1) To improve the few existing government schools by —

    a. employing only graduates or trained teachers;

    b. introducing a graded services for teachers...

    c. providing proper hostel accommodation;

    d. introducing a school course complete in itself with staff sufficient to teach what may be called the modern side with special attention to- the development of a historical and geographical sense;

    e. Introducing manual training and improving science teaching.

(2) To increase the grants-in-aid, in order that the aided institutions may keep pace with the improvements in government schools on the above mentioned lines, and to encourage the establishment of new aided institutions.

(3) To multiply and improve training colleges so that trained teachers may be available for public and private institutions.

(4) To found government schools in such localities as may, on a survey of local conditions and with due regard to economy of educational effort and expense, be proved to require them.

23. The Government of India also desire that the grant-in-aid rules should be made more elastic so as to enable each school, which is recognized as necessary and conform to the prescribed standards of management and efficiency, to obtain the special assistance which it requires in order to attain the fullest measure of utility. As larger grants become available and as the pay and the personnel of the teaching staff are improved, it will be possible for the inspecting officer to concentrate his attention more and more upon the general quality of instruction. Full encouragement then can be given to improved and original methods of teaching and courses; and gradually the grant-earning capacity of an institution will come to be judged on grounds of general efficiency and desert rather than by rigid rules of calculation.

24. The introduction of school course complete in itself and of a modern and practical character, freed from the domination of the matriculation examination, was recommended in the first instance by the Education Commission of 1882. In some provinces and particularly in Madras real progress has been made towards the accomplishment of this reform.

25. The Principal objects of the school final examination are adaptability to the course of study and avoidance of cram...

26. The value of external examinations cannot be overlooked...

27. A combination of external and internal examinations is required."[139]

The mushroom growth of secondary schools during 1882-1902, constrained thegovernment to adopt a policy of caution. To quote

---

139 *Indian Educational Policy, 1913*, Superintendent, Government Printing, Calcutta, 1913 As 4. pp. 16-24

Nurullah and Naik, "The new policy in secondary education has two important aspects — control and improvement."[140]

CALCUTTA UNIVERSITY (SADLER) COMMISSION, 1917

On September 14, 1917, the Government of India appointed the Calcutta University Commission under the Chairmanship of Dr. M. E. Sadler, Vice-Chancellor of the Leeds University. The other members of die Commission were Dr. Gregory, Mr. Philip Hartog, Prof. Ramsay Muir, Sir Asutosh Mukherjee, D. P. I. Bengal, and Dr. Ziauddin Ahmed. After a careful and thorough scrutiny, the Commission submitted its report after seventeen months in 13 parts. It is a comprehensive report. The Commission held that reforms in the secondary education are a *sine qua non* for effecting improvements of University education. Sir Arthur Mayhew termed this report as a 'constant source of suggestion and information', and its 'significance' as 'incalculable'.[141]Prof. A. N. Basu says that the recommendations of this report 'have gready influenced the subsequent course of secondary and higher education in India'.[142] Some of the major recommendations of this Commission relating to secondary education are as follows:

1. The stage of admission to the University should be that of the present intermediate instead of that of the present matriculation.

2. There should be two secondary school examinations, the first approximately corresponding to the present matriculation to be taken at the end of high school stage at the normal age of 16... and to be known as the high school examination; the second, approximately corresponding to the present intermediate, but much more varied in its range, to be taken at the end of the

---

140 J. P. Naik & Syed Nurullah, op. cit, Macmillan & co. of India Ltd., 1974. p. 258.

141 Arthur Mayhew, *The Education of India*, p. 213.

142 A. N. Basu,, op. cit, p. 62

       intermediate college course at the normal age of 18, and to be known as the intermediate college examination.

3. .... the intermediate stage should be transferred from the Universities to new institutions to be known as 'intermediate colleges', which should prepare not only for the degree course in arts and science but also for career in medicine, teaching engineering, agriculture, commerce, and industry. These colleges may be run as independent institutions or might be attached to selected high schools.

4. A Board of Secondary and Intermediate Education, consisting of the representatives of the Government, University, High Schools and Intermediate Colleges should be established in each State and entrusted with the administration and control of secondary and intermediate education.[143]

The Commission recommended that these Boards should be free from the control of the Education Department. The Commission recommended that the medium of instruction should be themother-tongue.

"But no action along the lines indicated herein was taken by Government partly because it was believed that an expert enquiry into the question was essential before any definite step could be taken and partly because of the outbreak of the Great World War."[144]

OTHER MAJOR EDUCATIONAL DEVELOPMENTS

In 1919, an Act of the Parliament was passed, which brought into effect changes in Government which Mr. Edwin Montague, the Secretary of the State for India, and Lord Chelmsford, the Viceroy of India had recommended. This Act introduced diarchy in provincial administration, and ushered in provincial autonomy. Education became a transferred subject. However, matters relating to European education

---

143 *Calcutta University Commission Report,* Vol. V, p. 298-299.

144 J. P. Naik & Syed Nurullah,, op. cit. p. 271.

and the Indian Education Service continued to be reserve subjects. The Government of India lost control over education and it was not in a position to frame policies for the entire country.

Mahatma Gandhi launched the Non-Cooperation Movement during 1919-1921. It had its deep repercussions on education. The Non-cooperation Movement advocated the boycott of Government schools by students and teachers and repudiation of State grants and recognition by private institutions. National Schools were established through-out the country and Vidyapeeths or National Universities were started at such centers as Calcutta, Poona, Patna, Banaras, Ahamadabad etc. The Jamia Milia Islamia (Muslim National University) was established at Aligarh in 1925 and was later transferred to Delhi. The muslims started Azad Schools. Hindi was taught in these schools and there was interest for spinning.

In May, 1928, Simon Commission (the Indian Statutory Commission) appointed a sub-committee under the Chairmanship of Sir Phillip Hartog to inquire into the growth of education in British India and to gauge its potentialities for progress. The Committee submitted its report in September, 1928. This Committee was of the opinion that the progress of secondary education was much better compared to primary education. It regretted the domination of the Matriculation Examination over secondary education. It recommended diversified curricula for rural schools toavoid the wastage of rural talent. It also recommended better training for teachers.

The Sapru Committee was appointed by the U. P. Government in 1943 to enquire into the causes of unemployment in the State. The Committee felt that at the root of unemployment lay the defective educational system. Therefore, it recommended the introduction of diversified courses and extension of secondary education by one year. It stated that vocational education should be imparted after the lower secondary stage.

The next important educational landmark was the Resolution of the Central Advisory Board of Education (CABE), 1935. The CABE had been revived in 1935. It stated that the lower secondary stage should have a self-contained course and in rural areas it should have a rural bias. There should be a public examination at the end of the lower secondary course. The higher secondary course should be preparatory to degree, professional and technical courses.

At the request of the CABE, Mr. A. Abbot and Mr. S. H. Wood visited India in 1937 and suggested improvements. The rural lower secondary course should have an environmental approach and the linguistic load be lightened; that the mother-tongue should be the medium of instruction; the importance accorded to English be lessened; greater stress be laid on manual work and art teaching. It recommended the institution of junior and senor technical schools for vocationalisation.

Mahatma Gandhi gave the general outlines of Basic Education in the 'Hariijan" of 1937. It was given an operational shape by the Zakir Husain Committee. It stated that mother-tongue should be the medium; that craft should be taught; that Hindi should be learnt and that the students should imbibe the spirit of nationalism and self-help. Self-sufficiency was advocated. It stated that all the subjects need to be inter-related and correlated.

As per the Government of India Act of 1935, education became, by and large, a State subject.

The Report of the Central Board of Education on the Post-War Educational Development in India was published in June, 1944. This Report is popularly known as the Sargent Report, 1944, after Sir John Sargent, Educational Adviser to Government of India. It was a comprehensive educational document.

It recommended the establishment of two types of high schools — the Academic and the Technical; the former imparting instruction in humanities and sciences and the latter in industrial and commercial subjects. The high school is to be seen as an institution for the children" who are well above the average in ability." The high school should cover six years. The age of admission should be 11+. Entry to high school should be on a selective basis. The high schools should have varied curricula.A large number of scholarships must be instituted to help the poor but able students. The intermediate course should be amalgamated in the high school. The tutorial system should be introduced. In brief, these were the major developments in the policy relating to secondary education up to 1947.

The Vernacular system of education was inaugurated on 1st January, 1901, in accordance with the terms of the Resolution No. 1 of the Government of Bengal. The old educational structure has been compared with the new structure of 1901 in Table No. 4.1.1.

TABLE 4.1.1

Comparison of the Vernacular System (1901) with the Pre-1901 System of School Education

Stage of Education	Sl. No.	High Schools (Pre-1901 System)	Middle Schools	Upper Primary Schools	Lower Primary Schools	New Standard under Resolution No. 1 of Govt. of Bengal (1901)	Equal to the Present (2007)	Stage of Education
High School	01.	Class I (Entrance Class)	...	...	...	XI	1st Yr of Higher Secondary course	Secondary Education
	02.	Class II	...	...	...	X	X	
	03.	Class III	...	...	...	IX	IX	
	04.	Class IV	...	...	...	VIII	VIII	
Middle School	05.	Class V	Class I	...	...	Standard VI	VII	Elementary Education
	06.	Class VI	Class II	...	...	Standard V	VI	
	07.	Class V	Class III	Class I	...	Standard IV	V	
	08.	Class IV	Class IV	Class II	...	Standard III	IV	
	09.	Class III	Class III	Class III	L.P.Class	Standard II	III	
Primary School	10.	Class II	Class II	Class IV	A Class	Standard I	II	
	11.	Class I	Class I	Class V	B Class	3rd Year of Infant Class	I	
	12.	Infant Class	Class IB	Class VB	C Class	2nd Year of Infant Class	Upper K.G.	
	13.	Infant Class (Preparatory)	Class IC	Infant Class	Infant Class	1st Year of Infant Class	Lower K.G.	

Note: Class I of the Entrance class was the top-most class of the high school.

"Under the existing conditions, the Upper Primary Standard (Standard IV) represents the limit of what is called primary education. Consequently the secondary education is imparted by the two highest classes of a middle school, and by the six highest classes of a high school. Now the Government Resolution, to which reference has been made above, laid down thatin all the six standards which it prescribed, the Vernacular must be the medium of instruction. English was, however, allowed as a second language in the middle and high schools in the classes which correspond to standards III to VI of the Vernacular system. As a result of these arrangements, there are two types of middle schools-(1) those that teach English as a second language in the four highest classes, and (2) those which do not teach English at all. The former are called Middle English Schools, the later Middle Vernacular Schools, and both are held to be imparting secondary education in the two highest classes. These two classes are sometimes called the middle stage and sometimes the lower secondary stage."[145]

The logic of this arrangement was criticized. Interpreted in terms of the English Board of Education, the lower secondary or middle school education was simply primary education. The additional instruction of English could not transform it into secondary education. Mr. Kuchler, Inspector of Schools, Bhagalpur Division, commented as follows:

"It is doubtful whether the line between primary and secondary education has been drawn at the proper stage. When we consider that the end of the lower secondary stage can be reached at the age of twelve, it would certainly appear more appropriate that this stage should be regarded as still belonging to primary education, and that the term 'secondary' should be reserved for that education which is at present given through the Medium of English. In the same way only high schools should in future be called secondary schools. The mere fact that English is taught in a school does not entitle the latter to be

---

145 *Progress of Education in Bengal. 1902-03 to 1906-07. The Third Quinquennial Review* pp. 33-34.

called a secondary school, but merely indicates that the instruction it is giving is preparatory to a course of secondary education."[146]

In the Report for 1905-1906, it had already been stated that 'it would be consistent to consider Middle Vernacular Schools as Primary'.[147] The Director of Public Instruction writes that, "there is a good deal to be said for Mr. Kuchler's proposal that the term *'secondary'* should be reserved for that education which is at present given through the medium of English."

The development of secondary education had not taken place uniformly in the entire Presidency of Bengal. Consequently, there were grave inter-regional imbalances. The Burdwan Division had 67 schools per district; the Presidency Division had 61.2; then Patna with an average of 12; then Orissa with an average of 11.8 and last Chotanagpur with an average of 10.2. The 17 Tributary States of Orissa had 16 secondary schools.[148]The development of secondary education in Orissa was very slow and highly unsatisfactory. The sorry state of affairs relating to the Tributaryslow and highly unsatisfactory. The sorryofaffairsrelating to the Tributary States of Orissa need not be commented upon. The native chiefs had cynical apathy towards education and the criminal neglect of education in these States is a sufficient indication of the lack of enlightenment amongst the wealthy aristocracy of the country of this part. The Tributary. States of Bonai, PalUahara, Rairakhol, and Tigiria did not have a single Middle English or Middle Vernacular School by 1907-1908.[149]

Table No. 4.1.2 represents the average strength of the various types of secondary schools in the Bengal Presidency at the close of the last four quinquennia:[150]

---

146 *JMd.* p. 34
147
148 *Ibid,* p. 36
149 L. E. B. Cobden-Ramsey, *Feudatory States of Orissa. Bengal Gazetteers.*1950
150 *Progress of Education in BenmL 1902-03 to 1906-1907*, p. 36.

TABLE 4.1.2

Average Roll Strength Secondary Schools in the Bengal Presidency (1891-92 to 1906-07)

The average monthly cost of a high school during 1906-07 was Rs. 383.8 as against

SI. No.	Year	Average Number of Students		
		High Schools	Middle English Schools	Middle Vernacular Schools
01.	1891-1892	207	67	60
02.	1896-1897	210	72	61
03.	1901-1902	218	71	57
04.	1906-1907	201	69	60

Rs. 356.5 in 1901-02; while that of a middle English school was Rs. 69.4 in 1906-07 as against Rs. 65.6 in 1901-02. The average cost of a middle Vernacular school during 1906-07 was Rs. 45.09 a month as against Rs. 38.49 a month in 1901-02.[151]

There had been no increase in the Government high schools. The tendency to make over to private management the control of the institutions of this class, which was evident from a comparison of the figures for 1891-92 with those of 1896-97, had been checked. The previous policy of the Government of India was to withdraw, wherever possible, from the direct management of secondary schools. This policy was set forth in the Resolution of 1894. But by 1896-97, the Government of India recognized that there were strong arguments against complete withdrawal. In 1904, Government school in each district. Fortunately, none of theGovernment high schools in the districts of Cuttack, Puri, Balasore and Sambalpur had been transferred to private management. However, the Berhampur Zilla School was transferred to private management by the Madras Government.

---

151 *Ibid*, p. 37.

By 1907, the D. P. I. of Bengal had stated that "secondary education has an importance of its own" and that it "ought to be able to do more for a boy than squeeze him through the matriculation examination of the Calcutta University."[152] He stated "the Government of India are quite alive to the urgency of improving secondary education system."[153]

The domination which the matriculation examination of the Calcutta University had hitherto exercised over the curriculum of secondary schools, had been most prejudicial not only to the schools, but also to the University. In a debate in the Senate on the report on the improvement of secondary education, the Vice-Chancellor had stated in 1906 that, "secondary education in India had languished mainly because secondary schools, instead of occupying an independent position and proposing to themselves aims of their own, had fallen to the place of mere feeders to the Colleges."[154]The nightmare of examinations is as real today as it was a century ago and its baneful influence on the curriculum has been a constant theme of discussion even to-day in 2007.

In the Report on the Progress of Education in Bengal for the quinquennium 1902-03 to 1906-07 it is stated that:

"Practically speaking there is not, nor ever has been, any secondary school curriculum. Government prescribes a course of studies which ends at standard VII, that is, at a point practically four years distant from the end of the secondary stage. This course obviously cannot be regarded as a course of studies for the secondary stage of education throughout as such. After this point everything is subordinated to an examination, the function of which is the selection of students who are considered fit to enter upon University courses, which as such, should be specialized and not general. Educational procedure in India has never been exactly logical. When you want to build anything, it is usual to begin with the foundations. In India, however, in educational structures

---

152 Ibid. p. 44
153 Ibid. p. 44
154

it has been usual to begin with the top story. We had Universities before we had secondary schools, and so University education came to be regarded as the goal to be attained by all who aspired to an education which went beyond the merely elementary. Accordingly the matriculation examination of a University was taken to represent a certain stage on the educational ladder, and consequently the utter and radical unsoundness of the state of affairs, which has always existed, failed until recently to attractthe general attention, which it would otherwise, perhapshave done."[155]

"No such thing as a secondary school, that is to say, a type of school which imparts an education which so far as it goes is given for its own sake, has ever existed or can ever exist until the conditions referred to are changed; for they bring all secondary schools to the educational level of cramming institutions."[156]

This had aptly been described in the first quinquennium of the 20th century by an Indian Principal in the following words,

"Secondary education, properly so-called, has not hitherto been organized on an independent basis of its own. The so-called secondary schools of the province simply serve as a training ground for entrance into the University. The great bane of all present day secondary schools in Bengal, therefore, has been the feverish anxiety with which both teachers and the taught look to matriculation as their goal. From the lowest class to the highest, boys in the name of education receive nothing more than bare instruction for passing class examinations, and ultimately the matriculation — their final aim: they are merely drilled from the earliest stage in the art of writing answers to probable questions to be set in examinations. Can anything be more disastrous to the cause of sound education? Some means, therefore, should be devised to separate secondary education from the incubus of matriculation."[157]

---

155 *Ibid*, p. 45
156 *Ibid* p. 45
157 *Ibid* p. 45

The Report on Public Instruction in Bengal for 1909-10 stated that a system of education must be self-sufficient. It continued to state:

"Enough has been said to show the urgent need for reform, and it is indeed fortunate that the subject has attracted the attention of the Government of India; for it is no exaggeration to say that the future work which the colleges and scientific and industrial institutions will be able to effect must largely depend upon the improvement of secondary schools.[158]

In 1908, at the instance of the Government of India, the Direct Method of teaching English was undertaken. The Report for 1909-1910 states that "it is an interesting experiment, and the measure of success which we achieve should be carefully weighed and compared with the cost."[159] Principal W. E. Griffiths of the David Hare Training College, Calcutta and Mr. L. Tipping, Headmaster of the Ranchi Zilla School had done a good deal in popularizing it. Inspector Cunningham of Chotanagpur Division was optimistic and thought that this scheme would succeed. However, Inspector Bhagavati Sahay of the Patna Division thought "the direct method of teaching English is not compatible with the Vernacular basis of instruction."[160]

The Government of Bengal submitted proposals relating to this scheme that would cost about 14 to 16 lakh of rupees.[161]

SECONDARY EDUCATION IN NORTH ORISSA, 1901-1912

The Districts of Cuttack, Puri, Balasore and Angul-Kondhamal were in the Orissa Division of the Bengal Presidency. In 1861, the Sambalpur district had been transferred to the Central Provinces. The Oriya-speaking States of Patna (i.e Bolagir-Patna), Kalahandi, Sonepur, Bamra,

---

158 *Ibidp.* 50
159 *Report on Public Instruction in Benval. 1909-10.p.12*
160 *Ibid,* p. 12
161 *Ibid.* p. 12

and Rairakhol were included in the Eastern States Agency and were under the superintendence of the Central Provinces. These States were transferred from C. P. and attached to Bengal on 16th October,1905. Amongst the Chotanagpur States, Bonai and Gangpur were retained in Bengal. The tributary States of Orissa were attached to Bengal. Ganjam and Koraput were in the Madras Presidency. In 1912, the Oriya-speaking tracts of Bengal were transferred to Bihar and Orissa. In 1936, Orissa became a separate Province when Ganjam and Koraput regions were transferred to Orissa from the Madras Presidency.

The area, population, and the number of towns and villages in the districts of Cuttack, Puri, Balasore, Sambalpur and Angul (including Kondhamals). as per the census of 1901 has been shown in Table No. 4.1.3.

TABLE 4.1.3

Area and Population of the Districts of the Orissa Division (1901)

SI. No.	District	Area in Sq. Miles	Number of		Population
			Towns	Villages	
01.	Cuttack	3,654	3	5,517	2,062,758
02.	Pun	2,499	1	3,101	1,077,264
03.	Balasore	2,085	2	3,358	1,071,197
04.	a. Angul	881	...	453	127,697
01.	b. Kondhamals	800	...	996	64,214
05.	Sambalpur	3,824	2	1,915	638,992
06.	Total	13,743	8	15,340	5,042,122

(Source: Census Report of the Bengal Presidency, 1901)

Note: Town means a habitation with more than 5,000 people in it.

In the Cuttack district there were 6 high schools during 1901-02. This number remained stationary up to 1906-07. during 1907-08, this increased to 7 and in 1908-09 to 8. However, due to the closure of Mrs. Reba Roy's school at Cuttack this number decreased to 7. There was no increase in the number of high schools for boys. Two high schools for Girls were started; but one survived. In the districts of Puri, Balasore, and Sambalpur the number of high schools remained constant during the entire decade. There were two high schools in the Puri district- Puri Zilla school and the school at Khurda. The four high schools of the Balasore district were - (1) The Balasore Zilla School at Balasore, (2) The Baptist Mission High School at Balasore, (3) Lakhannath High School at Lakhannath and (4) Bhadrak High School at Bhadrak. The Bhadrak high school became a full fledged high school during 1904-05. The monthly cost of educating a pupil in each of these schools was Rs. 32.38. Twenty candidates appeared at the Entrance Examination from these schools during 1904-05. During 1901-02 to 1910-11, the number of scholars studying in the high schools of the Cuttack district rose from 1,328 to 2,156; those of Puri district from 386 to 458; those of Balasore district from 584 to 696; and those of Sambalpur district from 33 to 330. There were no high schools in the Angul district. The number of Middle English schools in the district of Cuttack rose from 28 to 31; in the Angul district from 0 to 1; in the Puri district from 5 to 9; in the Sambalpur district from 0 to 5 during 1901-02 to 1910-11. The number of M. E. Schools remained constant at 11 during the above period in the Balasore district.

The number of scholars studying in the Middle English schools of Cuttack rose from 1,207 to 2,512; of Angul district from 0 to 62; of Puri district from 359 to 648; of Balasore district from 696 to 821; and of Sambalpur district from 0 to 451 during the period 1901-02 to 1910-11. The number of Middle Vernacular schools decreased from 7 to 4 in the Cuttack district; from 2 to 1 in the Angul district; from 15 to 10 in the Puri district; from 19 to 16 in the Balasore district; and from 6 to 3 in the Sambalpur district during the period1901-02 to 1910-11. According to Mr. L. S. S. O'Malley, "These schools were no long popular as the people generally attached but small importance to purely Vernacular education."[162]

The number of students studying in the Middle Vernacular schools decreased with the decrease in their numbers. During the period under

---

162 O'Malley, L. S. S.:. *Balasore. District Gazetteer,* 1905

review the decrease was from 533 to 327 in the Cuttack district; from 103 to 91 in the Angul district; from535 to 395 in the Puri district; from 886 to 821 in theBalasore district; and from 240 to 206 in the Sambalpur district.

During 1909-10, the average roll strength of a high school was 220. The average monthly cost of a high school was Rs. 445.00.[163]

163

TABLE 4.1.4

Secondary Education in North Orissa From 1901-02 to 1910-11

Sl. No.	Category	Year									
		1901-1902	1902-1903	1903-1904	1904-1905	1905-1906	1906-1907	1907-1908	1908-1909	1909-1910	1910-1911
	CUTTACK DISTRICT										
01.	(a) High School	6	6	6	6	6	6	7	8	8	7
	(b) Scholars	1328	1285	1390	1401	1491	1546	1683	1877	2067	2156
02.	(a) M.E.Schools	28	28	27	27	29	28	28	30	31	31
	(b) Scholars	1207	1573	1578	1607	1744	1824	1762	2141	2457	2512
03.	(a) M.V.Schools	7	7	7	7	5	5	5	5	5	4
	(b) Scholars	533	465	542	368	266	327	354	339	364	327
	ANGUL DISTRICT										
04.	(a) High School										
	(b) Scholars										
05.	(a) M.E.Schools									1	1
	(b) Scholars									46	62
06.	(a) M.V.Schools	2	2	2	2	2	2	2	2	1	1
	(b) Scholars	103	100	106	109	111	107	124	117	88	91

Sl. No.	Category	Year									
		1901-1902	1902-1903	1903-1904	1904-1905	1905-1906	1906-1907	1907-1908	1908-1909	1909-1910	1910-1911
	PURI DISTRICT										
07.	(a) High School	2	2	2	2	2	2	2	2	2	2
	(b) Scholars	386	394	409	390	391	389	383	365	431	458
08.	(a) M.E.Schools	5	6	7	8	8	8	8	7	8	9
	(b) Scholars	357	375	457	483	488	527	461	430	613	648
09.	(a) M.V.Schools	15	15	13	12	12	12	12	13	11	10
	(b) Scholars	535	449	468	394	431	464	417	472	431	395
	BALASORE DISTRICT										
10.	(a) High School	4	4	4	4	4	4	4	4	4	4
	(b) Scholars	584	607	583	603	531	500	541	565	628	696
11.	(a) M.E.Schools	11	11	11	11	11	10	12	11	11	11
	(b) Scholars	696	659	650	642	633	632	761	723	784	821
12.	(a) M.V.Schools	19	19	19	17	18	16	15	16	17	16
	(b) Scholars	856	870	854	750	840	741	694	769	828	821

Sl. No.	Category	Year									
		1901-1902	1902-1903	1903-1904	1904-1905	1905-1906	1906-1907	1907-1908	1908-1909	1909-1910	1910-1911
	SAMBALPUR DISTRICT										
13.	(a) High School	1	1	1	1	1	1	1	1	1	1
14.	(b) Scholars	33	31	35	35	175	214	236	278	300	330
15.	(a) M.E.Schools	...	...	...	...	...	...	...	3	3	5
	(b) Scholars	...	...	...	...	...	...	...	488	264	451
	(a) M.V.Schools	6	6	6	6	6	6	6	4	4	3
	(b) Scholars	240	279	888	946	1004	1027	1032	595	403	206

Of these institutions the Government was managing 4. high schools, 2 M. E. schools and 1 M. V. school. There were 13 M. E. schools and 12 M. V. schools under District Board Management. Nine high schools, 35 M. E. schools and 21 M. V. schools were aided institutions under private management. One high school at Lakhannath was managed by the local Zamidar. Seven M. E. schools and 2 M. V. schools were unaided institutions under private management.

The literacy level of the different districts in 1911 was as shown in Table No. 4.1.5.

TABLE 4.1.5

Literacy in the Orissa Division, 1911

SI. No.	District	Literacy percentage			Remarks
		Total	Male	Female	
01.	Cuttack	6	13	0.44	
02.	Puri	5	11	0.44	
03.	Balasore	7	14	0.45	Highest
04.	Sambalpur	3	6	0.20	Lowest
05.	(a) Angul	3	6	0.31	
	(b) Kondhamal (Phulbani)	4	7	0.20	

Source: Census Report of the Bengal Presidency,1911.

Balasore had the highest percentage of literacy and Sambalpur trailed behind all. In female literacy Balasore occupied the first position and Kondhamal (Phulbani) came last.

High Schools For Girls

During this period two high schools for girls sprang up at Cuttack. Orissa was very backward in female education up to this time. In 1908, a Girls high school was started at Cuttack. This was named as the Ravenshaw Girls' School in 1913. In 1908-09, another Girls' high school was started in Kaligali of the Cuttack town by Smt. Reba Roy. In this connection, Miss Brock, Inspectress of Schools remarked, "Both the schools at

Cuttack have been recognized by the University (i.e. Calcutta) though neither of them presented pupils at the last Matriculation Examination. One of these schools — the Ravenshaw Girls' School — is undoubtedly in a flourishing condition, having as many as 170 girls on the rolls, of whom 17 belong to the high stage. It thus justifies the high grant of Rs. 500-00 that it enjoys. The maintenance charges are high, as the Vernacular classes have to be duplicated to suit Uriya as well as Bengali girls. It is to be regretted that the authorities of the two schools do not see their way to combine and concentrate their energies. The fact is very clear, however, that although there may not be any room for two high schools at Cuttack at present, there is a demand for high education among the Uriya girls — so much so indeed that even married girls are being sent to the Ravenshaw school as boarders. The other school at Cuttack known as Mrs. Reba Roy's school was also fairly well attended, having 90 girls on theroll at the close of the year."[164] Mrs. Reba Roy's school in Kaligali, Cuttack was an ideal institution. Mrs. Roy was the daughter of the brother of the eminent educationist Raibahadur Madhusudan Rao, Joint Inspector of Schools of the Orissa Division. Miss Brock, Inspectress of Schools, Presidency, Burdwn and Orissa Divisions, visited the Ravenshaw Girls school and suggested that, (1) the Ravenshaw Girls school should be moved away from Mrs. Roy's school and (2) be held in a building with adequate compound so that girls from conservative families may also take advantage of it and that (3) conveyance be provided for the girls. In spite of these recommendations the Ravenshaw Girls school was languishing and the competition with Mrs. Reba Roy's school was too great for it. Mrs. Reba Roy's school got a grant of Rs. 300and as things stood Mrs. Roy's school had better chances of survival.

In 1908, the Managing Committee of the Ravenshaw Girls' school was reconstituted. Mr Madhusudan Das, C. I. E., the most venerated leader of the Oriya nation, became the President of the Managing

---

164 *Ibid.* 1910 pp. 35-36

Committee, Sri Bepin Behari Palit and the eminent lexicographer, Mr Gopal Chandra Praharaj along with some old members became the members of the Managing Committee. Shrimati Shailabala Das, the adopted daughter of Mr. Madhusudan Das, became the Honorary Lady Principal of the school. She had been to England and had studied the modern methods of instruction in the University of Cambridge. The intense efforts of Miss Das bore fruit and the Ravenshaw Girls' school began to prosper. The school was recognized and it presented two of its candidates at the Entrance Examination of the Calcutta University in 1909. In March, 1913 it was handed over to Government. In 1917, it moved to its present building near the Gouri Sankar Park.[165] The intermediate classes were opened in 1915.[166] In 1909, the Government stopped the grant to Mrs. Reba Roy's school and so finally it had to be closed. The failure of Reba Roy's school confirms the conviction that no school could thrive without Governmental patronage. The Ravenshaw Girls' school was first started in Kaligali; then due to the intense competition of Mrs. Reba Roy's school it was moved to the residence of Late Hariballav Ghose in Choudhary Bazar and finally shifted to its present buildings near the Gouri Shankar Park.[167] Mrs. Reba Roy's school was housed in the residence of Late Ganeshlal Pandit in Beharibag.[168]In March, 1913, when the Ravenshaw Girls'school was taken over by Government, Mrs Banks replaced Miss Shailabala Das as the new Lady Principal. The other teachers were Smt. Behar Sircar, Mrs. Maitra (youngest daughter of Sri Surendranath Bannerjee), Miss (later Mrs.) Charushila Ray, Smt Amarbala Pal etc. They were all Bengalees and were from Bengal. The teachers from Orissa were Nirmalabala Nayak, Chandramukhi Dash, Narmada Kar, Binodini Sarangi, Sarala Patra, Ester Patra, Suprabha Kar, Pratibha Kar, Mrs

---

165 *The Ravenshaw Girls' School Centrenary Souvenir. 1973. Editorial written by Mrs. Sahitri Rout,* pp. iv-vi
166 Thid. *Headmistress's Report.*
167 Ibid. Shanti Mukherji: Moro Chatree Jibanara Smruti, p. 31
168 Ibid. Smt. Binodini Sarangi's Pade Adhe, p. 3

Hazra and Mrs. Ghosal. Most of the students were Christians and the Hindu students were small in number.[169]

SECONDARY EDUCATION IN NORTH ORISSA, 1912-1935

The most important single event in the field of secondary education during the period 1912 to 1935 is the rise and fall of the Satyabadi school of Sakhigopal in the district of Puri. This school had played a crucial role in the socio-cultural regeneration of Orissa. Many of its teachers and students played an important role in the freedom struggle of India. Every Oriya remembers with sentimental nostalgia the glory of this school and its fate and fame still echo in the hearts of the people of this State. Therefore, a brief history of this school has prefaced the proceedings of this period.

The Satyabadi School, Sakhigopal (1912-21)

Pandit Gopabandhu, the selfless servant of the people of Orissa, had realized that education was the key to social re-engineering and political enlightenment. On 12th August, 1909, he founded the Satyabadi M. E. School at Sakhigopal. Sri Gopinath Das, a Deputy Magistrate, generously contributed for the school.

The school started with 19 students, "This was the nucleus of the Satyabadi Grove School with which the patriotism of Orissa is so intimately connected."[170] The school was started in the temple bunglow. The Sakhigopal Temple Management leased out two acres of land to the north of the Temple to the school. This area was covered with Bakul trees. Inspired by the sylvan settings of Tagore's Santiniketan, Pandit Gopabandhu Dash wanted to establish an open-air school with no buildings, whatsoever, so that the students can drink deep from the

---

169 Shanti Mukherjee, Moro Chatre Jibanara Smrutu in Ravenshaw Girls' school Centenary Souvenir,p. 30

170 Dr. S. C. Dash, *Pandit Gopabandhu Das* pp. 42-44.

fountains of nature. The torrential rains of Sakhogopal constrained Gopabandhu to change his plans and asolid structure was raised. The Education

Department accorded recognition to the M. E. School. Pandit Nilakantha Das, the noted literary giant of Orissa, joined this school as its Headmaster on 11th October,1911. He had passed his M. A. and had a fiery personality. The process of upgrading the school to a high school began with his arrival. Class IV corresponding to class VIII of the present day, was opened in January,1912. It was patterned after the Gurukula system of education. It strove to reform and rejuvenate the decadent Oriya society. It hoped to inspire the people with the greatest ideals of nationalism. It was run under the auspices of the Universal Education League of Orissa formed on the pattern of the Deccan Education Society. Pandit Gopabandhu Das was the Secretary of the school. Simplicity and austerity were the watchwords of the institution. The bold reformist stance of the Sakhigopal school created panic among the arch-conservative Brahmins of Puri. To destroy the school, some miscreants set fire to it on 22nd March,1912. The thatched school buildings were reduced to ashes, the valuable library books permanently destroyed and the morale of the organizers was thoroughly shaken. But Pandit Gopabandhu Das and Pandit Nilakantha Das were not cowed down. They were men with courage and vision. They had undaunted heroism to surmount the difficulties. They appealed for help and help poured in from different quarters of Orissa. By the time the rainy season commenced (June-August) two blocks of buildings had been completed. Later, when the permanent buildings were constructed, these blocks were converted into hostels of the school.

Necessity is the mother of invention. Now that the school-house was reduced to ashes, somehow the school must be kept-going. Pandit Gopabandhu Dash decided that the classes should be held in the small area 'well covered with a thick overgrowth of the branches of banyan, peepal, churiana, and bakul trees.' This area was known as 'Gupta Brundaban' and here raised masonry pedestals were constructed where from the teachers could teach. The experiment in open-air schooling had started. In 1913, the work on the new building started and it was complete by 1914.

During 1912, Acharya Harihar Das joined the school. Classes III and II (corresponding to classes IX & X of the present day) were opened in 1913. Pandit Godavarish Mishra, an M. A. in Economics from the Calcutta University joined the school. In 1914, class I (class XI of the present day) was opened. In 1914, Pandit Krupasindhu Misra joined the staff. The school applied for affiliation to the Calcutta University. However, acceptance of a nominal grant of Rs. 75was made a pre-condition for affiliation. The patriotic band of teachers spurned the idea because they were not prepared to compromise with the autonomy of the school. Consequently, affiliationwas delayed and the first batch of students had to appear as private candidates through other high schools. Finally, the Satyabadi High School was granted affiliation on 25th November 1914. Due to the efforts of Sri Ramabalav Mishra, the Collector of Puri, the school could get the permanent affiliation of the Calcutta University on 12th September 1917. The affiliation of the school was changed to the Patna University on its establishment on 1st October,1917. 15 Students out of the 22 who appeared at the Matriculation Examination came out successful.

Sri Asutosh Mukherjee visited the school on 12th June,1918 and remarked in the Visiting Book "such school should be held in every village of Bengal".

The Satyabadi high school was altogether a type by itself. It had set before itself the highest ideals of education. The finest elements of Santiniketan were incorporated into the school. It was the precursor of a model post-basic school. The teachers were the best that this State could produce. Every one of them has left behind a trail of glory in the annals of history. Pandit Gopabandhu Das was the greatest social worker and an eminent politician; Pandit Nilakantha Das was a forceful writer and also a front-rank freedom fighter; Pandit Godabarish Mishra with his chaste English pronunciation was an erudite scholar who was the Education Minister of the State and was responsible for the establishment of the Utkal University; Pandit Krupasinghu Mishra was an eminent historian, and Acharya Harihar, the saint and savant of Orissa, was the living embodiment of the finest Gandhian values. They were commonly known as the 'Five Friends' or 'Pancha Sakha'. Individually and collectively these Five Friends, have had a profound influence in transforming the socio-political scenario of Orissa. The other dedicated teachers were Sri Ramachandra Rath, Sri Satyabadi Tripathy, Sri Dhaneswar Maharana, Pandit Banchanidhi Mishra, Sri Gangadhar Mahapatra, Sri Paramananda Mishra, Sri Bhubaneswar Rath, Sri Madhusudan Misra etc. Sri Venu Gopalachari was a Tamilian working at Ranchi as a Professor in a Government College. He was a double M. A. He resigned his job and joined the Satyabadi band on a paltry pay of Rs. 50 per month. Sri Dhaneswar Maharana was the Art teacher. On 22nd January 1921, the Satyabadi school became a National Education Centre in response to Mahatma Gandhi's call to launch the Non-Cooperation Movement and so lost its affiliation.[171] Pandit Krupasindhu became the headmaster. On 26th March, 1921. Mahatma Gandhi visited the school and spent the night with its staff and students. Finally the school was closed. One of the gloriest experiments in the field of secondary education came to ahead end.

SECONDARY EDUCATION IN THE BIHAR & ORISSA PROVINCE

George High School, Bargarh started originally as an Upper Primary school in 1862, and was converted into a Middle Vernacular School in 1868, and again into a Middle English school in 1908. The fourth, third and second classes were opened in 1915, 1916 and 1917 respectively. The Patna University accorded sanction to the opening of the Matriculation class on the 22nd November, 1919, which was started from the beginning

---

171 *The Second Quinquennial Review on the Progress of Education in Bihar and Orissa 1917-1922*, Patna, 1992.

of the year 1920. The roll strength of the students rose from 140 in 1920 to 175 in 1930. The high school building was constructed with the help of a Government contribution of Rs. 23,000.00, Rs. 20,900.00 received from the sale proceeds of the old Middle Vernacular school building, and from a public donation of Rs. 8,994-8-7. There were two hostels attached to it. [172]The high schools at Kendrapara and Jajpur in Cuttack district were established by 1917. In Bihar & Orissa, during 1912-1917, there was an overall increase of high schools by 9, and of the M. E. schools by 38. However, the number of M. V. schools decreased by 3. Thus there was a net gain of 44 secondary schools in the entire province, In 1916-17 the total number of high schools, M. E. schools and M. V schools in the Province were 100, 226 and 130 respectively; and these increased to 117, 257 and 159 respectively by 1921-22. Three high schools were accorded recognition during 1917-1922 in Orissa. The school buildings of the Bargarh high school, the Khurda high school and the Kendrapara high school were completed during this quinquennium. The Government grant for buildings to the Bargarh school was Rs. 23,000, to the Kendrapara school Rs. 13,122 and to the Khurda high school Rs. 20,000. The two M. E. schools in the Angul district and the practicing M. E. school attached to the Government Training School, Cuttack were the three M. E. schools under the Government management. The four Zillah schools were Government schools.

In 1921, the fees in all government and non-government high and Middle English schools were raised 'in order to enable the pay of the teachers in aided schools to be improved.' This accounted for an increase from Rs. 16.27 to Rs. 18.77 in the average annual fee paid by a pupil in a High or Middle English school. At the same time public revenues paid 36.3% of the cost of these schools against 21.7% five years previously. The proportion of cost of secondary education which was met from fees could scarcely be termed excessive. The percentage

---

172 F. C. King, I. C. S., *Sambalpur District Gazetteer*, p. 232.

of free studentship were raised from 5 to 10in 1918 in all the High and Middle English schools.

The rise in school fees, the belief that Patna Matriculation course was suffer than the Calcutta Matriculation course, the poor pay of the teachers and their consequent apathy contributed to a general decrease in the roll-strength of the secondary schools during 1917-1922.

On 1st October, 1917 the Patna University was constituted and all the schools of Orissa were affiliated to this newly established University. In 1914, the institution of a School Leaving Certificate Examination for high schools was devised by a Committee. But it was not given effect to till the creation of the Patna University. An important feature of the period was the institution of special courses designed to prepare students for commercial or clerical careers. This examination was to be based on (1) the scrutiny of the school records. (2) the public examination and (3) in the case of those candidates who fail in one subject only at the public examination, an examination conducted *in situ* by the Inspector. In the Matriculation students destiny was determined on the basis of a single external examination; whereas in case of S. L. C, the school record was also given due weightage. The examination was conducted by an Administrative Board assisted by a Board of Studies. The Administrative Board consisted of the D. P. I. and Assistant D. P. I, five members nominated by the. Government, three members nominated by the University and two members were to represent the non-Government schools. At least three of the members were to be non-officials.

The first S. L. C. Examination was held in 1921. Two hundred sixteen candidates from 27 schools appeared. However, this examination was not popular as it was almost similar to the Matriculation Examination and the Matriculation was more prestigious than the S. L. C. Further the schools could not provide adequate optional for the S. L. C. course. The age limit for the Matriculation Examination was abolished in the year 1921.

In 1918, the Government decided to bear the entire cost of the Middle English Schools so that the Local bodies could devote their resources to the expansion of Primary and Vernacular education.

The Government was seriously considering the question of introducing Vernacular as the medium of instruction. An Education Committee was appointed to work out the details. An Association of Headmasters of High Schools was formed at Cuttack. Endeavours were also made, as far as possible, to see that the teachers in each school were fully consulted by the Headmasters and had opportunities of expressing their views. For this purpose each high school had its Teacher's Association, "though these did not meet as regularly as they should have done." The lack of trained teachers was acutely felt for which the Government was contemplating the opening of a Trainingwas acutely felt for which the Government was contemplating the opening of a Training college at Cuttack. The necessity of appointing whole-time clerks for high school was realized, so that one of the teachers may not be tied to clerical work. The scales of pay of teachers were revised in 1921-22. The schools were given grants to improve their furniture. There was an increase of 16 high school, 61 M. E. schools, and 83 M. V. schools during the quinquennium 1922-27. The high school at Rajkanika was closed.

The average annual cost per school during 1922-27 was as shown in Table No. 4.1.6.

TABLE 4.1. 6

Average Annual Cost per School, 1916-27

Sl. No.	Type of Schools	1916-17	1920-21	1921-22	1925-26	1926-27
01.	High School	Rs. 9,857.2	Rs. 11,261.5	Rs. 11,077.3	Rs. 12,494.1	Rs. 13,147.3
02.	M.E. School	1,721.7	2,151.8	2,152.8	2,344.3	2,347.5
03.	M.V. School	1,144.3	1,405.7	1,420.7	1,515.8	1,634.0

In 1926, the Government M. E. school at Angul was raised to the status of a high school with the opening of class VIII. In 1930, it became a full-fledged high school. It was the fifth Government school in Orissa. The Angul high school building was completed in 1929-30. During 1928-29, the high school at Olsing in the district, of Puri was recognized and. it sent its first batch of students to the Matriculation Examination. Classes VIII and IX were opened at Balasore Girls' High School and the Middle English was upgraded to an incomplete Girls' high school during 1930-31.

During 1932-33, the Nimapara high school at Nimapara in the district of Puri was recognized. During 1934-35, Banpur high school in the district of Puri was recognized. The extension of the school building of Balasore Zilla school was carried out in 1930-31. The building of the Sayeed Seminary at Cuttack was repaired during 1932-33.

The most important development was the constitution of a Board of Secondary Education during the year 1922-23. The constitution was revised during 1925-26.

Composition of the Board of Secondary Education (1925-26)

1. The Directorate of the Public Instruction, Bihar & Orissa was the *ex-officio* Chairman.
2. The Patna University elected three members
3. Five members elected by the non-official members of the Legislative Council, one from each Division. That means there was one member from the Orissa Division.
4. Principals of the Diamond Jubilee College and Nalanda College and the Headmaster of the Ranchi Zilla School were the *ex-officio* members.
5. A representative of female education.

6. Four representatives of the community which in the opinion of the Government is not adequately represented; to be nominated by the Government.

7. An Inspector of Schools to be nominated by the Government.

8. Four Headmasters of Schools to be nominated by the Government.

9. The Registrar of Examinations was the Secretary of the Board; but not a member.

The Board was a subsidiary of Patna University and worked under the overall supervision of the Syndicate of the University. The powers of recognition were vested with the Board. The S. L. C. Examination proved to be unpopular and only 71 candidates appeared at this examination 1925-26. Therefore, it had been described as *"an expensive luxury."*

The Grant-in-aid rules relating to high schools were modified in 1923-24 and again in 1925-26. In 1923 the grant-in-aid covered the extra expenditure incurred in connection with the payment of salaries to the clerk of the school and also to defray the additional expenses relating to annual repairs and the newly created Provident Fund. In 1925-26, *lump sum grant-in-aid was* given to schools on the basis of the teaching staff of the school.

In 1923 it was recommended that Vernacular should be the medium of instruction in the four highest classes of the secondary school. The regulations of the Patna University were revised in which it was provided that, "in subjects other than English and Mathematics, the medium of examination after the year 1928 may be the Vernacular offered by the candidate."[173] These, changes in the regulations were sanctioned by the Government with effect from 1st January, 1925.

In 1925, the Managing Committees of the Government high schools were reconstituted and enlarged by the addition of three non-official

---

173 Second Quinquennium Review on the Progress of Education in Bihar and Orissa, 1917-22

members, one of whom must be a Muhammadan. Previous to 1925 all the members of the Managing Committee were official members. The powers of the Managing Committees were substantially increased. [174]

Middle English schools were popular during 1922-1927; but many of them were not found efficient. A public examination was introduced at the end of class VII from the year 1927-28. A student must pass this public middle examination to be admitted to class VIII of the high school.[175]

The question of revising the system and rules in accordance with which recurring grants were made to high school was considered by a sub-committee of the Board of Secondary Education. The Report of the sub-committee was place before the Board's meeting held in March, 1928.[176] During 1928-29, for the first time, the Matriculation Examination was held for those students who had been taught throughout the Vernacular medium. During the same year a Committee was appointed by the Government to consider the alleged deterioration of quality in the standard of Matriculares.[177] The experiment relating to the introduction of the Vernacular medium in the four highest classes of the high schools which was in progress for the last five years was allowed to'be continued for two more years as the results of the experiment were inconclusive. It was noticed that the greatest handicap in working out this experiment was the lack of text books in the Vernacular languages.[178] The Committee appointed by the Government to consider the alleged deterioration in the merit of matriculates, met in November, 1929. It was of the opinion that the deterioration was only in some respects.

---

174 *Ibid.*

175 *Ibid*

176 *Report on the Prowess of 'Education in Bihar and Orissa.. 1927-28*, Patna, 1928 p. 18

177 *Report on the Progress of Education in Bihar and Orissa. 1928-29*, Patna, 1929p. 18

178 Report on the Progress of Education in Bihar and Orissa, 1929-30, Patna, 1930 p. 17

It recommended that the text-books in Mathematics and Geography should be in English.[179]

Vocational classes in the Government Middle English schools were made permanent with effect from 1st January, 1930.[180] Good reports were received of the vocational classes of the middle schools during 1930-31. The Government school, Cuttack, the M. V School at Subarnapur in Cuttack; the Narayan Chandra M. E. School, Balasore; the Janla Middle English school in Puri and the Patnayak Para M. E. school at Sambalpur each had a carpentry class. The Government M. E. School at Phulbani, the Anglo-Bengali M. E. School at Puri, the Ertal M. E. School at Balasore, the Rambag Middle English School at Cuttack had tailoring sections. Agriculture was taught at the Sidheswarpur M. E. School in Cuttack.[181]

By 1932-33 the D. P. I. was reporting that the experiment of teaching through the Vernacular medium had not been a success and needed to be abandoned.[182]

It was decided in 1933-34 that the public middle school examination was to be conducted by the Board; but in high schools the papers were to be evaluated by the teachers. The Examinations at high school would thus not be a public examination.[183]The same year the Cuttack District Board had appointed an auditor to audit the accounts of Middle English Schools aided by the Board.[184]

By 1935, there were 23 high schools and 116 Middle schools in North Orissa. There was an increase of 12 high school and 44 Middle schools during the period1900 to 1935 in North Orissa.

---

179 Ibid. p. 17
180 Ibid. p. 18
181 Report on the Progress of Education in Bihar and Orissa,1930-31 p. 19
182 Report on the Progress of Education in Bihar and Orissa, 1932-33 p. 18
183 Report on the Progress of Education in Bihar and Orissa,l 933-34, p. 17
184 Ibid p. 18

SECONDARY EDUCATION IN THE FEUDATORY STATES OF ORISSA UP TO 1912

There were three high English schools in 1911-12, at the headquarters stations of the States of Bamra, Dhenkanal and Mayurbhanj. The high school of the Bamra State was at Deogarh; of the Dhenkanal State at Dhenkanal; and the Mayurbhanj State at Baripada. All the three schools were affiliated to the Calcutta University. There were 20 Middle English schools and 6 Middle Vernacular schools in all the States taken together. Three thousand one hundred ten pupils were studying in all the secondary schools of the Feudatory States.

Up to 1905, the schools of Kalahandi, Sonepur, Bolangir, Patna, Rairakhol and Bamra States were receiving free aclministrative assistance from the Agency Inspector of Schools, Raipur. The States of Bonai and Gangpur were in the jurisdiction of the Inspector of Schools, Chotanagpur Division. The other States were under the Inspector of Schools, South West Division.

The total expenditure on education for the year 1907-08 was Rs. 2,50,000 of which Rs. 37,000 was paid by the Government, Rs. 1,36,000 by the several States and Rs. 77,000 from fees etc.[185]

Athagarh State had one M. E. School at Athagarh. It enjoyed the services of a Sub-Inspector of Schools and the Agency Inspector of Schools. Total expenditureon education was Rs. 1,047.00.[186]*Athamallik* State had a goodMiddle English school at Athmallik. The total expenditure on education was Rs. 2,629.00.[187]*Bamra* State had a high school at Deogarh. The total expenditure on education in the State was Rs. 7,162.00.[188]*Baramba* State had a single Middle Vernacular school at

---

185 L. E. B Cobden-Ramsey, Feudatory States of Orissa, 1905, pp. 106-107
186 *Ibid* P-112-113
187 *Ibid.*P-118
188 *Ibid*P-127

Barmba.[189]***Boudh*** State had one Middle English school at Boudh.[190]***Bonai*** State did not have a single Middle English or Middle Vernacular school or high school. Educationally it was an exceedingly backward State, "being inhabited by very wild aboriginal races scattered amongst the hill ranges and forests."[191]***Daspalla*** State maintained a Middle English school. Educationally the State was very backward. In 1907-08 the State had spent Rs. 2,658on education. It had received a grant of Rs. 279 towards education from the Government.[192]***Dhenkanal*** State maintained a High English school located in a building, "one of the finest in the Garhjats. "The cost of the upkeep of the school was Rs. 4,956 during 1907-08. The total fees collections amounted to Rs. 332. One hundred eighty six students were studying in the high school. The State had spent 5% of its income annually on education. The total cost of education in 1907-08, was Rs. 23,756 of which Rs. 10,385 was contributed by the State, Rs. 3,310by Government, Rs. 9,039 by school fees and the rest by subscriptions.[193]***Gangpur*** State had a Middle English school at Sundergarh. The school building 'was a fine one with a hostel attached'. There was also a Middle Vernacular school at Ujalpur, accommodated in a good house with a hostel attached. One hundred twenty eight students were studying in the Middle English school during 1907-08.[194]***Hindol'***State had a single Middle Vernacular school at Hindol. The total expenditure on education during the year 1907-08 was Rs. 1,434.[195]***Kalahandi*** State maintained a Middle English school at Bhawanipatna. A good hostel was attached to it. The State expenditure on education for the year 1907-08 was about Rs. 10,00.[196]***Keonjhar*** State had two Middle English schools, one was at Keonjhar and the

---

189 *Ibid*P-132

190 *Ibid*P-140

191 *Ibid*P-157

192 *Ibid*P-162

193 *Ibid*P-173

194 IbidP-188

195 *Ibid*P-192

196 *Ibid*P-211

other at Anandpur. The total educationalexpenditure was Rs. 8,055 in 1907-08.[197]*Khandapara*Statewas educationally backward. There was a single Middle Vernacular school at Khandapara.[198]*Mayurbhanj* State was the northern most and the largest of the States of Orissa. It had a high English school at Baripada with 271 students on rolls. The average daily attendance was 203. The cost of tuition per boy in 1907-08 was Rs. 19. This entire amount was borne by the State. Out of 271 pupils on the rolls, 258 were Hindus, 6 Muhammadans, 6 native Christians and one aborigine. The number of Middle English schools in the State was five. Four hundred nine students were reading in these schools. At the end of the year 1907-08 the cost of educating each pupil was Rs. 10.4. The expenditure from the State funds on account of education in all branches in 1907-08 was Rs. 35,541.52 or 2.9% of the gross revenue of the State.[199]*Narasinghpur* State had a single Middle Vernacular school at Narsinghpur. The educational expenditure of the State was Rs. 1,998 and in addition there was the Government grant of Rs. 1,397. 'Education is backward, but more advanced than in the neighbouring States,"[200]was the comment of Government. *Nayagarh* State had a single Middle English school at Nayagarh. Education was backward, but was making steady progress, and the intelligent section of the population were anxious to have high English education for their boys. The total annual expenditure in 1907-08 on education was Rs. 9,369.[201]*Nilgiri* State had one Middle English school at Nilgiri. The State expenditure on education was Rs. 2,347. "The people were appreciative of the benefits of education."[202]*Palahara* State did not have a single Middle English school or Middle Vernacular school. Educationally it was very backward.[203]*Patna* State had a Middle English school and a

---

197 *Ibid* P-231
198 *Ibid.*P-235
199 *Ibid*P- 257
200 *Ibid*P-261
201 *Ibid*P-270
202 *Ibid*P-274
203 *Ibid*P-280

Middle Vernacular school at Bolangir. There was an M. E. school at Patnagarh. The schools were looked after by a State Deputy Inspector of Schools.[204]*Rairakhol* State did not have a single secondary school. "Education was very backward in the state.'[205]*Ranpur* State maintained a Middle English school at Ranpur.[206]*Soneput*'State took great interest in education. There was a Middle English school at Sonepur established during 1894-95. There was a Middle Vernacular school also. 'The great advance and improvement made in the cause of education during recent years is one of the most marked features in the administration of the State.'[207]*Talcher* State maintained a Middle English school at Talcher.[208]*Tigiria* State had no secondary schools, whatsoever.[209]

The area, population and number of various types of secondary schools in the Feudatory States of Orissa in 1911-1912 has been depicted in Table No. 4.1.7.

TABLE 4.1.7

Area, Population & Secondary Schools in the 24 Feudatory State of Orissa

SI. No.	Name of the Feudatory State	Area InSq. Miles	Number of		Popu-lation in 1901	Schools in 1911-1912		
			Towns	Villages		High	Middle English	Middle Vernacular
01.	Athagarh	168	...	192	43,784	...	1	...
02.	Athmallik	730	....	460	40,753	...	1	...
03.	Bamara	1,988	1	931	123,378	1	...	...
04.	Baramba	134	...	181	38,260	...	...	1
05.	Baud	1,264	...	1,070	88,250	...	1	...
06.	Bonai	1,296	...	217	38,277	...	...	...
07.	Daspalia	568	...	485	51,987	...	1	...
08.	Dhenkanal	1,463	2	968	273,662	1	...	...

---

204 *Ibid*P-303

205 IbidP-312

206 *Ibid*P-316

207 *Ibid*. p. 328

208 *Ibid*. p. 334

209 *Ibid*. p. 37

SI. No.	Name of the Feudatory State	Area InSq. Miles	Number of		Population in 1901	Schools in 1911-1912		
			Towns	Villages		High	Middle English	Middle Vernacular
09.	Gangpur	2,492	...	806	238,896	...	1	...
10.	Hindol	312	...	234	47,180.	...	...	1
11.	Kalahandi	3,745	...	2,198	350,529	...	1	...
12.	Keonjhar	3,096	...	1,938	285,758	...	2	...
13.	Khandapara	244	...	325	69,450	...	...	1
14.	Mayurbhanj	4,243	1	3,593	610,383	1	5	...
15.	Narsinghpur	199	...	198	39,613	...	...	1
16.	Nayagarh	588	...	775	140,779	...	1	...
17.	Nilgiri	278	...	466	66,460	...	1	...
18.	Pal Lahara	452	...	265	22,351	...	...	...
19.	Patna	2,399	...	1,850	277,748	...	1	1
20.	Rairakhol	833	...	319	26,888	...	...	...
21.	Ranpur	203	...	261	46,075	...	1	...
22.	Sonepur	906	1	899	169,877	...	2	1
23.	Talcher	399	...	293	60,432	...	1	...
24.	Tigiria	46	...	102	22,625	...	...	...

Source: Bengal Gazetteers, Feudatory States of Orissa by L.E.B. Cobden-Ramsay, I.C.S., 1950, P.37

SECONDARY EDUCATION THE FEUDATORY STATES OF ORISSA, 1912-1935

In 1912-13, a high school was opened at Sonepur. In this connection the Administrative Report of the State for 1912-13 stated "There was one Rajkumar school and another Middle English school maintained in the town of Sonepur. After amalgamation of the two institutions into one, the school has been raised to the high English standard and is awaiting affiliation of the Calcutta University. To meet the requirement of the raised standard, extra expenditure will be provided in the new year's budget."[210] During 1913-14, "the teaching staff of the high school was strengthened by the appointment of two new teachers. It was expected that the high school would be affiliated to the Calcutta University; but owing to pressure of work, Calcutta University could not send out the team of Inspectors for reporting on the school to the University. The Jubaraj (heir-apparent) of the State was studying in the highest class of the schooland was to appear at the Matriculation Examination in 1915. The third son of the Chief was studying in the third class.[211] During 1914-15, the high school at Sonepur was affiliated to the Calcutta University.[212] The new building for the school was under construction.[213]

During 1913-14, three students were sent up as private candidates for the Matriculation Examination of Calcutta University from Bolangir under the efficient coaching of Babu Damodar Mohanty, Headmaster of the Middle English school at Bolangir. All the three passed the examination. During 1914-15, Bolangir School applied for affiliation to the Calcutta University. The Political Agent, Mr. Cobden-Ramsay evinced great interest in this regard. In 1915-16 as, the Prithviraj High School, Bolangir got temporary affiliation from the Calcutta University. Babu Damodar Mohanty was appointed the Headmaster of the school. Three students appeared at the Matriculation examination of 1915-16 as private candidates. In 1918-19, the school was affiliated to the newly established Patna University. In 1922-23, the Bolangir high school was described as a Very good school' and to have been on par with established schools at Baripada and Dhenkanal. In 1929-30, the results of the Prithviraj High School, Bolangir were excellent. Eight out of 9 candidates passed the Matriculation examination of 1930.

---

210 *Annual Report on the Administration of Feudatory States of Orissa and Chotanappur*1912-13

211 *Review on the Administration of Feudatory States of Orissa and Chotanappur,* 1913-14 p. 169

212 *Review on the Administration of Feudatory States of Orissa and Chotanappur,* 1914-15.

213 *Ibid,* for 1915-16

In the year 1913-14, there were 3 English and 4 Vernacular teachers in the Jubaraj School at Talcher. "But in January 1914 with the view of raising the status of the school to that of the high English school a new class corresponding to 3rd class was opened. Consequent!, a new English teacher was appointed. The number of students on roll was 166 against 158 of the previous year. The Jubaraj High School, Talcher was affiliated to the Patna University during 1918-19.

During 1915-16, two classes were added to the Middle English school at Bhawanipatna to make it a high school. In the following year further steps were taken in this direction. During 1918-19, the Bhawaqnipatna High School was recognized by the Director of Public Instruction, Bihar and Orissa. The teaching staff was improved and the institution was fully equipped according to rules.

The Middle English school at Sundergarh, the headquarters of the Gangpur State, was converted to a high school with the opening of the 3rd class during 1922-23. Class X was added during 1929-30. This school named as Bhawani Shankar HighSchool, Sundergarh sent its first batch of studentsto theMatriculation Examination in 1931-32.

Two classes corresponding to 3rd and 4th classes were added to the Middle English school at Athagarh in Athagarh State to raise it to the standard of a high English school during 1914-15. It was named Ramsay Secondary School after the name of Mr. L. E. B. Cobden-Ramsay, the then Political Agent. It was shown as a high school since 1924-25. It was a secondary school with instruction up to class IX up to 1931-32. Its progress was very slow and unsatisfactory.

Bamra High School was a full fledged high school up to 1922-23. However, in 1923 it was disaffiliated and it lost its recognition as a high school. Again in 1928-29, the school regained its original status as a full fledged high school and was recognized as such by the Patna University.

In 1912-13, attempts were made to start a high school at Baud. "A high English school was formally opened by the late Chief on 5th

October,1912, in the new buildings erected as a memorial to His Late Majesty the King-Emperor Edward VII. The local M. E. School was merged into it and a fourth class was opened during the year as a beginning". It was a bold venture no doubt. However, due to lack of adequate staff, the school had nominal existence for a year and a half when finally it was abolished. During 1931-32, the King Edward VII Middle English school at Baud was converted to a high school with the opening of class VIII from the beginning of 1932.

The progress of secondary education in the 24 Feudatory States can be gauged from Table No. 4.1.8.

TABLE 4.1.8

Secondary Education in the Feudatory States of

Qrissa, 1911 to 1932

SI. No.	Type of School	Year		
		1911-12	**1921-22**	**1931-32**
01.	High Schools	03	09	10
02.	M.E. Schools	18	26	30
03.	M.V. Schools	07	17	18
Total		**28**	**52**	**58**

The growth of secondary education was significant during the decade 1911-12 to 1921-22. There was a net gain of 24 institutions. The number of high schools rose from 3 to 9. There was also an increase of 8 Middle English schools and 20Middle Vernacular schools during this period. However, this tempo of expansion could not be maintained during the following decade i.e. 1921-22 to 1931-32, There was an increase of only one high school, one M. V. school and 4 M. E. schools. **Athagarh** State had only one Middle English school at Athagarh. It was raised to the status of a High English school during 1924-25. It continued to be a secondary school with instruction up to class IX till 1931-32. An M. V. School was established at Gurudijhatia during 1930-31. **Athamallik** State had one Middle English School by 1911-12. By 1931-32, it had one M. E. school and one M. V. school which was established at Kishorenagar in 1930-31. **Bamra** State had one high English school by 1911-12. This high school lost its recognition in 1922-23. The recognition was restored during 1928-29. There were one high English school at Deogarh and 3 Middle Vernacular schools in this State by 1931-32. **Baramba** State had one Middle Vernacular school at Baramba. During 1918-19, this school was converted in to a Middle English school. There was no further progress in the State up to 1931-32. **Bonai** State had not a single M. E. or M. V. school in the State during 1911-12. By 1931-32 there was one Middle English school at Bonai. The Middle English school was started during 1915-16. **Daspalla** State had by 1911-12, one M. E. school at Daspalla. There had absolutely been no further progress in the field of secondary education during 1911-12 to 1931-32. Gangpur State had by 1911-12, one M. E. school at Sundergarh, the headquarters of the Gangpur State. This M. E. school was raised to the status of a high school in 1930 and became a full fledged high school by 1931-32. In addition to this there were 4 more M. V. schools in the state by 1931-32. The M. V school at Rajgangpur was established in 1924-25. **Keonjhar** State had two Middle English schools at Keonjhar and Anandpur by 1911-12. By 1931-32, there were in all 2 M. E. schools and 2 M. V. schools in the State. **Khandapara** State had by 1911-12, a single Middle Vernacular school at Khandapara. This was converted into a Middle English school. There was no further progress up to 1936. **Narasinghpur** State had one M. V. school at Narsinghpur by 1911-12. By 1931-32, the only change was that it had been converted into a Middle English school. **Nayagarh** State had one M. E. school at Nayagarh by 1911-12. During 1924-25. one M. V school was established. By 1931-32, these were the two secondary school in the State. **Nilgiri** State had only one M. E. School at Nilgiri during the period 1911-12 to 1931-32. There was no progress whatsoever in the field of secondary education. **Pallahara** State had not a single secondary school by 1911-12. The U. P. school at Pallahara was raised to Middle Vernacular school on 1st January, 1913. During 1931-32, it was convertedinto a Middle English school. **Patna (Bolangir)** State had one M. E. and one M. V. school by 1911-12. In

1915-16, the Middle English school at Bolangir became the Prithviraj High School, Bolangir. By 1931-32, there were one high school, 2 M. E. schools and 3 M. V. schools in the Bolangir-Patna State. **Rairakhol** State was the most backward State educationally. Up to 1931-32, there was not a single secondary school in the State. **Boud** State unsuccessfully tried to establish a high school during 1912-13. by 1931-32, there was an incomplete high school with instruction up to class VIII. The U. P. School at Purunakataka was upgraded to an M. E. school during 1930-31. **Dhenkanal** State had only one high school at Dhenkana by 1911-12. During 1929-30, the M. V. school at Murhi (Kamakhyanagar) was converted into an M. E. school. By 1931-32, there were a high school, two M. E. schools, and two M. V. schools in the Dhenkanal State. **Hindol** State had one Middle Vernacular school at Hindol. This was converted into a Middle English school in 1916. There was no other progress up to 1936-37. **Kalahandi** State had one M. E. school at Bhawanipatna by1911-12. This was raised to a full-fledged high school during 1918-19. During 1916, one U. P. school was converted into an M. E. school. By 1936-37, there was a high school, an M. E. school and an M. V school in the Kalahandi State. **Mayurbhanj** State had one high school at Baripada; and there were 5 M. E schools in the Mayurbhanj State. Between the years 1925-28, the number of M. E. schools was 6. During 1928-29, an M. V. school was established at Rairangpur. During 1929-30, class VIII was added to the Nayabasa M. E. school. By 1936-37, there were one high school and 8 M. E. schools. **Ranpur** State had one M. E. school at Ranpur. This situation did not improve up to 1936-37. **Sonepur** State had 2 M. E. schools and one M. V school by 1911-12. In 1913, the Sonepur high school was started. During 1914-15, it became a full-fledged high school. The Tarbha M. V school was converted into an M. E. school in 1931-32. By 1936-37, there were one high school, 2 M. E. schools and 1 M. V. school in the Sonepur State. **Talcher** State had one M. E. school at Talcher by 1911-12. This became a full-fledged high school in 1918-19. There was no other secondary school in the State. **Tigiria** State did not have a single secondary school up to 1911-12. In 1914-15 two teachers were appointed to raise the Tigiria

U. P. school to an M. E. school. By 1936-37, there was only one M. E. school in the State.

Secondary education had made a fair progress in the States of Mayurbhanj, Sonepur and Bamra. The progress in all other States was not satisfactory.

SECONDARY EDUCATION IN SOUTH ORISSA

Secondary Education in the District of Koraput

The Middle English school at Jeypore was raised to the status of a high school in 1913. In 1917 it became a full-fledged high school and presented candidates for the Matriculation Examination of the Madras University. It had 182 students on rolls in 1922.

The Gunpur school was imparting instruction up to the third form with a roll strength of 68 students in 1922. Both these schools were Local Board schools. The Jeypore high school had rather inadequate buildings in the centre of the town and a hostel accommodating 12 boys. The Gunpur high school had a strength of 198 pupils in 1938, The Jeypore high school had a Headmaster and 14 assistant masters of whom 6 were graduates. In the Gunpur high school, there were 9 teachers including the Headmaster, of whom 4 were graduates (1938). It had an excellent building and a hostel. The total expenditure on account of Jeypore high school and the Gunpur Secondary school in 1922 was Rs. 12,129 and Rs. 3,975 respectively. A District Board was constituted for Koraput on 1st April 1934. The erstwhile Taluk Board schools were transferred to the management on the District Board.

A Board Middle English school was established at Nawarangpur in 1926. The Board Middle school at Kotpad was established in 1931 and the Board M. E. school at Rayagada in 1938. The Government used to make an annual grant to the District Board to aid it in the support of secondary education.

In 1938, there were eight Higher Elementary (M. V) schools in the district of Koraput. Six of them were managed by the Taluk Boards.

Two Higher Elementary schools were managed by the Schleswig-Holstein Evangelical Lutheran Mission.[214]

Secondary Education in the District of Ganjam (1917-22)

Ganjam and Koraput districts were in the Madras Presidency up to 1st April, 1936, when they were amalgamated, with Orissa. The development of secondary education in these two districts was linked to the developments in the Madras Presidency. The area and population of the Madras Presidency and the Ganjam district during 1921 were as shown in Table No. 4.1.9.

TABLE 4.1.9

Area & Population of Madras Presidency & Ganjam District, 1921

Sl. No.	Name of the Area	Area in Sq. Miles	Population 1921 Census
01	Madras Presidency	142,260	42,318,985
02	Ganjam District	4,798	1,835,562

The total number of educational institutions and scholars reading therein during 1916-17 and 1921-22 have been indicated in Table No. 4.1.10.

TABLE- 4.1.10

Educational Institutions & Scholars, 1916-17 & 1921-22

SI. No.	Name of the Area	1916-17		1921-22	
		Institutions	Scholars	Institutions	Scholars
01	Madras Presidency	36,045	16,61,012	40,647	18,37,022
02	Ganjam District	1,885	73,209	1,841	70,264

From the Table No. 4.1.10, it is evident that during the quinquennium 1916-17 to 1921-22, there was an overall decrease of 44 institutions and 2,942 scholars in the district of Ganjam.[215]

---

214 R. C. Bell, I. C. S., *Koraput District Gazetteer*, 1945, pp. 157-158

215 *Report on Public Instruction in the Madras Presidency for 1921-22 and for the. Quinquennium 1916-17 to 1921-22 VollMadras*, 1923 pp. 1-3

The percentage of scholars to population in respect of the Madras Presidency and the Ganjam district have been shown in Table No. 4.1.11.

TABLE 4.1.11

Percentage of Scholars & Population 1916-17 & 1921-22

SI. No.	Name of Area	1916-17			1921-22		
		Male	Female	Total	Male	Female	Total
01	Madras Presidency	6.5%	1.5%	4.0%	7.0%	1.8%	4.3%
02	Ganjam District	6.2%	0.7%	3.2%	7.4%	0.9%	3.8%

In 1916-17, the male literacy level of Ganjam was less than 0.3 of the Provincial norm. In so far as female literacy was concerned it was really backward. In the total percentage, Ganjam was the below the Presidency norms by 0.8% in 1916-17. By 1921-22, in male literacy Ganjam was above the provincial norm; however, in female literacy it was just half-way behind. In the total percentage Ganjam was below the Presidency norm by 0.5% and had made up 0.3% during the quinquennium.[216] The education of the Oriya speaking people in the Madras Presidency can be gauged from the statistics given in Table No. 4.1.12 [217]

TABLE 4.1.12

Oriya Speaking Scholars in Educational Institutions of the Madras Presidency

SI. No.	Name of Area	1916-17			1921-22		
		Boys	Girls	Total	Boys	Girls	Total
01	Public Institutions	45,672	4,422	50,094	51,507	5,729	57,226
02	Private Institutions	917	36	953	130	...	130
	Total	46,589	4,458	51,047	51,637	5,729	57,356

Berhampur and Paralakimedi with populations of 32,731 and 18,719 respectively were the two municipalities. By 1916, each had a College,

---

216 *Ibid* p.3
217 *Ibid* p.8

Berhampur had four secondary schools, 39 elementary schools and one school for Europeans. Parlakimedi had two secondary schools, 19 elementary schools and three special schools. Eight hundred sixty three boys and 164 girls were receiving secondary education at Berhampur. Seven hundred twenty nine boys and 2 girls reading in secondary schools at Parlakimedi. Parlakimedi was comparatively very backward in matters of secondary education of girls by 1922.[218]

The average cost of secondary education per pupil was Rs. 62.56 in and Rs. 56.44 in 1921-22. There was a reduction of Rs. 6.13 in the average cost of education per pupil during this period. The average per capita fee collection and average cost of education have been shown in Table No. 4.1.13.

TABLE 4.1.13

Average Per Capita Fee & Average Cost, 1916-17 & 1921-22

SI. No.	Institutions	191647		1921-22	
		Average fee in Rs.	**Average Cost in Rs.**	**Average fee in Rs.**	**Average Cost in Rs.**
01	Arts College	95.44	307.00	89.00	275.19
02	Secondary School	21.94	62.56	23.69	56.44
03	Primary School	0.19	13.13	0.13	11.25

The secondary school fees were almost one-fourth of the fees charged for Collegiate education; but was terribly costlier than primary education. The average cost of education had an overall decrease. The cost of secondary education was five times that of the primary education and was almost one-fifth of cost of the higher education.[219]

Ganjam had received a fairly good attention in matters of educational grants amongst the districts of the Madras Presidency. It received 3.41% and 3.75% grant-in-aid during 1921 and 1922 respectively. Eight

---

218 *Ibid* p. 10

219 *Ibid* p.27

districts had received higher grants-in-aid and 17 districts had received grant-in-aid less than this.[220]

The number of pupils attending secondary schools in the district if Ganjam by 31st March, 1921 was 5,166; and by 1922 it was 4,495, out of which 1,228 and 970 students were from outside the towns in which secondary schools were situated. One out of every four students was coming from outside the town in 1921; and in 1922 one out of every five students was such a pupil.[221]

The number of male pupils attending secondary schools on 31st March, 1917 was 4,828. This constituted 0.46 percent of the total male population according to 1911 census. As on 31st March 1922, the number of pupils studying in the secondary schools of Ganjam district was 4,459 which constituted 0.54 percent of the male population of the district according to the 1921 census. The total number of girls receiving secondary education was 176 in 1922 in the Ganjam district.[222]

There were 8 Sanskrit schools which had been classified as secondary schools imparting instruction to 180 scholars during 1922. This was the indigenous classical secondary education which had been recognized. However, there were 3 Sanskrit schools of the secondary level which were imparting instruction to 70 scholars which remained unrecognized.

By 1922, the following were the full-fledged high schools of the Ganjam district:

1. Russelkonda (Bhanjanagar) High School.
2. Aska High School.
3. Chatrapur Onslow Institute.
4. School Department of the Khallikote College, Berhampur
5. School Department of the Maharajah's College, Parlakimedi

---

220 *Ibid* p.32
221 *Ibid* p.34
222 *Ibid* p.34

Of the above high schools, the first three school were under Local Board Management up to 31st March,1934. Consequently on the constitution of a District Board on 1st April, 1934, these schools became District Board Schools. Now they are Government institutions. The Khallikote Collegiate High School, Berhampur and the Maharajah's Boys' High School, Parlakimedi were aided institutions.

The following secondary schools imparted instruction up to the Illrd form i.e. Class VIII.

1. Purushottampur (with primary classes attached)
2. Buguda
3. Surada
4. Gurandi
5. Berhampur Baptist Mission School
6. Dharakote
7. Digapahandi
8. Bairani (Now Kabi Suryanagar)
9. Khallikote

The first four were under Local Board management up to 1934; and then under the District Board management. The schools at Berhampur, Dharakote, Digapahandi, Bairani and Khallikote were aided institutions.

The following two schools were unaided institutions:

1. Chikiti with instruction up to IIIrd form and Primary classes attached.
2. Kodak Maradaraj School with instruction up to 1st form.[223]

The number of scholars studying in the various secondary class in 1922 was as shown in Table No. 4.1.14.[224]

---

223 *Ibid* p.34
224 *Ibid*. p. 34

TABLE 4.1.14

Scholars in Various Forms (i.e. Classes)

SI. No.	Classes	Equivalent to Classes	Board Schools	Aided Schools	Unaided Schools	Total
01.	VI Form	XI	99	159	...	258
02.	VForm	X	84	157	....	241
03.	IV Form	IX	84	137	....	221
04	III Form	VIII	103	282	04	389
05.	II Form	VII	114	250	09	373
06.	I Form	VI	152	271	26	449
	Total		**636**	**1256**	**39**	**1931**

In the secondary schools, 22 were trained graduates, and 82 were secondary grade trained teachers.

The following was the expenditure on account of secondary schools for Boys in the Ganjam district (1922)[225]

Rs.

1.	Government Revenue	...	19,460,00
2.	Local Funds	...	22,974.00
3.	Fees	...	7,471.00

Total ... **49,905.00**

The Berhampur Hindu School, Berhampur (now Government Secondary and Training School for Women), was the only secondary schools for girls with a roll strength of 140 imparting instruction up to the IIIrd form with a staff of 6 teachers. The total expenditure on account of this school was Rs. 3,732.00.[226]

---

225 *Ibid.* Subsidiary Tables p. 2
226 *Ibid-* Subsidiary Tables p. 33

SECONDARY EDUCATION IN THE GANJAM DISTRICT DURING (1922-1935)

The number of educational institutions and scholars reading therein during 1930 have been shown in Table No. 4.1.15.

TABLE 4.1.15

Institutions & Scholars

SI. No.	Areas	Number of Public Institutions	Number of Scholars
01.	Ganjam District	2,589	93,118
02.	Ganjam Agency	390	14,310
03.	Vizagapatam Agency (i.e.,the present districts of Koraput, Nawarangpur, Malkangiri and Rayagada)	460	13,810

Since 1922, there was an increase of 748 institutions and 22,854 scholars in the district of Ganjam.[227]

The percentage of scholars to population in respect of the Madras Presidency and South Orissa has been indicated in Table No. 4.1.16.[228]

TABLE 4.1.16

Percentage of Scholars to Population, 1921-22 & 1929-30

SI. No.	Area	1921-22			1929-30		
		Male	Female	Total	Male	Female	Total
01	Madras Presidency	7.0	1.8	4.3	10.6	3.1	6.8
02	Ganjam District	7.4	0.9	3.8	9.6	1.3	5.1
03.	Ganjam Agency	2.8	0.4	1.6	7.9	0.7	4.3
04.	Vizagapatam Agency (or undivided Koraput District)	2.8	0.4	1.6	2.5	0.3	1.4

227 *Report on Public Instruction in the Madras Presidency. 1929-30. Vol. IIp. 3*
228 *Ibid p. 4*

In 1921-22, Ganjam district was above the Provincial norms in so far as male literacy was concerned. By 1930, it fell behind the Provincial norm by 1%. The female literacy level of Ganjam was half that of the Provincial norm in 1921-22; it went down to less than one-third of the Provincial norm by 1929-30. In overall literacylevel the gap widened from 0.5% to 1.7%. In levels of literacy, Ganjam Agency was better off than Koraput district (i.e. Vizagapatam Agency).

The number of Oriya speaking scholars was as follows:[229]

| 1921-22 | ... | 57,356 |
| 1929-30 | ... | 77,617 |

No new secondary school was opened in the Ganjam district during the period due to the acute economic depression. The Berhampur Hindu School for Girls, Berhampur (now Government Secondary Training School for Women) became a full fledged high school in 1935. This was the first Girls' high school of South Orissa and the second of its type in Orissa. In the Ganjam Agency, a IIIrd Form Secondary school was opened at Linepada. It had 186 students and 9 teachers. The total expenditure for this school was Rs. 6,510.00.[230]

The Board Middle English school at Gunupur in the district of Koraput was raised to the status of a high school during 1929. Two Board M. E. schools were opened at Nawarangpur and Kotpad in 1926 and 1929 respectively. There were 283 students on the rolls of the Jeypore high school and 119 in the Gunupur high school. The Nowrangpur M. E. School had 92 students. The total number of teachers in these schools was 45. The total expenditure on account of these schools was Rs. 46,323.00 during 1929-30. Sri Vikram Deb Varma, Raja Saheb of Jeypore was conferred the D. Litt. (Honoris Causa) by the Andhra University. He was the first Oriya to get such a high prestigious academic recognition.

---

229 *Ibid.* p. 4
230 *Ibid.* p. 67

There was no increase in the number of secondary schools in the two municipal towns of Berhampur and Parlakimendi. In all there were 7 Local Board secondary schools, 8 aided secondary schools of which one was a Mission school. The total number of scholars receiving secondary education was 2,829 in 1929 as against 1,931 in 1922. There was a net increase of 898 in secondary school scholars. Twenty eight trained graduate teachers, 2 elementary trained teachers, one certified secondary teacher, 12 untrained graduates and 4 others were engaged in teaching in these secondary schools of Ganjam. The total expenditure on account of secondary education was Rs. 1,82,679 during 1929-30.

The Taluk Boards were abolished and District Board were set up for Ganjam and Koraput with effect from 1st April, 1934. A District Education Officer was appointed for Ganjam who also remained in charge of Ganjam and Ganjam Agency.

In so far as education of boys was concerned, Ganjam had the Madras Provincial average. However, the progress of women's education was far behind. The Vizag Agency, i.e. Koraput district was backward in every respect and was far behind the Provincial norms.

The number of secondary school students was 1,065 boys and 99 girls at Berhampur; and 791 boys and 1 girl at Parlakimedi. The number of girls receiving secondary instruction was definitely discouraging. During this period the number of secondary school students increased by 137 at Berhampur and 61 at Parlakimedi. One of the secondary schools at Berhampur was closed down. This indicates a sort of lull in the field of secondary education. There was a net increase of 419 male students during this five year period. The increase was only 0.05% of the total male population. There was an yearly increase of 0.01 %.[231]

The roll-strength, number of girls studying, average on rolls, average daily attendance, number of teachers and expenditure on each school in 1927 are depicted in Table No. 4.1.17.

---

231 *Ibid Statistical Tables*

TABLE 4.1.17

Profile of Schools of South Orissa, 1927

Sl. No.	Name of the School	Roll Strength on 31st March 1927	Average on rolls	Average daily attendance	Number of Girls studying in Boys Schools	Number of Teachers				Expenditure in Rs.
						Trained		Untrained		
						Grad-uate	Matric	Graduate	Matric	
	Aided Local Board Schools									
01.	Russelkonda (Bhanjanagar)	251	221	182	2	3	5	1	4	16,417.00
02.	Aska	330	320	288	…	3	7	4	2	18,302.00
03.	Chatrapur	329	327	278	1	5	6	0	3	18,694.00
04.	Purushottampur	30	28	24	0	1	2	0	0	3,766.00
05.	Surada	64	58	52	0	1	3	0	1	5,343.00
06.	Buguda	72	65	60	0	0	5	0	0	5,284.00
07.	Gurandi	80	80	66	0	1	4	0	0	6,157.00
08.	Baptist Christian School, Berhampur	130	130	113	29	4	0	0	0	3,840.00
	Aided Non-mission Schools									
09.	M.R.B.H. School, Parlakimedi	677	697	650	0	9	11	1	0	26,974.00
10.	K.C.H. School, Berhampur	845	828	709	0	8	15	3	0	29,193.00
11.	Dharakote	70	76	69	0	0	3	0	2	3,253.00
12.	Digapahandi	96	94	73	1	4	0	0	0	4,367.00
13.	Boirani	111	98	83	0	0	5	0	0	5,970.00
14.	Khallikote	95	91	77	0	0	5	0	1	5,450.00
15.	Chikiti	82	76	63	0	1	3	0	1	4,003.00
	Secondary School for Girls									
16.	Berhampur Hindu School	70	62	47	0	1	5	0	0	6,600.00
	Ganjam Agency									
17.	Linepada	186	166	156	0	1	8	0	0	6,510.00

The Madras University appointed a Committee to consider the question of revision of the Secondary School Leaving Certificate (S. S. L. C) Examination during 1929. This Committee recommended that the S. S. L. C. course "might be considered as an equivalent test for admission to the University Courses," and that "the University should be given greater representation on the Board...". This question was considered "with a view to meeting the wishes of the University without in any way, sacrificing the essentials of a sound secondary education...". Secondary education has its roots in the primary education and its fruits in the higher education. The search for a sound secondary education continued to haunt the educationists without yielding any concrete results.

Secondary education had curricular and structural drawbacks. Added to it and heightening their effects were the resultant defects of a faulty examination system. In this connection, the Report on the Public Instruction in Madras for 1927 statesthat, "The most disturbing element in connection with the public examination is the leakage of question papers. It is a humiliating fact that it is impossible to conduct any public examination in this Presidency unless elaborate arrangements are made, minute rules are laid down and every precaution which secrecy and ingenuity can devise adopted. Where there is a leakage, certainly was the case last March in a restricted area in one paper, it is practically impossible to get evidence. Leakage of question papers could be stopped at once if an articulate public opinion, condemned and was strong enough to require cooperation with the authorities and the supply of evidence as to the source of the evil. As it is, there is the annual specter of possible leakage and the reality of the case after case of malpractice. Each year there is the repellent task of dealing with these cases; and these, taken together with the thriving trade in bogus papers, form a sorry commentary on public examination morality. This year complaints were actually preferred by parent purchasers of bogus question papers because none of the questions appeared in the genuine papers ! and moral instruction forms part of the school curriculum. Optimism in such circumstances is difficult and one wonders if there is much educational advantage in retaining a public examination, a recurring feature of which is a struggle to baffle dishonesty".[232]

---

232 *Report on Public Instruction in the Madras Presidency, 1929 Vol. Lpp. 12-13*

It was decided that a uniform course of instruction should be followed in both the urban and rural schools. It was also decided not to convert the Higher Elementary schools into Middle schools. Revised rules for the election of members to the District Secondary Education Board were formed and issued in G. O. No. 1767, Law (Education) dated 24th August, 1928.[233]

The reorganisation of secondary education "was almost under continuous consideration" but no far-reaching changes were made. The Venkataratnam Report was reviewed and a Special Officer was placed on special duty "to survey and report on important questions relating to the finance and expansion of secondary education".

A Secondary Education Reorganization Committee was appointed by the Government. It noted with serious concern that the so-called literary side of secondary and collegiate education was rapidly expanding and, while nobody desired to restrict the spread of education or to press for utilitarian aims to the prejudice of the essential function of secondary education. It was increasingly becoming obvious that the aim and character of secondary education must be adjusted so as to equip young men not merely to embark upon professional careers; but to enter other occupations whichhad hitherto been little resorted to by the educated classes. Middle class unemployment had become a serious problem and the continued overproduction of one type of academically qualified students was feared to result in a positive danger to society. In view of this realization it was felt that the secondary school course should be recognized "so as to permit a larger number of students to fit themselves for technical courses and skilled occupations. Diversification at the end of the fourth form, rural bias to rural schools, vocationalization of courses etc. •were seen as possible alternatives."

---

233 *Ibidpp.* 13-14

It was stated by this Committee that "the use of the Vernacular as a medium of instruction, may indirectly assist in bringing about a changed attitude towards the value of secondary education", and that "... in any country there is a limit to the number of pupils that can reasonably be expected to be reading in secondary schools." However, the progress of time has belied both these contentions of the Committee. Today, the general medium of instruction is the Modern Indian Languages but that in no way has stopped the inundation of the universities. Limiting secondary education is the next to impossibility and every country considers secondary education as the basic education for its citizens. Without secondary education the manpower potential can hardly be developed. Another important feature of secondary education during this period is the closing down of unviable small secondary schools which were uneconomical.[234]

The rates of pay of teachers did not improve much either in the Ganjam district or the Koraput Agency tract during this five-year period.

As per the recommendations of the Secondary Education Reorganization Committee, District Secondary Education Boards were set up in January, 1923 to advise the Government on the various aspects of secondary education viz:

1. Application for teaching, building, and equipment grants.
2. Recognition of secondary schools
3. Aid to be given to secondary schools to be newly opened.
4. Coordination on the matter of text books and syllabuses.
5. Vocational training
6. Organization of education exhibitions
7. Organization of common playgrounds, field games and development of boy scout movement
8. Medical Inspection of Schools
9. Hostel accommodation.

---

234 *Report on Public Instruction in the Madras Presidency, 1921-22 to 1926-27*,pp. 55-57

10.   Religious and moral instruction
11.   Scholarships
12.   School libraries and laboratories

However, the constitution of these Boards was not easy and their working was not satisfactory. Sri P. Sitaramaya, Secretary to Government of Madras, comments, "The experiences gained by the working of the District Secondary Education Boards has led to doubts as to whether the Boards have justified their anticipation of Government as to their contribution to the development of secondary education and the question of reconstituting them is under consideration."[235]

EDUCATION IN THE GANJAM DISTRICT AT A GLANCE[236]

TABLE 4.1.18

Area and Population

SI. No.		Period		
		1901	1921	1931
01	Area in Sq.Miles	8,369	8,381	8,382
02	Population	20,10,256	21,68,460	24,11,619

TABLE 4.1.19

Percentage of Literacy

SI. No.	Year	Total		Hindus		Muslims		Christians		Others	
		Male	Female	Male	Female	Male	Female	Male	Female	Male	Female
01	1901	7.6	0.3	8.8	0.3	27.4	3.3	34.8	21.8	0.8	0.0
02	1921	11.4	1.6	13.0	0.6	34.7	7.3	54.1	43.3	1.67	0.3
03	1931	10.5	0.7	11.3	0.7	32.6	4.3	26.0	14.1	1.6	0.5

---

235 G O. No. 142 dated 26. 1. 1928 of the Government of Madras in the Education Department.

236 Source:
Madras District Gazetteers. 1905. Ganjam District Vol. II
Madras District Gazetteers, 1930, Ganjam District, Vol. II
Madras District Gazetteers, 1935, Ganjam District Vol. II.

TABLE 4.1.20

Educational Institutions

SI. No.	Year	Arts Colleges		Secondary Schools	
		Men	Women	Boys	Girls
01	1901	2	0	13	0
02	1921	2	0	22	1
03	1931	3	0	23	1

TABLE 4.1.21

Scholars in Secondary Schools

SI. No.	Year	Scholars in Secondary Schools	
		Boys	Girls
01	1901	1,296	0
02	1921	4,627	80
03	1931	5,373	143

TABLE 4.1.22

Expenditure on Education

SI. No.	Year	Expenditure in Rupees			
		Total	College Education	Secondary Education	Primary Education
01	1901	1,95,011	9,293	33,909	1,32,863
02	1921	8,63,867	37,394	2,46,010	1,12,004
03	1931	11,53,386	32,450	3,01,753	7,48,638

On 1st April, 1936, Orissa became a separate Province. Table 4.1.23 presents a picture of the educational situation of North Orissa and South Orissa in 1935 just prior to the formation of the separate State.

TABLE 4.1.23

Secondary Education in 1935 for Boys

Sl. No.	Region	High Schools	Middle Schools
01	North Orissa	23	116
02	South Orissa	09	53

SECTION II

INDEPENDENT LINGUISTIC IDENTITY

(Secondary Education in the Province of Orissa and 24 Feudatory Oriya States) (1936-1947)

The Government of India Order (Constitution of Orissa Province) was placed before the British Parliament on 21st January,!936. His Majesty the King of England and Emperor of India issued the Royal Order dated 3rd March,1936 which was entitled, "The Government of India (Constitution of Orissa) Order, 1936". It stipulated the formation of a Governor's Province to be known as Province of Orissa.

Orissa Province was created on 1st April,1936. Sir John Ausitn Hubback was its first Governor from 1st April,1936 to 8th December, 1938 with a short break from 11th August,1938 to 7th December 1938 when Mr. George Townsend officiated as the acting Governor. Mr. P. T Mansfield, I. C. S. was its first Chief Secretary.

The Districts of Cuttack, Puri, Balasore, Sambalpur and Angul-Khondmals of North Orissa and the districts of Ganjam and Koraput of South Orissa were brought together. However, the 24 Feudatory States of Orissa remained separate till 1948-49. The erstwhile Angul district became a sub-division of the Cuttack district. Kondhamal was attached to Ganjam district. The Angul-Kondhamal district was dissolved from 1st April,1936. The long drawn struggle of the Oriya speaking people for independent identity became a reality.

The area and population of the State of Orissa according to the 1931 and 1941 Census were as shown in Table No. 4.2.11.[237]

TABLE 4.2.1

Area and Population of the State of Orissa (1931 & 1941 Census)

SI. No.	Census Year	Area in Sq. Miles	Population
01	1931	32,211.42	80,21,117
02	1941	32,198.00	87,28,544

The Government of India Act, 1935 was a further step towards greater self-government and complete independence. This Act put to an end to the diarchy inaugurated by the 1919 reforms. Provincial autonomy came into operation in 1937. The provincial legislatures had overwhelming majority of elected members. TheMinistry was responsible to the legislature. The IndianEducation Service (IES) was a vanishing service and the European Officers were very few. The Congress Ministry was installed in Orissa. Capt. Krishna Chandra Gajpati Narayan Deo, Maharaja of Paralakimedi became the Prime Minister (at present Chief Minister) of the State from 1.4.1937 to 19.7.1937. He was succeeded by Mr. Biswanath Das (19.7.1937 to 6.11.1939). Again Krishna Chandra Gajapati became the Prime Minister from 24.11.1941 to 30.6.1944. However, the ministry did not hst long as the Congress Ministries throughout the country resigned in protest against the war policy of the Government of India. The Ministry of Orissa resigned on 30.6.1944. The Second World War was fought from 1939 to 1945. The economic situation was as bleak as it could be. Educational expansion and reconstruction had to wait.

EXPANSION OF SECONDARY SCHOOLS

The number of high schools for boys rose from 32 in 1936-37 to 83 in 1946-47. During the same period girls' high schools increased from 2 to 6. Thus the total number of high schools rose from 34 in 1936-37

---

237 Census Tables relating to Orissa of 1931 and 1941.

to 89 in 1946-47. The middle schools for boys rose from 169 to 253, and those for girls from 12 to 20 during this period. The total number of middle schools thus rose from 181 to 273 during the period. The growth of secondary schools during 1936-37 to 1946-47 has been shown in Table No. 4.2.2.[238]

TABLE 4.2.2

Expansion of Secondary Schools (1936-37 to 1946-47)

SI. No.	Year	High Schools			Middle Schools		
		Boys	Girls	Total	Boys	Girls	Total
01.	1936-37	32	02	34	169	12	181
02.	1937-38	33	03	36	182	11	193
03.	1938-39	36	03	39	186	12	198
04.	1939-40	38	03	41	194	14	208
05.	1940-41	39	03	42	202	14	216
06.	1941-42	45	03	48	213	14	227
07.	1942-43	49	03	52	214	14	228
08.	1943-44	52	05	57	218	12	230
09.	1944-45	58	05	63	227	16	243
10.	1945-46	64	06	70	239	19	258
11.	1946-47	83	06	89	253	20	273

There was a rapid growth of student population of the secondary schools during this period. There was sudden decrease during the War years 1941-44. The tempo was picked up again by 1946-47.

The number of boys studying in high schools rose from 9,490 in 1936-37 to 12,742 in 1940-41. Due to the stringent war situation the number began to decrease and there was definite and marked recession up to 1945-46. However, by 1946-47, the student population increased

---

238 Computed from the Statistical Tables of Reports on the Progress of Education from 1936-37 to 1946-47.

again and stood at 22,373. The same trend was also discernible in the girls high schools, boys middle schools and girls middle schools. The number of girls studying in high schools was 515 in 1936-37 which increased to 709 by 1940-41. Then a sharp fall was noticeable. This recession continued up to 1944-45. In 1945-46, the enrolment rose to 737 and in 1946-47 to 1,390. The total enrolment of students in all high schools in 1936-37 was 10,005 and it increased to 13,451 in 1940-41. The total enrolment declined during the period 1941-1946. The roll strength began to rise only in 1946-47, when it stood at 23,763.

The number of boys studying in Middle schools was 18,316 in 1936-37. This rose to 22,917 by 1940-41. Then the enrolment showed an abrupt fall and in 1944-45; it was the lowest being 10,827. In 1945-46, there was a slight improvement when the enrolment was 11,980. By 1946-47, normalcy had returned when the harsh war years were gone. The total enrolment of boys in 1946-47 was 26,329. The number of girls studying in Middle English schools, rose from 1,876 in 1936-37 to 2,095 in 1940-41. The war years badly affected female education and enrolment went down. It picked up slighdy in 1945-46 and by 1946-47 the enrolment was 2,252. The total enrolment of the Middle Schools was 20,192 in 1936-37 which rose to 25,012 in 1940-41. The war years almost halved the total enrolment. In 1946-47, the enrolment was 28,581.

The year-wise enrolment of boys and girls in High and Middle schools during1936-37 to 1946-47 has been depicted in Table No. 4.2.3.

TABLE 4.2.3

Enrolment of Scholars in High Schools and Middle Schools (1936-37 to 1946-47)[239]

SI. No.	Year	High Schools			Middle Schools		
		Boys	Girls	Total	Boys	Girls	Total
01.	1936-37	9490	515	10005	18316	1876	20192
02.	1937-38	10142	616	10758	19680	1817	21497

---

239 *Ibid.*

SI. No.	Year	High Schools			Middle Schools		
		Boys	Girls	Total	Boys	Girls	Total
03.	1938-39	10998	663	11661	20739	2187	22926
04.	1939-40	12104	681	12785	22225	2405	24630
05.	1940-41	12742	709	13451	22917	2095	25012
06.	1941-42			**Figures not** available			
07.	1942-43	7611	460	8071	11116	827	11943
08.	1943-44	8711	557	9268	11713	932	12645
09.	1944-45	9417	640	10087	10827	963	11790
10.	1945-46	10678	737	11415	11980	1217	13197
11.	1946-47	22373	1390	23763	26329	2252	28581

The average cost of education per boys was Rs. 54.68 and for a girl it was Rs. 106.60. The cost of education per girl was almost double that of a boy. The few girls high schools that existed in 1936 had not enough scholars on the rolls. Naturally, the costs were high. By 1943-44, this cost per a boy was Rs. 52.61 and per girl was Rs. 89.87. The per capita cost of education showed a decline which was a healthy indication. In 1946-47, the cost of education a boy was Rs. 49 in a high school and Rs. 27 in a middle school. In 1936-37, the per capita cost for scholar was Rs. 21.24 for boys and Rs. 25.82 for girls. The glaring disparity in cost per scholar which was evident in high schools was not there at the middle school level. In 1943-44, the cost per pupil was for a boy Rs. 22.89 and for a girl it was Rs. 36.55. This widening of the gap was due to the opening of new middle schools for girls which were not optimally utilized.[240]

---

240 *Ibid.*

TABLE 4.2.4
Cost per Scholar

Sl. No.	Year	High Schools		Middle Schools	
		Boys	Girls	Boys	Girls
01.	1936-37	54.68	106.60	21.24	25.55
02.	1937-38	55.10	102.77	20.74	21.42
03.	1938-39	50.00	97.30	19.00	21.33
04.	1939-40	51.08	90.45	19.99	24.16
05.	1940-41	47.72	89.87	19.20	23.01
06.	1941-42	Figures not available			
07.	1942-43	Figures not available			
08.	1943-44	52.61	86.60	22.89	36.55
09.	1946-47	49.00	N.A	27.00	N.A

Note: (Old coinage of rupees, annas and pies has been converted to new coinage of rupees and naya paise)

The expenditure on account of high schools for boys was Rs. 5,31,456 during 1936-37 which rose to Rs. 11,11,564 in 1946-47. The total amount spent on girls high school was Rs. 54,901 in 1936-37. Expenditure on this account had gone up to Rs. 1,19,227 by 1946-47. An amount of Rs. 3,88,997 had been spent during 1936-37 to run the boys middle schools and this rose to Rs. 7,28,184 by 1946-47. The total money spent for girls schools was Rs. 47,796 in 1936-37 and this rose to Rs. 76.781 in 1946-47. The total expenditure on high school education was Rs. 5,86,357 and on middle school education it was Rs. 4,36,793. The total amount spent for secondary schools was Rs. 10,23,150 out of a total educational expenditure of Rs. 39,48,139 for the year 1936-37. The total expenditure on high schools rose to Rs. 12,30,791 and on middle schools to Rs. 8,04,965 by 1946-47. The total expenditure on secondary was Rs. 20,35,756 in 1946-47 out of the total education expenditure of Rs. 91,54,701 for the year.[241]

DIFFERENCES RELATING TO THE SECONDARY EDUCATION IN NORTH & SOUTH ORISSA

There were 32 high schools, 122 middle English schools and 47 middle vernacular schools and 7568 primary schools on 1st April 1936, when the separate Provincecame into existence. North Orissa was part of BengalPresidency up to 1912, and of Bihar and Orissa Province up to 31st March 1936. The development and pattern of secondary education were determined by the developments in these provinces. The Feudatory States of Orissa were also influenced by Bengal and later by Bihar and Orissa. However, Ganjam and Koraput districts were in die Madras Presidency. The secondary education of these two districts was based upon the Madras pattern. Sambalpur district was part of the Central Provinces from 1861 to 1905. Therefore, it had been influenced by that Province. However, by 1936 Sambalpur had fully accepted the North Orissa pattern. The fundamental differences relating to secondary education in North and South Orissa and the attempts made to establish a uniform pattern throughout the State is an administrative exercise of unifying two patterns into one.

In North Orissa, the age of entry to the primary school was 5+. In South Orissa it was 6+.

The lower primary classes in North Orissa were the infant class and classes 1,11 and III. There was no infant class in South Orissa where standards I, II, III, IV and V constituted the lower elementary classes. Classes IV and V constituted the upper primary classes of North Orissa. The lower elementary school of South Orissa corresponded to the upper primary school of North Orissa. North Orissa had the additional infant class which south Orissa did not have. The upper primary course

---

241 *Ibid*

of north Orissa lasted for six years and the lower primary course of South Orissa for 5 years.

Classes VI and VII constituted the lower secondary course in North Orissa. In case English instruction was provided in these classes, it was termed as a middle English school; and without English it was the middle vernacular school. In South Orissa classes VI, VII and VIII constituted the higher elementary course. The entire instruction up to the higher elementary stage was vernacular education. Eight years of schooling constituted middle school education in North Orissa; and in South Orissa it constituted higher elementary education. By this time the child was 13+ in North Orissa and 14+ in South Orissa.

The age of entry to the Primary School is 6+ in U. K., France, Germany, Italy, Austria, Rhodesia, Nigeria, Hongkong, Uganda, Malaysia, Lesotho, Swaziland, Gambia, Ghana, Guyana, West Cameroon, Seychelles, New Hebrides, Papua, New Guinea. It is 7+ in U. S. A., Sweden, Norway, Russia, Denmark, Sudan, and Tanzania. According to Basil Berstein, the English sociologist, the age of entering and leaving school are defining factors of the notion of childhood. The Kothari Commission of 1966 hadrecommended 6+ as the right age of entry to primary schools.[242] South Orissa had the right pedagogical approach in this respect. The schooling started rather too early in North Orissa. Of course, if the infant class can be viewed as a nursery class, then real primary education began at the age of 6+ in North Orissa also. Further, instruction up to the age of 14 is really elementary education and cannot be termed as secondary education. Therefore, the South Orissa nomenclature was appropriate. In South Orissa classes IV and V and Forms I, II and III constituted the middle school.

In high schools of North Orissa there were eight classes from IV to XI. In high schools of South Orissa there were classes IV and V and Forms I to VI. In both the regions, high school instruction lasted 8 years. Table

242 Bharati Mohapatra, A Critical Analysis of the Primary School Curriculum, unpublished M. Ed. Dissertation, Utkal University, 1976.

No. 4.2.5 depicts the comparative situation of North and South Orissa relating to School Education.[243]

TABLE 4.2. 5

Comparison of the School Systems of North & South Orissa with Reference to the School System of 2007

Age of Entry to School: North Orissa 5+

South Orissa 6+

Orissa in 2007: 6+

In north Orissa, all grades were called *"Classes"*. In south Orissa the grades of

Grade	Stage of Education	North Orissa 1936		South Orissa			
		Stage of Education	Class	English School		Vernacular School	
				Form	Stage of Education		
XI	1st Yr of HSSC	Secondary	XI	VI	Secondary		
X	Secondary	Secondary	X	V	Secondary		
IX	Secondary	Secondary	IX	IV	Secondary		
VIII	Upper Primary	Secondary	VIII	III	Lower Secondary or Middle	Higher Elementary VIII Std.	
VII	Upper Primary	Lower Secondary or Middle	VII	II	Lower Secondary or Middle	Higher Elementary VII Std.	
VI	Upper Primary	Lower Secondary or Middle	VI	I	Lower Secondary or Middle	Higher Elementary VI Std.	

---

243 Report on the Progress of Education, 1936-37 (Orissa)

Grade	Stage of Education	North Orissa 1936		South Orissa		
		Stage of Education	Class	English School		Vernacular School
				Form	Stage of Education	
V	Primary	Upper Primary	V	Class V	Lower Secondary or Middle	Lower Elementary V Std.
IV	Primary	Upper Primary	IV	Class IV	Lower Secondary or Middle	Lower Elementary IV Std.
III	Primary	Lower Primary	III	Std-I	Lower Elementary	Lower Elementary III Std.
II	Primary	Lower Primary	II	Std-II	Lower Elementary	Lower Elementary II Std.
I	Primary	Lower Primary	II	Std-III	Lower Elementary	Lower Elementary I Std.

Vernacular schools were called *"standards"*; and in English schools the top six grades were called *"forms"* and the lower two grades were called *"Classes"* After completing standard III in an elementary school, a scholar may proceed to a *"higher elementary school"* which imparted instruction up to standard VIII in Vernacular; or to an English school which imparted instruction up to the VIth form.

'Grade' is a grouping of students on the basis of age and academic achievement. *"Class"* is a general term for group of students brought together for teaching. Students belonging to the same school year are designated to be belonging to a *'form'* especially in the United Kingdom. A *'standard'* demands accepted levels of *attainment* in academic work and personal, moral and social behaviour. Attainment of predetermined

levels of achievement is essential to progress from one standard to the next higher one.

In the Bengal Presidency *'Class'* — the general term for a group of students-wasgenerally used. In the Madras Presidency *'standard'* was the term specifically used to describe classes of the Vernacular schools. The fourth and fifth year instruction in English schools was termed as *'classes'*. Real secondary education commenced from *'Form I'* at the age of 11+; and closely conforms to the *'post 11+ Grammar school'* approach of U. BC

Vernacular education of eight years provided from the age of 6+ in the Madras Presidency is real elementary education for the masses. It is the precursor to the eight year elementary schooling recommended by the Kothari Commission of 1964-66.

The English education was meant for the classes, and the transition from concrete thinking to the abstract level as suggested by Piaget is rigorously practiced. It is the formative period through progress from 'form' to 'form'.

Elementary education is expected to lay the foundation of learning and sharpen the basic skills of learning. Secondary education is transitional intellectual stage to take off to higher levels of intellectual attainment and/or attaining life-skills for upward mobility.

A *'class'* denotes only homogeneity of a group, *'standard'has* in-built quality control semantics. The shaping force of education is reflected in *the. form. Grade* has in-built upward mobility as its guiding principle. The nomenclatures of *'standard'* and *'form' widely used in the Madras Presidency seems to have better academic semantics than the colourless* 'class'.

On completion of the High School course, students in North Orissa were presented for the Matriculation examination conducted by the Patna University, while those in South Orissa were presented for the S. S. L. C. examination conducted by the Government of Madras. The qualification of South Orissa candidates who were declared eligible for admission to the University course of study was considered equivalent to that of Matriculation in North Orissa. At the end of the middle school course, the students of North Orissa appeared at a public examination known as the Middle School Certificate examination conducted by the School Examination Board, while in South Orissa there was no such public examination. For such students in South Orissa, a house examination used to be conducted in high and middle schools by the respective Headmasters, and a school leaving certificate examination was held in the Higher Elementary Schools by the Deputy Inspector.[244]

There were essential differences in the management of schools in North and inSouth Orissa. In South Orissa, the recommendations of Commission of 1882 were scrupulously followed, and, therefore, the Government completely withdrew from secondary education. The Ganjam Zilla School was handed over to the District Board management and there were no government high schools in South Orissa by 1936. In North Orissa, Government continued to maintain the four Zilla Schools at Cuttack, Puri, Balasore and Sambalpur and the Government High School at Angul. In North Orissa the practicing Middle English School at Cuttack was a Government M. E. School. In Kondhamal, the Tikabali & Phulbani Middle Schools were the only two Govt. M. E. Schools. The District Boards of North Orissa concerned themselves with primary and middle schools because they were not permitted to spend their resources on high school education. In South Orissa, the Ganjam District Board managed 4 high schools and the Koraput District Board managed 2 high schools. In both the parts of the State there were aided schools.[245]

This situation relating to management of high schools had deep repercussions on the educational administration of Orissa in latter years. The Headmasters and trained graduate teachers of North Orissa belonged to Government service. In due course, they occupied all the

---

244 Report on the Progress of Education, 1937-38. (Orissa)
245 Report on the Progress of Education,1936-37, (Orissa)

important and strategic posts in the field of educational administration of the State. The experienced and veteran educationists of South Orissa were all District Board employees. Naturally, they remained outside the Governmental stream. The North Orissa administrators with their background thought that the North Orissa educational system was better and so in the name of amalgamation and introduction of uniformity, the North Orissa pattern was imposed on South Orissa. Some of the excellent features of South Orissa like the teaching of Science and Manual instruction in secondary schools, the higher elementary system of education (also the age of entry) were completely abandoned. A fine fusion of the elements available in the secondary education system of both the parts of Orissa would have been better. But South Orissa did not have adequate representation in the educational administration of the State in the post-1936 years.

In each of the high schools of South Orissa drill teacher, a manual teaching instructor and a physical training instructor had been provided; while there was no such provision in the high schools of North Orissa. In the South Orissa middle schools there was provision for an Oriya Pandit and a combined drill and drawing instructor. There was no such provision in North Orissa.[246] The grant-n-aid rules also differed greatly in North and South Orissa.

The Oriyas were classified as a backward class by the Madras Government. Therefore, the Oriya students of South Orissa were paying only half the school-fees and the government was making good the loss incurred by the schools on this account. The formation of Orissa, though a boon by itself, brought in its wake greater financial burden to the South Orissans as this concession was withdrawn.

The Director of Public Instruction, Orissa had a word of commendation for the Higher Elementary Schools of South Orissa in his report for

---

246 *Ibid.*

1936-37 which reads "There seems no doubt, however, that the best school for rural areas is one from which English is entirely excluded."[247]

In North Orissa, there was greater emphasis on the provision of hostels than in South Orissa. "No provision existed for medical inspection of secondary school students in South Orissa on 1st April,1936. The system was in vogue in North Orissa."[248]

The recognition of Middle English Schools in South Orissa vested in the Director of Public Instruction. The District Education Council, Ganjam had the powers of recognizing Higher Elementary Schools in Ganjam plains. The Special Assistant Agent to the Governor of Koraput Agency and Ganjam Agency had the power of recognizing Higher Elementary Schools in their respective jurisdictions. The Middle English Schools and Middle Vernacular Schools for boys in North Orissa were recognized by the respective District Inspectors of Schools and the Middle Schools (English & Vernacular) for girls were recognized by the Inspectress of Schools.[249]Obtaining recognition for a middle English school was comparatively more difficult in South Orissa than in North Orissa. Hence, the preponderance of Vernacular Schools in South Orissa. In 1936, there were 108 Middle English Schools and 8 Middle Vernacular schools in North Orissa. In South Orissa, on the other hand, there were only 13 middle English school, but there were 39 Higher Elementary Schools comparable to Middle Vernacular Schools of North Orissa.

In South Orissa, the staff of a middle English school consisted of one trained graduate Headmaster, 3 assistant teachers, an Oriya Pandit, a physical training instructor, and a combined Drill and Drawing Master. In North Orissa, the staff of Government Middle English School consisted of two trained graduates and 5 trainedinstructor, and a combined Drill and Drawing Master. In NorthOrissa,the staff of Government Middle English School consisted of two trained graduates

---

247 *Ibid.*
248 *Ibid.*
249 Report on the Progress of Education,! 942-43, p. 28 (Orissa)

and 5 trained matriculates.[250] In North Orissa, the scale of pay of teachers in aided middle schools or in those managed by local bodies were (1) Headmaster-Rs.50, Assistant Master (Trained graduates) - Rs. 35, other teachers - Rs. 25, Rs. 20 and Rs. 15per month. In South Orissa, the scale of pay of teachers working under the aided schools were — (1) Trained graduates Rs. 65-5/2-100, (2) Trained matriculates Rs. 30-2/2-50. The teachers of South Orissa had a running scale of pay and their salaries were better. In North Orissa, the salary was fixed and there were no increments. In Government Schools of North Orissa and Board Schools of South Orissa the scale of pay of teachers were as depicted in Table No. 4.2 6.[251]

TABLE 4.2.6

Scale of Pay of Teachers in Government Schools of North Orissa and Board Schools of South Orissa

SI. No.	Category of Teachers	North Orissa (Government)	South Orissa (District Board)
01.	Trained Graduates (Men)	Rs. 65-4/2-105	Rs. 65-5/2-100
02.	Trained Graduate (Women)	Rs. 70-5/2-120	Rs. 65-5/2-100
03.	Trained Matriculates (Men)	Rs. 30-3/2-45-2/2-55	Rs. 30-3/2-45-2/2-50
04.	Trained Matriculates (Women)	Rs. 40-1-55	Rs. 30-3/2-45-2/2-50
05.	Physical Training Instructor		Rs. 30-2/2-50
06.	Drawing Master		Rs. 25-2/2-45
07.	Pandits		Rs. 30-3/2-45-1-55

---

250 Report on the Progress of Education, 1942-43, p. 29,(Orissa)
251 *Ibid.* p. 30-31

The School fees charged by the schools varied in North and South Orissa as shown in Table No. 4.2.7.[252]

TABLE 4.2.7

School Fees Charged by the Schools of North and South Orissa

SI. No.	NORTH ORISSA				SOUTH ORISSA				
	Class	School Fee per month			Class	School Fee per year			
		General Boys	S.T. and S.C.	Girls		General	Oriyas Muslim Girls	S.T.	S.C.
01.	IV	1.25	0.25	(i) @ 0.25 to 0. at the discretion of the local Committee	IV	10	5		
02.	V	1.25	0.38		V	10	5		
03.	VI	1.50	0.50	(ii) No fee in the Schools of Local Body	Form I	22	1		
04.	VII	1.50	0.63		II	22	11		
05.					III	22	11		

Note: S.T. = Scheduled Tribe, S.C = Scheduled Caste

The school fees for classes TV and V was higher in North Orissa being Rs. 15 per year compared to South Orissa's Rs. 10. In classes VI and VII, the North Orissa fees was less than that of South Orissa. Scheduled Caste and Scheduled Tribe students were better off in South Orissa; Oriya students in South Orissa used to pay half-fees. In South Orissa, scholarships were awarded to the Middle English and Higher Elementary Scholars on the basis of merit-cum-poverty. In North Orissa, 10% of the students on rolls got free studentship on merit-cum-poverty basis.[253] In South Orissa, school building and their equipments were satisfactory. In North Orissa itwas not so.[254]

In North Orissa, Middle English and Middle Vernacular Schools for boys were inspected by District Inspectors and Deputy Inspectors. The

---

252 *Ibid.* p. 31-31
253 *Ibid.,* p. 32
254 *Ibid.,* p. 34

girls' schools were inspected by the District Inspectress of Schools. In South Orissa, the middle English school were inspected by the District Education Officer, Ganjam plains and by the Special Assistant Agent to the Governor of the area in Koraput and Ganjam Agency. Higher Elementary Schools for boys were inspected by the Sub-Inspector of Schools. The Higher Elementary Schools for Girls were inspected by the Deputy Inspectors of Schools.[255]

The high schools of North Orissa were under the administrative control of theInspector of Schools, North Orissa. The high schools of South Orissa wereunder the administrative control of the District Education Officer, Ganjam. The Director of Public Instruction had the powers of recognition and sanctioning aid.[256]

Standard staff of an eight-class High School in North and South Orissa was follows.[257]

TABLE 4.2.8 (a)

Standard Staff of an Eight-class High School

NORTH ORISSA		SOUTH ORISSA	
One	Headmaster (O.E.S.II)	One	Headmaster
Six	Trained Graduate Teacher (S.E.S)	Three	Trained Graduate
Two	Oriental Teachers (S.E.S.)	Four	Trained Matriculate
Two	Vernacular Teacher (LSES) (Matric C.T)	One	Pandit
One	Drawing Master (S.E.S.)	One	Drawing Master
One	Drilling Instructor (LSES)	One	Dril Master
One	Clerk	One	Commercial Instructor

The scales of pay of High School Teacher in North and South Orissa were as shown in Table No. 4.2.8 (b). [258]

---

255 *Ibid.,* p. 28
256 *Ibid,*p. 37
257 *Ibidp.,* 37-38
258 *Ibidp.,* 39

TABLE 4.2.8 (b)

Scales of Pay of Teachers

SI. No.	Posts	High Schools in North Orissa		High Schools in South Orissa	
		Government	Aided Rs.	Government	District Boards & Aided
01.	Head Master	200-25-300-20-500	100	250-25-300-20-500	110-10/2-170
02.	Trained Graduate (a) U.D. (b) L.D	128-12/2-200 65-4/2-105	50	65-4/2-105	65-5/2-100
03.	Trained Matric	30-55	40	30-3/2-45-2/2-55	30-3/2-45-2y$_2$/2-50
04.	Oriental Teacher or Pandit	65-4/2-105	50	30-3/2-45-2/2-55	45-2/2-75 (30-2/2-50)
05.	Darwing Master	65-4/2-105	40	50-5/2-100	25-2/2-45
06.	Drill Master	30-55	25	25-1-50	30-2/2-50 (20-2/2-45)
07.	Commercial Instructor	214-35		35-1-45	30-2/2-50

The scales of pay in the aided high schools in North Orissa were really bad and needed urgent revision. In North Orissa there were separate scales for men and women. There were upper division scales and lower division scales. Such distinctions did not exist in South Orissa. The aided high schools of South Orissa accepted the scale of pay of the Board Schools. There was provision for a clerk in the Government High Schools of North Orissa which did not exist in South Orissa.

The variations in school fees charged from pupils in North and South Orissa are indicated in Table No. 4.2.9.[259]

TABLE 4.2.9

School Fees

SI. No.	Class	NORTH ORISSA				Class/ Form	SOUTH ORISSA			
		Govt.	Aided	SC & ST	Girls High Schools		General	Oriyas & Muslims	SC & ST	Girls
01.	IV	1.75	1.50	0.25	1.00	Class-IV	1.25	1.63	....	0.63
02.	V	1.75	1.75	0.38	1.25	Class-V	1.25	0.63	....	0.63
03.	VI	2.00	2.00	1.00	1.50	Form-I	1.38	...	1.63	....
04.	VII	2.50	2.00	1.00	1.75	Form-II	2.75	1.38	...	1.63
05.	VIII	3.00	2.50	0.25	2.00	Form-Ill	2.75	1.38	....	1.63
06.	IX	3.00	3.00	1.50	2.25	Form-IV	5.25	2.63	...	2.63
07.	X	3.50	3.50	1.75	2.50	Form-V	5.25	2.63	....	2.63
08.	XI	3.75	3.50	1.75	2.75	Form- VI	5.25	2.63	...	2.63

Note: S.T. = Scheduled Tribe, S.C = Scheduled Caste

In class IV and V, the school fees in South Orissa was less than that of North Orissa. From Class VI to Class XI, the school fees in South Orissa was rather high. The philosophy of the Madras Government seems to be to keep primary education cheap and within the reach of the people and to make secondary education comparatively costlier. Scheduled Caste and Tribe students did not pay any fees in South Orissa.

Free studentship up to 10% of the total enrolment existed in the high schools of North Orissa. Similar provisions existed in the aided high schools of South Orissa; but none in the Government institutions.

AMALGAMATION

The first step towards bringing uniformity in both the halves of the State was taken in 1939-40. New and uniform scales of pay were

---

259 *Ibid.*

introduced for all the various classes of Educational Services excepting the Class I Services.[260] Pending the formation of the Utkal University, all the high schools of Orissa were affiliated to the Patna University with effect from 1st January,1943. The affiliation of the high schools of the South Orissa was transferred from the Andhra University to the Patna University. Patna University made special provisions for conducting the examination in Telugu by constituting a separate Board of Studies. The Secondary School Leaving Certificate Examination conducted by the Madras S. S. L. C. Board was to be discontinued from the examination of 1945. The Director of Public Instruction, Orissa was authorized to conduct the S. S. L. C. Examination for South Orissa as per the Patna University syllabus.[261] The Orissa S. S. L. C. was introduced in form IV in the high schools of Orissa in place of the Madras S. S. L. C. [262]During 1943-44, the syllabus was unified in both halves of the State. Infant class was added to the schools of South Orissa. The syllabuses of the Middle and Middle English Schools in both the halves of the State were unified and all the schools followed the courses of studies prescribed by the Department. In line with the South Orissa pattern, elementary science was introduced as an optional subject for the high school classes. The Utkal University was established on 23rd November, 1943.[263]The affiliation of all the schools of Orissa and those of the FeudatoryStates was transferred to this University with effect from 1945-46.[264]

RECOGNITION AND UPGRADATION OF SECONDARY SCHOOLS

The Mission M. E. School, Balasore was converted into a girls' high school during 1937-38. This was the third girls' high school of the State. Three middle English schools were opened in the Cuttack district

---

260 Report on the Progress of Education in Orissa, 1939-40
261 Report on the Progress of Education in Orissa, 1942-43.
262 *Ibid*
263 Report on the Progress of Education in Orissa, 1943-44
264 Report on the Progress of Education in Orissa,!945-46.

and one in the Balasore district. Nine Middle Vernacular Schools were opened viz. 2 in Sambalpur district; 3 in Ganjam district and 4 in the Koraput district. In all, 13 Middle Schools were opened in the State during 1937-38.

Three high schools and 4 middle schools were opened for boys during 1938-39. In the same year one Girls' Middle English School was opened. The Girls Middle Vernacular School at Puri was converted into a Middle English School for Girls. Two middle schools were opened in the Cuttack district, 2 in the Balasore district and one M. E. School in the Sambalpur district. One Higher Elementary School was closed down in the Koraput district. The three new high schools which gained recognition during the year were Agarpara, Jagatsinghpur, and Bhingarpur high schools.

During 1939-40, the number of high schools rose from 35 to 37. Two M. E. Schools of Ganjam district were converted into high schools. Five new M. E. Schools were opened viz. three in Balasore, and one each in Puri and Koraput districts. Class XI of the Angul Government High School was duplicated owing to the increase in the number of students. The George Middle School at Chikati was transferred from the management of the Zamindar of Chikati to that of the Ganjam District Board with a subsidy of Rs. 833 per year. The Board Higher Elementary School at Rayagada was converted into an middle school.

During 1940-41, the Government Middle English School, Tikkabali in the Ganjam Agency was converted into a High School with effect from 1st September, 1940. It was named Hubback High School after Sir John Austin Hubback, first Governor of the Orissa Province. In 1941, it was shifted to Phulbani.

Eight Middle Schools for boys were opened during the year viz. 2 each in the district of Cuttack, Sambalpur and Koraput and one each in the district of Puri and Ganjam. Of these 8 Middle Schools, 4 were M. E. and 4 were M. V. Schools. A high school was established at Olsingh in 1940. Sri Dasarathi Patnaik, a rich man of the locality, was mainly instrumental in establishing this school.

The Ranihat M. E. School of Cuttack town became a proposed high school in1940 with the opening of class VIII. The M. E. school at Tangi (then in Puri district) was upgraded and became a proposed high school in January,1943 with the opening of class VIII. The first batch of this school appeared at Matriculation Examination of the Utkal University in 1947. In 1947, it was named Balaramdeb High School after the local presiding deity.

In 1946, a high school was established at Sarankul. It was named after the local ruler Narayan Singh Mandhata and is known as Narayan High School, Sarankul.

During 1943-44, the Board M. E. Schools at Kotpad and Nabarangpur were upgraded to the status of proposed high schools. These two schools became full-fledged high schools in 1946; and presented candidates for the Matriculation examination of the Utkal University in 1947. In all, there were four high schools in the undivided Koraput district by 1947. They are Board High Schools of Jeypore, Gunupur Nabarangpur and Kotpad headed by four pioneering veteran headmasters of high caliber and tremendous commitment namely Late Oruganti Hanumantha Rao, B.A. L.T. of Jeypore High School; Late Gagadhar Panda of Gunupur High School; Late Nabin Chandra Patra of Nabarangpur High School and Late Gangadhar Nanda, B.A. B.Ed, of Kotpad High School. Kotpad was a big agricultural village near Orissa border of Chattishgarh. But even in this far-flung place there were outstanding teachers like Late Vedula Ramamurty, B. A. B. Ed. (the author's revered father), Late Vajjhala Venkateswarulu, B.A. B.Ed.; Late Damodar Tripathy B.Sc, B. Ed. The other teachers of extra ordinary eminence were Mr. V. A. N. Sharma (who later joined the Civil Service and retired as an IAS officer) and Pandit Nityananda Padhi. Late D. Sundaram Patnaik, Late Brundaban Mishra, and Mr. Sunam Patro Boro were the other teachers. Mr. V. A. N. Sharma, M. A. (Economics), M.D. PA (IIPA, New Delhi)

M.B.A. (IGNOU), M.A. D.E. (IGNOU) & Rashtra Bhasha Ratna is the author's teacher, elder brother and role-model. His students of Kotpad High School from 1947 to 1954 remember his erudition and excellent teaching skills. The middle schools at Koraput and Rayagada became proposed high schools in 1957 and full-fledged high schools in 1961. Late Biswaranjan Mahapatra, M.A. B.Sc. B.T. was the headmaster of the Government High School, Koraput with Mr. R. N. Pani as the seniormost teacher. Dr. R. N. Pani earned his M. Ed. and became the first Ph.D. in Education of the state from the Utkal University. He was the Principal of the Demonstration Multipurpose School (of the NCERT), Bhubaneswar. There were other illustrious teachers like Late Gopinath Bhatta, an outstanding mathematics teacher; Mr. Umakant Dash, M.A. B.Ed, a teacher of extraordinary repute; and Sri Chandra Sekhar Rathwho was endowed with the finest qualities of head and heart of an outstanding teacher. The author too was a teacher in the Govt. High School, Koraput from 1962 to 1967. These outstanding teachers and their tribe did their best to spread secondary education in a far-flung district like Koraput. The author received his secondary education in the Board High School, Kotpad; and the entire credit for this work belongs to his teachers. However, they are in no way responsible for the blemishes and short-comings of this document.

During the year 1940-41 no new high school was recognized as a full fledged high school in North Orissa, but permission was accorded to the opening of one or more high school classes at the following places.

Puri District	1. Edward Middle English School, Puri
	2. M. E. School, Bhubaneswar
Balasore District	1. Jamalpur
	2. Jaleswarpur
	3. Soro
Cuttack District	1. Ranihat M. E. School, Cuttack
Sambalpur District	1. Patnaikpara M. E. School,Sambalpur
	2. Larmbha M. E. School

The question of opening a High School at Jharsuguda and Khariar was considered, but the classes were not recognized. During 1941-42, six Boys High Schools were opened.

During 1942-43, the Government of Orissa made a policy decision to have a Middle English School for Girls in each sub-division of the province and one high school for Girls in each district.

A single Middle English School was started during the year. The practicing Upper Primary School attached to the Secondary Training School, Berhampur became a Government Middle English School. The Board/Higher Elementary School at Koraput was converted into a Government M. E. School. The Government M. V. School for Girls at Biribati, Balasore was converted into a Government M. E. School. Four high schools for boys were opened during the year.

During 1943-44, the number of Middle English Schools increased by 9, and the number of Middle Vernacular Schools decreased by 7. The number of recognized Schools rose from 52 to 57 during the year. One High School for girls was opened. Besides, there were 7 incomplete and 20 unrecognised High Schools.

During 1945-46, 12 Middle Schools for boys and 6 Middle Schools for girls wereopened. There was a net addition of 6 boys high schools during the year. The number of girls' high schools remained stationary at 5.

In 1945-46, there was an increase of 15 M. E. Schools and 7 high schools. The Stewart School at Cuttack was for Anglo-Indians and the Hubback High School at G. Udayagiri was exclusively for scheduled tribes. Of the seven new high schools, six were for boys and one was for girls. Of the Middle English Schools, 12 were for boys and 3 for girls.

In 1945-46, the number of high schools for boys increased from 63 to 83. Nineteen new schools sprang up. The number of Grils' High School remained stationary at 6. There was an increase of 14 middle schools for boys and one for girls.

Administrative Developments

1. During 1936-37, a separate Directorate of Public Instruction was created for the newly formed province. Mr. H. Dippie became the first Director of Public Instruction. The functions of the Text-book Committee were entrusted to him. An Advisory Committee was set up to assist him. The text-books recommended by the Bihar and Orissa Text Book Committee remained in force in North Orissa and those prescribed by the Madras Text Book Committee remained in force in South Orissa.

2. The Government of India in their letter No. F. 1.6 (a)/36 C. A. B dated 30th April, 1936 intimated the Orissa Government of the contemplated far-reaching changes in the field of secondary education. To supply the information and opinions requested by the Government of India, a small Committee was set-up and this made important recommendations. Consideration was deferred till the coming into operation of the new provincial constitution.

3. During 1937-38, a Committee was set-up to consider several questions relating to the reorganization of secondary education including (1) the deprovincialization of Government High Schools, (2) the establishment of Statutory Board of Secondary Education and (3) Grant-in-Aid system. Pandit Godavarish Mishra was the President of the Committee.

4. The Utkal University was established on 24th November, 1943 with Dr. Prana Krishna Parija as the Vice-Chancellor & Prof. V. V. John as the Registrar. It started functioning at Cuttack. It conducted the first Matriculation Examination of 1946.

5. The start of the school session was changed from January to July from 1945.

6. A Director of Physical Education was appointed for the secondary schools of Ganjam by its District Board. A Physical

Training Instructor was appointed on a temporary basis for the Middle and Primary Schools of Cuttack by its District Board.

7. Unification of syllabus in North and South Orissa was accomplished during 1943-44

8. The nomenclature of 'forms' in South Orissa was changed to Classes.

9. During 1942-43, more facilities were provided for the spread of education among the Scheduled Tribes. Scheduled Tribe students of Hubback High School, G Udayagiri and Government M. E. School at Koraput were exempted from the payment of school-fees. The Savara students of Serango in Ganjam Agency were sanctioned high stipends

Curricular & Co-Curricular Changes

1. The decision of the Provincial Government to introduce Indian languages as the medium of instruction for the Matriculation Examination of 1942 was announced.

2. Oriya became the medium of instruction in all the High Schools of North Orissa in accordance with the new regulations of the Patna University. Oriya was introduced as the medium of instruction in three complete and two incomplete High Schools of Ganjam district in accordance with the rules laid down in the Secondary School Leaving Certificate Scheme.

3. During 1938-39, arrangements were made for the teaching of Hindustani in some High and Middle Schools of Orissa. A scheme for introducing the subject in all schools was under consideration of the Government.

4. Teaching of Music was introduced in the Government Secondary and Training School for Women, Berhampur during 1940-41.

5. Agricultural Botany was introduced in the Mission High School, Cuttack

6. 'Basic English' was introduced in all Middle English Schools of the Sambalpur district.

7. The second year course of Basic English was introduced in the Middle English Schools of the Sambalpur district.

8. Teaching of Civics and General Knowledge was continued in some schools of North Orissa with good results.

9. Diversification of studies was provided in High Schools of the State during 1942-43. Instruction in such practical subjects like woodwork, agriculture, typewriting etc. was introduced.

10. Drill Masters of Government High Schools and Training Schools were deputed to attend a refresher course at Saidpet, Madras during 1939-40.

11. A number of Middle English School teacher were trained in bee-keeping to introduce it as a hobby among the pupils.

12. A growing desire to introduce vocational training in Middle and Higher Elementary Schools was noticeable.

13. The following Middle Schools had Vocational Classes attached to them: Lakshidhar, Sidheswarpur (Agriculture), Rambag (Agriculture), Cuttack Practising (Carpentry), Janla (Carpentry), Gop (Gardening, Carpentry and Cane work), Begunia (Poultry), Rameswar and Bolgarh (Weaving), Puri Anglo-Bengali (Tailoring), Banpur (Tailoring), Bhadrak W. C. (Carpentry), Tihiri (Agriculture), Basta and Bagurai (Tailoring), Hatigarh (Agriculture & Carpentry), Rampella (Weaving), Sambalpur Patnaikpara (Carpentry), Berhampur Municipal Oriya (Weaving), Kukudakhandi (Weaving) and Phulbani (Tailoring).

14. Vocational classes were attached to a few more secondary schools during 1942-43.

15. Schools were encouraged to have small work-shops

16. Gardening was taught in almost all the Middle Schools and Vernacular courses were introduced in a few Middle Schools

17. Daily health inspection of the students worked well.

18. Competitive sports were becoming a regular feature of many schools.

19. *Grow-More-Food* campaign gave an impetus to gardening

20. The hostel of the Ravenshaw Girls' School, Cuttack was electrified

21. The unprecedented floods of the year damaged many school buildings in the districts of Cuttack and Puri

22. Grants were paid to secondary school buildings damaged in cyclone

23. The Scout Movement was started and a number of teachers were trained by the Hindustan Scout Association

24. Headmasters were advised to introduce Students' Councils and Class-Monitors and to invest them with adequate powers.

25. Informal weekly or fortnightly tests were introduced in the High Schools in addition to the usual terminal examination during 1944-45.

26. Calcium Lactate as a substitute for milk was experimented on undernourished children.

For secondary education in Orissa the year 1936-37 is often described as *'one of marking time'* and *'stock-taking'*. The year 1946-47 may be described as *'one on the threshold of development'*.

SECONDARY EDUCATION IN THE FEUDATORY STATES OF ORISSA DURING 1936-1948

The progress of secondary education in various Feudatory States of Orissa demands separate treatment as these states were not part of Orissa. The Feudatory States were amalgamated with Orissa in 1948-49 and Orissa attained its present size and shape from 1st January,1949.

On 1st April, 1936, there were 3 High Schools, 20 Middle English Schools and 6 Middle Vernacular Schools in the Feudatory States of Orissa. The State-wise progress during 1936-1948 in the field of secondary education was as follows:

The Middle Vernacular School at **Athagarh** was raised to the status of a High School during 1934-35. It became a full-fledged High School in 1937. It was named King George V. High School, Athagarh on 8th July

1937. It was recognized by the Patna University. The new buildings of the School were opened by the Ruling Chief on 2nd April,1937. The candidates of this school appeared at the Matriculation Examination of the Patna University in 1937.[265] During 1942-43, Dr. Mayadhar Mansingh, M. A., D. Ed. (Patna), Ph.D. (Durham), a creative genius of outstanding stature in literature and ace educational administrator, joined as its Headmaster. Consequent on his appointment to the post of Educational Advisor to the Eastern States Agency, he relinquished the job to take up his new assignment. The staff of the school consisted of 5 teachers. The roll strengths of the High School during 1942-43, 1943-44 and 1944-45 were 243, 254, 287 respectively. There was a steady increase in the roll strength. The M. V. School at Gurudijhatia was converted into anM. E. School in 1944-45. It had five teachers.[266]

During the period under review, there was no progress in the field of secondary education in the **Athamallik State.** The Kishorenagar M. V. School was converted into a M. E. School. The Victoria M. E. School, Athamallik had 114 students on rolls and the Kishorenagar M. E. School had 53 students on rolls during 1944-45.[267]

By 1936, there was one high school and three M. V. Schools in the **Bamara State.** The Rajkumar High School, Deogarh had 12 teachers on the staff. The Headmaster was Mr. D. Dehuri. The roll strength of the school was 211 in 1941-42, 192 in 1942-43, 258 in 1943-44, 260 in 1944-45 and 258 in 1945-46. The results of the School were uniformly excellent, being not less than 88% in any year. The results were 12 out of 13 in 1939-40, 10 out of 10 in 1941-41, 19 out of 19 in 1941-42, 15 out of 15 in 1942-43 and 22 out of 25 in 1945-46. The M. V. School for girls had 3 students on rolls during 1941-42, 15 in 1942-43, and 7 in 1943-44 and the same number in 1944-45. The roll strength of the

---

265 Report on the Administration of the Athagarh State, 1937-38, p. 4
266 Report on the Administration of the Athagarh State, 1942-43, 1943-44, 1944-45.
267 Report on the Administration of the Athamallik State, 1944-45.

school was very low. But still it was kept alive and this is an indication of the progressive outlook of the ruler of the State. During 1944-45, 2 M. E. Schools were opened in the State. Thus by 1946-47, there was one High School, 4 M. E. Schools and one M. V. School for girls. The roll strength of the Middle English Schools for boys registered a steady increase. In 1941-42, in all 160 students were studying in these Schools which went up to 168 in 1942-43, 188 in 1943-44, 224 in 1944-45. The expenditure on account of secondary education was Rs. 8,920 and Rs. 9,570 in 1940-41 and 1941-42 respectively. This rose to Rs. 12,127 and Rs. 13,553 in 1944-45 and 1945-46 respectively.[268]

The M. E. School at **Baramba State** became a full-fledged High School during the period. The School was named Rai Sahib Madan Mohan Subudhi High English School. The Headmaster of the School was Sri Kulamani Rath, B. A. The staff consisted of 7 teachers. There were 98 students studying in the secondary classes of the school. The results at the Matriculation Examination of 1944 were creditable being 14 out of 14.[269] By 1946-47, there was only one high school in this State and there was no other secondary school.

The M. E. School at Bonaigarh in **Bonai State** had been established during 1915-16. Up to 1946-47, there was no further expansion in the field of secondaryeducation. The M. E. School, Bonaigarh had 7 teachers on the staff. Sri Lalit Mohan Biswal, B. A. was the Headmaster during 1944-45 and Sri U. N. Jena, M.A. B.Ed., during 1945-46. The roll strengths of the school for the period 1942-43 to 1945-46 were 162,163,133 and 181 respectively. During these years the respective roll strengths of girl students studying in this institutions was 2,4,6 and 8 respectively. Both the hostels attached to the school were in a deplorable condition during 1944-45 and so were repaired during 1945-46.[270] The Bonai State,

---

268 Report on the Administration of the Bamra State, 1941-42, 1942-43, 1943-44, 1944-45 and 1945- 46

269 Report on the Administration of the Baramba State, 1943-44.

270 Annual Administrative Report on the Administration of the Bonai State, 1942-43, 1943-44, 1944- 45 and 1945-46.

which was one of the most backward Feudatory State, was making rapid headway and the progress was heartening when compared with the other States.

There was no development in the field of secondary education in the **Daspalla State** up to 1942-43. There was only one M. E. School, the Gupta M. E. School at Daspalla. It had a spacious building and a hostel attached to it. The staff consisted of a Headmaster, 4 teachers and a Weaving teacher in 1945-46. The roll strength of the school increased from 98 in 1941-42 to 131 in 1945-46. A Middle English School for girls was founded in the year 1942-43 at Kunjabangarh due to the personal initiative of the Regent Raj Sundari Dei. The School was named Raj Sundari Preparatory Middle English School for Girls. The roll strength of the Girls' M. E. School was 111 and it was 92 in 1945-46.[271]

In 1940-41, there was one High School, the Bhawanishankar High School, Sundargarh in the **Gangpur State.** The M. E. Schools were the Rajgangpur M. E. School and the Harihar M. E. School at Kuanrmunda. There were 4 Middle Vernacular Schools in addition. The number of M. E. Schools for boys increased to 3 in 1943-44. An M. E. School for Girls was established at Kesrimal in 1943-44. Thus two new M. E. Schools were established during the year. By'1945-46, the number of M. E. Schools for boys increased to 11 (with 46 teachers) and the Girls' M. E. Schools to 2. New M. E. Schools were established at Hemgiri and Jhunmur. The roll strength of the B. S. High School was 284 in 1941-42, 309 in 1942-43, 328 in 1943-44 and rose to 337 in 1945-46. The staff of the High School consisted of a Headmaster, 4 trained graduates, one untrained graduate, one untrained I. A., 5 trained Matriculate, one post was vacant during 1945-46. The Headmaster of the School during 1945-46 was Sri Madan Mohan Pradhan. The expenditure on the High

---

271 Report on the Administration of Daspalla State, 1940-41, 1941-42, 1942-43, 1943-44, 1944-45, and 1945-46

School was Rs. 10,715 in 1940-41, Rs. 10,903 in 1941-42, Rs. 14,936 in 1942-43, Rs. 16,317 in 1943-44 andRs. 21,137-5-9 in 1945-46.[272]

The Middle English School at **Keonjhar State** was raised to the status of a High School on 30th August, 1934. It was named the Gibson High School after Mr. Gibson, I. C. S., Agent to the Governor-General for Eastern States Agency. Later, it was renamed as Dhanurjaya Narayan High School. In July 1945, another High School was started at Anandpur. There were one Middle English School and two Middle Vernacular Schools in 1940-41. By 1944-45, both the M. V. Schools were converted into M. E. Schools. In July 1945, the M. E. School at Anandpur became a High School. A new M. E. School was started during the year. Thus by 1945-46, there were in the State of Keonjhar 2 High School, and 4 M. E. Schools. There were M. E. Schools at such important places of the district like Deogaon, Kalikaprasad and Champua by 1945-46. The total roll strength of the 4 Middle English Schools was 269. The roll strength of the Gibson High School, Keonjhar was 344 in 1945 and 364 in 1946. There was a hostel attached to the School in which 94 boarders were residing during 1945-46. The results of the School at the Matriculation Examination was 90% during 1940-41. Therefore, it may be stated that the School was quite good. The staff consisted of the Headmaster, 11 teachers and a clerk in 1940-41. Sri Bhabagrahi Mohanti, M.A. L.T., was the Headmaster of the School. By 1945-46, the staff of 11 teachers increased to 19 teachers. The expenditure on account of this school was Rs. 12,766.13 in 1939-40, Rs. 12,465.56 in 1940-41 which rose to Rs. 14,783.69 in 1944-45 and Rs. 16,013.45 in 1945-46. The B. N. High School, Anandpur was established in July,1945 by converting the Local Middle English School into a High School. The roll strength of the School was 229 during the year, and the staff consisted of a Headmaster and 8 teachers. Sri R. C. Patnaik was the Headmaster of the School. The

---

272 Annual Administrative Reports of the Gangpur State, 1940-41, 1941-42, 1942-43, 1943-44, and1944-45,

total expenditure on account of this school was Rs. 3,412-2-0 during the year.[273]

The local M. E. School in **Khandapara State** was raised to a High School during 1944-45. In 1945-46, it became a full-fledged High School. It was named the Ramachandra High School. It was affiliated to the Utkal University. It was formally inaugurated on 5th January,1946 by the ruler in an opening ceremony presided over by Sri Syamacharan Tripathy, I. E. S., Director of Public Instruction, Orissa and attended by Sri H. Mishra, Inspector of Schools. The roll strength of the School was 300. The staff consisted of a Headmaster and 10 teachers. The expenditure on accountof the school for the year 1945-46 was Rs6,107[274] There were no other secondary schools in the State.

In the **Narasinghpur state** there was absolutely no expansion whatsoever in the field of secondary education since 1911-12. 157 students were studying in the only M. E. School during the year 1945-46.[275]

The Middle English School at **Nayagarh State** was upgraded to a High School. In 1940-41, it became a full-fledged High School in 1944 and sent up candidates for the Matriculation Examination of 1945 of the Patna University. It had two hostels with 107 boarders. The only Middle Vernacular School was converted into an M. E. School. In all, there were two M. E. Schools at Sarankul and Odagaon besides the High School at Nayagarh by 1945-46.[276]

Throughout the period 1911-12 to 1945-46, there was absolutely no progress in the field of secondary education in **Nilgiri State.** The roll strength of the Nilgiri M. E. School was 184 including 6 girl students

---

273 Annual Report on the Administration of the Keonjhar State, 1940-41, 1941-42 and 1942-43.

274 Annual Administrative Report of the Khandapara State, 1944-45. Annual Administrative Report of the Khandapara State, 1945-46.

275 Annual Administrative Report of the Narasinghpur State, 1945-46.

276 Nayagarh State Administrative Report, 1945-46

in 1945-46. There was an attached hostel in which 38 boarders were staying.[277]

The Middle Vernacular School established in 1913 was converted in to a Middle English School in 1931-32 in **Pallahara State.** There was no further expansion in the field of secondary education up to 1946-47. Eighty students were studying in the schools during 1946-47 and the percentage of attendance was 96.2 Provision had been made for imparting vocational training to the students.[278]

Since 1936, three new Middle English Schools for boys and one M. E. School for girls were opened in the **Patna (Bolangir) State.** By 1946-47, there were one High School, 5 Middle English Schools for boys, one M. E. School for girls and 3 Middle Vernacular Schools in the State. The roll strength of the Prithiviraj High School, Bolangir was 513 during 1943-44. Twenty nine candidates passed the Matriculation Examination in 1942-43 and 23 in 1943-44. The staff consisted of a Headmaster and 20 assistant masters. Sri Balamukunda Hota was the Headmaster of the High School. Expenditure amounting to Rs. 16,289.20 and Rs. 15,884.73 were incurred in 1942-43 and 1943-44 respectively. Six hundred ninety four students were studying in the M. E. Schools of the State. It is heartening to note that a Girls' M. E. School was openedincurred in 1942-43 and 1943-44 respectively. Six hundred ninety four students were studying in the M. E. Schools of the State. It is heartening to note that a Girls' M. E. School was opened in the State. The total expenditure for all the Middle English School was Rs. 10,279.25 and Rs. 10,636.88 during 1942-43 and 1943-44 respectively. There was no increase in the number of Middle Vernacular Schools. They were 3 in number. Four hundred fifty two scholars were enrolled in these schools during 1943-44. Amounts of Rs. 3,190.38 and Rs. 3,170.75 were spent respectively during 1942-43 and 1943-44.[279]

---

277 Annual Administrative Report of Nilgiri State, 1944-45
278 Annual Administrative Report of Pallahara State, 1946-47.
279 Report on the Administration of Patna State, 1942-43, 1943-44 and 1946-

Rairkhol State was the most backward State in so far as secondary education was concerned. There was not a single Middle English School up to 1936. During the period 1936 to 1946, a Middle English School was started at Rairkhol. Twelve out of the 18 candidates that appeared at the M. E. Examination passed in 1944-45. An amount of Rs. 2,679 was spent for this school during 1944-45. There was no further progress up to 1947.[280]

By 1937, there was a full-fledged High School at Boud in **Boud State.** It was named the King Edward VII High School The staff consisted of a Headmaster, eight trained teachers and four untrained teachers in 1945-46. Sri R. N. Baliarsingh was the Headmaster of the School. The roll strength of the School was 278 and 301 respectively during 1943-44 and 1945-46. It was a co-educational institution where girls studied with boys. Ten girls were studying in the High School during 1943-44 and five during 1945-46. An amount of Rs. 10,964was spent for this school during 1945-46. During 1936 to 1947 one new Middle English School was opened in the State. In all, there were two Middle English Schools with nine teachers out of whom 4 were trained teachers. The expenditure on account of the Middle Schools was Rs. 4,680in 1945-46 as against Rs. 4,254.90 in 1943-44. In 1946-47 there was one High School and two M. E. Schools in the Boud State.[281]

By 1936-37 there was one High School, two Middle English Schools and two Middle Vernacular Schools in the **State of Dhenkanal.** By 1942-43 the two M. V. Schools had been converted to M. E. Schools. There was practically no expansion of secondary education in the Dhenkanal State from 1936-37 to 1946-47. The number of scholars studying in the Dhenkanal High School registered a steady increase. The roll strengths were 382, 415,410 and 425 during the 1942-43,1943-44,1944-45 and1945-46 respectively. This was a co-educational institution and as many as 5 girls were studying in this High School during 1945-46.

---

280 Annual Administrative Report on Raiakhol State,1 944-45
281 Report on the Administration of Baud State, 1943-44, 1945-46

The total roll strength of all the Middle English School rose from 694 in 1942-43 to 718 in 1944-45. Eighteen girl students were studying in these four M. E. Schools.[282]

The only Secondary school in **Hindol State** was the Middle English School at Hindol by 1936-37. It was raised to the status of a High School during 1943-44 by opening Class VIII. During 1944-45 class IX was started to make it a full-fledged High School. The school session commenced from July instead of January. The staff of the school consisted of a Headmaster, six teachers and one music teacher. The roll strength of the school was 98. There was no further progress in the field of secondary education up to 1946-47.[283]

By 1946-47, there were one High School, one M. E. School for boys and one M. E. School for girls in the **Kalahandi State.** The High School and the M. E. School for girls were located at Bhawanipatna. The M. E. School for boys was located at Junagarh and was a popular M. E. School. The Bhawanipatna High School was affiliated to the Utkal University in 1944. The roll strength was 332 in 1944-45. The staff consisted of a Headmaster and fourteen teachers. Sri Basudev Mohanty, B.Sc. D. Ed., was the Headmaster of the School. The school had two blocks of buildings which were adequate for it. The School showed 60% results in the Matriculation Examination of the 1944. An amount of Rs. 13,241.90 was spent during 1942-43 and Rs. 13,661.89 during 1943-44. The State was contemplating opening of a new High School in Pahilpur area. The M. E. School, Junagarh was a popular and thriving institution. An amount of Rs. 1,610was expended for this institution during 1943-44 as against Rs. 1,373during 1942-43. The Girls M. E. School at Bhawanipatna was started in 1943-44 by upgrading the existing U. P. School for Girls. The roll strength of the School was 124 during 1943-44 and 134 during 1944-45. The expenditure for this school was Rs. 826in 1943-44 and Rs. 1,207during 1944-45. Music,

---

282 Dhenkanal State Administration Report. 1942-43, 1943-44, 1944-45, 1945-46 and 1946-47
283 Hindol State Administration Report, 1944-45. p. 29 and 1946-47

sewing and cooking were introduced in the School as inducement. It was noted in the report that it was, "yet to be popular".[284]

There was one High School and eight Middle English Schools in **Mayurbhanj State** during 1936-37. By 1946-47, the number of High Schools was two and that of the Middle English Schools was twelve. The Rairangpur M. E. School was upgradeto a High School in 1943 by opening of Class VIII. Class XI was opened in 1946. It was affiliated to the Utkal University and its first batch of students passed the Matriculation Examination in 1947. The total roll strength of both the High Schools was 962 during 1946-47. In the same year the total roll strength of the 12 Middle English School was 1,507.[285]

There was absolutely no development in the field of secondary education since 1911-12 up to 1946-47 in **Ranpur State.** There was only one M. E. School at Ranpur. A hostel was attached to it. The staff consisted of a Headmaster and four teachers. The roll strength was 125.[286]

There was a High School and three Middle English Schools in the **Sonepur State** by 1944-45. The total number of pupils in secondary schools was 573 in 1943-44 and 638 in 1944-45. Fourteen boys appeared at the Matriculation Examination of 1944 and 8 passed,42 appeared at the M. E. School Examination and 6 at the M. V Examination out of which 19 and 3 passed respectively. The expenditure on High Schools was Rs. 11,677.63 during 1944-45. Sri Heramba Chandra Dasgupta, M. A. B. L.,D. Ed., was the Headmaster of the High School,. Sri Rakrishna Mishra, B. A., B. Ed. was the Inspector of Schools, Sonepur State. By 1946-47 the number of High Schools was one and that of Middle Schools was three.[287]

---

284 Kalahandi State Annual Administration Report, 1942-43, 1943-44, 1944-45, 1945-46 and 1946-47
285 Annual Administration Report of the Majoirbhanj State 1943-44 to 1946-47.
286 Ranpur State Administration Report, 1943-44 to 1946-47
287 Report on the Administration of the Sonepur State 1943-44m 1944-45 and 1946-47

The Jubraj High School, Talcher had been established in 1918-19 and since then there was no expansion of secondary education up to 1946-47 in **Talcher State.** The roll strength of the High School was 210 in 1944-45 and 278 in 1945-46. The staff consisted of a Headmaster, nine teachers, a clerk and a peon in 1946-47. Twenty three candidates out of the 38 that appeared passed the Matriculation Examination in 1944-45.[288]

There was one M. E. School in the **Tigiria State** by 1916-17 and the situation had not changed in the subsequent four decades. There was only one M. E. School in Tigiria by 1946-47. Tigiria was very backward in the field of secondary education.[289]

India attained independence on 15th August, 1947. The English left this country. The Indian bureaucracy who had been conditioned to rule with the colonial mindset was the greatest beneficiary of freedom. The politicians and administrators behaved exactly like their British predecessors. In the annual report of the EducationDepartment of the Government of Orissa for the year1947-48, there is no mention of this great even. We had Indian masters in place of the British. A burning sense of urgency to change the old order was totally lacking. Education continued to be the bastion of conservatism; and perpetuated the colonial culture of education. Macaulay must have smiled with satisfaction in his heavenly abode. English colonialism was dead; but long live the educational legacy left by the English. Independence inebriated the people and made them forget the radical departures that they had to take. New roads were beckoning; but those roads were not taken. India preferred to walk on the beaten track. There was evident lack of courage and conviction. The educational system of post-independent India was more of the colonial educational system with cosmetic changes here and there. The imported imposed educational order persists. Independent indigenous educational ethos is yet to

---

288 Annual Administration Report of Talcher State, 1944-45 to 1946-47
289 Annual Administration report of Tigiria State from 1943-44 to 1946-47.

emerge. In 1947, Indians marched ahead with great expectations and high aspiration. India floated on educational rhetoric; and the harsh realities were not squarely faced.

* * *

CHAPTER-5

INNOVATIVE INITIATIVESIN INDEPENDENT INDIA (1947-85)

HIGHLIGHTS

- University Education Commission, 1948
- Secondary Education Commission, 1952
- Indian Education Commission, 1964-66
- Other Committees
- Implementation of 10+2+3
- Vocationalization of Secondary Education
- Education in Concurrent List, 1976
- Secondary Education, 1947-85

SECTION I

EDUCATIONAL POLICIES

India became independent on 15th August, 1947. lt adopted its own constitution and became a Republic on 26th January, 1950. Gandhiji, the father of the nation, was assassinated on 30th January,!948. the Age of Gandhi and its associated value system came to an end. The Gandhian system of education envisioned by the Zakir Husain Committee of 1937 was cleanly forgotten; and lip-service continued to be paid to his ideals. His name, fame, ideas and ideals have been utilized as tools of political convenience to gain electoral mileage. Political idealism and national development were guiding forces; the culture of real politics and Machiavellian manipulations had not yet gained strength.

Reservations for the Scheduled Tribes and Scheduled Castes was accorded constitutional sanctity. On 2nd October, 1952 the Community Development Programme was launched. The first six five year plans were implemented during the period from 1951 to 1985. Four censuses were conducted in 1951,1961,1971 and 1981 Eight general elections were held to the Parliament of India by 1985[290]. India was safely and securely progressing ahead on the road of democracy and planned development.

The old currency of rupees, annas and pies was replaced by the decimal coinage from 1st Aprill957. Metric weights were introduced from 1st

---

290 Source: Census of India Reports, 1951, 1961, 1971 and 1981 of relating to
Orissa State
*Note: A 'town' is a habitation with more than 10,000 people in its.
According to the

April 1962. The switch over to the decimal system in coinage and weights necessitated the rewriting of books on mathematics, geography etc. The reorganization of States of India on linguistic basis; amalgamation of princely states; abolition of zamindaris created new challenges for preparing date bases. This problem was further confounded by the creation and abolition of districts and changes in their territorial jurisdictions. In the flush of independence old names were changed and new names came in their place. It was an age of great expectations for the officialdom which had inherited the colonial behaviour, mindset and administrative style. The freedom fighters were demanding their pound of flesh for the sacrifices (real or fancied) that they had made. By 1966, India was staring at an uncertain future complicated by the explosion of population and ever increasing levels of poverty.

Indian Constitution, *"Education"'*was prima facie, a State subject up to 1976. Entry 11 of the list II of the Seventh Schedule to the Constitution lays down that, "Education including Universities, subject to the provisions of entries 63,64,65 and 66 of List I and entry 25 of the List III should be a State subject."[291]Therefore, secondary education was primarily a State responsibility. The state legislatures are concerned with education and are entirely responsible for it. The Government of India appointed the University Education Commission in 1948, Secondary Education Commission in 1952, and the Indian Education Commission in 1964. The Reports of these Commissions have provided the broad guidelines for the development of education. The inauguration of the Community Development Projects in 1952 ushered in an era of accelerated development on all fronts including education. The Five Year Plans provided the financial allocations for educational development and a period of planned progress with clear-cut priorities began from 1951. The major recommendations of the various Committees and

---

291 Constitution of India, Publication Division, Govt, of India, New Delhi, 1950

Commissions of Education relating to Secondary Education have been briefly discussed.

UNIVERSITY EDUCATION COMMISSION (1948-49)

Dr. S. Radhakrishnan was its Chairman. It was appointed to enquire into university education. Incidentally, it made certain recommendations relating to secondary education. According to this Commission, secondary education was really the weakest link of our educational system. It recommended that:

- Intermediate stage of education should be part of school education;
- Well-equipped Intermediate Colleges should be started;
- A large number of occupational institutions should be opened to divert students to different vocations;
- There was need for separate schools for boys and girls during the ages 14 to 18; and
- Adequate stress should be laid on general studies to develop a broad outlook and avoid narrow specialization.[292]

Tarachand Committee (1949)

It was appointed by the Government of India in 1949. Dr. Tarachand, Educational Advisor to the Government of India, was its Chairman. The Central Advisory Board of Education considered its recommendations in 1949. The following were its major recommendations:

- School education should be of 12 years duration.
- Secondary Schools should be multi-lateral instead of being the one-track institutions they were.
- The teaching of Hindi and English should be compulsory at the secondary stage.

---

292 University Education Commission Report, 1949. p. 747

- There should be a public examination at the end of the school course. Universities might lay down conditions of eligibility of admission to colleges.
- The pay and conditions of service of teachers should be as recommended by the Central Advisory Board of Education.[293]

SECONDARY EDUCATION COMMISSION (1952)

On September 23,1952, it was appointed under the Chairmanship of Dr. A. Lakshmanswamy Mudaliar, Vice-Chancellor of the Madras University, to examine the prevailing secondary education system and to suggest suitable reforms. The Commission submitted its report in June,1953. The major recommendations of the Commission were:

- School education should be of 11-12 years duration. The Higher Secondary stage should be of 4 years duration. One year of the Intermediate course should be included in the higher secondary stage. As a consequence, the first degree was to be of three years duration. For those who pass out from high schools there should be a provision for a one-year pre-university course. Admission to professional colleges should be open for those who have completed the higher secondary course. One-year pre-professional course should be provided in professional colleges.
- Multi-purpose schools should be established wherever possible to provide varied courses of interest to students with diverse aims, aptitudes and abilities. Access to polytechnic and technological institutions should be there for those who complete these courses.
- All States should provide special facilities for agricultural education.
- A large number of Technical Schools should be started either separately or as part of the Multi-purpose Schools near or

---

293 Report of the Committee on Secondary Education in India, 1948. p. 11.

around industrial areas. Central Technical Institutes should be established. Apprenticeship training should be provided.

- Public Schools might continue to exist. "Residential Day Schools" should be established.
- There should be no distinction between the education imparted to boys and girls. "Separate girls Schools" might be opened if there is demand. Special needs of girl students and women teachers should be taken care of in co-educational institutions.
- Mother-tongue should be the medium of instruction. Hindi and English should be taught at the Middle English School stage.
- There should be a core-curriculum at the middle school stage and the diversified courses at the higher secondary stage.
- Discipline, character, moral instruction and extra-curricular activities should receive due importance.
- Guidance and counseling should receive greater attention.
- A properly organized school medical service should be built up.
- Physical education should be geared to the needs capacities and aptitudes of children. All teachers below the age of 40 should participate in physical education.
- Urgent examination reforms were recommended.
- Improvement of teaching personnel, improvement of methods of inspection, management and conditions of recognition, hours of working and vacations, and educational finance engaged the attention of the commission and many useful recommendations had been put forward.[294]

On the basis of the recommendations of the Secondary Education Commission (1952) attempts were initiated to introduce "a national pattern of education of 11 years — five years of lower primary, three years upper primary and three years of higher secondary classes. This was to be followed by a three-year course for the first degree in arts and

---

294 Secondary Education Commission Report, 1953, New Delhi, 1965 pp. 186-198

science and a further two-year course for the second degree". Attempts were made to upgrade the high schools to convert them into higher secondary schools. In spite of central assistance, this pattern did not find favour and it remained as an unfulfilled academic agenda. The higher secondary scheme was not "given a fair trial".

Diversification of courses and vocationalisation was proposed to commence at the end of class-VIII. This was criticized as early pushing and was not acceptable to the middle class which constitutes the most forceful opinion group. The scheme of multi-purpose higher secondary schools proposed by it was not put into practice with rigour and commitment.

This commission focused its attention on the appropriate methods of techniques of teaching. It noted with regret that teaching methods had not improved andcontinue "to be dominated by the old besetting evil of verbalism .... And remainsas dull and uninspiring as before". It recommended for breaking the isolation of the teachers. Bureaus of Education and Vocational Guidance and Centres of Educational Extension were set-up to improve the quality and competence of the teachers. It recommended a new approach to school evaluation. The Central Examination Unit was set-up by the Government of India. Teachers accepted the new ideas relating to evaluation; but they were never seriously practiced. The recommendations of the Secondary Education were pragmatic, purposive andpointed, but they were not put into practice by the state governments who had inherited a "no-change mindset".

In November 1957, a Committee was appointed for the **Integration of Post-Basic Schools and Higher Secondary Schools.** The Post-Basic Schools were the products of the deliberations at Sevagram in 1945 and the Higher Secondary Schools were founded as a consequence of the recommendations of the Secondary Education Commission, 1952. This Committee recommended that:

Craft of the Post-Basic Schools should be considered as an equivalent to an electivesubject of a Higher Secondary Schools; that the techniques of correlation should be adoptedin Higher Secondary Schools; that there should be a common examination for both types ofschools etc.[295]

In 1960, **"A Panel on School Buildings"** was appointed to recommend the model designs for higher secondary schools.[296]

In May 1961, the Ministry of Education of the Government of India appointed the **"Committee on Emotional Integration"** under the Chairmanship of Dr. Sampurnananda to study the role of education in promoting the process of emotional integration. It suggested that,"At the secondary stage the curriculum should include, among other things, the study oflanguage and literature; social studies, moral and religious instruction and co-curricularactivities."[297]

India was steadily progressing ahead on the road of democracy. The network of community development blocks were ushering in fundamental and far reaching changes in rural India. There were more hospitals and more schools. With the success of the green revolution people had practically forgotten the harrowing hungry days of early 1940s when food scarcity loomed large on the horizon. Peace and prosperity promoted population growth. By 1981, the population of India was more than 68.33 and literacy was 53.57% (1981) The six five-year plans implemented during 1951-1985 were steadily changing the social landscape. From 1966 to 1969, there was a plan holiday; and again another one from 1979 to 1980.

India's first atomic power station had become functional at Tarapur on 1st April,1969; and its first nuclear detonation took place at Pokhran (Rajsthan) in May,1974. India had become an atomic power. The indigenously designed Indian satellite "A. *ryabhatta* was launched in 1975. India entered the space-age. The nationaltelevision network

---

295 Report of the Committee for the Integration of Post-Basic and Multipurpose Schools, 1957.
296 Report of the Panel on School Buildings,1961
297 Report of the Emotional Integration Committee, 1961.

Doordarshan was launched on 1st April,1975 which greatly assisted in promoting national integration and distance education.

The Indian Education Commission appointed in 1964 submitted its comprehensive report in 1966. The National Policy on Education of 1968 practically endorsed all its recommendation. The 42nd Amendment to the Indian Constitution shifted 'Education' from the 'State List' to the 'Concurrent List' and thereby accorded constitutional validity to the pro-active initiatives of the central government in the field of education. In 1978, a Committee was set-up under the Chairmanship of Ishwar Bhai Patel to review the NPE, 1968. In 1983, the National Commission on Teachers (School Teacher) was set up under the Chairmanship of Professor D. P. Chattopadhyaya which submitted its report in 1985. "Curriculum Load at the School level: A Quick Appraisal' with Prof. Yash Pal as its Chairman was undertaken by the NCERT in 1985. Five All India Education Surveys were conducted by the NCERT at the behest of the Government of India by 1986. Twenty years had elapsed after the submission of the Indian Education (Kothari) Commission of 1966. Its recommendations were implemented at varying paces in the various States and Union Territories. The post - NPE, 1968 developments needed to be reviewed. The Government of India appointed a task-force. Its findings have been documented as "Challenge of Education" (1985).

In 1966, the Indian Education Commission Report was published. It created a stir in the educational scene. Mr. M. C. Chagla, the eminent jurist and ex-Education Minister of India termed it as 'a unique report' Critics alleged that it had ignored 'intellectual discipline'. The year 1966 closed with the publication of this classic report on education whose repercussions influenced the educational developments of the subsequent decades.

INDIAN EDUCATION COMMISSION (1964-66)

On 14th July, 1964 the Government of India appointed the Indian Education Commission as per Resolution No. F. 41/3(3)/64/E.

T of the Ministry of Education. Dr. D. S. Kothari who was the Chairman of the University Grants Commission was designated as its Chairman. Hence, this Commission is very often referred to Kothari Commission. Mr. J. P Naik was its member-secretary and the driving force. Mr. J. F. McDougall of UNESCO was its associate secretary. The Commission comprised of 15 eminent intellectuals - ten from India; and one each from Japan, France, U. K., U. S. A., U. S. S. R. The Indian members were Dr. K. G. Saiyidain (who was also anarchitect of the Gandhian system of Basic Education chiseled by the Zakir Husain Committee of 1937), Dr. Triguna Sen (later Central Minister of Education), Mr. A. R. Dawood, Mr. R. A. Gopalaswamy, Dr. V. S. Jha, Mr. P. N. Kripal, Prof. M. V. Mathur, Dr. B. P. Pal, and Kumari S. Panandikar. The foreign members were Mr. H. L. Elvin (U K), Mr. Sadatoshi Ihara (Japan), Mr. Roger Revelle (USA) and Mr. Jean Thomas (France). The Commission submitted its report entided *"Education **and** National Development"* on 29th June, 1966 to Hon'ble Mr. M. C. Chagla, Minister of Education, Government of India. It is needless to reiterate that the appointment of the Commission was "largely due to his initiative and vision."

The Indian Education Commission had rightly reiterated that education holds the key to national development. Aptly, the tide of the report of the Commission was "Education and National Development". It stated that:

"1.01. The destiny of India is now being shaped in her classrooms. This, we believe, is no mere rhetoric. In a world based on science and technology, it is education that determines the level of prosperity, welfare and security of the people. On the quality and number of persons coming out of our schools and colleges will depend our success in the great enterprise of national reconstruction whose principal objective is to raise the standard of living of our people. In this context, it has become urgent

- to re-evaluate the role of education in the total programme of national development;
- to identify the changes needed in the existing system of education if it is to play its proper role, and to prepare a programme of educational development based on them; and
- to implement this programme with determination and vigour."

"1.02. The task is neither unique nor is it quite new. But its magnitude, gravity and urgency have increased immensely and it has acquired a new meaning and importance since the attainment of independence and the adoption of the policy and techniques of planned development of the national economy. If the pace of national development is to be accelerated, there is need for a well-defined, bold and imaginative educational policy and for determined and vigorous action to vitalize, improve and expand education."

The population explosion, the unprecedented expansion of educational institutions and the exponential growth in enrolment have generated a matrix of complicated problems. "The size and complexity of these problems argue the need for rapid action and in evolving an appropriate education policy...." (1.03). It appropriately commented, "... education cannot be considered in isolation or planned in a vacuum. It has to be used as a powerful instrument of social, economic and political change...." (1.04). The major national problems recurrendy haunting India are the absence of self-sufficiency in food and freedom from hunger; viable solution to unemployment and under-employment through sustained economic growth; safe-guarding nationalunity; and reinforcing the democratic way of life. Education needs to be utilized as the main instrument of social change to solve the national problems. Education should be pragmatic and should be "related to life, needs and aspiration of the people" (p. 5). Education and productivity must be linked to each other; and to realize this goal greater emphasis needs to be accorded to science and work-experience. Education should promote modernization and fight against obscurantism and obsolescence. All stages of education including secondary education test the strength of the nation and its capability to solve the emerging contingencies.

The structure of education attracted the attention of the Kothari Commission. It stated that:

"2.02. To begin with, we would like to state our approach to the problems of structure and standards. The standards in any given system of education at a given time depend upon four elements (1) the structure or the division of the educational pyramid into different levels or stages and their inter-relationships; (2) the duration or total period covered by the different stages; (3) the extent and quality of essential inputs such as teachers, curricula, methods of teaching and evaluation, equipment and buildings; and (4) the utilization of available facilities. All these elements are inter-related, but they are not of equal significance. For instance, the structure, which may be regarded as the skeleton of the educational system, is of the least importance. The duration or total period of education plays a more significant role; but it becomes crucial only when the available facilities are utilized to the full and no further improvement can be expected without the addition of time. The quality of different inputs is even more important, and with an improvement in these, it is possible to raise the standards considerably without affecting the structure or increasing the duration. But the utilization of available facilities is probably the most significant of all elements on which standards depend. For any self-accelerating process of development, it is essential in the first place to improve efficiency at the level of the existing inputs and to add more inputs only if they are crucial to the process. An increase of inputs assumes significance only at a later stage".

"2.03. In this context it may be interesting to note that until recently, the general tendency everywhere has been to over-rate the importance of the duration of the school course. There is a reason for this. When the quantum of knowledge covered in the school was not very large, the pace of school work was leisurely and when one learnt more outside school than within school, it was natural to suppose that the longer one stayed at school the better one gained in knowledge and maturity. All this has changed now. The knowledge explosion has imposed an altogether new pressure on schools and colleges. Formal education now plays a much greater part than it did previously at any time in history and the efficiency of the educational system has become a very important factor."

The explosion in knowledge and fierce competition from other countries in a knowledge-based world order constrained the Commission to reduce the 11-yearschool to a 10-year school system. The savings of one year plus one year rolled back from the college system together would form the 2-year Higher Secondary Education component where specialization and skill learning would commence. This is the +2 stage of education. The first degree shall be of three years duration - increased duration for in-depth specialization. The total time spent by a student for completing the first degree remained to be 15 years. The old "11+2+2" structure was retuned, and became the "10+2+3" system as suggested by it.. It categorically stated that:

"The idea that every secondary school should be raised to the higher secondary status should also be abandoned... It is only the biggest and better type of high schools that should be upgraded. If one-fourth of the total number of high schools were raised to the higher secondary status, they would meet all the needs of the situation... An essential requirement is that the institution should be large, centrally located and equitably distributed between the urban and rural areas... The existing higher secondary schools that are too small and uneconomic or of very poor quality may be reconverted into high schools" (2.18 P. 30).

Integrated approach to education must come to an end at the end of Class-X; and specialization must commence at the higher secondary stage. It recommended vocationalization of Higher Secondary Education. The structural changes is not a revised arithmetic process of addition of 10+2+3 in place of the erstwhile 11+2+2. The rationale has been explained thus:

"2.33. The principal object of the changes in structure and duration which have beendiscussed above is to raise standards. In this context, however, it is essential to note that:

- structure and duration play a significant but secondary role in improving standards;
- the changes proposed in structure and duration will be rather slow in making an impact on quality, because their full implementation has been spread over twenty years; and
- the most serious weakness of the existing educational system lies, not in its structure, but in its feebleness. We are getting relatively much less than what we should from the system as it exists and the resources that go into it. No reorganization of structure or addition of time can remedy this basic weakness.

It is, therefore, necessary to place a much greater emphasis in all our plans of educational reconstruction on programmes of intensive utilization of facilities available, and on improving the extent and quality of the inputs other than time, and particularly on the improvement of teachers. These will yield immediate and far-reaching results".

Further, it recommended that:

- The instructional days for schools should be increased to about 234 days in schools in an academic year.
- 'Vacations' should not be wasted. They should be utilized for research work, participation in NCC; social service camps; work experience; 'earning for maintenance'; hikes, excursions, tours, cultivation of hobbies and activities like literacy drives.
- Every instructional day must have six hours of teaching and self-study. In an academic year the instruction time should be at least 1000 hours at the secondary stage; and preferably raised to 1100-1200 hours.

- Steps should be taken to optimally utilize the institutional facilities available. It recommended that:

.... an intensive effort should be made through measures for reorganization of the structure, increase of duration, intensive utilization and improvement of the quality and extent of inputs other than time, to raise standards continually at all stages of education" (P. 42). It envisaged the "linking of secondary and primary schools" through *school-complexes*.

It stated that class VTII to X or IX to X shall constitute '**Lower Secondary Education**'; and shall be imparted in high schools; and that classes XI & XII shall constitute the '**Higher Secondary Education**' imparted in High or Higher Secondary Schools.

The Commission boldly envisioned a *"National Enrolment Policy"*. It pertinendy asked, "How can available resources be best deployed to secure the most beneficial form of educational development ? How much education, of what type or level of quality should society strive to provide and for whom?" (5.01 p.89). It suggested:

- "To expand lower secondary education on as large a scale as possible.
- To provide higher secondary education to those who are willing and qualified to receive such education...." (5.02 P. 89)

This critical aspect had been explained thus:

5.04. Provision of Secondary and Higher Education: Several complex problems relating to the amount, type and quality of education to be provided arise in respect of secondary and higher education. It is not easy to determine the size of total enrolments in the absence of clear and precise targets about overall expansion rates. Moreover, as education at these stages has to be diversified into a large number of courses to meet varied individual aptitudes as well as social requirements for trained man-power, it becomes even more difficult to decide the precise extent of provisions for each course. Unfortunately, an understanding of these problems is still limited. Enrolment policy must, therefore, be based on the pragmatic combination of four different criteria; the public demand for such education; the full development of the *pool of ability*; the capacity of the society to provide the educational facilities needs at given levels of quality; and manpower needs for national development".

5.05. Public Demand for Secondary and Higher Education: During recent years, the demand for secondary and higher education has increased enormously. There are several reasons for this such as:

- the traditional social status attached to a university degree;
- the growing hunger for education among the urban people and the middle classes who have realized that the best and probably the worthwhile legacy they can leave to their children, is to give good education;
- the awakening among the rural people and the lower classes who are now seeking social advancement just as the urban and middle classes did during the last hundred years-through education and government service;
- the disappearance of the old 'values' attached to primary education which makes secondary education the 'minimum' and higher education the 'optimum' qualification for any worthwhile job;
- the absence of adequate employment opportunities for young persons so that many of them are forced to go in for secondary or university education simply because they have nothing else to do.
- The increasing provision which is being made by State Governments for free secondary education and for the liberal grant of free studentships, stipends and scholarships at the university stage; and
- A rapid multiplication of educational institutions at this level which has made them easily accessible to young persons in thousands of small and out-of-the-way places."

5.06. This situation could have been met in two ways, either by expanding facilities in secondary and higher education strictly on the basis of available real resources in terms of teachers and materials and adopting a policy of selective admissions to bridge the gap between the public demand for such education and the facilities actually provided, or by adopting a policy of open-door access and providing all the resources needed to create the required facilities and to maintain them at the optimum level of efficiency. But as it was neither possible to resist the demand nor to raise all the needed resources, a compromise approach was attempted: the access to all secondary education was provided on an open-door basis; and in higher education, both the selective and open-door policies were operated upon simultaneously in different sectors.

5.07. This policy has had several undesirable consequences. As overall resources were limited and were absorbed in programmes of expansion of general education, it became impossible to pay adequate attention to programmes of qualitative improvement or vocationalisation. Most of this expansion has also been non-egalitarian since secondary schools and colleges enrolled students who had access to them and who could afford the expenditure involved, although their preparation and motivation were often inadequate. On the other hand they failed to enroll a large proportion of talented students who were prevented from studying further by social or economic handicaps. The benefits of expansion thus went largely to the privileged rather than to the under-privileged classes. Moreover, there grew up an imbalance between the development of general and vocational education, the former far exceeding demand and the latter generally failing much below it. Consequently, the output of matriculates and of graduates in arts and commerce was in excess of demand and created problems of educated unemployment while trained personnel for the development of agriculture, industry or research remained in short supply."

5.08. During the next two decades, the demand for secondary and higher education will increase still further as primary education becomes universal and the general economic conditions improve. Under these circumstances, a continuation of the earlier enrolment policies will merely accentuate these evils. It is, therefore, necessary to adopt some definite policy of 'selective admissions' so as to relate enrolments to facilities available and to maintain standards."

5.09. The Pool of Ability: Providing secondary and higher education to all the potentially able students generally sets up a very high target which even affluent societies find it difficult to achieve. It will be obviously beyond our reach, at least in the immediate future, in view of the limited resources available. This should, however, be the goal towards which we should continually move. In the transitional period, immediate effect should be given to one important implication of this policy, viz., to ensure that all gifted students (at least the top 5-15 per cent of all students), who complete primary or secondary education are enabled to study further in institutions of secondary (or higher) education. For this purpose, it will be necessary to provide a large number of scholarships on the lines to be discussed later".

5.10. Capacity to Provide Facilities: In planning enrolment facilities, it is essential to take into consideration the real resources available and the capacity of the society' to create the educational facilities needed or in demand. There are internal constraints in every educational system which limit expansion of facilities, especially in secondary and higher education. These are the availability of competent teachers, of physical plant and of finance. Even in affluent societies, these built-in constraints make it almost impossible to provide all those facilities, quantitatively and qualitatively, which would be required on the basis of public demand or for the development of the total pool of ability."

The need for creation of *'a pool of ability'*, *'capacity to provide facilities'*, and *'manpower needs'* should be the guiding parameters of expanding access **to** secondary/higher secondary education. It suggested the following guiding principles.

7.43. Expansion of Secondary Education:

1. Enrolments in secondary education should be regulated during the next 20 years by (a) proper planning of the location of secondary schools, (b) maintaining adequate standards and to that end, by determining the enrolment in terms of facilities available, and (c) selecting the best students.

2. A development plan for secondary education should be prepared for each district and implemented in a period of ten years. All new institutions should satisfy essential standards, and existing institutions should be raised to the minimum levels.

3. The best students should be selected for admission into secondary schools, through a process of self-selection at the lower secondary stage, and on the basis of external examination results and school records at the higher secondary state."

7.50 & 7.51. Vocationalizing Secondary Education:

1. Secondary education should be vocationalised in a large measure and enrolments in vocational courses raised to 20 per cent of total enrolment at the lower secondary stage and 50 per cent of total enrolment at the higher secondary stage by 1986.

2. A variety of part-time and full-time facilities in vocational education should be available at both these stages to meet the needs of boys and girls, in urban and rural areas. Special sections should be set up in the Education Department to help young people who drop out after Class VII or VIII to obtain training on a full-time or part-time basis, and to be in overall charge of the organization of these courses.

3. The Central Government should provide special grants to State Governments in the centrally sponsored sector for the vocationalization of secondary education". (86.S)

7.52 &7.53. Part-time Education: Facilities for part-time education should be provided on a large scale at the lower and higher secondary stages, in general and vocational courses. A desirable target would be 20 per cent of the total enrolment, at the lower secondary stage and 25 per cent at the higher secondary stage. Special emphasis will have to be placed on agricultural courses for those who have taken to farming as a vocation and on courses in home science or household industries for girls."

7.54. Education of Girls: Secondary Stage:

1. Efforts should be made to accelerate the expansion of girls education so that the proportion of girls to boys reaches 1:2 at the lower secondary stage and 1:3 at the higher secondary stage in 20 years.
2. Emphasis should be placed on establishing separate schools for girls, provision of hostels and scholarships, and part-time and vocational courses. (88.S)

7.55. Planning and Location of Schools:

1. A national policy for the location of new institutions of each category should be adopted so as to avoid waste and duplication. The second education survey should be used for the careful planning of the location of educational institutions.
2. Public opinion should be educated to accept mixed schools at the primary stage and the sharing of bigger and efficient schools in common. Villages should be grouped so as to make the economic provision of primary schools possible.
3. At the secondary stage, the establishment of small and uneconomic institutions should be avoided, and existing uneconomic schools should be consolidated.
4. Vocational schools should be located near the industry concerned." (89.S)

It stressed the need for guidance and counseling at the school stage. Its specific recommendation for secondary schools were:

9.51. Guidance at the Secondary Stage:

1. Guidance at the secondary stage should among other things, help in the identification and development of the abilities and interests of adolescent pupils. The ultimate objective should be to introduce adequate guidance services n all secondary schools with a trained counselor in charge of the programme. But in view of the limited financial and personnel resources, a short-range programme should be adopted for the next 20 years consisting of:

   (i) a rninimum guidance programme for all secondary schools through a visiting school counselor for a group of ten schools, assisted by the school teachers in the simpler guidance functions;

   (ii) comprehensive guidance programme in selected schools, one in each district, to serve as models; and

   (iii) provision of necessary supervisory staff in the State Bureaus of Guidance.

2. All secondary school teachers should be introduced to guidance concepts through pre or in-service training. The training colleges should be suitably staffed for the purpose.

3. General. Arrangements should be made for the professional training of guidance workers by the State Bureaus of Guidance and training colleges. Advanced training should be organized at the national level.

4. Ancillary programmes should include the production of guidance literature and materials and research into problems of guidance in the Indian situation."

9.58-64. Search for and Development of Talent:

1. The search for talent must be a continuous process, pursued at all stages, but the secondary stage is the most crucial.

2. In addition to programmes of enrichment and advanced curricula, a variety of extra-mural programmes should be organized for the talented such as summer schools, visits to places of educational interest and provision of hostels and day-centres for those whose home environment is not conducive to study.

3. Teachers should be oriented to the special techniques of dealing with the talented children, especially to the need for providing an atmosphere for free expression and creative work (108.S)

9.58-64. The Backward Child: Neglect of backward children leads to wastage of educational facilities and human resources and it is necessary for a developing country to reduce this wastage to the minimum. In particular, attention has to be given to the under-achievers who represent a loss of potential manpower often of high ability. Steps should, therefore, be taken to diagnose the cause of under-achievement and to formulate and implement remedial programmes within the school system, with the help of interested teachers and child guidance clinics, where available, and parent-teacher associations. (109.S)"

92. Organization of the Curriculum:

1. In non-vocational schools, a common curriculum of general education should be provided for the first ten years of school education, and diversification of studies and specialization should begin only at the higher secondary stage.

2. Standards of attainment should be clearly defined at the end of each sub-stage.

3. At the lower secondary stage, study of subjects will gain in rigour and depth.

4. At the higher secondary stage, courses will be diversified in such a manner as to enable pupils to study a group of any three subjects in depth with considerable freedom and elasticity in the grouping of subjects. In order to ensure the balanced development of the adolescent's total personality,

the curriculum at this stage should provide half the time to the electives, on-fourth of the time to the languages, and one-fourth to physical education, arts and crafts, and moral and spiritual education.

5. At the higher primary stage, enrichment programmes should be provided for the talented children. It may take the form of additional subject or greater depth in the same subject.

6. At the secondary stage, courses should be provided at two levels-ordinary and advanced-beginning with Class VIII. The programme may be done within or outside school hours or on a self-study basis. A beginning may be made with advanced courses in mathematics, science and languages at the lower secondary stage and in all the specialized subjects at the higher secondary stage. (92.S)"

8.30. Study of Languages:

1. The language study at the school stage needs review and a new policy regarding language study at the school stage requires to be formulated.

2. The modification of the language formula should be guided by the following guiding principles:

   a. Hindi as the official language of the Union and enjoys an importance next only to that of the mother-tongue;

   b. A working knowledge of English will continue to be an asset to students;

   c. The proficiency gained in a language depends as much upon the types of teachers and facilities as upon the length of time in which it is learnt.

   d. The most suitable stage for learning three languages is the lower secondary (classes VIII-X).

   e. The introduction of two additional languages should be staggered;

    f. Hindi or English should be introduced at a point when there is greatest motivation and need;

    g. At no stage should the learning of four languages be made compulsory.

3. The three language formula modified on these principles should include (a) the mother-tongue or the regional language; (b) the official language of the Union or the associate official language of the Union so long as it exists; and (c) a modern Indian or European language not covered under (a) and (b) and other than that used as the medium of education.

4. At the lower primary stage the pupil will ordinarily study only one language-the mother-tongue or the regional language. At the higher primary stage, he will study two languages-the mother-tongue (or the regional language) and the official language of the Union (or the associate language). At the lower secondary stage, he will study three languages, the mother-tongue (or the regional language); the official or associate official language; and a modern Indian language, it being obligatory to study the official or the associate official language which he had not studied at the higher primary stage. At the higher secondary stage, only two languages will be compulsory.

5. The study of important modern library languages other than English should be made possible in selected schools in each State with option to study."(93.S)

96. Work-Experience:

1. Work-experience should be forward-looking in keeping with the character of the new social order. It will take the form of simple handwork in the lower primary classes, and of craft in the upper primary classes. At the lower secondary stage, it will be in the form of workshop training, and at the higher secondary stage, work-experience will be provided in the school workshop, farm or commercial and industrial establishments.

2. Where school workshops cannot be provided, suitable kits of. tools and materials should be made available at low cost.

3. The training of teachers, provision of workshops, mobilization of local resources, preparation of literature and the phased introduction of the programme are essential to the success of the scheme."(96.S)

97. Social Services:

1. Programmes of social service and participation in community development should be organized at all levels as suited to the different age-groups, in a phased manner.

2. Labour and social service camps should be run throughout the year; and for this purpose, a special organization set up in each district. These camps will facilitate the organization of social service programmes in schools. Such programmes may be started as a pilot project in 5 per cent of the districts and extended gradually to the others."(97.S)

98. Physical Education: Physical education is important for the physical fitness and efficiency, mental alertness and the development of certain qualities of character. The programme of physical education, as it is in force today, needs to be re-examined and redesigned in the light of certain basic principles of child growth and development."(98.S)

99. Education in Moral and Spiritual Values:

1. Organized attempt should be made for imparting moral education and inculcating spiritual values in schools through direct and indirect methods with the help of the ethical teachings of great religions.

2. One or two periods a week should be set aside in the school time-table for instruction in moral and spiritual values. The treatment of the subject should be comprehensive and not divorced from the rest of the curriculum."(99.S)

100. Creative Activities:

1. The Government of India should appoint a committee of experts to survey the present situation of art education and explore all possibilities for its extension and systematic development.
2. Bal Bhawans should be set up in all parts of the country with substantial support from the local community.
3. Art departments should be set up in selected university centres to carry out research in art education.
4. A variety of co-curricular activities should be organized to provide pupils opportunity for creative self-expression."(100.S)

101. Differentiation of Curricula for Boys and Girls: The recommendations of the Hansa Mehta Committee that there should be no differentiation of curricula on the basis of sex is endorsed. Home science should be provided as an optional subject but not made compulsory for girls. Larger provision should be made for music and fine arts; and the study of mathematics and science should be encouraged."(101.S)

102. The New Curriculum and Basic Education: The essential principles of basic education, namely, productive activity, correlation of curriculum with productive activity and the environment, and contact with local community, are so important that they should guide and shape the educational system at all levels, and this is the essence of the proposals made in this report. No single stage of education need be designated as basic education."(102.S)

> **Note:** Pages 155 to 168 relating to the recommendation about different aspects of Secondary Education of India are based on Indian Education Commission, 1964-66 entitled *"Education and National Development,* 1st Edition, 1966, Publication Devision, GOI, New Delhi, 1966.

The major recommendations of the Commission pertaining to Secondary Education in India were:

- Ten years schooling of which the "last 3 to 2 of general education or one to three years of vocational education" shall be the lower secondary stage of education.
- A Higher Secondary Stage of two years of general education or one to three years of vocational education.
- Vocationalisation of Secondary Education.
- The first degree shall be of three years duration.
- Special emphasis on the training of teacher;
- Introduction of work experience; and
- Stress on moral education;

The pattern of education recommended by it is commonly known as "10+2+3." The higher secondary education came to be commonly known as "+2 course". The universities stopped conducting the pre-degree courses or Intermediate courses and these were transferred to the Boards of Secondary Education or newly constituted Councils/Boards of Higher Secondary Education.

The basic structural changes of secondary education suggested by the Kothari Commission (1966) were:

- A Higher Secondary stage of either general or vocational education.
- At the higher secondary stage, courses should be diversified in such a manner as to enable pupils to study a group of any three subjects in-depth with considerable freedom and elasticity in the grouping of subjects.
- A tuition-free lower secondary stage of two years duration (classes IX & X).
- At the secondary stage, courses should be provided at two levels — Ordinary and Advanced — beginning with class VIII. A beginning may be made with advanced courses inMathematics, Science and Languages at the lower secondary stage and in all the specialized subjects at the higher secondary stage.[298]

---

298 Report on the Progress of Education in Orissa, 1947-48, Supdt. Orissa Govt. Press, Cuttack1948. p. 1

- At the lower secondary stage, study of subjects should gain in rigour and depth.
- A national policy for the location of new institutions of each category should be adopted to avoid waste and duplication.
- The establishment of small and uneconomic institutions should be avoided, and existing uneconomic schools should be consolidated
- Accelerated expansion of girls' education so that the proportion of girls to boys reaches 1:2 at the Lower Secondary stage and 1:3 at the higher secondary stage in 20 years (i.e. by 1985).
- Regulated expansion and planned location of schools to augment the steady development of quality institutions.
- Emphasis should be placed on the establishment of separate schools for girls, provision of hostels, and part-time and vocational courses.
- Improved methods of teaching, extensive guidance facilities and better supervision.

NATIONAL POLICY ON EDUCATION, 1968

On the basis of the recommendations of the Indian Education Commission, 1964-66's Report entided "Education and National Development", the Government of India announced the "National Policy on Education,1968". The Government of India emphatically stated that, "… radical reconstruction of education on the broad lines recommended by the Education Commission is essential for economic and cultural development of the country, for national integration and for realizing the ideal of a socialistic pattern of society. This will involve a transformation of the system to relate it more closely to the life of the people, a continuous effort to expand educational opportunity, a sustained and intensive endeavour to raise the quality of education at all stages, and emphasis on the development of Science and Technology and cultivation of moral and social values." The Policy statement endorsed the need "to have a broadly uniform educational structure in all parts of the country." The "10+2+3" pattern of education was strongly endorsed by it. The 'Ten-year Schooling' and 'Higher Secondary Education' became the two critical components that transformed the erstwhile 11+2+2 pattern of general education which had totally failed to inculcate 'work experience'. It was deficient in providing designed purposive moral and spiritual education, and vocationalization.[299]

EDUCATION IN THE CONCURRENT LIST

The Constitution of India which came into force with effect from 26th January, 1950 envisaged a Union of India with a federal type of government. In such a constitutional arrangement the operational spheres of the Central Government and the State Governments must have to be demarcated clearly. There is a 'Central List' which clearly states the absolute prerogatives of the Central Government in such matters as defense, foreign affairs, atomic energy etc. Similarly, the 'State List' spells out the sphere of activity assigned to State Government like the prerogative of maintenance of law and order, providing health care and education etc. Both the Lists - the Central and the State are long. There are certain common areas where both the Centre and the States can play a role; and these have been included in the Concurrent List.

The 42nd Amendment Act of the Constitution passed in 1976, had removed *'Education'* from the State List and placed it in the Concurrent List. It was suggested by Sardar Swaran Singh Committee which remarked:

"Agriculture and Education are subjects of prime importance to the country's rapid progress towards achieving desired socio-economic changes. The need to evolve all-India policies in relation to these two subjects cannot be over-emphasised."[300]

---

299 Report on the Progress of Education in Orissa, 1960-61, p. 64
300 Report on the Progress of Education in Orissa, 1947-48, p. 1

The provision of the 42nd Constitutional Amendment Act of 1976 are as follows:

"Entry 25 of the Concurrent List includes, 'Education, including technical education, medical education and universities subject to entries 63, 64, 66 of List I,[301] vocational and technical training, training of labour".

The Government of India had consistently and continuously been playing a constructive, counseling and cajoling role in educational affairs right from 1948. It had appointed the University Education Commission (1948) under the Chairmanship of Dr. S. Radhakrishnan; the Secondary Education Commission (1952) under the Chairmanship of Dr. Laxmanswami Mudaliar; and finally the Indian Education Commission (1964) under the Chairmanship of Dr. D. S. Kothari. It had also appointed a large number of Committees relating to different aspects of education. The Ministry of Education, Central Advisory Board of Education (CABE), the National Council of Educational Research and Training; and the National Institute (now University) of Education Planning and Administration were already playing a highly pro-active role in matters pertaining to education. The 42nd Amendment provided the much needed constitutional sanctity and legal authority to the Centre to play an active role in all spheres of education.

OTHER COMMITTEES AND COMMISSIONS (1966-85)

The Government of India had appointed the following Committees, Commissions, Study Groups and Working Groups whose reports have greatly influenced the different aspects of secondary education in India. They are:

1. Committee on Improvement of Art Education.
2. Committee on School Text-Book, 1966,

---

301 Report on the Progress of Education in Orissa, 1960-61, p. 54

3. Study Group on Supervision and Inspection, 1969, NCERT, 1969.
4. Committee on Examination, 1970, NCERT, 1967.
5. Committee on School Building, 1970, Ministry of Education (1972).
6. Review Committee - Ishwar Bhai Patel, NCERT, 1977
7. Working Group on Organisation of Vocational Education, 1977, Ministry of Education, 1977.
8. National Review Committee on Higher Secondary Education with Special Reference to Vocationalisation, 1977, Ministry of Education and Social welfare, 1978.
9. Report on Autonomous Schools, CBSE, 1981.
10. Curriculum Load at the School level: A Quick Appraisal, NCERT,1985.
11. National Commission on Teachers-I (School Teachers), 1983-85/(1986).
12. Challenge of Education: A Policy Perspective, 1985.

The reports of all these Committees, Commissions and Working Groups tried to clarify issues raised by the Indian Education Commission,1966. They suggested modalities of implementation. These reports have influenced the educational policies and programmes of all the States of India.

DEVELOPMENT OF SECONDARY EDUCATION IN ORISSA (1947-1966)

Right from 2nd December,1766 when the East India Company took possession of Ganjam region to 1st January, 1949 (and even prior to it), the Oriya speaking tracts of India lay dispersed in Bengal, Bihar and Orissa, Central Provinces, Madras Presidency and the 24 feudatory states. In 1936, a separate Orissa Province was formed with the six districts under British administration. On 1st January, 1948, 23 feudatory states were amalgamated with Orissa. On 1st January, 1949, Mayurbhanj State was also merged. The present day Orissa has thus taken its shape and size from 1st January, 1949. On 19th August,1949 Bhubaneswar was declared the capital of Orissa. Cuttack was the capital from 1816 to 1949; and Puri from 1803 to 1816.

Orissa was divided into 13 administrative divisions, known as districts with effect from 26th January,1950. The erstwhile feudatory states of Athagarh, Baramba, Narasinghpur, Tigiria were merged in the Cuttack district. The Feudatory States of Dhenkanal, Talcher, Hindol, Pal Lahara, Athamallik together with Angul which was a direcdy British administered territory formed the new district of Dhenkanal. Nilgiri was merged with Balasore district. Daspalla, Khandapara, Nayagarh and Ranpur States were merged with the Puri district. Kalahandi and Mayurbhanj became separate districts by themselves. Bonai state and Gangpur State together constituted the new Sundergarh district. Rairakhol and Bamra states were merged with the Sambalpur district.

Sonepur and Patna merged together to form the new Bolangir district. Baud State and the direcdy administered territories of Kondhamals and Balliguda area of Ganjam Agency formed the new Phulbani district. Keonjhar State became the Keonjhar district. There was no addition to either Ganjam or Koraput districts. Table No. 5.2.1 shows the 13 reorganized districts of Orissa of 1950.

TABLE 5.2.1

Revised Jurisdiction of the 13 Reorganized Districts of Orissa (1950)

SI. No.	Name of the District	The previous area which it comprises	Headquarters	Area in Sq.Kms.
01	Cuttack	Cuttack District, Baramba State, Athagarh State, Narasinghpur State and Tigiria State	Cuttack	11,211
02	Puri	Puri District, Daspalla State, Khandapara State, Nayagarh State and Ranpur State	Puri	10,159
03	Balasore	Balasore District and Nilgiri State	Balasore	6,393
04	Ganjam	Ganjam District	Chhatrapur	12,527
05	Koraput	Koraput District	Koraput	27,020
06	Sambalpur	Sambalpur District, Bamra State, Rairkhol State	Sambalpur	17,570
07	Mayurbhanj	Mayurbhanj State	Baripada	10,412
08	Keonjhar	Keonjhar State	Keonjhar	8,240
09	Kalahandi	Kalahandi State	Bhawanipatna	11,835
10	Bolangir	Patna State and Sonepur State	Bolangir	8,903
11	Sundergarh	Bonai State and Gangpur State	Sundergarh	9,675
12	Dhenkanal	Angul Sub-Division of Cuttack district Dhenkanal State, Pal Lahara State, Hindol State, Talcher State and Athamallik State	Dhenkanal	10,826

SI. No.	Name of the District	The previous area which it comprises	Headquarters	Area in Sq.Kms.
13	Phulbani	Kondhamal Sub-Division of Ganjam district, Boudh State and Balliguda area of Ganjam Agency	Phulbani	11,070
	Orissa State	6 formerly Bridsh administered districts + 24 Feudatory States	Bhubaneswar	155,842

In the subsequent discussion references shall be made to these newly reconstituted districts and the old treatment has necessarily been abandoned.

Population and literacy are the defining factors of the requisite magnitude of secondary education. Urbanization is an accelerating factor. Population and percentages of urbanization and literacy of India and Orissa have been provided to understand the adequacy (or inadequacy) of access to secondary education.

TABLE 5.2.2

Population, Percentages of Urbanization AND Literacy of
India and Orissa (1951 to 2001)

SI. No.	Census Year	Population		Percentage of urbanization		Percentage of Literacy	
		India	Orissa	India	Orissa	India	Orissa
1.	1951	36,10,88,090	1,46,45,946	17.3	4.06	18.33	15.80
2.	1961	43,92,34,771	1,75,48,846	18.0	6.32	28.30	25.24
3.	1971	54,81,59,652	2,19,44,615	19.9	8.41	34.45	30.53
4.	1981	68,33,29,097	2,63,70,271	23.3	11.79	43.57	40.96
5.	1991	84,63,87,888	3,16,59,736	25.7	13.38	52.21	49.09
6.	2001	102,70,15,247	3,68,04,660	27.70	14.97	64.84	63.61

Higher the population greater is the latent demand for all stages and phases of education. Increased levels of literacy intensify the demand for elementary and secondary education. Higher the rate of urbanization greater is the available access to secondary education. The dream of universalization of secondary education can become an operational reality, if and only if, universalization of elementary education becomes a success.

EXPANSION OF SECONDARY EDUCATION IN ORISSA (1947-48 TO 1960-61)

Schools

In 1946-47, there were 89 high schools in Orissa - 83 for boys and 6 for girls.[302]By 1960-61, the number of high schools (including 2 Post-Basic Schools) rose to 450.[303] Of these, 35 were for girls and the rest 415 (including the 2 Post-Basic Schools) were for boys. There was an increase of 400% in case of high schools for boys and 483.2% increase in case of High Schools for girls. There was almost a fourfold increase in the total number of high schools in the State during the period 1946-47 to 1960-61.

In 1946-47, there were 273 middle schools in all - 253 for boys and 20 for girls.[304]By 1960-61, the total number of middle schools went up to 1,241. Of these, 1241 middle schools, 88 institutions were for girls. The rest 1,153 were for boys.[305] Of these boys schools, 23 were Senior Basic Schools. The First Five Year Plan and the Second Five Year Plan accelerated the pace of educational expansion.

Inl951-52, one Senior Basic School was opened.[306] This number increased to 6 in 1953-54,[307] 15 in 1954-55,[308] 16 in 1955-56, [309]18 in

302 Report on the Progress of Education in Orissa, 1951-52, p. 2
303 Report on the Progress of Education in Orissa, 1953-54, p. 2
304 Report on the Progress of Education in Orissa, 1954-55, p. 2
305 Report on the Progress of Education in Orissa, 1955-56, p. 2
306 Report on the Progress of Education in Orissa, 1956-57, p. 2
307 Report on the Progress of Education in Orissa, 1957-58, p. 2
308 Report on the Progress of Education in Orissa, 1954-55, p. 2
309 Report on the Progress of Education in Orissa, 1956-57, p. 2

1956-57,[310] and 23 in 1957-58[311]and remained stationary there up to 1960-61. The Senior Basic Schools are middle schools following the Basic educational curriculum with its stress on craft, manual labour, and emphasis on the mother tongue. A Post-Basic School is a higher secondary school of the Basic type. The first Post-Basic School was opened in 1954-55,[312] and this number increase to 2 in 1956-57.[313] The number of these schools did not increase up to 1960-61.

The growth of secondary schools during 1946-47 to 1960-61[314]has been depicted in Table No. 5.2.3.

TABLE 5.2.3

Growth of High & Middle Schools in Orissa, 1946-47 to 1960-61

SI. No.	Year	High Schools			Middle Schools		
		Boys	Girls	Total	Boys	Girls	Total
01	1946-47	83	06	89	253	20	273
02	1947-48	99	07	106	265	21	286
03	1948-49	132	07	139	414	*34	448
04	1949-50	146	07	153	453	36	489
05	1950-51	165	07	172	468	33	501
06	1951-52	183	09	192	490+01*	35	526
07	1952-53	190	10	200	522+01*	37	560
08	1953-54	199	11	210	542+06*	35	583
09	1954-55	210+01**	13	224	578+15*	39	632
10	1955-56	244+01**	13	258	628+16*	44	688

---

310 Data collected from die Report on the Progress of Education in Orissa, from 1946-47 to 1960-61.

311 Report of the Progress of Education in Orissa, 1946-47 p. 5 & Report on the Progress of Education in Orissa, 1960-61. p. 54

312 Report of the Progress of Education in Orissa, 1946-47 p. 5 & Report on the Progress of Education in Orissa, 1960-61. p. 55

313 Data collected from the Report on the Progress of Education in Orissa from 1946-47 to 1960-61

314 Report on die Progress of Education in Orissa, 1947-48 (Section Education p. 11), and Report on the Progress of Education in Orissa 1960-61. p. 59

SI. No.	Year	High Schools			Middle Schools		
		Boys	**Girls**	**Total**	**Boys**	**Girls**	**Total**
11	1956-57	263+02**	13	278	655+18*	50	723
12	1957-58	288+02**	16	306	697+23*	54	774
13	1958-59	318+02**	23	343	802+23*	59	884
14	1959-60	372+02**	31	405	952+23*	73	1048
15	1960-61	413+02**	35	450	1130+23*	88	1241

During 1957-58, the Ravenshaw Collegiate School, Cuttack, the Government Girls' High School, Puri and Khallikote Collegiate High School, Berhampur were converted into Higher Secondary Schools. During 1958-59, Larambha High School, Onslow Institute, Chhatrapur, B.B. High School, Dhenkanal and B. M. High School, Bhawanipatna were converted into higher secondary schools. The multi-purpose syllabus was introduced in these schools.

During 1950-51, the Tribal and Rural Welfare Department establishes *Ashram Schools* for Scheduled Caste and Scheduled Tribe students. These Middle Schools were not under the administrative control of the Education Department though they were being inspected by the Inspecting staff of the Education Department. During 1950-51, a number of middle schools were amalgamated with the neighbouring high schools.

Management

In 1946-47, there was not a single high school under the management of the Government of India. By 1960-61, only such school was the Sainik School at Bhubaneswar.

In 1946-47, there were only 6 high schools for boys and 4 for girls under the management of the Government of Orissa. These schools constituted 11.2% of the total high schools. By 1960-61, the total number of Government high schools in the State had risen to 84 — 60 for boys and 24 for girls. The high schools in the ex-State had to be taken over as government schools after the merger of the feudatory states. The District

Board Schools of Ganjam and Koraput districts were also taken over by the state government. Thus the number of government high schools swelled from 10 in 1946-47 to 84 in 1960-61. In 1960-61, the government high schools constituted 18.6% of the total number of schools.

There were 14 District Board High schools in 1946-47. These were taken over by the Government of Orissa. So there were no District Board Schools by 1960-61. There were three high schools managed by the Municipalities. The District Boards and Municipal Boards were Local Self-Government institutions. There was perceptible and definite decrease in the number of schools under the management of local self-government institutions during this period.

The aided schools under private management were 59 in 1956-57 and this number rose to 234 in 1960-61. These schools constituted 67.4% of the total number of schools in 1946-47, and by 1960-61 they were 52% of the total number.

There were four unaided schools under private management in 1946-47 and such schools had increased to 126 by 1960-61. The maximum increase was in this field. This indicates the growing desire and the increasing initiative for education on the part of the people.

TABLE 5.2.4

Comparative Statement of Management of High Schools/Higher Secondary Schools in 1947-48 and 1960-61 [315]

SI. No.	Management	Number of Institutions				Increase/ Decrease	
		1946-47		1960-61			
		Boys	Girls	Boys	Girls	Boys	Girls
01	Central Government			01		+01	
02	State Government	06	04	60	24	+54	+20

---

315 Report on the Progress of Education in Orissa, 1947-48 (Sec. Edn. p. 1), and Report on the Progress of Education in Orissa 1960-61. p. 60.

SI. No.	Management	Number of Institutions				Increase/ Decrease	
		1946-47		1960-61			
		Boys	Girls	Boys	Girls	Boys	Girls
03	District Board	14				-14	
04	Municipal Board	02		04	01	+02	+01
05	Private Aided	57	02	224	10	+167	+08
06	Unaided	04		126		+122	
	Total	83	06	415	35	+332	+29

In 1946-47, the number of state government middle schools was 21 and this rose to 190 by 1960-61. This increase was due to the merger of the feudatory states in Orissa and the taking over of the Board Schools. There were 54 middle schools in 1946-47 under District Board management. In 1960-61, there was no middle school under District Board management. They had all become government schools with effect from 1959-60

In 1946-47, there were no middle schools under Municipal management. By 1960-61, there were 10 such schools. The role of the local self-government was negligible in the field of middle school education.

In 1946-47, the total number of aided Middle schools under private management was 139 which rose to 721 in 1960-61. The total number of unaided middle schools was 54 out of the total 273 in 1946-47; and 297 out of 1,218 in 1960-61. The growing demand for education as well as the initiative of the people was clearly evident. By 1960-61, there were 70 aided middle schools for girls which were only 11 in 1946-47. Girls' education was steadily progressing.

TABLE 5.2.5

**Comparative Statement of Management of Middle Schools in
1946-47 and 1960-61** [316]

SI. No.	Management	Number of Institutions				Increase/ Decrease	
		1946-47		1960-61			
		Boys	Girls	Boys	Girls	Boys	Girls
01	Central Government						
02	State Government	17	04	175	15	+158	+11
03	District Board	54	05			-54	-05
04	Municipalities			08	02	+08	+02
05	Private Aided	128	11	651	70	+523	+59
06	Private Unaided	54		296	01	+242	+01
	Total	**253**	**20**	**1130**	**88**	**+877**	**+68**

Scholars

There was a phenomenal increase in the number of scholars. Approximately, the total high school student population increased $1^X A$ times and the middle school student population by almost 7 times.

In 1946-47, the total number of students studying in high schools was 13,129 of which 12,393 were boys and 763 were girls. By 1960-61, the total enrolment had shot up to 100,976. The total number of boys had risen to 88,509 and that of girls to 12,467. Evidently, there was great imbalance of education amongst boys and girls. During this period, the total number of boys increased from 12,393 to 88,509 and the total number of girls studying in high schools from a mere 736 to 12,467. The increase in respect of enrolment in high schools of boys was 7.1 times and that of the girls by 16.9 times. The proportion of total male scholars to females was 7:1 approximately. The number of scholars studying in Post-Basic schools rose from 26 in 1954-55 to 2,961 in 1959-60.

---

316 Computed from the data available in the Reports on Progress of Education in Orissa from 1946-47 to 1960-61.

In these schools 24 boys and 2 girls were studying in 1954-55. By 1959-60, 2,367 boys and 592 girls were studying in these institutions.

The enrolment of all the middle schools was 14,818 in 1946-47 which rose to 97,716 in 1960-61. When the enrolment figures of 1960-61 of Senior Basic schools are added to this total, the overall enrolment was around 101,200. Thus it is seen that the enrolment in high schools and middle schools stood almost at par. But in a desirable educational situation, the enrolment of middle schools ought to be at least twice or thrice that of the high school enrolment. The craze for high school education was evident from the enrolment figures. The total number of middle schools was 2.75 times that of the total high schools. But the enrolment figures are almost equal. The high schools had higher enrolments whereas the middle schools were all very small institutions with low enrolments. The enrolments of boys increased from 13,724 in 1946-47 to 82,539 in 1960-61 and of girls the increase was from 1,094 to 15,177 during this period. Senior Basic schools were started in 1950-51. The total enrolment in Senior Basic Schools in 1950-51 was 129 boys and 102 girls which in 1958-59 was 3,066 and 726 respectively. The total enrolment in Senior Basic Schools rose from 231 in 1950-51 to 3,792 in 1958-59.

The total number of scholars in High schools and Middle Schools from 1946-47 to 1960-61[317] was as follows:

---

317 *Ibid.*

TABLE 5.2.6

Scholars in Secondary Schools from 1946-47 to 1960-61

SI. No.	Year	High Schools			Middle Schools		
		Boys	Girls	Total	Boys	Girls	Total
01	1946-47	12393	736	13129	13724	1094	14818
02	1947-48	13508	854	14362	15904	1193	17097
03	1948-49	35299	2675	37974	38279	5321	43600
04	1949-50	40582	3311	43893	40647	5570	46217
05	1950-51	44523	3400	47923	42179+129*	5619+102*	47798+231*
06	1951-52	48567	4417	52984	41876+121*	5945+83*	47821+204*
07	1952-53	50903	5205	56108	43066+184*	6208+03*	49274+187*
08	1953-54	51798	5663	57461	43068+576*	6238+160*	49306+736*
09	1954-55	52362+24**	6413+02**	58775+26**	45635+1501*	6647+402*	52282+1903*
10	1955-56	58234+42**	7111+03**	65345+45**	48273+1754*	7679+430*	55952+2184*
11	1956-57	63039+68**	7950+06**	70989+74**	51294+2069*	7499+509*	58795+2578*
12	1957-58	70887+88**	9315+03**	80202+91**	56083+2842*	8455+682*	64538+3524*
13	1958-59	74899+69**	10173+00**	84772+69**	64279+3066*	2599+726*	73878+3792*
14	1959-60	80133+2101**	10272+592**	90405+2691**	74019	12610	86629
15	1960-61	88509	12467	100976	82539	15177	97716

* Senior Basic Schools (SBS) ** Post-Basic Schools (PBS)

Teachers

In 1947-48, in all there were 1,381 teachers working in the various high schools of Orissa as against 5,314 during 1960-61. The total male teachers working in high schools in 1946-47 was 1,295 out of which 612 (i.e. 47.2%) were trained and 683 (i.e. 52.8%) were untrained. In 1960-61, there were 4,936 male teachers who were working in the high schools of the State. Of these 2,203 (i.e. 44.6%) were trained and 2,733 (i.e. 55.4%) were untrained. During the period under review the numberof trained male teachers decreased by 2.6%. The growth of high schools was slowly pushing the demand for trained teachers higher and higher; and due to the lack of trained manpower the schools had to employ untrained teachers because schools cannot be shut down for dearth of trained personnel.

TABLE 5.2.7

Teachers in High Schools[318]

SI. No.	Year	Men			Women			Total
		Trained	Untrained	Total	Trained	Untrained	Total	
01	1947-48	612	683	1295	69	17	86	1381
02	1960-61	2203	2733	4963	298	80	378	5314

In 1947-48, there were 86 female teachers in high schools of whom 69 (i.e. 80.2%) were trained teacher and 17 (i.e. 19.8%) were untrained. By 1960-61,there were 378 female teachers of whom 298 (78.8%) were trained and 80 (i.e. 21.2%) were untrained. With the growth of female education the steady increase of untrained teachers is discernible. Table No. 5.2.7 indicates the position of teachers in High School.

The total number of male teachers in middle schools in 1947-48 was 1,390, out of which 747 (53.7%) were trained teachers and 643 (46.3%) were untrained teachers. By 1960-61, the number of male teachers in

---

318 *Ibid*

middle schools rose to 4,546; out of which 1.329 (29.2%) were trained teachers and 3,217 (70.8%) were untrained.

The total number of female teachers in middle schools in 1947-48 was 107, out of which 83 (77.5%) were trained and 24 (22.5%) were untrained. By 1960-61, the number of female teachers went up to 305, out of which 170 (55.8%) were trained and 135 (44.2%) were untrained.

There were more untrained teachers among male teachers. The situation called for urgent remedial action by opening adequate training colleges and schools.

The total number of teacher in 1947-48 in middle schools both male and female was 1,497, out of which 830 were trained and 867 were untrained. By 1960-61, the total number of Middle School teachers shot up from 1,497 to 4,851; of these 1,499 were trained and 3,352 were untrained. Table No. 5.2.8 depicts the situation of teachers in Middle Schools in 1947-48 and 1960-61. [319]

TABLE 5.2.8

Teachers in Middle Schools

SI. No.	Year	Men			Women			Total
		Trained	Untrained	Total	Trained	Untrained	Total	
01	1947-48	747	643	1390	83	24	107	1497
02	1960-61	1329	3217	4546	170	135	305	4851

The standard staff of a High School was revised in 1949-50. It was fixed as three trained graduates, one I.Sc. teacher, one classical teacher and 2 trained matriculates.[320] During 1950-51, the standard staff of a Middle School was revised and a fifth teacher was added. [321]In 1947-48, the

---

319 Report on the Progress of Education in Orissa, 1947-48 (Sec. Edn. Middle schools) © iii.

320 Report on the Progress of Education in Orissa, 1947-48, 1957-58, Table 26.

321 Report on the Progress of Education in Orissa, 1947-48,. Middle schools (c) iii

pay of teachers in Government Schools was revised with effect from 1st April 1947.[322] In 1949-50, the Government of Orissa in their Resolution No. 3061/E dated 10.4.1949 revised the scales of pay of Aided School teachers. The Government prescribed model scales of pay for the teachers of aided schools.[323] The scale of pay of teachers were again revised in 1959-60.[324]

Pre-service training facilities were extended for teachers by the establishment of a number of Secondary Training Schools and Basic Training Schools in the State. During 1955-56, the Basic Training College, Angul was started with an intake capacity of 48 students.[325] During 1959-60, an Extension Service Department was started and was attached to the Radhanath Training College, Cuttack. It was started at the instance of the All India Council of Secondary Education. During 1960-61, this was transferred to the Government. It purported to provide in-service training and academic guidance to serving teachers. During the same year the Board of Secondary Education conducted two Refresher Courses for secondary school teachers — one in Mathematics and one in Science*[326]

The total expenditure on Education in 1947-48 was Rs. 24,88,475which rose to Rs. l,38,83,287in 1960-61. The expenditure in 1960-61 was 5Vz times that of 1947-48.

The expenditure for High schools — both boys and girls, went up from Rs. 15,80,120in 1947-48 to Rs. 87,72,268in 1960-61. The expenditure on account of Middle Schools went up from Rs. 9,08,358to Rs. 51,11,109during the same period. The expenditure on account of secondary education includes the expenditure incurred on Higher Secondary Schools also.[327]

---

322 Report on the Progress of Education in Orissa, 1947-48, 1949-50. p. 19
323 Report on the Progress of Education in Orissa, 1947-48 to 1960-61.
324 Report on the Progress of Education in Orissa, 1949-50, p. 18
325 Report on the Progress of Education in Orissa, 1954-55. p. 40
326 Report on the Progress of Education in Orissa from 1947-48 to 1960-61
327 Report on the Progress of Education in Orissa,! 949-50, p. 17

TABLE 5.2.9

Expenditure on Secondary Education

Sl. No.	Year	High Schools			Middle Schools			Total expenditure on Secondary Educadon
		Boys	Girls	Total	Boys	Girls	Total	
01	1947-48	1453141	126977	1580120	793826	114529	908355	2488475
02	1948-49	....	....	2165372	....	....	1341206	3506578
03	1949-50	2327853	228950	2556803	152666	126245	1628911	4185714
04	1950-51	2976318	237070	3213388	1971412	153467	2124879	5338267
05	1951-52	3177596	223467	3401063	1912325	161462	2073787	5474850
06	1952-53	3586718	269902	3856620	2376366	171809	2548175	6404795
07	1953-54	3919101	323133	4242234	2561076	204521	2765597	7007831
08	1954-55	4331403	334969	4666362	2742668	201965	2944633	7610995
09	1955-56	4625223	409935	5035158	2881400	213710	3095110	8130268
10	1956-57	5012319	440875	5453194	3154019	263614	341763	8870827
11	1957-58	5701841	465258	6167099	3371105	302767	3673872	9840971
12	1958-59	....	....	6716305	....	....	3965495	10917806
13	1959-60	....	....	7781945	....	....	4616582	12398527
14	1960-61	....	....	8772268	....	....	5111019	13883287

During 1947-48, the cost per pupil in a Boys' High School was Rs. 50.75 and that of a Girls' High School was Rs. 80.25. Girls' High schools were few and the enrolment was low. Therefore, the cost per pupil was higher in the Girls' High schools. By 1960-61, there was an appreciable expansion of High schools for both boys and girls and the per capita cost was Rs. 86.90 for both boys and girls studying in high schools.

The per capita cost duringl 947-48 for a pupil in the Boys' Middle School was Rs. 29.25 and that in the Girls' Middle Schools was Rs. 45.56. By 1960-61, the per capita cost of a pupil in a Middle School was Rs. 52.19. Of course, the per capita cost has been stated in terms of current prices and not constant prices. In this connection, it may be stated that unification in the rates of tuition fees of boys and girls in all classes of secondary schools was effected in 1949-50.[328]

---

328 Report on the Progress of Education in Orissa, 1950-51, Chapter V, Control item iv.

Examination Results

From the examination results, it is seen that the number of candidates appearing at the Matriculation Examination (called the High School Certificate Examination since 1955) and Middle School Examination and passing the said examinations was increasing from year to year.

Only 4,712 boys and 194 girls had appeared at the Matriculation Examination in 1947-48, out of whom 2,744 boys and 129 girls passed it. By 1960-61, the number of boys and girls appearing at this examination had risen to 17,647 and 1,355, out of which 8,010 boys and 704 girls passed the said examination.

The number of boys that appeared at the Middle School Examination was 10,593 and that of girls was 603 in 1949-50. Out of these 8,702 boys and 534 girls passed the examination. By 1960-61, the number of boys and girls appearing at the Middle School Examination increased up to 28,914 and 3,071 respectively and the number of passes were 24,267 and 2,460 respectively.

Table No. 5.2.10 indicates the examination results of the period under review.[329]

TABLE 5.2.10

Results at the Matriculation and Middle School Examinations

MATRICULATION RESULTS

No.	Year	Appeared			Passed		
		Boys	Girls	Total	Boys	Girls	Total
01	1947-48	4712	194	4906	2744	129	2872
02	1948-49	Figures not available					
03	1949-50	6150	262	6412	2885	168	3053
04	1950-51	6471	359	6830	3003	149	3152
05	1951-52	7528	403	7931	2887	**167**	3055
06	1952-53	Figures not available					

---

329 Report on the Progress of Education in Orissa, 1947-48. p. 5

No.	Year	Appeared			Passed		
		Boys	Girls	Total	Boys	Girls	Total
07	1953-54	8379	447	8826	3634	208	3842
08	1954-55	9974	534	10508	4463	287	4750
09	1955-56	8600	561	9161	4258	335	4583
10	1956-57	9874	673	10520	4804	366	5170
11	1957-58	11799	852	12651	6103	517	6620
12	1958-59	13684	895	14579	7267	548	7815
13	1959-60	17497	1163	18660	8313	691	9004
14	1960-61	17647	1355	19002	8010	704	8714

MIDDLE SCHOOL RESULTS

No.	Year	Appeared			Passed		
		Boys	Girls	Total	Boys	Girls	Total
01	1949-50	10593	603	11196	8702	534	9236
02	1950-51	9818	525	10343	8444	434	8878
03	1951-52	12222	763	12985	10763	676	11439
04	1952-53	Figures not available					
05	1953-54	13979	1091	15070	5701	426	6127
06	1954-55	15460	1282	16744	12222	1063	13285
07	1955-56	15541	1274	16815	12096	1079	13175
08	1956-57	16846	1537	18303	13186	1153	14339
09	1957-58	17730	1836	19566	14020	1361	14381
10	1958-59	21080	2041	23121	17435	1795	19230
11	1959-60	Figures not available					
12	1960-61	28914	3071	31985	24267	2460	26727

During 1955-56, the Middle English Examination was reorganized and the students of High School were made eligible to appear at this examination.

Ten per cent of the students studying in High School were granted free-studentships as before. Education was made free in all Middle Vernacular Schools in1947-48. With effect from 1955-56 education up to class V was made free. Consequendy, students studying in Class IV and V of the M. E Schools and High schools were exempted from payment of fees. To make good the loss incurred by the aided schools due to this scheme, they were compensated by the Government.[330]During 1957-58, the system of scholarships was revised. One hundred seventeen Middle School Merit Scholarships @ Rs. 5 per month and 398 Middle School Merit-cum-Poverty Scholarships at the rate of Rs. 15 per month were instituted.[331]

It was realized that the Scheduled Castes and the Scheduled Tribes are the weaker sections of the society. They were educationally disadvantaged. To encourage the Scheduled Caste and Scheduled Tribe students to prosecute studies, they were exempted from payment of fees in the Middle English Schools during 1947-48.[332]During 1949-50, Scheduled Caste and Scheduled Tribe students were granted stipends and lumpsum grants. The total expenditure on this account came to Rs. 3,45,456 during the year.[333]

The total amount spent on scholarships during 1947-48 was Rs. 2,06,960. By 1960-61, the Government was spending yearly Rs. 18,28,399on this account. The increase was almost eighteen times. Equalization of educational opportunities and providing access to education to the weaker sections of the society compelled the government to increase the expenditure on this account from year to year. Table No. 5.211 depicts the amount of money expended on scholarships from 1947-48 to 1960-61.[334]

---

330 Report on the Progress of Education in Orissa,1949-50. p. 18
331 Report on the Progress of Education in Orissa, 1959-60, Sec. Edn. Administration. Item 4 & 5
332 Report on the Progress of Education in Orissa,1955-56. p. 30
333 Report on the Progress of Education in Orissa,1959-60 p. 72
334 Report on the Progress of Education in Orissa,1956-57. p. 69

TABLE 5.2.11

Amount Expended on Scholarships

SI. No.	Year	Amount spend on Scholarships
01	1947-48	2,06,960
02	1948-49	5,16,278
03	1949-50	6,91,345
04	1950-51	9,52,720
05	1951-52	2,53,032
06	1952-53	Not available
07	1953-54	3,92,580
08	1954-55	4,01,752
09	1955-56	6,81959
10	1956-57	8,99,051
11	1957-58	10,93,101
12	1958-59	14,14,409
13	1959-60	14,91,766
14	1960-61	18,28,399

It is observed from the above table that there was a sharp rise of expenditure on scholarships from 1947-48 to 1950-51. Then, there was a sudden fall in 1951-52. This is because prior to 1951-52, the stipends and lump grants given to Scheduled Caste and Scheduled Tribe students were administered by the Education Department. However, consequent upon the creation of a new Department of Tribal and Rural Welfare of the Government of Orissa to look after the welfare of the Scheduled Caste and Scheduled Tribes, the administration of these scholarships, stipends and lump grants was transferred to the new Department. Consequendy, the expenditure on scholarships of the Education Department showed a sharp decline in 1951-52.

Size of the Class

During 1949-50, the Government decided that the maximum number of students in secondary classes should not exceed 40. In view of this roll strength of the class, the size of the classroom was prescribed as 24' X 15'. Every student was to be provided with 10 to 12 sq. feet of space. 18" desk space was to be provided for every pupil.[335]In 1954-55, the Government revised its previous decision and stated that the maximum size of the Class VI and VII should not exceed 45 students and in cases of VIII, IX and X, XI the maximum roll strength should not exceed 50 in each class. Therefore, the size of the classroom, it was stated, should be 26' X 20'. In cases where adequate breadth of the classes could not be maintained, the length should be extended.[336]

School Buildings

There were no residential schools. However, many schools had hostels attached to them. During 1947-48, grants were paid to schools for repair under the post-war reconstruction programme. Table 5.2.12 indicates the expenditure on account of buildings and repairs in the various years.[337]

TABLE 5.2.12

Expenditure on School Buildings and Repairs

SI. No.	Year	Expenditure on Buildings and Repairs
01	1949-50	2,00,000
02	1950-51	75,000
03	1951-52	75,000
04	1953-54	2,04,632
05	1954-55	2,50,303
06	1955-56	8,61,026
07	1956-57	4,58,852
08	1957-58	31,53,000

---

335 Report on the Progress of Education in Orissa, 1955-56,p. 39
336 Report on the Progress of Education in Orissa, 1959-60 p. 68.
337 Report on the Progress of Education in Orissa, Sec. Edn. High schools, item vii.

Many schools in the ex-State areas had inadequate buildings and buildings were in disrepair. These required to be repaired and money was spent under the post-war reconstruction programme. The unprecedented floods and cyclone of 1954 did great damage to the schools in the costal areas. Consequently, there was heavy expenditure on this account in the subsequent years. Expenditure relating to the years 1959-60 and 1960-61 have not been mentioned in the official reports.

BOARD OF SECONDARY EDUCATION, ORISSA

It had long been felt that a separate Board of Secondary Education ought to be constituted for the State of Orissa. As early as 1946, a Committee had been appointedunder the Chairmanship of Pandit Godavarish Mishra to consider this question. As per the Orissa Secondary Education Act, 1953, the Government was authorized to constitute a statutory body to look after secondary education to be known as the Board of Secondary Education, Orissa. The Board of Secondary Education thus constituted by the Government had its first meeting in the month of April,1956.[338]Bye-Laws were framed and appointment of members to different Committees was made at this meeting. The Board conducted the High School Certificate Examination of July, 1956 for the first time.[339] In 1959-60, it conducted the Higher Secondary Examination (Part-1) for the first time.[340] The Utkal University was freed from conducting the Matriculation Examination from July, 1956.

Innovations of Importance

Some of the noteworthy experiments in the field of secondary education immediately after independence were:

(i) During 1950-51, special schools for Scheduled Tribe students were established. They were known as Ashram Schools and were patterned on the Gandhian philosophy of education. Sri Chintamani Mishra, a

---

338 *Ibid.*

339 *Ibid.*

340 Report on the Progress of Education in Orissa,1949-50

Veteran Gandhian and freedom fighter, was the first Director of the Tribal & Rural Welfare Department and was mainly instrumental in establishing these schools with a new deal for the tribal children. (ii) The Multi-Purpose Higher Secondary Schools recommended by the Secondary Education Commission (1 952-53) were established. Some high schools were upgraded and converted into Higher Secondary Schools in 1957-58. (iii) In 1951-52, one Senior Basic School was started; and by 1960-61, there were 23 such schools. They were schools with classes I to VIII based on the Gandhian approach to education. (iv) In 1954, a Post-Basic School was started at Mendhasala and by 1956-57 their number was two. A Post-Basic School is a higher secondary school based on the Gandhian principles of Basic Education. (v) Board of Secondary Education, Orissa was established in 1955.

Curricular Changes

i. During the academic session 1947-48, the North Orissa syllabus wasintroduced in the high schools of South Orissa.

ii. Teaching of General Science was made compulsory in all the high schools of the state. Necessary grants were given to Aided High Schools to provide the necessary facilities to introduce the teaching of General Science.

iii. Oriya was made the medium of instruction in all the high schools of Orissa from 1947-48. However, the bi-lingual high schools of Ganjam and Koraput districts and the Orient Paper Mill High School, Brajrajnagar were exempted from this stipulation.

iv. Teaching of Hindi was made compulsory in classes VT to XI in 1949-50.

v. Two periods for Supervised Study and one period for General Knowledgeper week were allotted in 1949-50.

vi. Technical subjects were introduced in some high schools of Orissa during 1951-52.

vii. Vocational subjects like Carpentry, Agriculture, Paper-making were introduced in some high schools during 1947-48

viii. Agriculture was introduced as an optional subject in the high schools at Nawarangpur, Hinjilicut, G. Udayagiri, Khurdha, Nayagarh, Karanjia, Champua, Sonepur and Tihidi. A grant of Rs. 550 per school was sanctioned for the purchase of agricultural implements.

ix. The new courses of studies for classes VI & VII prescribed by the Board of Secondary Education, Orissa were introduced in the academic session 1960-61.

x. During 1947-48, teaching of Hindustani was introduced in the middle schools on an experimental basis. Teaching of Hindi became compulsory in the middle schools from 1949-50.

xi. Vocational training on agriculture, carpentry, canework, tailoring and paper-making was given in 26 middle schools in 1947-48.

xii. During 1950-51, some features of the Basic Schools patterned after the Gandhian system of education were introduced in the middle schools. An amount of Rs. 1,80,000 was spent during 1956-57 for the introduction of the features of Basic Education in the middle schools. During 1957-58, Craft was introduced in 60 Middle English Schools.

xiii. During 1953-54, a sum of Rs. 24,000was spent for the improvement of 24 school libraries and during 1955-56, a sum of Rs. 1,00,000 was also spent for the improvement of the school libraries.

xiv. The Board of Secondary Education, Orissa mooted the idea of experimenting with the Structural Approach to the teaching of English in October,1960.

Co-Curricular Activities

Physical education and co-curricular activities were accorded greater importance. Mass Drill, Boy Scouts and Girl Guides, and sports competitions were organized. School excursions and dramatic performances gained increasing popularity. Auxiliary Cadet Corps was introduced in some high schools from 1955-56. In 1956-57, it was named the National Cadet Corps.

The Inspectors of Physical Education were placed under the administrative control of the Inspectors of Schools with effect from 1947-48 to streamline the supervision of physical education. Daily health inspection and Hygiene Parades had become common school practices. The School Medical Officers was in charge of the examination of the health of the students in government schools. In case of other school this aspect was looked after by the District Health Officer and doctors of local dispensaries.

Nutritional deficiency was noticed among school children and especially of those belonging to the Scheduled Castes. In 1947-48, multivitamin tablets were distributed among the students. Dry milk powder was distributed free of cost to sickly and needy students. Free mid-day meals were provided in some schools.

Class Councils, Courts of Honour, Co-operative Societies, Poor Boys, Fund, Self-government in the schools, thrift and small savings were experimented in a few schools.

FIRST EDUCATIONAL SURVEY, 1957

From 1947-48 to 1960-61, there was phenomenal growth in the field of secondary education. However, the growth rate was not uniform in all the districts. Grave inter-district and even intra-district imbalances were visible by 1957. The district-wise details of secondary education have been presented in Table No. 5.2.13.[341]

---

341 *Ibid.* p. 19

TABLE 5.2.13

District-wise Details of Secondary Education (31.12.1957)

SI. No.	Name of the District	Area in sq. miles	No. of Secondary Schools		No. of Pupils in		Average No. of Pupils attending		Area Served by one school in Sq. Miles	
			High and HSS	ME	High and HSS	ME	High and HSS	ME	High and HSS	ME
01	Cuttack	4210	129	299	31810	31710	247	106	19	14
02	Puri	4043	50	144	13367	12580	267	87	81	28
03	Balasore	2507	53	150	11042	11705	208	78	46	17
04	Sambalpur	6765	32	117	7027	6947	220	59	218	58
05	G an jam	3315	53	76	15018	4896	383	65	63	44
06	Mayurbhanj	4021	25	85	4141	6522	167	77	161	47
07	Keonjhar	3216	18	55	2570	3856	143	17	178	58
08	Dhenkanal	4226	25	85	4811	5418	192	64	167	50
09	Bolangir	3412	12	38	2832	3226	194	35	287	90
10	Sundergarh	3768	18	65	3136	6052	184	82	235	57
11	Phulbani & Ganjam Agency	5692	10	32	1382	1833	138	57	569	178
12	Kalahandi	5057	13	31	1346	1643	104	53	391	163
13	Koraput	8975	12	41	2993	1329	248	55	822	219

Source: First Educational Survey, 1957

Cuttack was the most populous district with 25.2 lakhs of population. It had the largest number of high schools as well as middle schools compared to any other district. The enrolment was also the highest in respect of high schools and middle schools. There was one High School for every 19 Sq. Miles and a middle school for every 14 sq.miles of area of this district. There was one high school for every 18,727 persons of the population and middle schools for every 3,459 persons. Cuttack was the most advanced district in respect of secondary education in 1960-61. Next to Cuttack, Puri district had the maximum number of scholars in secondary schools. The average number of pupils attending the high schools was 267 per school which is second highest among the districts. High school education was very good in Ganjam;but middle school education was lagging behind. Phulbani was the most backward district in respect of secondary education. The position of Kalahandi and Koraput was equally deplorable. Among the ex-State areas Dhenkanal had made maximum headway leaving Mayurbhanj behind. The inter-district imbalances needed to be remedied. The First All India Educational Survey conducted in 1957-58 brought out in clear relief these glaring disparities and the educational planners became sensitive to the problem.

SECONDARY EDUCATION IN ORISSA (1961-1966)

High Schools

There were 344 recognised High Schools for boys and 22 High Schools for girls; the total being 366 in 1961-62. The number of boys' high schools increased to 654, that of the girls' High School to 52 and the total to 706 by 1965-66.

There were two Higher Secondary Schools in 1960-61 which rose to 11 by 1965-66. The 11 Higher Secondary Schools of 1965-66 included 2 Post-Basic Schools.

Table No. 5.2.14 indicates the number of High schools in Orissa during 1961-62.[342]

---

342 *Ibid.* p. 20

TABLE 5.2.14

Number of High Schools in Orissa 1961-62 to 1965-66

SI. No.	Year	Number of High Schools recognized during the year	Total number of High Schools in the State in the year
01	1961-62	53	366
02	1962-63	59	422
03	1963-64	109	530
04	1964-65	80	606
05	1965-66	106	706

The expansion of women's education was noteworthy.[343] Table No. 5.2.15 indicates the growth of secondary school population during the quinquennium under review.[344]

TABLE 5.2.15

Enrolment in High Schools of Orissa 1960-61 to 1965-66

SI. No.	Year	Class VIII	Class IX	Class X	Class XI	Total
01	1961-62	20030	18853	14326	10176	63385
02	1962-63	26404	22046	18176	13170	79796
03	1963-64	NA	NA	NA	NA	NA
04	1964-65	34716	34716	24354	18729	107680
05	1965-66	37921	37921	26889	21080	119604

The total High School population rose from 63,385 to 1,19,604. There were 284 students studying in Class XII of the Higher Secondary Schools in Orissa in 1962-63. The number rose to 598 in 1965-66. Higher Secondary Schools did not flourish well. Four of the Higher Secondary Schools were converted into High School during 1965-66.

---

343 Report on the Progress of Education in Orissa, 1951-52, p. 7 and Report on the Progress of Education in Orissa, 1956-57 p. 68

344 Report on the Progress of Education in Orissa,! 947-48, p. 14 (viii Experiments)

Middle Schools

The number of Middle schools rose from 1,218 in 1960-61 to 3,310 in 1965-66.[345]The number of scholars studying in Middle schools rose from 97,716 in 1960-61 to 2,51,000 in 1965-66.[346] By 1965-66, both High schools and Middle schools had expanded greatiy and enrolment in these schools was spiraling. It was a period of rapid quantitative growth. Out of every 100 students in class I, 14 students were attending the middle schools and only 3.3 students were studying in high schools. This indicates the magnitude of wastage and drop-out rates at the secondary level. The percentage of rural population with Middle School facility within their own habitation or within a distance of 3 kms. Was 74.8.[347]Percentage of population served by High schools was 65.1% in 1965-66.[348] The average population served by a Middle section was 5,522 and by a High School section was 22,070 in 1965-66.[349] The number of teachers working in the Middle schools was 11,184 in 1965-66. Table No. 5.2.16 indicates the qualifications and training of Middle school teachers.[350]

---

345 Report on the Progress of Education in Orissa, 1949-50, p. 20

346 Report on the Progress of Education in Orissa, 1950-51, Secondary Education Reorganisation & Development, item 1.

347 Report on the Progress of Education in Orissa, 1956-57, p. 67

348 Report on the Progress of Education in Orissa, 1957-58 p. 55

349 Report on the Progress of Education in Orissa, 1960-61, p. 71

350 Report on the Progress of Education in Orissa, 1950-51, Reorganisation & Development, item 6.

TABLE 5.2.16

Qualifications and Trainingof Teachers of Middle Schools, 1965-66

SI. No.	Qualification	Men			Women			All Teachers		
		Trained	Un-Trained	Total	Trained	Un-Trained	Total	Trained	Un-Trained	Total
01	Less than Matriculation	167	143	310	20	38	58	187	181	368
02	Matriculation	2178	6113	8291	221	367	588	2399	6480	8879
03	Intermediate	446	705	1151	22	57	79	468	762	1230
04	Graduate	211	162	373	29	37	66	240	199	439
05	Post-Graduate	8	7	15	4	1	5	12	8	20
06	Others	164	54	218	24	6	30	188	60	248
	Total	3174	7184	10358	320	506	826	3474	7690	11184

The number of untrained teachers was more than double that of the trained teachers.

There were 7,831 teachers working in the various high schools of Orissa in 1965-66. Table No. 5.2.17 indicates the qualification and training of high school teachers during 1965-66.[351]

TABLE 5.2.17

Qualification and Training of Teachers of High Schools, 1965-66

Sl. No.	Qualification	Men			Women			All Teachers		
		Trained	Un-Trained	Total	Trained	Un-Trained	Total	Trained	Un-Trained	Total
01	Less than Matriculation	22	25	47	7	1	8	29	26	55
02	Matriculation	312	516	528	71	38	109	383	554	937
03	Intermediate	354	1068	1422	23	33	56	377	1101	1478
04	Graduate	1990	1506	3496	277	62	306	2234	1568	3802
05	Post-Graduate	129	91	220	21	11	32	150	102	252
06	Others	688	537	1225	64	18	82	752	555	1307
	Total	3495	3743	7238	430	163	593	3925	3906	7831

[62] Report on the Progress of Education in Orissa, 1953-54, Chapter V. Item xiii.

351

In case of high schools the number of untrained teachers was more than that of the trained teachers. During the period 1961-62 to 1965-66, there was great progress both in case of middle schools and high schools. The enrolment was increasing at a much more rapid pace. But the number of trained teachers was steadily declining. The quantitative expansion adversely affected the qualitative aspect of secondary education.

SECTION-III

DEVELOPMENT OF SECONDARY EDUCATION IN ORISSA (1966-1985)

LEGISLATION RELATING TO SECONDARY EDUCATION

The following Acts passed by the Orissa Legislature have influenced the implementation of the National Policy on Education, 1968 which had endorsed almost all the recommendations contained in the Indian Education (Kothari) Commission Report of 1966. These legislations were:

- Orissa Education Act, 1969.
- Orissa Secondary Education (Amendment) Act,1979.
- Orissa Aided Educational Institutions (Appointment of Teachers Validation) Act 1978 & 1981.
- Orissa Educational Institutions (Supersession of Managing Committee) Validation Act,1979.
- Orissa Subordinate Education Service (Validation of Appointment) Act, 1982.
- Orissa Higher Secondary Education Act,1982.

IMPLEMENTATION OF NPE, 1968

(i) 10+2+3 Pattern and Orissa

The Board of Secondary Education, Orissa accepted, in principle, the introduction of vocational education in the context of 10+2+3 pattern during 1973-74.[352]

During 1974-75, the Board decided in principle to introduce the 10+2+3 scheme.[353]The Board had introduced the new pattern of education from die school session 1976-77.[354] The frame-work for the studies for grades 7 tolO has been prepared. Necessary approval was obtained from Government for amendment of the Regulations for incorporating the changes in the courses of studies. It accepted 'work-experience' as an integral part of the new curriculum. It introduced work-experience programmes in some High Schools in collaboration with the Khadi and Village Industries Board. The instructions received from Government of Orissa in 1977-78 for conversion of the 11 years structure to the 10 year pattern were as follows:[355]

"That Class XI has been renamed grade 10, Class X grade 9 and so on up to Class I which has been renamed grade I. The age of entry for grade I will be 6+. As the Board of Secondary Education used to deal with the curriculum of the four High School classes from grade 7 to grate 10., the framework of the courses of studies was prepared by the Board for these four classes." An intensive programme was taken up in hand for re-orientation and revision of the syllabi for grades 7-10 during 1977-78.[356] It was also decided to introduce the new syllabus with effect from the academic session 1978-79.[357]

---

352 Report of the Indian Education Commission, 1964-65.
353 National Policy on Education, 1968
354 Report of Sardar Swaran Singh Committee
355 Constitution of India, 42nd Amendment
356 Annual Report of Board of Secondary Education, Orissa, 1973-74
357 Annual Report of Board of Secondary Education, Orissa, 1974-75

At this juncture, the Government of India announced the appointment of a Review Committee under the Chairmanship of Sri Iswarbhai Patel with regard to the pattern, course and content of school education. The Board at its General Body Meeting held on 30th September,1977 decided to postpone introduction of the new curriculum under 10+2 pattern of education by one year, as it anticipated certain fundamental changes in the whole set up. In the mean time, the Report of the Review Committee was published and the Board decided to set up a Committee consisting of specialists from different areas and of representatives from Government to give their specific views on the Report.[358] Consequent upon the re-thinking that was being given to the pattern of education, the Board for the time being suspended its programme for curriculum revision till final decisions are taken on the vital points. It had been decided to introduce the new curriculumfrom 1979-80 with the anticipation thatfirm decision would have been taken by that date. During 1978-79, an intensive programme was taken up in hand for reorientation and revision of the syllabi for grades 7 to 10 as per the guidelines provided by the National Council of Educational Research and Training (NCERT). The new pattern was introduced with effect from the academic session 1979-80.[359]It has generated a lot of opposition from students, teachers, parents, Teachers' Union etc.

(ii) Establishment of Council of Higher Secondary Education, Orissa

In pursuance of the provisions of the Orissa Higher Secondary Education Act,1982 the Council of Higher Secondary came into existence with effect from 7th September,1982. Its major functions are to regulate, control and develop higher secondary education in the State of Orissa in close collaboration and liaison with the Board of Secondary Education, Orissa on the one hand and the several Universities of the State on the other. It accords recognition to the institutions offering higher secondary education; prescribes detailed courses of studies for

---

358 Annual Report of Board of Secondary Education, Orissa, 1976-77
359 Annual Report of Board of Secondary Education,Orissa, 1977-78

each branch of study; prescribes or prepares textbooks for the courses conducts examinations and publishes results.

(iii) Vocationalization of Higher Secondary Education

Though the Indian Education Commission,1966 had strongly advocated the vocationalization of secondary education, no tangible action had been initiated in this regard by the Government of Orissa during the period 1966 to 1985. It was in a state of hibernation or suspended animation. The idea was attractive; but it did not gain any momentum during this period.

(iv) Changes in the Structure and Semantics of Secondary Education

The concept of secondary education was radically changed by the Indian Education Commission,!966' and had officially been endorsed by the National Policy onEducation, 1968. The classical concept of secondary education was that it is the "education of the adolescents" i.e. of boys and girls in the age group 12 years to 19 years. The education of the children 5+ or 6+ to 11+ was recognized as Primary education. Secondary Education has three divisions:

a. Lower Secondary Education comprised of post-primary education. It was the education of the pubescent and early adolescent years of 11+, 12+ and 13+; and was the education provided in classes VI, VII & VIII. These classes were located either in High Schools or Middle Schools.
b. Secondary Education comprised of the education provided to children of the ages 14+, 15+ & 16+ in classes IX, X and XI.
c. High Secondary Education was known as First Arts Classes (F.A), Intermediate Classes (I.A/I.Sc./I.Com) and later Pre-University course + Pre-Degree Course for youth of the ages 17+ & 18 +.
d. University education for the first degree commenced at the age of 19+.

Briefly, 'education for the children is primary education', 'education of the adolescents is secondary education', and 'education of the adults is higher or tertiary education'.

Article 45 of the Constitution of India states that, "The State shall endeavour to provide within a period of ten years from the commencement of this Constitution, for free and compulsory education for all children until they complete the age of 14 years."

The Constitution of India came into force with effect from 26th January, 1950. Therefore it ought to have provided basic education needed for optimum survival in a democratic ethos of eight years schooling comprising of five years of Primary Education plus three years of Lower Secondary Education. Even the Kothari Commission has referred to class VIII as being part of secondary education. But the bureaucrats who preside over the destinies of education from Shastri Bhawan of New Delhi termed the entire spectrums of the first eight years of schooling as 'Elementary Education'. Elementary education has two stages — primary stage consisting of classes I to V; and upper primary stage consisting of classes VI, VII & VIII. Administrative consideration took precedence over sound psychological and pedagogical arguments. The Table No. 5.3.1 below depicts the change in the education scenario. The age of entry was raised to 6+ in place of the earlier 5+.

Class	Structure of Education up to 1968		Post-NPE (1968) structure of Education	
	Age	Stage of Education	Age	Stage of Education
I	5+	Lower Primary	6+	Primary
II	6+	Lower Primary	7+	Primary
III	7+	Lower Primary	8+	Primary
rv	8+	Upper Primary	9+	Primary
V	9+	Upper Primary	10+	Primary
VI	10+	Lower Secondary	11 +	Upper Primary

Class	Structure of Education up to 1968		Post-NPE (1968) structure of Education	
VII	11 +	Lower Secondary	12+	Upper Primary
VIII	12+	Lower Secondary	13+	Upper Primary
IX	13+	Secondary	14+	Lower Secondary
X	14+	Secondary	15+	Lower Secondary
XI	15+	Secondary	16+	Higher Secondary
XII	16+	Higher Secondary Higher Secondary	17+	Higher Secondary
XIII	17+	Higher Secondary (also called IA/ PU+PP)	18+ 19+ 20+	B. A/B. Sc/B. Com First Degree Higher Education
First Degree	18+	B. A/B. Sc/B. Com		
	19+	Higher Education		

The total time required for completing the first degree is 15 years in both the cases - (a) 11+2+2 and (b) 10+2+3. However, the importance and duration of primary education has increased; Middle school education is classified as elementary education; class VIII has been incorporated in elementary education.

Middle school education has become an organic part of elementary education with the acceptance of 10+2+3 pattern of education. Higher secondary education has become part of the spectrum of secondary education. Hence discussion relatingto middle school education has been omitted, and higher secondary education has been accorded special importance in view of the changed context.

Different agencies report the expansion of secondary education in different ways - some restrict them to full-fledged schools recognized by the Board of Secondary Education; some include higher secondary schools in this category; and some include or exclude secondary schools which impart instruction through Sanskrit or Urdu. Hence, there are differences.

The number of high schools which are full-fledged and are recognized by the Board of Secondary Education, Orissa have been shown in Table No. 5.3.2.

TABLE 5.3.2

Full-fledged High Schools Recognized by Board of SecondaryEducation, Orissa

SI. No.	Year	Number of Schools		
		Boys	Girls	Total
01	1966-67	759	71	830
02	1967-68	887	88	973
03	1968-69	1029	111	1140
04	1969-70	1198	134	1332
05	1970-71	1260	147	1407
06	1971-72	1350	178	1528
07	1972-73	1429	190	1619
08	1973-74	1515	191	1706
09	1974-75	1594	195	1789
10	1975-76	1656	199	1855
11	1976-77	1679	200	1879
12	1977-78	1822	213	2035
13	1978-79	1880	219	2099

Source: Records of Board of Secondary Education, Orissa.

These 2,099 secondary schools are full-fledged institutions. If the incomplete proposed high school are included, the number of high schools stood at 2,167 on 30.9.1978.

The number of teachers according to sex and training working in the recognized full-fledged high schools of Orissa has been shown in Table No. 5.3.3.

TABLE NO. 5.3.3

Training and untrained/Male & Female Teachers working in the High Schools of Orissa 1965-66 to 1978-79

Sl. No.	Category of Teachers	1965-66	1973-74	1978-79
1	Men	7238	14077	18080
2.	Women	593	1751	2929
	Total	**7831**	**15828**	**21009**
3.	Trained	3925	9873	14255
4.	Untrained	3906	5955	6754
	Total	**7831**	**15828**	**21009**

During 1978-79, every high school was serving a population of 11,388 as against 11,832 in 1973-74. Development of secondary education was not uniform in all the districts of Orissa and the district-wise position has been shown in TableNo. 5.3.4.

TABLE 5.3.4

High Schools District-wise 1978-79

Sl. No.	Name of the District	Complete	Incomplete	Total
1.	Phulbani	37	02	39
2.	Kalahandi	67	05	72
3.	Bolangir	87	01	88
4.	Koraput	85	13	98
5.	Keonjhar	100	02	102
6.	Sundergarh	116	03	119
7.	Dhenkanal	120	06	126
8.	Ganjam	154	01	155
9.	Sambalpur	154	04	158
10.	Mayurbhanj	160	03	163
11.	Puri	242	03	245
12.	Balasore	294	02	296
13.	Cuttack	551	06	561
	Orissa State	2167	51	2218

The Board of Secondary Education, Orissa had recognized 2099 out of the total 2167 complete high schools; and the cases of 68 were under consideration. Cuttack, Balasore and Puri were advanced in secondary education and Kalahandi-Bolangir-Koraput (KBK) districts and Phulbani were very backward. The inter-district imbalances need immediate remediation to counteract simmering discontent in these disadvantaged districts.

The expansion of secondary education on the basis of 2nd, 3rd, 4th & 5th Educational Surveys has been depicted in Table No. 5.3.5

TABLE 5.3.5

Growth of High Schools, Number of Teachers, Enrolment & Teacher-Pupil Ratio[360]

Year	No. of High Schools	No. of Teachers	Enrolment in Classes IX & X	Teacher-Pupil Ratio	Remarks
1965-66	1,030	7,831	1,01,000	12.89	2nd Survey
1973-74	1,974	15,828	1,94,000	12.26	3rd Survey
1978-79	2,167	21,009	2,63,000	12.5	4th Survey
1986-87	3,955	35,313	4,08,000	11.55	5th Survey

There were 1,030 High Schools during 1965-66 and their number had increased to 3,955 by 1986-87. The net increase in number was 2,925. Almost 133 schools were established in an year on an average. The growth was more than 3.8 times during the period. There were 7,831 teachers working in these schools during 1965-66; and their number had increased to 35,313. It is an accretion of 27,462 teachers; and on an average every year more than 1,294 teachers were joining the work-force of the teaching community of the high schools. 1,01,000 students were studying in classes IX & X during 1965-66 and by 1986-87 their number had increased to 4,08,000. 3,07,000 additional students had gained access to secondary education. It amounts to an increase of

---

360 Ibid, p. 3

13,954 additional students every year on an average. The teacher-pupil ratio was 12.89 in 1965-66; 12.26 in 1973-74; 12.5 in 1978-79 and 11.55 in 1986-87. It is abysmally low and the teachers are not being utilized to the optimum level. The average student strength of a secondary class was 42 during 1965-66 and 1973-73. It had increased to 60.7 during 1978-79 and decreased to 51.6 during 1986-87.

As per the 3rd and 4th Educational Surveys of 1973 and 1978 the drop-out rates have been depicted in Table No. 5.3.6.

TABLE 5.3.6

Drop-out rates in Secondary class & Retention Index[361]

(For Every 100 Students enrolled in Class I)

Class	3rd Educational Survey,1973		4th Educational Survey 1978	
	Stay-in	Drop-outs	Stav-in	Drop-outs
VIII	10.69%	89.31%	17.61%	82.39%
XI	6.04%	93.96%	9.46%	90.54%

If 100 students were admitted in class I only 6.04 in 1973 and 9.46 students in 1982 could reach class XI, the highest class of the secondary school. There is an improvement of 3.42% retention over a period of 4 years and 9 months. Schools were performing better. The secondary school had become a common feature of rural areas; and it had lost its exclusive urban identity.

During 1978-79, every Middle School was serving a population of 3,792 as against 4,432 during 1973-74, and every High School was serving a population of 11,388 as against 11,832 in 1973-74.

The development of secondary education has not been uniform in all the districts of the State. The district-wise position of secondary schools in 1978-79 was as shown in Table No. 5.3.7.[362]

---

361 Ibid

362 Ibid

TABLE 5.3.7

District-wise Figures of Secondary Schools 1978-79

SI. No.	Name of District	High Schools		Middle Schools	
		Total	Incomplete	Total	Incomplete
01	Cuttack	551	06	1412	
02	Balasore	294	02	823	
03	Puri	242	03	679	04
04	Mayurbhanj	160	03	489	01
05	Sambalpur	154	04	550	06
06	Ganjam	154	01	434	01
07	Dhenkanal	120	06	413	01
08	Sundergarh	116	03	334	
09	Keonjhar	100	02	336	...
10	Bolangir	87	01	329	...
11	Koraput	85	13	.319	03
12	Kalahandi	67	05	218	02
13	Phulbani	37	02	171	08
	Orissa State	2167	51	6507	25

Of these 2,167 High schools in the State, 2,099 High schools were recognized by the Board of Secondary Education, Orissa. The rest of the Schools were awaiting recognition.

The most advanced district was Cuttack and the most backward district is Phulbani. The inter-district imbalance needs to be eliminated through proper planning.

The district-wise development of secondary education in Orissa from 1979-80 to 1985-86 has been depicted in Table No. 5.3.8.

TABLE 5.3.8[363]

Districtwise Development of High Schools from 1979-80 to 1985-86

District	1979-80	1980-81	1981-82	1982-83	1983-84	1984-85	1985-86
Koraput	77	84	87	102	107	112	123
Bolangir	87	93	103	110	119	124	143
Kalahandi	64	66	66	81	92	92	106
Phulbani	35	39	39	45	49	50	53
Dhenkanal	128	137	140	165	194	214	247
Keonjhar	110	130	147	158	176	190	214
Mayurbhanj	170	187	210	220	239	243	256
Sundergarh	117	122	125	132	135	139	149
Sambalpur	154	167	181	207	228	239	264
Ganjam	155	167	175	194	231	243	244
Puri	277	285	310	351	407	428	457
Balasore	318	345	376	405	450	458	501
Cuttack	585	618	660	732	793	828	900
Orissa	2277	2443	2619	2902	3220	3360	3657

The Koraput-Bolangir-Kalahandi (KBK) districts and Phulbani had the least number of high schools. The coastal districts of Cuttack, Balasore, Puri and Ganjam as well as Sambalpur had high levels of access to high school education. The ex-state areas and agency areas of south Orissa were lagging behind

Enrolment figures and number of teachers of secondary schools provide the picture of access and also the quality of instruction provided therein.

---

363 Annual Report of Board of Secondary Education, Orissa, From 1966-67 to 1977-78

TABLE 5.3.9

Enrolment of students in Secondary Schools[364]

District	1979-80	1980-81	1981-82	1982-83	1983-84	1984-85	1985-86
Phulbani	4	4	4	5	6	6	6
Kalahandi	6	7	8	8	8	9	11
Bolangir	9	10	14	14	14	15	15
Koraput	8	11	14	14	14	14	14
Keonjhar	12	14	15	15	15	16	17
Dhenkanal	14	16	17	17	17	20	22
Mayurbhanj	17	19	23	24	24	24	24
Sundergarh	18	20	21	21	21	23	25
Sambalpur	20	23	25	25	26	29	29
Ganjam	25	26	27	27	29	29	29
Balasore	32	37	40	41	41	48	50
Puri	36	43	46	47	49	50	52
Cuttack	82	90	99	100	100	104	109
Orissa	283	320	353	356	364	389	403

Source: Education in Orissa 1988-89, pp. 54 & 55

The high school enrolment of Cuttack district stood at 1,09,000 in 1985-86; and the enrolment of all the secondary schools of the seven districts i.e. Phulbani, Kalahandi, Bolangir, Koraput, Keonjhar, Dhenkanal and Mayurbhanj in the same year was also exacdy the same. Glaring regional disparities were clearly evident.

---

364 Educational Surveys of Orissa 2nd, 3rd, 4th & 5'

CHAPTER-6

NEW POLICY AND RENEWED HOPES

SECONDARY EDUCATION

FROM 1985 TO 2007

HIGHLIGHTS

- Challenge of Education, 1985
- National Policy on Education, 1986
- with modifications of 1992
- Programme of Action, 1986
- Ramamurti Review Committee, 1990
- Janardan Reddy Committee, 1991
- Programme of Action, 1992
- Initiatives to Augment Quality of Secondary
- Education
- National Curriculum Framework, 2000
- National Curriculum Framework, 2005
- Quantitative Growth of Secondary Education and Impact of:
  - Freedom
  - Planning
  - Growth of Population
  - Urbanization
  - Literacy

Growth of Secondary Education as per the Survey Reports, 1ˢᵗ to 7ᵗʰ

The Report of the Indian Education Commission, 1966 was a holistic appraisal of the total educational spectrum of India. The radical reforms recommended by it to put back the system on the rails of democracy and economic development were not implemented with the seriousness that they deserved. The National Policy on Education of 1968 practically endorsed its recommendation in their totality. 'Education' was in the 'State List' as per the Constitution of India that came into force with effect from 26ᵗʰ January, 1950. Every State of India was free to follow its own independent course of action relating to all educational matters. The well thought out recommendations of the various Commission and Committees were never implemented with sincerity and dedication. Every State was tinkering education with a few insignificant cosmetic changes. No state exhibited a revolutionary fervour to change the old order of education to suit the emerging needs of an independent nation wedded to a democratic philosophy and fast marching ahead to create a new social order based on the principles of equality. The *status quo ante* persisted. The legacy of the colonial educational system expanded and thrived. The Government of India appointed a task-force in 1985 to review the post-NPE, 1968 educational scenario. Its report entitled "Challenge of Education" (1985) made an in-depth analysis of the drawbacks and recommended remedial measures. The National Policy on Education, 1986 was formulated on the basis of these recommendations. Acharya Ramamurti Committee and Janandan Reddy Committee reviewed it. It was reformulated in 1992. A Programmes of Action were prepared to operationalise the NPE,1986 and its reformulation in 1992. Salient features relating to secondary education contained in these seminal documents have been highlighted.

CHALLENGE OF EDUCATION: A POLICY PERSPECTIVE (1985)

Twenty years had elapsed after the publication of the Indian Education Commission,1966 which had recommended many radical reforms in the field of education. The National Policy on Education, 1968 endorsed almost all the recommendations of the Commission of 1966. It also clearly stipulated "...a five yearly review of progress and working out of new policies and programmes."[365] During the British colonial rule, the Education Departments of the Provinces used to publish annual reports and quinquennial reports describing, in detail, all the aspects of education. In Orissa, the publication of annual reports of the Education Departmentwas discontinued from 1966 onwards due to thelethargyand lack of vision of the educational administrators of the times. In 1985, the Government of India constituted a Task Force to Review the post-NPE (1968) educational scenario. It contained, "...an overview of the State of education and pointers to the direction of future initiatives."Mr. K. C. Panth, Union Minister for Education, Government of India, frankly admitted in the Foreword to this document that,

> "The analysis of developments over die last two decades makes it. clear that desired improvements have not materialized because neidier the resources nor the measures for restructuring were commensurate with the imaginative and purposeful thrust of the educational policy adopted in 1968"

This document generated a lot of debate across the nation and provided the basis for the formulation of the National Policy on Education, 1986. This document admitted that:

- "A five-yearly review of the policies and programmes of education to be essential
- The challenges of the technological progress demand urgent reorientation of education to make it relevant and resilient
- The chasm of economic disabilities, regional imbalances and social injustice will widen further, resulting in the building up of disintegrative tensions"[366]

---

365 National Policy on Education, 1968, Govt, of India, New Delhi
366 *Ibid,* Para 1.1

In Chapter IV of this document entitled "An approach to Educational Reorientation", it has made certain cogent observations relating to secondary education. They are:

1. "By rolling back the first 2 years of college into the school structure, the age specific competence of children was fitted into the pedagogical system of school education. The rationale for the +2 system has, however, to some extent been undermined in the States where a large number of the students in the +2 stage have been enrolled in Junior Colleges". Orissa belongs to this category of States.[367]

2. The expenses in equipping schools with +2 stage are high.[368]

3. "...amongst practically all sections of the population and even amongst various sections of the intelligentsia, there is considerable difference of opinion about what constitutes the core of the 10+2 system. Some regard the +2 system as an innovation of great importance because of its accent on vocationalisation, while a sizeable proportion of experts in education regard it the new initiative to be concerned more with the content and pedagogy of education up to class 10 than with vocationalisation."[369]

It acknowledged 'the phenomenal expansion of secondary education during the period 1947-48 to 1982-83'.[370] "While a fourteen-fold increase has taken place in thenumber of schools, there has been a twenty-fold increase in enrolment with onlya ten-fold increase in teachers"[371], it noted. It aptly anticipated that "the pressure for expansion will most certainly continue and may indeed increase as the country progresses towards universal elementary education."[372] It emphasized

---

367 *Ibid,* Chapter IV p. 102 to 103
368 *Ibid.,* P. 105
369 *Ibid,* P. 104
370 *Ibid,* P.43
371 *ibid.*
372 *Ibid.*

the major challenge in the field of secondary education" "...on the one hand, meet the growing demand for Secondary Education and Higher Secondary Education and, on the other hand, ensure that the objective of qualitative viability does not get diluted."[373] It stated that "Norms have to be laid down regarding the minimum facilities to be provided to every secondary school in terms of laboratories, libraries, playgrounds etc."[374] It stated that equal opportunities need to be provided to both boys and girls in urban and rural areas to study science and mathematics so that the then prevailing "discriminatory situation...for the scientific and technological professions in favour of the urban and more affluent section of the society" [375]could be appropriately corrected. It exhorted the introduction of a common curricular system and the need for examination reforms.

NATIONAL POLICY ON EDUCATION 1986 (WITH MODIFICATION OF 1992)[376]

The National Policy on Education, 1986 stated after forty years of independence that:

> "**1.1.** Education has continued to evolve, diversify and extend its reach and coveragesince the dawn of human history. Every country develops its system of education to expressand promote its unique socio-cultural identity and also to meet the challenges of the times. There are moments in history when a new direction has to be given to an age-old process. That moment is to-day."

A sense of urgency and seriousness to evolve a country-specific relevant educational system is clearly evident. It reiterated the achievements in

---

373 *Ibid*, P.44
374 *Ibid*
375 *Ibid.*
376 National Policy on Education, 1986, MHRD, New Delhi, 1986, pp. 20 to 22.

the field ofeducation after the adoption of NPE,1968 and claimed that it had promoted,

"a sense of common citizenship and culture, and to strengthen national integration". During the period 1968 to 1986, there had been considerable expansion in educational facilities all over the country at all levels. It recognized, "...the acceptance of a common structure of education throughout the country and the introduction of the 10+2+3 system by most states" as the most notable development of the period. The inadequacy and irrelevance of the prevailing educational system was recognized; and stated:

"1.9. Education in India stands at die cross roads to-day. Neither normal linear expansion nor die existing pace and nature of improvement can meet the needs of the situation".

It candidly admitted that, "India's political and social life is passing through aphase which poses the danger of erosion to long-accepted values. The goals of

secularism, socialism, democracy and professional ethics are coming under increasingstrain" (1.11 P. 3). The urban-rural divide seems to be widening. The policy stated:

"1.12. The rural areas, with poor infrastructure and social services, will not get thebenefit of trained and educated youth, unless rural-urban disparities are reduced anddetermined measures are taken to promote diversification and dispersal of employmentopportunities" (p.4).

It could visualize that, "Life in the coming decades is likely to bring new tensions together with unprecedented opportunities" (1.14 P. 4) and that "new challenges and social needs" have to be met. It agreed with the basic theorem of Economics of Education that, "Education is a unique investment in the present and the future" (P. 5). The aims of School Education of which secondary education is the critical finishing stage have been outlined thus:

"The National System of Education will be based on a national curricular framework which contains a common core along with other components that are flexible. The common core will include the history of India's freedom movement, die constitutional obligations and other content essential to nurture national identity. These elements will cut across subject areas and will be designed to promote values such as India's common cultural heritage, egalitarianism, democracy and secularism, equality of the sexes, protection of the environment, removal of social barriers, observance of the small family norm and inculcation of the scientific temper. All educational programmes will be carried on in strict conformity with secular values."

"India has always worked for peace and understanding between nations, treating the whole world as one family. True to this hoary tradition, Education has to strengthen this world view and motivate the younger generations for international cooperation and peaceful co-existence. This aspect cannot be neglected".

"To promote equality, it will be necessary to provide for equal opportunity to all not only in access, but also in the conditions for success. Besides, awareness of the inherentEquality of all will be created through the core curriculum. The purpose is to remove prejudices and complexes transmitted through the social environment and the accident of birth".

"Minimum levels of learning will be laid down for each stage of education. Steps will also be taken to foster among students an understanding of the diverse cultural and social systems of the people living in different parts of the country. Besides the promotion of the link language, programmes will also be launched to increase substantially the translation of books from one language to another and to publish multi-lingual dictionaries and glossaries. The young will be encouraged to undertake the rediscovery of India, each in his own image and perception." (PP. 6 to 7 of NPE)

The inclusion of *'Education'* m the concurrent list of the Constitution of India in 1976 through the 42nd Amendment it was described as a 'meaningful partnership' between the Central and State Governments. It re-assured, '...the removal of disparities and to equalize educational opportunity by attending to the specific needs of those who have been denied equality so far" (4.1 P. 9). It also promises that, "Education will be used as an agent of basic change in the status of women" (4.2 P. 10)

It assured 'equalisation with non-SC population' of the SC population'. It also spelt out a new deal for the Scheduled Tribes and expansion of educational access to these socio-economically disadvantaged groups. In short, it promised to correct the inadequacies in access to education to all the socio-culturally and economically disadvantaged groups like the rural people, residents of hill and desert areas, those living in remote and inaccessible areas and islands; and to the minorities and the handicapped.

5.12. "Resolve: The New Education Policy will give the highest priority to solving the problem of children dropping out of school and will adopt an array of meticulously formulated strategies based on micro-planning, and applied at the grass roots level all over the country, to ensure children's retention at school. This effort will be fully coordinated with the network of non-formal education. It shall be ensured that free and compulsory education of satisfactory quality is provided to all children up to 14 years of age before we enter the twenty-first century. A national mission will be launched for the achievement of this goal."

In the overall educational philosophy under-pinning the NPE,1986, the role of secondary education needs to be viewed. The national goals and commitment would remain as fluttering angels in the void unless they are translated into interesting instructional experiences especially at the formative stage of secondary education. The National Policy on Education, 1986 (with modifications undertaken in 1992) had stated the purpose and thrust of Secondary Education thus:

Secondary education begins to expose students to the differentiated roles of science, the humanities and social sciences. This is also an appropriate stage to provide childrenwith a sense of history and national perspective and give them opportunities to understand their constitutional duties and rights as citizens. Access to secondary education will be widened with emphasis on enrolment of girls, SCs and STs, particularly in science, commerce and vocational streams. Boards of Secondary Education will be reorganized and vested with autonomy so that their ability to improve the quality of secondary education is enhanced. Effort will be made to provide computer literacy in as many secondary level institutions as possible so that the children are equipped with necessary computer skills to be effective in the emerging technological world. A proper understanding of the work ethos and of the values of a humane and composite culture will be brought about through appropriately formulated curricula. Vocationalisation through specialized institutions or through the refashioning of secondary education will, at this stage, provide valuable manpower for economic growth.

It is universally accepted that children with special talent or aptitude should be provided opportunities to proceed at a faster pace, by making good quality education available to them, irrespective of their capacity to pay for it.

Pace-setting residential schools, Navodaya Vidyalayas, intended to serve this purpose have been established in most parts of the country on a given pattern, but with full scope for innovation and experimentation. Their broad aim will continue to be to serve the objective of excellence coupled with equity and social justice (with reservation for the rural areas, SCs and STs), to promote national integration by providing opportunities to talented children from different parts of the country, to live and learn together, to develop their full potential, and, most importantly, to become catalysts of a nationwide programme of school improvement."

Teaching shall be subject-based and intellectual discipline shall be instilled. The secondary school curriculum would attempt to translate the national commitments into vibrant instructional realities. Its centrality in shaping the future citizens has amply been recognized.

PROGRAMME OF ACTION 1986[377]

The Parliament of India discussed and adopted the "National Policy on Education, 1986' in its budget session of 1986. During the course of the debate the Minister of Human Resource Development promised to present the Programme of Action for the implementation of the policy in the monsoon session of the Parliament. Immediately thereafter twenty three Task Forces were constituted and each was assigned a specific subject of the Policy. Each Task Force had eminent educationists, experts and senior representatives of the Central and several State Governments.

One Task Force dealt with Secondary Education and Navodaya Vidyalayas. It outlined the parameters, priorities and strategies of programme implementation relating to secondary education.

The Task Force was requested to examine the present situation relating to Secondary Education and 'to elaborate the implications of the specific statements contained in the NPE.' It was 'also expected to project the actions that would be necessary and indicate the broad targets and the phasing of the programme;., and 'to indicate the broad financial implications...' Such detailed exercises had not been undertaken earlier; and that is one of the major reasons for the non-implementation of the earlier policies with rigour.

The Reports of the Task Forces were ready by July, 1986. These reports were discussed at length in a series of meetings convened by the Ministry of Human Resource Development. The POA,1986 was discussed in a meeting of the Secretaries of the Education Departments of the several

---

377 POA of NPE, 1986, MHRD, GOT, Aug. 1986, pp. 22 to 26.

State and Union Territory Governments. The Central Advisory Board of Education attended by the Education Ministers of the State & UT Governments considered it on 1ˢᵗ and 2ⁿᵈ August,1986. Many valuable suggestions that emanated from the deliberations were taken note of in retuning the POA,1986. The POA,1986 relating to *"Secondary Education and Navodaya Vidyalayas"* read thus:

Present Situation

There were 56323 secondary/higher secondary schools and 1,23,000 upper primary schools in 1983. This would give a ratio of 1:2.5. The enrolment at secondary level was 97,45,519 and at higher secondary level 51,01,435. There are unserved areas in the country where there is no school for 10 to 20 kms like in some tribal areas, desert or hilly areas where the low density of population does not allow enough children to be enrolled. An area may also be unserved though near a school if a physical barrier like river or mountain separates it.

Pre-Requisites & Broad Parameters of Strategy Envisaged

Secondary and higher secondary education is on the one hand terminal for those who enter the world of work after this stage. For such people a strengthened vocational scheme should form the main plank of strategy. For the rest it is preparatory to higher education and, therefore, a good grounding in the subject area should be provided along with learning orientation. The improvement in management systemof which perhaps the school complex system and improved supervisory system are the most important should be the main programmes during the 7ᵗʰ Plan and would continue thereafter. A flexible and interactive teaching programme supported by adequate laboratories and libraries would be a pre-requisite for learning-oriented education. A programme of curricular reform and examination/evaluation reform would provide conditions for a good grounding in subject areas.

The policy relating to secondary education implies extension of the school system in the unserved areas consolidating the existing facilities and providing special arrangements for the gifted children and the high achievers. This would mean that it would require—

a. Programme to ensure access to secondary education being widened to cover unserved areas:
b. Programme **of** consolidation in other areas/schools: &
c. Programme of setting up Navodaya Vidyalayas.

Programmes & Implementation[378]

As a **short** term measure the State Governments would be persuaded to open secondary schools in unserved areas taking blocks as a unit having a lower ratio than 1:2,5 duly considering the present distance of habitation from the nearest secondary school and population in the unserved habitations. As a medium and long term measure a programme **of** school mapping in each state for locating schools to cover all areas will be taken up. The technique of school mapping will be followed both for planning and implementation for location of secondary schools on the basis of clearly defined norms and standards. Special emphasis will be laid in this study on backward areas, areas predominandy inhabited by SC/ST and schooling facilities for girls. School clusters will be established with secondary school as its lead school and upper primary schools in the catchment areas. The ratio of upper primary to primary schools will be attempted to be kept at 1:3 as recommended by the Kothari Commission. This programme would be taken up by NIEPA in cooperation with SCERTs. This exercise can be completed by 1988 and from 1989 onwards it could be implemented. By 2000 the unserved areas will be fully served. The funds required **for** this purpose which cannot be estimated now will be fully met by the State Governments only.

1. For the products of non-formal education at elementary stage many of whom will continue to find it difficult to attend full time school and for the working people who have missed the

---

378 *Ibid.*

secondary school and others of this type, a flexible, non-formal arrangement is needed at secondary and higher secondarylevel.

This requirement is proposed to be met by Open Schools. Open Schools would be established in a phased manner by 1990 with a resource centre in each district. These resource centres should be located in or linked to the selected secondary teacher training institutions or the district institutes of education.

2. It is known that the secondary and higher secondary schools are under- provided particularly in the rural areas in terms of buildings, teachers and school facilities but the extent of these shortages have not been surveyed in all aspects. The programme of consolidation envisaged in the policy will have the following components of which the cost cannot be precisely estimated:

   a. Adequate playground facilities where needed will have to be provided by making available nearby vacant land and in other places by arranging for sharing of such facility with neighbouring school as a priority programme during the 7th Plan.

   b. A programme for construction of additional classrooms and laboratory facilities in schools to the extent they are deficient will be taken up. School education is mainly looked after by the State Governments and local bodies. If possible the Central Government may consider supplementation of resources.

   c. Every school must have laboratories and other facilities as specified in the terms of recognition of the Board of Secondary/Higher secondary education to which it is affiliated. These norms have been developed by the NCERT and KVS also. Taking into consideration the past experience that the equipment once given is not replaced and even maintained it is suggested that community participation by way of student contribution at the rate of Rs. 10 to 15 per month should be levied, except from girls and other exempt from payment of tuition fee. This collection should remain in the school for replacement and maintenance purposes.

d. The teacher competencies would be improved by attracting better qualified people to the profession as envisaged in the policy and by improving the pre-service and in-service training programmes through strengthened secondary teacher training institutions. The process will begin straightaway and will be continued for consistently upgrading teachers' competencies.

e. An envisaged in the Policy the core-curriculum will play an important role in educational consolidation. This will be followed by overall improvement in curriculum, the textual material, teaching practices and examination/evaluation methods.

f. The Kothari Commission suggested that the ratio of higher secondary and secondary schools should be 1:3. This should be ensured. A large number of higher secondary schools have only one or two streams out of humanities, science and commerce and most do not have vocational stream. As an important programme in the process of consolidation, schools should be helped to have all the three streams and a vocational stream in selected schools. This will be the responsibility of the State Government concerned. Vocational stream would be set up with the assistance of the Government of India as may be determined.

3. The programme for bright children has two parts — one is for potentially high achievers particularly in the areas who are substantially left uncovered by the present system and the other is the programme for the gifted students who can be expected to make original contribution in their subject areas if properly nurtured.

Under the scheme of Navodaya Vidyalayas for catering to the category of high achievers one such Vidyalaya will be set up in each district during the 7th Five Year Plan period. These schools will make available good quality education irrespective of the parents' capacity to pay and their socio-economic background. In these schools there will be 75% reservation for children from rural areas. There will be reservation for SC and ST as per their actual population in the district subject to a minimum of nationally prescribed figure of 15 and *IVi* for SC & ST respectively. An effort will be made to cover girls to the extent of $^1/_3$ in a school. Education will be free including boarding and lodging in these schools. These schools will be affiliated to the Central Board of Secondary Education.

The gifted students frequently have pronounced competence in a limited subject area accompanied by indifference in certain other areas. Therefore, arrangements for such students cannot be fitted into regular courses of study. Special arrangements for such students will have to provide teaching/learning on modular basis for every small group of students in a small number of subjects of interest to them. Such arrangements will be characterized by large facilities, higher teacher-student ratio and regular participation by professionals in teaching programmes. A detailed project for this purpose should be worked out by a specially constituted group within one year. Arrangements will be designed for implementation within the present system for such students.

RAMAMURTI REVIEW COMMITTEE (1990) ON NPE 1986

The National Policy on Education, 1986 was formulated during the Congress Party's regime. The National Front with the Janata Dal as the dominating party came to power in 1989. In its election manifesto, the Janata Dal had promised to review the NPE, 1986. After assuming office in 1989, the National Front Government at the Centre appointed a Review Committee of NPE,1986 under the Chairmanship of Acharya Ramamurti on 7th May,1990. It submitted its Report entitled, *"Towards an Enlightened and Humane Society"* on 9th January,1991. The major recommendations of the Review Committee relating to school education were:

Development of a common school system to ensure equity and social justice in education. It recommended that the present schools should be transformed into vibrant 'neighbourhood schools'. There should not be schools for the 'haves, and the 'have-nots'. It noted with concerned the neglect of the schools in rural areas and tribal areas. The deficit in infrastructural facilities of the schools in these areas was glaring, compared to the urban schools. The 'urban-rural' and 'general-tribal' divides need to be bridged. It recommended that steps need to be taken to eliminate regional imbalances and developmental distances. It advocated that launching of pro-active educational programmes for the socially and economically disadvantaged groups like STs, SCs, women, physically handicapped and the backward minorities. Elimination of education disparities was emphasized. It boldly stated that education of the women is not simply limited to increased access to education only. It should be viewed as a process of empowering women through education of all on the basis of equality of sexes. Vocationalization of education is an urgent imperatives and should not be viewed as "one meant for the less fortunate". It recommended "a single stream of school education with vocational as well as the non-vocational components of different mixes" as a healthy academic alternative.

The other recommendations pertained to examination reforms, regional languages as the media of education, decentralized planning and management of education, university autonomy, concept of participative education, value education and mobilization of resources for education, etc. Its recommendations have freshness, vigour, and vitality with deep concern to usher in a humane social order.

JANARDAN A REDDY REVIEW COMMITTEE (1991) ON NPE, 1986

The Congress Party came back to power at the Centre. The Central Advisory Board of Education (CABE) appointed a Committee in May 1991 under the Chairmanship of N. Janardana Reddy, Chief Minister of Andhra Pradesh who was also holding the Education portfolio, to examine the relevance of the Ramamurti Committee. It stated that only a few of the recommendations of the Ramamurti Review Committee on National Policy, 1986 have policy implications. It suggested a few modifications.

PROGRAMME OF ACTION, 1992

The National Policy on Education (NPE), 1986 was adopted in 1986. The in-depth reviews conducted by the Acharya Ramamurti Committee and Janardan Reddy Committee provided intellectual inputs. The administrative difficulties in operationalisation of the Policy from 1986 to early 1992 also impelled the necessities of pragmatic reformulation of the policy. The Revised Policy formulations provided the basis for the modification of the NPE,1986 in 1992. The Central Advisory Board on Education (CABE) endorsed the Revised Policy formulation in its meeting held on 5th & 6th May, 1992. The Revised Programme of Action (POA), 1992 was formulated as per the method followed in 1986. Mrs. (Dr.) Chitra Naik, Member, Planning Commission was the Chairperson of the Steering committee. The Task Force on Secondary Education had Dr. K. Gopalan, Director, NCERT, New Delhi as its Chairperson. A separate Task Force delved into affairs connected with the Navodaya Vidyalayas. The draft POA,1992 was discussed in a conference of the Secretaries and Directors of Education of the States and Union Territories. CABE endorsed it in its meeting held on 3rd & 4th August,1992. It was described as, 'more practical and action oriented'. The details of the POA,1992 relating to secondary education have been reproduced for reference. It stated:

1. PRESENT SITUATION[379]

(a) Access

8.1.1. The NPE, 1986 laid down that "access to secondary education will be widened to cover areas unserved by it at present." There has been a significant increase in the number of secondary and higher

---

379 POA, 1992 to the Revised Formulation of NPE, 1986.

secondary schools and in enrolment during the period from 1987-88 to 1990-91. During this period enrolment at secondary stage increased by 16.8 per cent and at the higher secondary stage by 17.6 per cent. The number of secondary schools increased from 54,845 in 1987-88 to 59,468 in 1990-91; corresponding figures for higher secondary schools are 16,460 and 19,151 respectively. The ratio of secondary and higher secondary schools to upper primary schools had declined from 1:1.98 in 1987-88 to 1:1.86 in 1990-91.

8.1.2. Gender disparities in enrolments are significant. In 1990-91 girls accounted for 33.4% of the enrolment at the secondary stage and 32% at the higher secondary stage. The SCs and STs also lag in regard to enrolment. Thus, SCs account for 11.85% at the secondary stage and 9.7% at the higher secondary stage; corresponding figures for STs are 4.21% and 3% respectively.

(b) Structure[380]

8.1.3. Though a considerable degree of uniformity has been achieved in regard to common education structure of 10+2+3, there is a considerable diversity regarding thelocation of the +2 stage. In quite a few states it is not part of the school system.

(c) National Curricular Framework

8.1.4. The secondary stage is divided into two very distinct sub-stages – secondary (up to class X) which is the stage of general education and higher secondary (classes XI and XII) which is marked by differentiation and diversification. The National system of education, as stated in the NPE,1986 envisages a National Curricular Framework. Such a framework has already been prepared for the secondary education though its implementation has been uneven. The work of curriculum revision for the secondary stage was undertaken in almost all the States and the Union Territories (UTs). The NCERT

---

380 *Ibid.*

also prepared the guidelines, syllabi and textbooks for all stages of school education. For the higher secondary stage, however, the Curricular Framework has not yet been authorized. The NCERT had developed a draft document in 1988, but that document requires to be reviewed keeping in view the emerging concerns. However, several States used the draft National Curricular Framework for the higher secondary stage prepared by the NCERT.

* The term 'higher secondary' used in this report refers to all post-secondary (high school, class X) and pre-degree education and includes Higher Secondary of the 10+2 pattern, Pre-University (one year course) Pre-Degree/Pre-University (Two year course) and intermediate Junior colleges.

** The issues relating to computer literacy, vocationalisation of education, Navodaya Vidyalayas, Open Learning Systems, Examination Reforms and Teacher Training, though linked with secondary education, have not been discussed here. They were discussed separately.

(d) Facilities for Qualitative Improvement

8.1.5. The POA, 1986 specified programmes for providing adequate playground facilities, construction of additional classrooms and provision of laboratory facilities, as specified in terms of norms developed by various organizations. Although no systematic studies have been conducted to assess the progress of diversification of courses at the higher secondary stage improvement in curriculum, the textual materials, teaching practices, examination/evaluation methods, and for the improvement of pre-service and in-service training programmes, there is a general feeling that the progress has not been marked.

2. POLICY CHANGE[381]

8.2.1. The Revised Policy Formulations take note of the increased demand for secondary education and go beyond NPE,1986 by calling

---

381 *Ibid.*

for a planned expansion of secondary education facilities all over the country. Secondly, they call for higher participation of girls, SCs and STs, particularly in science, vocational and commerce streams. Thirdly, they call for reorganization of Boards of Secondary Education and vesting them with autonomy 'so that their ability to improve the quality of secondary education is enhanced'. Fourthly, they envisage that effort will be made to provide computer literacy in as many secondary level institutions as possible so that the children are equipped with necessary computer skills to be effective in the emerging technological world.

3. BROAD PARAMETERS OF THE STRATEGY ENVISAGED[382]

8.3.1. They include:

- Extending access to secondary education by setting up new schools in the unserved areas and by extending and consolidating the existing facilities, with particular emphasis on ensuring substantially increased enrolment of girls, the SCs and the STs.
- Progressively bringing in the higher secondary stage (and all its equivalents) as a part of the school system in all States.
- Formulating a National Curriculum Framework for the higher secondary stage as well as development of new curricula and instructional packages based on the semester pattern.
- Reviewing and revising the curricula of secondary education (classes IX and X).
- Implementing a comprehensive scheme of examination reform.
- Improving considerably the physical and infrastructural facilities in secondary and higher secondary schools.
- Providing for diversity of courses in higher secondary schools.
- Reviewing afresh the existing system of pre-service teacher education for the secondary stage and formulating and implementing an improved teacher education system.

---

382 *Ibid.*

- Institutionalising in-service teacher training.
- Transforming the role of the Boards of Secondary Education.
- Strengthening the academic institutions and bodies concerned with research and development in the areas of curriculum, instructional materials and equipment for secondary schools.

4. WIDENING ACCESS TO SECONDARY EDUCATION[383]

8.4.1. The following steps are envisaged:

i. As a short term measure, the State Governments would be advised to provide in existing institutions necessary facilities for a diversity of courses, including science, commerce and vocational courses. They would also be advised to immediately initiate services for locating unserved areas and open High (i.e. Secondary) Schools in unserved areas taking the block as a unit so that the ratio of Secondary Schools to Upper Primary Schools is not lower than 1:1.86. The distance of the existing schools from the unserved habitations will be duly considered. Special emphasis will be laid on opening schools in backward areas, areas inhabited predominantly by the SCs and the STs.

ii. As a medium and long term measure, the programme of school mapping in each State for locating schools on the basis of clearly defined norms and standards will be revised. This exercise, to be carried out by NIEPA in collaboration with educational authorities in the States, will be completed by the end of 1994 and a programme to fully serve the unserved areas will be completed by 2000 A.D. In this exercise the educational needs of girls, SCs and STs would receive special consideration.

iii. The States/UTs will be urged to formulate a special enabling plan to ensure increase in enrolment of girls, the SCs, the STs and other educationally backward sections. Necessary guidelines to formulate the plan/mechanism will be developed

---

383 *Ibid*

by the NCERT in consultation with the education authorities of the States/UTs. (iv) The educational needs of those who find it difficult to attend full-time school and for the working people who have missed the secondary school will be met by extending and strengthening the Open School system.

5. COMMON EDUCATIONAL STRUCTURE[384](a)

8.5.1. In order to ensure that during the Eighth Plan period, a common educational structure of school education, that is, 10 (5+3+2) +2, is established throughout the country, the following steps are envisaged:

i. As an immediate steps, States/UTs that have not yet switched over to the nationalcommon educational structure will be urged to see that every new school whichis opened follows the 10 (5+3+2) +2 structure. States/UTs that have already initiated the process of bringing the +2 stage into the school system will beurged to intensify the effort in this regard.

ii. A task force will be set up to work out the modalities in consultation with the educational authorities of States/UTs, for solving the difficulties and problems of switching over to the common structure.

6. QUALITATIVE IMPROVEMENT AND FACILITIES[24 (b)]

8.6.1. The key issues in secondary education, apart from access, are quality, modernization and diversification. Standards regarding minimum facilities such as classrooms, sanitary facilities, science laboratories/equipments, libraries, etc., will be evolved by the NCERT in consultation with the Boards of School Education and similarly norms in respect of number and qualifications of teachers will also be laid down. The States and UTs and Boards of Secondary Education would be advised to enforce these norms. Taking into consideration the past experience that the equipment once given is not replaced

---

384 (a) *Ibid.*

24 (b)

and even maintained it is suggested that community participation by way of student contribution at the rate of Rs.10 to Rs.15 per month should be levied, except from girls and others exempt from payment of tuition fee. This collection should remain in the school for replacement and maintenance purposes. States and UTs will conduct surveys from time to time about the facilities available in schools so that they can plan their school improvement programmes on sound database. These surveys will also be meshed with the All India Educational Survey.

7. STRENGTHENING THE ROLE OF THE BOARDS OF SECONDARY EDUCATION

8.7.1. The Boards of Secondary Education occupy a key position as they prescribe the courses of study, prescribe/recommend and, in some States prepare textbooks and other instructional materials, lay down the standards of achievement of students, and 'pass judgments on the quality of performance of the learners at the secondary stage'. A number of other institutions at the national and state levels such as the NCERT, the NIEPA, the SCERTs, the Directorates of School Education, etc. also play an important role in strengthening secondary education. While the mutual interaction and collaboration among the various institutions working in the area of secondary education will be strengthened and institutionalized, the role and functions of the Boards will be redefined to enhance their ability to improve the quality of secondary education. This would require, a greater autonomy for the Board and strengthening them in terms of their structure and composition.

8.7.2. The much needed examination and evaluation reform will require the Boards of Secondary Education to play a greater role in improving and monitoring the quality of secondary education. The Boards will also be expected to play a central role in enforcing the norms with regard to academic and infrastructural facilities in secondary education.

8.7.3. A Task Force will be set up to study the existing position and status of the Boards throughout the country and to draw up a scheme to transform the Boards into effective instruments for bringing about qualitative improvement of secondary education. The Task Force would have due representation to the States/UTs, State Boards of Education and other institutions concerned. This Task Force will submit its report by March, 1993 and the States/UTs will be advised to implement its recommendations within the Eighth Plan Period.

8. PROFESSIONAL DEVELOPMENT PROGRAMMES FOR HEADS OF SECONDARY/HIGHER SECONDARY SCHOOLS[24 (c)]

8.8.1. Suitable programmes for Heads of Secondary/Higher Secondary schools will be designed to facilitate the effective implementation of the reforms outlined above.

9. CONTENT AND PROCESS

8.9.1. The programme of reorientation of content and process needs to be worked out separately for the two stages of Secondary Education, viz., the secondary stage (classes IX-X) and higher secondary stage (classes XI-XII). This is because in terms of both content and process, the two stages are very different while the former is a. continuation of, and forms the conclusion stage of general education, the latter marks the beginning of differentiation and diversification. There is a much clear understanding of nature of education at the secondary state to at the higher secondary stage. The National Curricular Framework visualized as a basis of the National System of Education in the NPE has been formulated and programmes for implementing it has been carried out by the educational authorities in almost all States/UTs. However at the higher secondary stage, as mentioned earlier while a draft of the curricular framework was prepared in consultation with educational agencies and organizations of experts throughout the country, its acceptance as a national document cannot be said to have been achieved. It was not even printed for wide circulation though educational authorities of many States/UTs have used it in varying degrees in the programmes of reorienting the content and process. Many issues relating to the modernization of its structure and content imparting it a greater degree of relevance and its transaction and evaluation are related to the question of semesterization recommended by the NPE.

8.9.2. At the secondary stage of education, where knowledge areas become increasingly important, the content and process education has to undergo continuous reorganization an upgradation. Though, ideally, various learning experiences basis on the school curriculum should make an integrated whole, they have to be classified under various subject areas for the sake of convenience. The planning of objectives, learning activities and strategies under each curricular area have to be further guided by considerations such as the requirements of the various stages of education and the developmental stages of the learners.

Secondary Stage

8.9.3. The NCERT, in 1988, brought out the modified version on the *National Curriculum for Elementary and Secondary Education. A Framework* in the light of the major thrusts and recommendations, including the core curricular areas, of the NPE. It dealt with various aspectsof the reorientation of content and process of education as a whole and in various subject areas up to the secondary stage. This Framework formed the basis of the guide-lines and syllabi as well as textbooks and other instructional materials in various subjects brought out by the NCERT. According to the framework the content of secondary education which is the terminal stage of general education will be built around the following curricular areas:

- Languages (mother tongue, Hindi, English)
- Mathematics
- Science
- Social Sciences (History, Geography, Civics, Economics)
- Work Experience
- Art Education
- Health and Physical Education

8.9.4. Languages: One of the major thrusts in the Framework was the effective implementation of the Three Language Formula. It recommended the study of three languages before the child completes her/his Secondary Education with one language — the mother tongue/regional language — to be studied from the primary stage to the end of the secondary stage and the study of the second and the third language from the upper primary stage to the secondary stage.

8.9.5. Mathematics: The secondary stage (classes IX-X) marks a beginning for the transition from functional mathematics studied till the upper primary stage to the study of mathematics as a discipline. The logical proofs of proposition, theorems, etc. is introduced at this stage. Apart from being a specific subject, it should be treated as a concomitant to any subject involving analysis and reasoning.

8.9.6. With the recent introduction of computers in schools, educational computing and the emergence of learning through the understanding of cause-effect relationships and the interplay of variables, the teaching of Mathematics will be suitably redesigned to bring it in line with modern technological devices.

8.9.7. Science: The aim of teaching science at this stage is primarily directed towards problem-solving and decision-making through the learning of key concepts which cut across all the disciplines of science. The content of science should be organized on the basis of two guidelines, namely contemporary science and the learning ability of the pupil. It should reflect that science is a continuing human endeavour and that it is international in character and method.

8.9.8. The instructional materials in science based on the Framework will be reviewed to ensure that the approaches followed are in consonance with the objectives of science education as laid down in the policy, viz., to develop in the child well-defined abilities and values such as spirit of inquiry, creativity, objectivity, courage to question, and aesthetic sensibility. Learning of science will be oriented to ensure that the learners discover the relationship of science with health, agriculture, industry, and other aspects of daily life.

8.9.9. Social Science: The Framework recommended that social sciences at the secondary stage may comprise elements of History, Geography, Civics and Economics topromote an understanding of contemporary India. The general framework of objectives of teaching social sciences at this stage had three major components. These were:

i. deepening the pupil's understanding of contemporary India and its social, economicand political development as an independent nation, and its composite culture;

ii. developing in the pupil a world perspective and an understanding of the problems of the contemporary world, particularly those relating to international peace and human rights and the establishment of a just world order; and

iii. inculcating in the pupil a spirit of enquiry, a scientific and forward looking outlook and aversion to injustice and bigotry.

8.9.10. Art Education: The framework defined the aim of art education up to the secondary stage as sensitization of the learners so that they may learn to respond to the beauty in line, colour, form, movement and sound, and knowledge and understanding of the cultural heritage.

8.9.11. Work Experience: The framework visualized work experience - 'purposive and meaningful manual work, organized as an integral part of the learning process and resulting in either goods or services useful to the community' — as an essential component at all stages of education. Its introduction through well-structured and graded programmes comprising activities in according with the interests, abilities and needs of learners was recommended. The Framework also laid stress on the inculcation in the learners respect for manual work, values of self-reliance, cooperativeness, perseverance, helpfulness, inquisitiveness, work ethics, attitudes and values related to productive work, and concern for the community. For the secondary stage, the imparting of a pre-vocational orientation to the programme was recommended to facilitate the choice of the vocational courses at the higher secondary stage.

8.9.12. Health and Physical Education: Health and Physical education was visualized as an integral part of education up to the secondary stage. The Framework laid emphasis on the total health of the learner and the community by promoting desirable attitudes, understanding and practices with regard to nutrition, health and sanitation and developing health, strength and physical fitness of the body through games and sports activities, yoga, scouting, guiding, N.C.C., social service, etc."

INITIATIVES TO AUGMENT QUALITY IN SECONDARY EDUCATION (* Based on MHRD Reports.)

Every educational policy contains in itself the mosaic vision of education and embedded in it are the envisaged reforms. But an educational policy is only a 'rhetoric', and to translate it into reality a detailed road-map is essential. NPE,1968 could not be implemented because it was not accompanied by a detailed scheme for implementation. The Programme of Action accompanying the NPE,1986. and its revised formulation of 1992 took note of this deficiency, and remedied it. The POAhad envisaged certain centrally sponsored schemesthat would act as demonstrative examples to emulate. The Centrally Sponsored Schemes were launched to effect radical qualitative changes in the secondary school system. They are:

- National Population Education Project, 1980
- Computer Literacy and Studies in Schools, 1984-88
- English Language Teaching Institutes,1986
- Indian Culture, Arts and Value Education,1987
- Revised Educational Technology Scheme, 1987
- Scheme for Improvement of Science Education, 1987-88
- Reorganisation of Teacher Education,1988
- Environmental Orientation to School Education,1 988-89
- Centrally Sponsored Scheme of Vocational Education, 1988-89

- Centrally sponsored Scheme of Yoga
- School Computer Programme Everywhere (SCOPE)
- Scheme of Navodaya Vidyalayas
- National Curriculum Framework, 2000
- National Curriculum Framework, 2005

Quality is praised and prized in all fields of production. In the service sector, it is not universal. An effective engineer, an outstanding lawyer, a specialist doctor, an able adman, and even a competent chef are recognized and are paid highly. Quality in education is quietly ignored though it is its quintessence. In 1962, Stiles *et al* remarked with anguish that in USA. "Teaching is perhaps the only profession that does not identify and reward quality".[385] It is a truth that holds good in today's (2007) India. In 1966, the Indian Education (Kothari) Commission stated with great concern that "...the standards reached at the end of the first ten years of school education at present are far from satisfactory..."[386] and recommended that "...for the next tent years the principal effort in all the States and Union Territories should be directed towards the qualitative improvement of this stage of education."[387] The "Challenge of Education" (1985) very briefly summed up the dilemma relating to secondary education in these words, "The major challenge before educational planners is to devise an educational system that would, on the one hand, meet the growing demand for secondary education and, on the other, ensure that the objective qualitative viability does not get diluted."[388] The National Policy on Education, 1986 (with modification undertaken in 1992) reiterated the resolve for quality in secondary education and stated: "5.13. Boards of Secondary Education will be reorganized and vested

385 Stiles, J. Linidsay et al., "Secondary Education in the United State." N.Y. Harcount, Brace & WorldInc. 1962 P.244.
386 Ministry of Education, GOI, "Report of the Education Commission, 1964-66, New Delhi, GOIPress 1st Edition, P.268
387 *Ibid.*
388 Challenge of Education op.cil p. 41

with autonomy so that their ability to improve the quality of secondary education is enhanced."[389]

Like Janus, the Roman God, who had two faces - one looking to the front and the other towards back, secondary education is organically linked to both elementary and tertiary education. It is the sturdy bridge that links these two stages of education, but is getting rusted and weak. Secondary schools have lost classes VI, VII and VIII to elementary education, which has encroached into the bonafide territory of secondary education i.e the education of the adolescents. Higher secondary education has lived with the first degree of the college for almost one and half centuries and is reluctant to enter into the main stream of secondary education. Today, the Indian high school has only two classes — IX and X. It has become a small school and a neglected sector of education.

(i) National Population Education Project, 1980

The National Population Education Project was launched in April, 1980. It aimed to institutionalize population education, and infuse integrated population related concepts into the school curriculum. The United Nations Fund for Population Activities, UNESCO, Ministry of Health and Family Welfare of the Government of India assisted and collaborated with this critical programme. NCERT was the nodal agency for the county, and the SCERTs were the nodal agencies for implementing this project in the States and Union Territories. Awareness generation and value orientation were the two main focal activities. The Directorate of Teacher Education & SCERT, Orissa implemented it in Orissa with great enthusiasm and commendable results.

(ii) Computer Literacy and Studies in School (CLASS) 1984-85

During 1984-85, this scheme was initiated and operationalised in 28 select schools. The Department of Education and the Department

---

389 MHRD, GOT, "National Policy on Education, 1986" with modifications undertaken in 1992, p. 21

of Electronics, Government ofIndia collaborated in this project. The scheme wassteadilyextended to 2598 schools by 1995. The scheme was introduced in the secondary and higher secondary schools of Orissa during 1994-95.

(iii) English Language Teaching Institute (ELTI) (1986)

The English Language Teaching Institute was established in 1986. It has three broad objectives: teaching, in-service training, and research with a view to enhance the standards of English language teaching and learning in the State. The Institute has also introduced courses in French and Japanese languages. The Institute has under its control three District Centres for English Language Teaching at Baripada, Sambalpur and Berhampur. It has to its credit specific research work and training course for tribal learners.

(iv) Indian Culture, Arts and Value Education,1987

The rich cultural heritage of India needs to be preserved and cultural awareness needs to be augmented. Art Education is another important but grossly neglected area of the school curriculum. Value Education provides the survival skills for the nation. All these three areas are of extreme importance. The Government of India has formulated schemes of financial assistance to augment teaching, research, and awareness etc. in these areas.

(v) Revised Educational Technology Scheme, 1987

Educational Technology Scheme had been launched during 1972. Centre for Educational Technology was set-up in the NCERT. Educational Technology Cells were started in the States. There was one such E.T. Cell operating in Orissa. It was attached to the Directorate of Public Instruction.

The Educational Technology Scheme was revised in 1987 keeping the emerging demands of NPE, 1986 in view. Satellite-based ETV programmes were telecast in Oriya every day for 45 minutes. Such programmes were available in Hindi, Telugu, Gujarati and Marathi also.

State Institute of Educational Technology (SIET) was set-up by the Government of India (MHRD) in 1986 to provide technological support to school education. The main objectives of SIET are: production of educational/enrichment programmes for telecast/broadcast through TV/Radio and communication through audio/video cassettes-players; interacting with and educating children through TV/Audioprogrammes; designing and producing of teaching aids, administering the educational technology programmes; imparting training to production personnel, teachers and teacher educators; programme support to total literacy campaign activities, communication research and evaluation, dissemination of TV, radio (audio visual) programmes through available commercial channels; patronizing production of educational materials by outsiders; development of teachers' guides; and telecast of education news which contains all the instructions, or-ders, circulars etc. of the government relating to education to bridge the communication gap.

(vi) Scheme for Improvement of Science Education, 1987-88

The Centrally-sponsored Scheme for Improvement of Science Education was launched towards the end of 1987-88. Under this scheme, the Central Government provided financial assistance to the States and Union Territories to provide Science Kits to upper primary schools. The laboratories of secondary and higher secondary schools were upgraded and strengthened with the funds made available under this scheme. The libraries were better equipped with books on science. District Resource Centres for Science Education were set up. The training of teachers of science and mathematics was encouraged. Development of instructional material in Science and Mathematics was encouraged. 27,037 secondary and higher secondary schools of India were provided financial assistance to upgrade and strengthen their science laboratories 27,396 secondary/higher secondary schools received grants for strengthening their libraries.

(vii) Reorganisation of Teacher Education,1988

The NPE, 1986 envisaged the empowerment of teachers. Upgraded pedagogic skills empower teachers. In November 1987, the Education Consultants of India (A Government of India Enterprise) came forth with a document entitled "Programme for Improvement of Secondary Teacher Education". In it, it was clearly mentioned that the term 'secondary' means the classes 9th to 12th and includes senor/or higher secondary stage. It suggested the 'Restructuring and Re-organisation of Secondary Teacher Education'. It envisaged the setting up of 50 Institutes of Advanced Study in Education (IASEs) and 200 Colleges of Teacher Education (CTEs). These institutions were expected to undertake recurrent in-service training programmes, research, extension, publication etc. It also envisaged the closure of "B.Ed. Shops" by closing down non-viable B.Ed, colleges.

SCERTs were strengthened. NCTE was set up as a statutory authority. The IASEs, CTEs could not live up to the high pedagogic expectations. The SCERTs are more bureaucratic and less pedagogic. The NCTE has promoted *"Teacher Education Myopia"* by visualizing very small Teacher Education Institutes with an intake of (usually less than 100 students). Thanks to the NCTE and its flexible norms, the mushrooming of non-viable Secondary Teacher Education Institutions is on the increase. It blissfully forgot the recommendation of the Kothari Commission (1964-66) which stated:

"With a view to ensuring economy and efficiency, training institutions should be of a fairly large size. The minimum size of a training institution at the primary stage offering a two-year course should be 240 and that at the secondary stage should be 200. Existing institutions should be raised to this size.... by expansion and/or amalgamation. With regard to new institutions the size should not be less than 400. The classes for the training of primary teachers attached to secondary schools as well as teacher education departments attached to colleges for arts and science should be abolished and replaced by large-sized training institutions"

(Report of the Education Commission," Teacher Education' P. 84. Min. of Education, New Delhi, 1966)

(viii) Environmental Orientation to School Education, 1988-89

The Centrally-sponsored Scheme of Environmental Orientation to School Education was launched in 1988-89. The NPE, 1986 had envisaged the integration of educational programmes in schools with local environmental conditions and the ecological ethos. This scheme aimed to translate it into a transactional reality. The Government of India provided 100% grants to schemes that aimed to promote environmental consciousness among the school students, and to undertake projects related to it. The projects under this category included — development, incorporation or revision of environmental curricula, preparation of books, instructional materials, booklets, brochures, posters, slides, audio tapes, films etc. to promote environmental consciousness and the related corpus of knowledge. It assisted projects that aimed to investigate ecological problems. Orientation of teachers and seminars on this area were also funded by this scheme. The State Departments of School Education, in collaboration with the Ministry of Human Resources Development, Government of India are jointly implementing this scheme.

(ix) Centrally Sponsored Scheme of Vocational Education, 1988-89

The Centrally-sponsored Scheme of Vocational Education at the higher secondary stage was introduced in the State from 1988-89 initially in 31 institutions on a pilotbasis. Later on, 150 more vocational higher secondary institutions were sanctioned by the Government of India during 1992-93 and another 50 institutions during 1993-94. These institutions were attached either to a secondary school or to a college.

The primary aim of this programme was to provide diversification of educational opportunities so as to enhance individual employability, to reduce the mismatch between demand and supply of skilled manpower and to provide an alternative for those who do not wish to pursue higher general education. There are 15 different trades in five different areas which include:

1. *Agriculture Area.*—Crop Production, Horticulture, Sericulture, Poultry Farming, Dairy Farming, Inland Fisheries and Farm Mechanic

2. *'Engineering Area.*—Repair and Maintenance of Radio and TV Receivers, Repair and Maintenance of Electrical Domestic Appliances,

3. *Commerce Area*—Office Management, Tax Assistance and Insurance

4. *Home Science*—Creche and Pre-School Management, Commercial Garment Designing and Making, Food Preservation and Processing

5. *Health and Para-medical.*—Area X-Ray Technician and Medical Laboratory Technician.

(x) Centrally-Sponsored Scheme of Yoga

Yoga is physical and mental discipline. It has its roots in ancient Indian thought. It is widely practiced in different parts of India. The English being Westerners could not appreciate its worth. Its importance is being realized increasingly. It has caught the imagination of the West. This scheme was launched to revitalize the school curriculum. The greatest hurdle in implementing it, is the lack of adequately trained manpower.

(xi) School Computer Programme Everywhere (SCOPE)

It is a programme of the Government of Orissa in collaboration with privately managed computer education agencies. The Government of Orissa provides rent-free room with adequate facilities of electricity in high schools where this programme was introduced.. The private agencies supply the computer hardware, software and training personnel. It is operating in 56 select high schools of Orissa. Computer Education is provided to children studying in Class VIII or above.

(xii) Scheme of Navodaya Vidyalayas

A Navodaya Vidyalaya is a residential and co-educational institution. It provides quality modern education to the talented children predominantly from rural areas. These institutions impart education up to class XII and are affiliated to the CBSE. Government of India in the Ministry of Human Resource Development fully bears the financial liability of these schools. They are for bright rural children. It has two parts - one is for potentially high achievers, particularly in the areas, which are substantially left uncovered by the present system, and the other is the programme for the gifted students, who can be expected to make original contribution in their subject areas, if properly nurtured.

These schools were expected to emerge as high quality public schools for the rural areas, irrespective of the parent's capacity to pay and their socio-economic background. In these schools, there is 75% reservation for children from rural areas. There is reservation for SC and ST as per their actual population in the district subject to a minimum of nationally prescribed figure of 15% and 7.5% for SC and ST respectively. Girls constitute at least one-third of the total intake,. Education is free including boarding and lodging. These schools are affiliated to the Central Board of Secondary Education.

In Orissa, there are 24 Navodaya Vidyalayas located at different places of the districts of Dhenkanal, Keonjhar, Koraput, Cuttack, Phulbani, Balangir, Sambalpur, Sundergarh, Balasore, Kalahandi, Ganjam, Mayurbhanj, Puri, Nuapada, Kendrapara, Angul, Sonepur, Nawarangpur, Gajapati, Rayagada, Jharsuguda, Malkanagiri, Khurda, and Boudh. Steps are afoot to start seven more schools in Orissa in the near future.

(xiii) National Curriculum Framework, 2000

The National Curriculum Framework,2000 (NCF,2000) admits that "curriculum development is not a one-time venture, but an on-going process", and that it is "a device to translate national goals into educational experiences." The NCERT started this academic exercise of 'developing a new curriculum framework' in September,1999. The faculty of the NCERT did the spadework and developed "National Curriculum Framework". This was followed by interaction with eminent experts. Nation-wide debates and discussions were organized, and by September,2000 the NCF,2000 was finalized.

Its emphases were on (a) Minimum Levels of Learning (b) Value Education, (c) Use of ICT, (d) Management and Accountability of the educational system. Theother major concerns were (i) Healthy, enjoyable and stress-free Early Childhood Care and Education, (ii) Sustenance and nurturing of talent for securing excellence, (iii) Reduction of the curricular load, (iv) Integration of Environmental Education with different curricular areas of the school curriculum, (v) Introduction of the "Art of Healthy and Productive Learning" encompassing art education, health and physical education and work education, (vi) Education about Religions, (vii) Integrated Approach to teaching of Social Sciences, (viii) Integration of Science and Technology, (ix) Bringing Mathematics closer to life, (x) Empowerment of Teachers, (xi) Participation and Accountability of parents and community, (xii) Introduction of oral-aural as well as individual and group approaches to Evaluation, etc. It exhorted the States and the several Boards of School Education and others concerned to abhor 'the tendency to maintain status quo ante' and to make the curriculum relevant and 'in tune with regional needs'.

This document generated a lot of heat and dust, and some of the basic pedagogic messages embedded in it were lost sight of. For the first time in India, the curriculum debate degenerated into a political debate. All political parties without any exception realized that the school curriculum is an effective tool for political indoctrination and a means to gain political mileage. The NCF,2000 faced vitriolic criticism from the word 'go'. The intended curriculum was caustically criticized, and its operational strategies attracted greater criticism. Curriculum has become more a political affair than a balanced pedagogical exercise.

The 21st century started with an unprecedented awareness relating to curriculum. Curriculum is under constant watch and critical scrutiny. It is the master-key to quality of education.

(xiv) National Curriculum Framework, 2005

In the meeting held on 14th and 19th July 2004, the Executive Committee of the NCERT took the decision to revise the NCF,2000. A National Steering Committee consisting of 35 eminent intellectuals of India was constituted of which Prof. Yash Pal was the Chairperson and Prof. M. A. Khader, Professor of Education and Principal, RIE, Bhubaneswar was the Member-Secretary. Twenty-one National Focus Groups were set-up to examine the various facets of the School Curriculum. It was placed before the Central Advisory Board of Education (CABE) at its meeting held on September,6 and 7, 2005.

Professor Yash Pal candidly stated that curriculum is *'what should be taught to our children and how'*, and ended with a note of hope that NCF,2005 'might start a freedommovement for the education of our young — away from the tyrannies in which we have enveloped ourselves'.

Some of its approaches have novelty and creative vision. The salient features are:

- Language skills are basic and cut across the school subjects and disciplines, and that the multilingual character of Indian society should be viewed as a resource for the enrichment of school life.
- Creative, constructive, comfortable and congenial imaginative approach to mathematics was advocated as a process of 'mathematization'.
- The wider context of science, its process and method were accorded precedence over the labyrinth of scientific facts and formulae.

- The inter-disciplinary nature and conceptual understanding of social sciences were stated to be central.
- Work education vehemently advocated by Zakir Husain Committee of 1937 had been blissfully forgotten by the nation and grossly neglected by educationists was restored: and was viewed as a 'pedagogic medium' with great learning potentials.
- The heritage of folkloristic was re-emphasized in Art Education.
- India had practically forgotten Peace Education. Peace had degenerated into ill-understood rhetoric of Gandhian thought. Peace Education received the rightful important position.
- Health and Physical Education including Yoga were viewed as magnetic attractive forces to be utilized by the school for enrolment, retention and promotion of success.

QUANTITATIVE GROWTH

Describing the quantitative growth of education is considered to be a relatively easier task than portraying the qualitative development of education which is intangible, abstract and elusive. However, this task is not as easy as it is imagined to be due to great political changes as creation of Burma as a separate country on 1st April, 1936 or of Pakistan on 14th August, 1947; the integration of the erstwhile feudatory states, reorganization of states on the basis of language, and intra-territorial reorganization by creation or abolition of districts etc. Firm data-base is not available and this creates problems.

The quantitative expansion is triggered by freedom, implementation of five-year plan, population explosion etc. Comparison of growth rates during different periodsof times provides information relating to the momentum of quantitative development. Developmental distances can be assessed on the basis of disparities in the urban-rural, male-female, ST and Non-ST population etc. Assessment of quantitative growth from time to time is essential to know the adequacy or otherwise of access to education.

India was under the British Rule from 1757 to 1947. During the period 1841 to 1947 i.e. over a period of 106 years only 106 high schools in Orissa had been established. In 1947-48, there were 106 High Schools in Orissa and by July, 2007, their number had risen to 7,128 i.e. a net increase of 7022 high school over a period of almost sixty years. The growth rate of high schools was one per year during the colonial period, and one per every three days after freedom. Freedom is a definite accelerating factor of education.

Planning has been accepted by India as an effective strategy to augment social development. The Five-Year Plans have effectively contributed to the universalization of primary education and thus prepared the requisite foundation for the development of secondary education. The growth of secondary education plan-wise has been depicted in Table No. 6.1.

TABLE 6.1

Plan-wise Growth of Secondary Schools in Orissa

Plan	No. of Secondary School	Growth during the Plan period
1st Plan		+73
1951	172	
1956	245	
2nd Plan		+121
1956	245	
1961	366	
3rd Plan		+350
1961	366	
1966	716	
Plan Holidays: 1966-67 to 1968 due to Chinese War		
4th Plan		+374
1969	1,332	
1974	1,706	
5tn Plan		+174
1974	1,706	
1979	1,880	

Plan	No. of Secondary School	Growth during the Plan period
Plan Holidays: 1978-79 to 1979-80		
6th plan		+1211
1980	2,243	
1985	3,454	
7th Plan		+1,110
1985	3,220	
1990	4,330	
Plan Holidays: 1990-91 ro 1991-92		
8^{.h} Plan	+1,294	
1992	4,774	
1997	6,068	
9^{rh} Plan		+330
1997	6,068	
2002	6,398	
10th Plan		+730
2002 2007	6,398 7,128	

(*Source:* Directorate of Elementary Education, Orissa)

Growth of secondary education at the rate of more than 1000 schools per plan period is noticed from the 6th Plan onwards. Resources can never keep pace at this growth rate; and quality is the natural casualty.

The following table depicts the population of Orissa census-wise and the growth in the number of secondary schools of Orissa.

TABLE 6.2

Decadal Growth of Population and the Growth in Number of High Schools

Census Year	Population	No. of High Schools	One High Schools per a population of
1951	1,46,46,000	172	85,151
1961	1,75,49,000	415	42,287
1971	2,19,45,000	1,407	15,597

Census Year	Population	No. of High Schools	One High Schools per a population of
1981	2,63,70,000	2,443	10,794
1991	3,16,60,000	4,641	6,822
2001	3,67,07,000	6,431	5,708

(*Source:* Directorate of Elementary Education Statistical Cell)

The demands of an ever increasing population have to be fulfilled in a democracy. The demands if ignored amount to open invitation to unpopularity and eventual loss of power for the party that has failed to fulfill the needs of the people. The secondary schools increased by more than 2000 in the decades of 1981-91 and 1991-2001.

The urban areas are always privileged in so far as educational facilities are concerned. The magnitude of urbanization in Orissa has been on the increase from 2.47% in 1901; 2.42% in 1911; 2.52% in 1921; 2.54% in 1931, 3% in 1941. The process of urbanization increased after independence. Bhubaneswar, Rourkela, Hirakud, Brajarajnagar, Sunabeda, Bargarh, Jatni, Barbil, NALCO civil township etc. have sprung up only after independence. As per the census of 2001, there were 138 towns. The urban population has increased from 4.06% in 1951 to 14.97% by 2001. The total urban population was 54,96,318 in 2001. As per the 7th Educational Survey (date of reference 30.09.2002) there were 709 secondary schools in the 138 urban areas. The secondary schools of urban areas are better off quality-wise. Most of the elite secondary schools managed by DAV Trust and the missionaries are all located in urban areas.

The community has always evinced keen interest in the promotion of secondary education. The following table depicts the support of the community to secondary education.

TABLE 6.3

Management of High Schools (1993)

Area	Govt.	Private Aided	Private Unaided	Total
Rural	1071	2487	1119	4677
Urban	331	212	90	633
Total	1402	2699	1209	5310

The Governmental support to secondary education in the urban areas was 52.3% as against its support to the rural areas which was just 22.9%. The Govt, aided schools were 33% in urban areas as against 53.2% in the rural areas. The totally privately managed schools without any aid accounted for 14.2% in the urban areas and 23.9% in the rural areas. The willing support of the community to 1119 secondary schools without any government assistance speaks volumes regarding the educational awareness and proactive initiative of the rural populace in this field. The efforts of the urban community in this regard are almost insignificant.

This scenario has changed and by 2007 the number of high schools functioning in Orissa was 7128 out of which 3556 were Government High Schools and 657 were aided high schools. The number of fully unaided high schools completely supported by the community was 2915. This increasing tendency of rendering support to secondary education by the community is satisfying. However, the people living below poverty line in the economically backward districts are unable to support private schools.

STATUS SITUATION AS PER SURVEY REPORTS

The growth of secondary education has to keep pace with the growth of population. The increase in the number of schools per one lakh of population indicates the available levels of access. The plentiful information relating to infra-structural facilities, playgrounds, laboratories embedded in the seven Educational Surveys conducted by the Government of India from 1957 to 2002 provide the possibilities of success attainable in these institutions..

The Educational Surveys have been conducted in 1957, 1965, 1973, 1978, 1986, 1993 and 2002. The census data for population is available as on 1st March of 1951, 1961, 1971, 1981, 1991 and 2001. The population for the specific year of the Educational Survey has been calculated and is approximate population for the corresponding year of education survey.

TABLE 6.4
Growth of Secondary Education in Orissa (1947-48 to 2006-07)

Sl. No.	Year (Date of Reference)	Number of		School & Enrolment per 1,00,000 of population		No. of teachers	Teachers per School	Teacher Student ratio
		High Schools	Enrolment in Classes IX & X in lakhs	High Schools	Enrolment in Classes IX & X in lakhs			
1.	1947-48 Independence Year (31.3.1948)	106	0.15	0.73	104.23	1,505	14.2	10
2.	1950-51 Pre-plan Year (31.3.1951)	172	0.16	1.17	109.24	2,247	13.1	7.1
3.	Ist Survey,1957 (31.12.1957)	178	0.72	1.67	432.96	3,601	13	20
4.	2nd Survey,1965 (31.12.1965)	1,030	1.01	5.23	513.38	7,831	7.6	12.9
5.	3rd Survey,1973 (31.12.1973)	1,974	1.94	8.5	836.25	15,828	8	12.3
6.	4th Survey,1978 (30.9.1978)	2,167	2.63	8.56	1039.5	21,009	9.7	12.5
7.	5th Survey,1986 (30.9.1986)	3,955	4.08	13.48	1391.11	35,313	8.9	11.6
8.	6th Survey,1993 (30.9.1993)	5,310	5.23	16.1	1586.24	49,525	9.3	10.6
9.	7th Survey,2002 (30.9.2002)	6,398	6.79	17.02	1806.87	55,124	8.6	12.3
10.	1st July 2007	7,128	7.0+	17.58	NA	NA		

Note: Exact enrolment figures for 2007 are not yet available
Source: Directorate of Elementary Education, Orissa

DISTRICT-WISE DISTRIBUTION OF HIGH SCHOOLS

There were 13 revenue districts in Orissa. For administrative convenience they have been reorganized into 30 districts in early 1990s. The data for 1986-87 relates to the undivided districts. The newly created districts carved out of the old districts have been shown in column-2 of Tables No. 6.5 & 6.6. The date reveals the relative progress of secondary education in the different districts of Orissa

TABLE 6.5

District-wise High Schools (1986-87 to 2001-02)

SI. No.	New Districts	SI. No.	Old Districts	No. of High Schools		
				1986-87	1993-94	2002-03
1.	Balasore	1.	Balasore	505	421	459
2.	Bhadrak				227	277
3.	Bolangir	2.	Bolangir	177	187	219
4.	Sonepur				79	88
5.	Cuttack	3.	Cuttack	930	342	376
6.	Jagatsinghpur				194	266
7.	Jajpur				322	334
8.	Kendrapara				285	320
9.	Dhenkanal	4.	Dhenkanal	270	188	242
10.	Angul				153	190
11.	Ganjam	5.	Ganjam	281	356	437
12.	Gajapati				38	61
13.	Kalahandi	6.	Kalahandi	121	142	172
14.	Nuapada				63	99
15.	Keonjhar	7.	Keonjhar	224	318	421
16.	Koraput	8.	Koraput	151	85	98
17.	Malkangiri				38	50
18.	Nawarangpur				49	77
19.	Rayagada				57	84
20.	Mayurbhanj	9.	Mayurbhanj	266	377	391

SI. No.	New Districts	SI. No.	Old Districts	No. of High Schools		
				1986-87	1993-94	2002-03
21.	Kondhamal	10.	Phulbani	62	70	95
22.	Boudh				42	44
23.	Sundergarh	11.	Sundergarh	177	255	258
24.	Sambalpur	12.	Sambalpur	308	122	159
25.	Deogarh				52	58
26.	Bargarh				192	245
27.	Jharsuguda				74	93
28.	Pun	13.	Puri	483	203	289
29.	Khordha				220	323
30.	Nayagarh				159	173
	Orissa			3955	5310	6398

Source: Directorate of Elementary Education, Orissa

TABLE 6.6

District-wise Enrolment in High Schools (1986-87 to 2001-02)

SI. No.	Netricts	SI. No.	Old Districts	No. of Students		
				1986-87	1993-94	2002-03
1.	Balasore	1.	Balasore	52,000	56,617	77,101
2.	Bhadrak				36,598	59,739
3.	Bolangir	2.	Bolangir	15,000	26,354	41,116
4.	Sonepur				10,898	17,265
5.	Cuttack	3.	Cuttack	1,10,000	64,705	86,237
6.	Jagatsinghpur				38,097	54,970
7.	Jajpur				50,398	72,553
8.	Kendrapara				48,435	59,048
9.	Dhenkanal	4.	Dhenkanal	23,000	28,382	45,177
10.	Angul				26,410	40,730
11.	Ganjam	5.	Ganjam	29,000	58,373	95,738
12.	Gajapati				6,061	14,978
13.	Kalahandi	6.	Kalahandi	11,000	18,843	34,744
14.	Nuapada				7,081	15,336

SI. No.	Netricts	SI. No.	Old Districts	No. of Students		
				1986-87	1993-94	2002-03
15.	Keonjhar	7.	Keonjhar	17,000	37,350	64,133
16.	Koraput	8.	Koraput	14,000	14,194	16,197
17.	Malkangiri				4,281	9,832
18.	Nawarangpur				7,276	16,688
19.	Rayagada				9,043	19,438
20.	Mayurbhanj	9.	Mayurbhanj	24,000	45,233	61,993
21.	Kondhamal	10.	Phulbani	6,000	9,445	21,162
22.	Boudh				4,784	6,587
23.	Sundergarh	11.	Sundergarh	25,000	48,079	59,782
24.	Sambalpur	12.	Sambalpur	30,000	18,807	35,037
25.	Deogarh				5,819	8,374
26.	Bargarh				26,031	51,402
27.	Jharsuguda				11,320	21,493
28.	Puri	13.	Puri	52,000	38,019	67,274
29.	Khordha				51,819	94,307
30.	Nayagarh				22,245	29,159
	Orissa			4,08,000	8,30,997	12,97,590

Source: Directorate of Elementary Education, Orissa

On the basis of the data of the Seventh AH India Educational Survey: Provisional Statistical Tables of Orissa (date of reference 30.9.2002) it can be stated that:

- The nine coastal districts of Balasore, Bhadrak, Cuttack, Jagatsinghpur, Jajpur, Kendrapara, Puri, Khorda and Ganjam have 3081 i.e. 48.2% of the high schools of Orissa.
- The rest 21 districts together have 3,317 high schools. The KBK districts of Koraput, Malkangiri, Nawarangpur, Rayagada, Kalahandi,Nuapada, Bolangir and Sonepur plus Gajapati - the backward nine districts together have 948 high schools i.e. 14.82% high schools.

- The nine coastal districts have a total enrolment of 6,66,967 i.e. 51.4% of the total secondary school enrolment.

- The nine backward districts of KBK plus Gajapati together have secondary schools enrolment of 1,85,594 in the high schools which is 27.8% of the total enrolment of the nine advanced coastal districts and constitutes 14.3% of state's total secondary school enrolment.

- These glaring imbalances need to be urgendy remedied to check future social unrest.

- The UNICEF had righdy warned that, "There is a clear and growing danger that both the present potential and past achievements may be overwhelmed, in the years ahead, by the growing crises of absolute poverty, rapid population growth, and increasing environmental pressure". The KBK and Gajapati districts present the darker side of failure of developmental efforts of the past.

The secondary stage of education of Orissa is under the administrative control of the Department of School & Mass Education of Government of Orissa and the academic control of the Board of Secondary Eduction. By 31st March 2007, 7,128 high schools were functioning in the State During 2003-04 about 6.79 lakh students were enrolled in these schools. There was one High School for every 21.84 sq.kms. area and for a 5,163 population on an average during 2003-04.

TABLE 6.7

Number of High Schools, Students Enrolled and Teachers in Orissa

SI. No.	Aspect	1999-00	2000-01	2001-02	2002-03	2003-04	2006-07
1.	No. of High Schools	6,094	6,165	6,282	6,811	7,011	7,128
2.	No. of Students (in thousand)	1,076	1,083	1,134	1,288	1,296	NA
3.	No. of Teachers	51,568	51,570	52,389	58,136	60,960	NA

Source: Director, Elementary Education, Orissa, Bhubaneswar

Besides the above, 140 Madrasas, 253 Sanskrit tols, 56 Kendriya Vidyalayas and 24 Navodaya Vidyalayas are providing secondary education. Apart from these, a number of privately managed secondary schools are imparting education which are affiliated to the ICSE or the CBSE. The National Institute of Open Schooling and the Correspondence Cell of the Board of Secondary Education, Orissa are providing secondary education through the distance mode; but the coverage and reach is marginal and negligible. The Sainik School and the Navodaya Schools, are pace-setting secondary schools with special features.

The dropout rate in high school stage is showing a decreasing trend. During 2001-02 the overall dropout rate in High Schools was 69.5% which has decreased to 64.4% during 2003-04. The dropout rate among SC & ST boys is higher than their female peers, while in general category the dropout rate among girls is higher than boys. Though the dropout rate in all categories of high school students have decreased, it is still higher among SCs/STs. The dropout rate in high schools for the year 2000-01 to 2003-04 is as follows.

TABLE 6.8

Dropout rate in High Schools in ORISSA

SI. No.	Community/Gender	2000-01	2001-02	2002-03	2003-04
1.	**All** Communities				
	(i) Boys	68.4	67.0	65.9	62.5
	(ii) Girls	73.4	72.0	68.5	66.7
	(iii) Total	70.6	69.5	67.2	64.4
2.	Scheduled Castes				
	(i) Boys	76.2	75.0	74.1	74.3
	(ii) Girls	78.0	77.0	76.5	73.7
	(iii) Total	77.0	76.0	75.3	74.0
3.	**Scheduled Tribes**				
	(i) Boys	79.3	79.0	78.0	76.3
	(ii) Girls	78.1	77.0	76.5	74.9
	(iii) Total	80.2	78.0	77.3	75.8

Source: Vision, 2020, SME Department, Govt, of India.

During 2003-04, 218 High Schools including 55 for girls were functioning in the State under ST and SC Development Department with an enrollment of 56,063 students in these schools, of which 65.7% were STs and 16.9% were SC. The sanctioned strength of teachers in these schools was 3803. 3924 STs and SCs students (3135 ST and 789 SC) appeared in the HSC Examination,2004 out of which 2506 (1992 ST and 514 SC) students came out successful. The percentage of success rates among the ST and SC candidates were 63.5% and 65.1% respectively during 2004 as against 58.8% and 55.7% during 2003. These rates are higher than the over-all percentages of success of candidates of all communities.

In order to make education popular among the STs and SCs, the State Government is providing hostel facilities at pre-matric and post —matric Levels. There are 218 residential High Schools. Hostels (40 seated each) are functioning in the Tribal Sub-plan (TSP) areas of the State. Besides, there are 7 special hostels for tribal students including 2 for tribal girls (one at Bhubaneswar and the other at Rourkela) in Orissa.

During 2002-03, construction of 15 forty-seated hostel buildings were taken up in 11 districts at an estimated cost of Rs.8.50 lakh/Rsx. 10.00 lakh each for SC/ST students. For KBK districts, an amount of Rs,34.00 crore was provided for construction of 40 seated ST girls' hostel buildings. By the end of 2003-04, about 400 hostel buildings were completed.

With the objective of providing quality education to meritorious tribal students, ten model schools have been established in eight districts under the management of Orissa Model Tribal Education Society (OMTES). Each of the schools will ultimately have class VI-XII with residential facilities for 60 students including 30 girl students in each class. Government have named these Model Schools as Ekalavya Model Residential Schools.

Sex ratio and gender disparity are highly important demographic and social indicators. These negative symptoms need to be corrected.

The Constitution of India categorically states that no discrimination whatsoever should be tolerated due to sex differences. Equality of sexes is the corner-stone of a healthy egalitarian society. Every girl must be able to walk with dignity and 'head held high' with her male peers.

TABLE 6.9

Sex-ratio and Female Literacy of Orissa

Census Year	Sex ratio	Female Literacy rate
1951	1,022	4.52%
1961	1,001	8.65%
1971	988	13.92%
1981	981	20.60%
1991	971	34.68%
2001	972	50.97%

Source: Censuses of 1951 to 2001

It is highly disturbing to note that a persistent decline in the number of females was evident from the census of 1921 and onwards. This symptom got aggravated after 1951. The sex ratio which was steadily declining and the glaring disparity in female literacy portray a disturbing societal picture with its adverse impact on secondary education.

TABLE 6.10

Gender Disparity in Secondary Education

(The Scenario of Orissa 1947-48 to 2002)

(One lakh 100,000)

Year	Enrollment in classes IX & X in Lakhs			Gender Disparity in (%)
	Total	Boys	Girls	
1947-48	0.15 (100%)	0.14 (93.3%)	0.01 (6.7)	86.60%
1950-51	0.16 (100%)	0.15 (93.75%)	0.01 (6.25%)	87.50%

Year	Enrollment in classes IX & X in Lakhs			Gender Disparity
	Total	**Boys**	**Girls**	**in (%)**
1957 (1st Survey)	0.72 (100%)	0.63 (87.5%)	0.9 6. 25%)	70.00%
1965 (2nd Survey)	1.01 100%)	0.90 (89.1%)	0.11 (10.9%)	78.20%
1973 (3rd Survey)	1.94 (100%)	1.57 (80.9%)	0.37 (19.1%)	61.8%
1978 (4th Survey)	2.63 (100)	1.95 (74.4%)	0.68 (25.6%)	49.3%
1986 (5th Survey)	4.08 (100%)	2.76 (74.76%)	1.32 (25.24%)	49.52%
1993 (6th Survey)	5.23 (100%)	3.22 (61.57%)	2.01 (38.43%)	23.14%
2002 (7th Survey)	6.79 (100)	3.79 (55.8%)	3.00 (44.2%)	11.6%

Gender disparity has drastically decreased from 86.6% in 1947-48 to 11.6% by 2002. Education of the girls is definitely progressing. But this satisfaction is negated by the mind-boggling drop-out rates. The entire system of secondary education seems to be in disarray and needs to be streamlined before it totally become irrelevant andirreversibly sub-standard. Bureaucratic bludgeoning can never be the answer. Academic approach needs to be adopted for the reconstruction of secondary education and restoration of its critical role.

CHAPTER-7

HIGH HOPES FROM HIGHERSECONDARY EDUCATION

HIGHLIGHTS

- Evolution
- Recommendation of relating to Higher Secondary Education of:
  - Challenge of Education
  - NPE, 1986 & 1992
  - POA, 1986
  - POA, 1992
- False Start, 1955-85
- Higher Secondary Education, 1985-2002

HIGHER SECONDARY EDUCATION (1981-2007)

Higher Secondary Education is the post-secondary education and provides the essential preparation for higher or tertiary education. The first three universities of India were established in 1857. The preparatory course for the first degree, which is the higher secondary education, was part of the collegiate education. It was known as the First Arts or Intermediate in Arts/Science/Commerce (I.A/I.Sc./I.Com.), and later Pre-university (PUC) plus Pre-Degree Courses. It was of two years duration. The Sadler Commission of 1917; the Radhakrishnan Commission on University Education, 1948; the Mudaliar Commission on Secondary Education, 1952; the Kothari Commission on Indian Education (1966) had time and again reiterated the urgent need for transferring the Higher Secondary Education to the school branch and make it an integral part of secondary education. Multi-purpose higher secondary schools were started in the wake of the recommendations of the Secondary Education Commission (1952). However, it did not find favour with the educational administrators of the times who had inherited conservative no-change mind-set. The higher secondary schools died one by one, and the educational system of Orissa reverted back to the classical "11+2+2" pattern

The Indian Education Commission (1966) advocated the "10+2+3" pattern of education. It was endorsed by the National Policy on Education, 1968. However, the *status quo ante* persisted. The expansion of Higher Secondary Education (i.e. Class XI & XII) from 1950-51 to 1965-66 in India has been depicted in Table No. 7.1.

TABLE 7.1

Expansion of Higher Secondary Education from 1950-51 to 1965-66

Year	Enrolment			Enrolment as percentage of population in the corresponding age group		
	Boys	Girls	Total	Boys	Girls	Total
1950-51	2,45,000 (12.0)	37,000 (13.9)	2,82,000 (12.2)	3.3	0.5	1.9
1955-56	4,31,000	71,000	5,02,000	502	0.9	3.1
1960-61	7,17,000 (10.3)	1,32,00 (11.4)	8,49,000 (10.5)	8.0	1.6	4.9
1965-66	11,72,000 (7.7)	2,26,000 (11.6)	13,98,000 (8.3)	11.5	2.3	7.0

CHALLENGE OF EDUCATION, 1985

The stock-taking exercise of Post-NPE 1968, is evident in the "Challenge of Education" (1985). The Kothari Commission (1966) had recommended the rolling back of the higher secondary courses from the universities to the school system in its recommendation of 10+2+3. The "+2" is the higher secondary education component of the total educational system envisaged from Class I to the end of the first degree. The Challenge of Education noted with deep concern the non-acceptance and non-implementation of the 10+2+3 pattern in states like Punjab, Rajasthan and Madhya Pradesh. Further, even in the states that had accepted the new pattern, "The standards of education available in different schools is also a cause of concern." It further adverted that, "... the change of pattern is not mere arithmetical exercise. It involves the introduction of methods of teaching and evaluation and modernization of curricula as well as the upgradation of standards. The new system is more expensive than the old one."

"By rolling back the first 2 years of college education into the school structure, the age specific competence of children was fitted into the pedagogical system of school education. The rationale for the +2 system has, however to some extent been undermined in the States where a large number of the students in the +2 stage have been enrolled in Junior Colleges". [390]This is the case of Orissa. Higher Secondary Education has not been integrated into the holistic scheme of a vibrant secondary education catering to the needs of the late adolescents.

The "Challenge of Education" lists the criticisms leveled against the 10+2 system.[391] They are:

i. "Equipping secondary schools for imparting +2 education is expensive."
ii. The +2 course has "...imposed on students a load of textual material quite beyondtheir competence"
iii. There are deep differences of opinion "amongst practically all sections of the population and even amongst the various sections of the intelligentsia, what constitutes the core of the 10+2 system".

However, advocates in favour of 10 +2 system state that:

i. It introduces a uniform pattern of education through out the country.
ii. The alleged increased cognitive load is due to failure to develop 'integrated packages of education.'
iii. It is an "innovation of great importance".
iv. It emphasizes vocationalisation of higher secondary education.
v. "It is a new initiative with the content and pedagogy of education".[392]

NATIONAL POLICY ON EDUCATION, 1986 (With modification undertaken in 1992)

According to the National Policy on Education, 1986 with the modification under in 1992:

---

390 *Ibid*, Para 4.104, p. 103
391 *Ibid*, Para 4.105, p. 103
392 *Ibid*, Paras 4.104, 4.105, 4.106 & 4.107 pp.102 to 104

   i.   Secondary Education means education of the children of the age group14+to 17+

  ii.   The secondary classes are four and they are classes IX,X,XI & XII

 iii.   They are preparatory courses for the first degree

 iv.   Vocationalisation is advocated in classes XI and XII i.e. the +2 stage.

PROGRAMME OF ACTION, 1986

The Programme of Action, 1986 had diagnosed the basic maladies haunting secondary and higher secondary education in India. The major short-comings of secondary/higher secondary schools are—

   i.   They are grossly under-provided especially in rural areas.

  ii.   The magnitude of deficit of basic infra-structural facilities have not correctly been assessed. A holistic deficit-picture and a definite road map for remediation and augmentation is not available.

 iii.   Glaring inadequacies of play-grounds are harsh realities.

 iv.   Inadequacy of class-rooms to accommodate the increasing enrolment areabundantly clear.

   v.   The laboratories are in a bad shape and require recurrent-replenishment.

 vi.   Teacher competencies need upgradation.

 vii.   Lack of a core curriculum is a major problem. Continuous programme ofcurriculum renewal and improvement is an urgent need.

viii.   The ratio of higher secondary schools and secondary schools should be 1:3.

 ix.   Students must have access to a variety of streams at the +2 stage.

   x.   Special programmes need to be designed for potential high achievers' and 'a programme for the gifted students'.

 xi.   Providing quality secondary and higher secondary education with reservations of 75% for gifted rural children, 15% for the

Scheduled Caste children, and 7.5% for the Scheduled Tribe children. At least one third of the total enrolment in every category shall be reserved for girls to ensure gender-justice. These schools shall be known as "Navodaya" (New Dawn) schools, and shall be developed as pace-setting exemplar models of integrated secondary and higher secondary education.

PROGRAMME OF ACTION, 1992

The National Policy on Education, 1986 was modified in 1992 on the basis of the intellectual in-puts provided by the Ramamurti Commission and the Janardana Reddy Committee. The Programme of Action, 1986 was also reformulated in 1992. The Programme of Action,1992 reiterated the role of higher secondary education thus:

Higher Secondary (+2) Stage

"8.9.15. The senior secondary (+2) stage is a crucial stage of school education as after this stage students become eligible to complete for professional courses to be future engineers, technologists, doctors, teachers or for pursuing academic courses at the tertiary stage. A large number of them also join the world of work. Therefore, it is at this stage that students are to be exposed to the structure of individual subject disciplines such as Physics, Chemistry, Biology, Mathematics, Geology, History, Geography, Political Science, Economics, Sociology, Philosophy, Psychology, Languages and Arts."

"8.9.16. The content of each subject has to take into account the recent developments in the subject in as much as they are relevant to the +2 stage, and providing all the needed foundations in each subject so that the needs of the different professional courses and the other areas of their further education can be met with in reference to these subjects".[393]

---

393 Ministry of HRD, **GOI**, (1992), Programme of Action, 1992, para 8.915, 8.9.16 p. 91

The POA, 1992 recommended the following steps for implement higher secondary education in India.

i. The ratio of higher secondary schools to secondary schools was envisaged to be 1:3. However, by 1995-96 this had actually decreased to 1:1.186. The promise remains unfulfilled.

ii. Gender disparities are significant.

iii. Though the 10+2+3 pattern has been accepted, "there is considerable diversity regarding the location of the +2 stage. In a few States, it is not a past of the school system".

Orissa is one of the most prominent States belonging to this category. Higher Secondary Education is controlled and directed by the Department of Higher Education of the Government of Orissa through:

a. The Directorate of Higher Education, Orissa

b. The Directorate of Vocational Education, Orissa, and

c. The Council of Higher Secondary Education, Orissa.

iv. The National Council of Educational Research and Training (NCERT), NewDelhi prepared the National Curriculum Framework in 1988, 2000 and 2005. The NCF,1988 never saw the light of the day, the NCF-2000 was mired bycontroversies, and NCF-2005 is attracting violent criticisms. It is suspectedthat every party in power at the Centre is trying to implement its politicalagenda through the instrumentality of a National Curriculum Framework. Curriculum has come to centre-stage and is facing the worst cross-fire. Curriculum is no more the expertise and erudition of the teachers, but issuspected to be sub-serving to ensure political interests of vested politicalparties. However, the public apathy towards curricular matters is fastvanishing, and the common man's concern for curriculum is conspicuouslyevident.

v. Implementing a comprehensive scheme of examinationreforms

vi. Providing diversity of courses in Higher Secondary Schools

vii. Reviewing afresh the pre-service and in-service teachers' training programme.

FALSE START OF HIGHER SECONDARY EDUCATION IN ORISSA, 1955-1985

Higher Secondary Education is the link between secondary and university education and is the terminal stage of school education. For those, who would continue their studies in the universities, it is a preparatory stage and for those, who would enter the world of work, it is the terminal stage of school education, It would, therefore, cater to the needs of both the groups. For the former group it should provide liberal education and for the latter vocational and technical education. Catering to the needs of both the groups is a difficult task.

Higher Secondary Education in Orissa had been traditionally a part of college education. Higher secondary institutions formed part of degree colleges. But such institutions are regarded as initial stages for establishment of degree colleges. Concurrently, there are a few higher secondary schools running under various managements like Kendirya Vidyalaya Sangathan, NCERT, Dayanand Anglo-Vedic Trust, Navodaya Vidyalaya Samiti etc. The academic courses of these higher secondary schools are regulated by the Central Board of Secondary Education (CBSE) or Indian Council of School Education (ICSE).

The Secondary Education Commission, 1952 recommended the establishment of multi-purpose higher secondary schools. The first higher secondary school was established at Mendhasala in 1954-55, it was a post-basic school, and this number increased to two during 1956-57. during 1957-58, the Ravenshaw Collegiate School, Cuttack, Khallikote Collegiate School, Berhampur (Ganjam), Government Girls' High School, Puri were converted into higher secondary schools. During 1958-59, the higher schools at Larambha, Onslow Institution, Chhatrapur, B. B. High School, Dhenkanal, and B.M. High School,

Bhawanipatna were upgraded as Higher Secondary Schools, and the multi-purpose syllabus was introduced in these schools.

The Board of Secondary Education, Orissa had been entrusted with the responsibility of conducting the Higher Secondary School Certificate (HSSC) Examination. It conducted the first HSSC Examination in 1961 in which 193 candidates appeared. The number of candidates who appeared at the HSSC Examination was - 193 in 1961, 408 in 1962, 448 in 1963, 649 in 1964, 670 in 1965, 786 in 1966, 564 in 1967, 329 in 1968, 370 in 1969, 375 in 1970, 385 in 1971, 134 in 1972, 134 in 1973, 94 in 1974, 108 in 1975, 425 in 1976, 396 in 1977 and 424 in 1978. The educationists of Orissa of that time did not appreciate the utility of higher secondary schools. After the initial start, these schools lost sight of their new mandate. They reverted back to their original status as high schools. The development of Higher Secondary Schools in Orissa is depicted in the following table.

HIGHER SECONDARY EDUCATION IN ORISSA

Higher Secondary Education was part and parcel of the higher education system from 1857, (the year in which the first three universities of India Viz. Calcutta, Madras and Bombay had been founded) to 1982, the year in which the Council of Higher Secondary Education was established. There was insistent pedagogical demand to roll back the erstwhile intermediate classes to the secondary schools. However, theeducational administrators did not implement the scheme on one plea or the other. The traditional psychological perception that the intermediate classes were preparatory courses for higher studies in the colleges had its overpowering sway. Half-hearted measures were taken to upgrade some high schools of Orissa to the higher secondary level in the wake of the recommendation of the Secondary Education Commission,!952. However, the experiment failed and the temporarily upgraded higher secondary schools again reverted back to their original status as high schools. Even the post-basic schools which imparted Higher Secondary Education also steadily withered and vanished.

The acceptance of the "10+2+3" scheme and its implementation from the academic session 1970-80 created a situation whereby independent recognition to higher secondary education became unavoidable. The erstwhile Pre-University Course (PUC) and Pre-Professional Course (PPC) were clubbed together and came to be commonly known as "+2 courses" and a few independent higher secondary schools and "Junior"/"+2 colleges" were established.

The Department of Education and Youth Services was the administrative Department. These institutions offering "+2 courses" were controlled by the Director of Higher Education, The Universities of Orissa were conducting the PUC and PPC examinations, and they desired to wash off their hands of this responsibility.

EMERGING HIGHER SECONDARY EDUCATION (1985 TO 2007)

Higher Secondary Education (classes XI and XII) commonly known as the "+2 course" is provided in higher secondary classes attached to secondary schools or degree colleges. With effect the from the academic session 2001-02, the "+2 class" attached to Government and Government aided colleges were designated as "Junior Colleges". There are institutions which are managed by the Government of India like the Demonstration Multi-purpose School, Bhubaneswar, The Kendriya Vidyalayas (also known as Central Schools), the Navodaya Vidyalayas, DAV Schools and some private schools affiliated to the Central Board of Secondary Education, New Delhi which are out of the purview of the CHSE, Orissa.

There were 272 higher secondary institution recognized by CHSE, Orissa in 1985, the year in which it first conducted the higher secondary examination. All the universities of Orissa stopped conducting all examinations that lead to the pre-university and pre-professional courses of one year each and combinedly of two years duration and successor to the erstwhile Intermediate courses. By September2007, there were 1084 higher secondary institutions recognized by the CHSE, Orissa.

TABLE 7.2

Development of Higher Secondary Education in Orissa

Sl. No.	Year	Number of Higher Secondary schools
1.	1978	11
2.	1986	36
3.	1993	383
4.	2007	1084

It is not possible to provide a clear picture of higher secondary education in Orissa as only a few of these institutions are functioning separately. Traditionally it was considered as part of the higher education system. So, separate firm statistics for this phase of education are not available.

A well-planned need-oriented network of higher secondary schools has not yet been developed in the state of Orissa. The emerging scenario of higher secondary education in Orissa is awaited with bated breath, and its over all functional picture is not yet clear.

The Sixth All India Educational Survey collected information from 383 independent higher secondary institutions. An analysis of various aspects of these institutions is given. The date of reference of this Survey is 30.09.1993.

There were 383 independent higher secondary schools as on 30.09.1993. Their spatial distribution and management has been depicted in Table No.7.3.

TABLE 7.3

Spatial Distribution and Management of

Higher Secondary Schools of Orissa (as on 30.9.1993)

Sl. No.	Management	Number of Higher secondary Schools		
		Rural	Urban	Total
1.	Government	53	42	95
2.	Local Body	23	2	25
3.	Private Aided	109	14	123
4.	Private Unaided	117	23	140
	Total	302	81	383

It may be seen that 78.85 per cent higher secondary institutions were in rural areas and 21.15 per cent in urban areas. Management-wise distribution shows that 24.80 per cent were under Government management and 140 higher secondary institutions constituting 36.55 per cent were under private management. Among the Government institutions 55.78% of higher secondary institutions were in rural area. But taking the total number of higher secondary institutions into consideration, it will be seen that 24.80 per cent of them were only Government institutions.

The average enrolment was 223 students. 135 out of the total 383 higher secondary schools had six or less than six rooms. The availability of different streams of courses viz. Arts, Science, Commerce, Agriculture and Vocational and other have been depicted in Table No. 7.4.

TABLE 7.4

Availability of different streams of courses in Higher Secondary Schools of Orissa, 1993

Area	No. of H. S. Schools	Arts	Science	Commerce	Agriculture	Vocational	Others
Urban	81	46	33	10	2	24	10
Rural	302	262	56	20	2	11	9
Total	383	308	89	30	4	35	19

(*Sources:* "Vision 2020" p. 163, Dept. of SME, Govt, of Orissa, Vol. II, p. 163

The district-wise provision of higher secondary education is evident from tableNo. 7. 5.

TABLE NO. 7.5

District-wise Number of Higher Secondary Schools in Orissa, 1993

SI. No.	District	Government	Local Body	Private Aided	Private Unaided	Total
1.	Boudh	0	1	0	0	1
2.	Malkangiri	1	0	1	0	2
3.	Sonepur	0	0	2	1	3
4.	Nawarangpur	0	0	4	0	4
5.	Gajapati	2	0	0	2	4
6.	Nuapada	1	3	2	0	6
7.	Deogarh	2	1	1	3	7
8.	Kandhamal	6	0	2	0	8
9.	Jharsuguda	1	0	0	7	8
10.	Sambalpur	3	0	3	3	9
11.	Koraput	5	0	0	4	9
12.	Rayagada	2	0	0	*6	10
13.	Bhadrak	1	1	8	0	10
14.	Dhenkanal	0	1	5	4	10
15.	Angul	6	0	2	3	11
16.	Baragarh	2	0	2	7	11
17.	Nayagarh	1	0	4	6	11
18.	Jagatsinghpur	4	3	4	2	13
19.	Cuttack	4	1	5	4	14
20.	Keonjhar	2	0	7	6	15
21.	Kalahandi	2	1	4	8	15
22.	Jajpur	3	0	6	9	18
23.	Khurda	7	0	4	8	19
24.	Puri	6	8	1	4	19
25.	Ganjam	6	0	10	4	20
26.	Mayurbhanj	3	0	9	9	21
27.	Sundergarh	9	1	6	9	25

SI. No.	District	Government	Local Body	Private		Total
				Aided	Unaided	
28.	Kendrapara	6	0	11	9	26
29.	Balangir	5	0	8	14	27
30.	Balasore	5	4	10	8	27
	Total	95	25	123	140	383

Sources: Sixth All India Educational Survey Report (Orissa), Published by the Directorate of Elementary Education,Orissa,2000.[394]

It is evident from the above table that the districts of Boudh, Malkangiri, Sonepur, Nawarangpur, Gajapati, Nuapada, Deogarh, Kandhamal, Jharsuguda, Sambalpur, Koraput, Rayagada and Dhenkanal are grossly deficit in the provision of higher secondary education. Neglect of this field of education has deep sociological implications, as it is likely to engender developmental distances and domination of certain well-provided regions in all general and professional fields.

There were 42 higher secondary schools exclusively for girls (1993) out of which 18 were in urban areas. Of the total 383 higher secondary schools, 81 were in urban areas.

It may be observed that 308 higher secondary institutions constituting (80.41 per cent) offer Arts courses, 88 (23.23 per cent) Science courses, 30 (7.83 per cent) Commerce courses, 4 (1.04 per cent) Agriculture courses, and 35 (9.14 per cent) Vocational courses.

It may be further observed that 262 higher secondary institutions out of the 302 in the Rural sector constituting 86.75 per cent have Arts courses against 56.79 per cent in the urban sector. 18.54 per cent rural higher secondary institutions have Science courses against 40.74 per cent in urban areas.

The enrolment of students in higher secondary schools has been depicted in Table No.7.6.

---

394 NCERT, Sixth All India Educational Survey, 2000

TABLE NO. 7.6

Enrolment in Higher Secondary Schools

Area	Girls			Boys			Total		
	ST	SC	General	ST	SC	General	ST	SC	General
Urabn	363	691	7096	475	474	6529	838	1465	13625
Rural	1288	2768	18842	4312	6247	36315	5600	9015	55175
Total	1651	3459	25938	4787	7021	42844	6438	10480	68780

Sources: Sixth All India Educational Survey Report (Orissa), Published by the Directorate of Elementary Education,Orissa, 2000

The size of the higher secondary schools varied significantly. In some schools the enrolment was below 100, whereas in some it was more than 600. The average enrolment stood at 305.75 per school. There were 158 institutions with enrolment between 201-400, and only 34 schools had enrolment exceeding 600 students.

At the higher secondary stage, the highest enrolment was in the Arts stream 70,213 (81.92%) followed by Science stream 9,538 (11.13%), Commerce stream 2,043 (2.38%), the employment oriented streams of Agriculture had an enrolment of 409 students (0.47%), and Vocational stream 2,788 (2.67%). The Sixth all India Survey did not cover the "Higher Secondary Classes" attached to degree colleges. However, the Seventh All India Education Survey whose date of reference is 30th September,2002 has provided detailed data

SEVENTH ALL INDIA EDUCATIONAL SURVEY (2002)

The NCERT had conducted the Seventh All India Educational Survey. The Directorate of Teacher Education and SCERT, Orissa took up this responsibility for Orissa[395]. The final report has not yet been published by the NCERT. However, provisional data relating to school education as on 30.09.2002 is available for down-loading from the internet. The profile of higher secondary education in Orissa (2002) is based on this data.

395

There were 993 institutions offering higher secondary courses in Orissa, out of which 426 were higher schools and 567 were 'higher secondary classes' attached to degree colleges or 'junior colleges'. The distribution of these schools in rural and urban areas has been depicted in Table No. 7.7.

The rural schools abound in Arts course, Science and Commerce courses were highly inadequate. The presence of the "Agricultural streams "is marginal and negligible.

TABLE NO. 7.7

Higher Secondary Schools & Junior Colleges, 2002

SI. No.	District	Higher Secondary Institutions				Total Higher Secondary Institutions
		Higher Secondary Schools		Junior Colleges		
		Rural	Urban	Rural	Urban	
1.	Angul	8	5	16	4	33
2.	Bolangir	35	2	8	6	51
3.	Balasore	19	3	30	9	61
4.	Bargarh	21	2	14	7	44
5.	Boudh	1	2	4	1	8
6.	Bhadrak	14	0	13	6	33
7.	Cuttack	2	1	30	15	48
8.	Deogarh	5	0	3	1	9
9.	Dhenkanal	21	1	12	7	41
10.	Gajapati	3	1	4	3	11
11.	Ganjam	15	8	16	31	70
12.	Jagatsinghpur	18	1	16	2	37
13.	Jajpur	5	0	34	3	42
14.	Jharsuguda	13	7	1	4	25
15.	Kalahandi	21	8	2	1	32
16.	Kondhamal	6	0	5	3	14
17.	Kendrapara	11	0	27	5	43

SI. No.	District	Higher Secondary Institutions				Total Higher Secondary Institutions
		Higher Secondary Schools		Junior Colleges		
		Rural	Urban	Rural	Urban	
18.	Keonjhar	18	2	19	8	47
19.	Khurda	13	13	19	21	66
20.	Koraput	2	2	8	2	14
21.	Malkangiri	4	2	1	2	9
22.	Mayurbhanj	14	0	39	5	58
23.	Nawarangpur	2	2	3	2	9
24.	Nayagarhi	10	1	12	5	28
25.	Nuapada	4	3	4	1	12
26.	Puri	15	1	15	7	38
27.	Rayagada	5	0	8	3	16
28.	Sambalpur	13	9	6	5	33
29.	Sonepur	8	1	7	3	19
30.	Sundergarh	18	5	14	5	42
	Orissa	344	82	390	177	993

The district of Boudh (8), Malkangiri (9), Deogarh (9), Nabarangpur (11), Gajapati (11), Nuapada (12) and Rayagada (16) have the least facilities for higher secondary education. The districts of Ganjam (70), Khurda (66), Balasore (61) have the highest access to higher secondary education. Higher secondary education is the stepping stone to higher education. Its inadequacy generates developmental distances and regional imbalances culminating in far reaching socio-political and economic problems in the future. A well-designed action plan to spread higher secondary education evenly through out the state is an urgent necessity.

Existence of educational in institutions is not enough. Enrolment is the critical factor. The present day enrolment figures would delineate the social-political contours of the future. Enrolment in educational institutions has a direct and visible impact upon economic progress and upward social mobility. The trends of enrolment in the higher secondary courses have been indicated in Table No. 7.8.

TABLE NO. 7.8

Trends of Enrolment in the Higher Secondary Courses[396]

No.	District	Total Enrolment in Classes XI and XII		Total
		Higher Secondary Schools	**Junior Colleges**	
1.	Angul	2290	8566	10856
2.	Balangir	5336	9652	14988
3.	Baleswar	5219	21945	27164
4.	Bargarh	3460	9692	13152
5.	Boudh	204	1031	1235
6.	Bhadrak	2516	11765	14281
7.	Cuttack	480	15821	16301
8.	Deogarh	925	1778	2703
9.	Dhenkanal	3699	9978	13677
10.	Gajapati	237	2012	2249
11.	Ganjam	5226	19757	24983
12.	Jagatsinghpur	3526	11063	14589
13.	Jajpur	1668	17815	19483
14.	Jharsuguda	2503	4460	6963
15.	Kalahandi	4380	6344	10724
16.	Kandhamal	619	3001	3620
17.	Kendrapara	1816	15289	17105
18.	Keonjhar	2772	10851	13623
19.	Khurda	4457	23200	27657
20.	Koraput	317	2604	2921
21.	Malkangiri	608	1256	1864
22.	Mayurbhanj	2842	14122	16964
23.	Nawarangpur	446	1798	2244
24.	Nayagarh	2185	6947	9132

No.	District	Total Enrolment in Classes XI and XII		Total
		Higher Secondary Schools	**Junior Colleges**	
25.	Nuapada	974	2123	3097
26.	Puri	3062	12822	15884
27.	Rayagada	660	2946	3606
28.	Sambalpur	5212	8597	13809
29.	Sonepur	1409	3600	5009
30.	Sundergarh	4479	11836	16315
	Orissa	**73527**	**272671**	**346198**

Records of the Council of Higher Secondary Education, Orissa 1982 to 2006.

As has been mentioned earlier the higher secondary classes (Classes XI and XII) have been detached from the degree college with effect from 2001. The institutions are named as junior colleges/higher secondary institutions. The total number of this institution is 1086 at present with a teaching staff of 2710 and an enrolment of 48000, 35.2 thousand boys and 12.8 thousand girls.

From 2010 onwards every field of employment is surely going to be dominated by districts of Khurda, Balasore, Ganjam and Jajpur, which have the highest enrolment figures in the higher secondary courses in 2002. Similarly the districts of Boudh, Malkangiri, Nawarangpur, Deogarh, Gajapati, Koraput, Nuapada and Rayagada are likely to recede further backward. Educationally most backward area of KBK (Koraput, Bolangir and Kalahandi) with eight districts has just 12.85 of the total state's enrolment at the higher secondary stage.

* * * * *

CHAPTER-8

EDUCATION FOR SKILLS

VOCATIONAL HIGHER

SECONDARYEDUCATION

HIGHLIGHTS

- Evolution
- Recommendation Relating to Vocationalization of Secondary Education of:
    - University Education Commission, 1948
    - Secondary Education Commission, 1952
    - Kothari Commission, 1966
    - Challenge of Education, 1985
    - NPE, 1986
    - POA, 1986
    - POA, 1992
- Progress of Vocational Higher Secondary Education:
    - Directorate of Vocational Education and R.O.V.E.S.
    - Programmes Offered
    - Management Structure
    - Proposed Provision, 2000-07

Documentary evidence relating to vocational education is sketchy and scanty in the educational literature of ancient India. However, vocational education had been described as the basis on which, "ancient India was able to build up her own economic life and prosperity and figured in the ancient world as the chief exporting country; supplying foreign countries from time immemorial and through the ages with luxuries and other articles turned out by her cottage industries and handicrafts. India has a continuous and glorious legacy of vocational education; and that was the secret of India's glorious civilization."[397]

All forms of vocational education flourished in ancient India. There are profuse references to Medical Education, which Indians termed as the "wisdom for longevity" or Ayurveda; to military education which was called Dhanurveda or the "wisdom of shooting", to sculpture; music, metallurgy; and a host of other crafts and industrial activities. The guilds of the respective crafts functioned both as schools of industrial training and agencies of recognizing levels of skill proficiency.

The Buddhist texts profoundly refer to the rich tapestry of vocational and technical education of the times. It refers to such types of occupational education as clerical (lekham); accountancy (ganana); drawing (roopam); medicine and surgery etc. The Vinaya texts and Milinda Panha abound in references to a variety of arts, crafts and trades and vocational education. Islamic India inherited the culture of the past and interacted with the muslim countries. The result was an enrichment of all arts and crafts.

The Wood's Despatch (1854) pointed out the need for "occupational education for a large segment of the student population". The Indian Education Commission of 1882, commonly known as the Hunter Commission after its chairman WW Hunter, had recommended two Matriculation courses. "A" 'general' and; "B" 'Technical'. Mr. T. S. Slater, Principal, Sibpore Engineering College, formulated the details for the

---

397 Radhakumud Mookerji, Ancient Indian Education, Motital Banarasidass, New Delhi, 1998.

Matriculation (Technical Course). Dr. Voeleker, Agricultural Chemist to the Royal Society, visited India in 1889 to advise the Imperial Government on agriculture. He recommended that agricultural education should be integrated into primary education. In 1890, the Committee of Experts examined Dr. Voeleker's recommendation and approved them as 'most desirable'. The Calcutta University Commission (1917) recommended the bifurcation of higher secondary education into general and technical branches. The Hartog Committee (1929) recommended the introduction of industrial and commercial courses into higher education. The Wood-Abbot Committee (1936) recommended that general education should have a technical counterpart. The Zakir Husain Committee Report (1937) recommended the introduction of "... some suitable form of productive work" as "the most effective approach to the problem of providing an integral all-sided education"; and to relieve the children from the "tyranny of... academic and theoretical instruction". The Post-War Reconstruction Report of Sir John Sargent visualized two streams of secondary education: general and technical.

UNIVERSITY EDUCATION COMMISSION (1948)

The University Education Commission, (1948) suggested the introduction of vocational education to meet the multifarious social needs and emphasized the need for a 'vocational bias' to education.

SECONDARY EDUCATION COMMISSION (1952-53)

The Secondary Education Commission (1952) recommended 'streaming' and the introduction of multi-purpose secondary schools. It stated: "There should be much greater emphasis on crafts and productive work in all schools; and in addition diversification of courses...at the secondary stage so that students may take up agricultural, technical, commercial or other practical courses which will...enable them either to take up vocational pursuits or to join technical institutes for further training...". It recommended that:

- Multi-purpose schools should be established to provide varied courses of interest to students with diverse aims, aptitudes, and abilities. Access to Polytechnics and Technological Institutions should be there for those who complete these courses.

- All States should provide special facilities for Agricultural Education.

- A large number of Technical Schools should be started either separately or as part of the Multi-purpose Schools near or around industrial areas. Central Technical Institutions should be established. Apprenticeship training should be provided.

INDIAN EDUCATION COMMISSION (1964-66) AND AFTER

The Indian Education Commission (1964-66) recommended, "Vocationalisation of secondary school curriculum, so that 20% of the lower secondary level students and 50% of the higher secondary students may be diverted to these vocational courses by 1986. Diversification and specialization was to begin at the higher secondary stage only."

It strongly recommended the vocationalisation of higher secondary education. This was approved in the NPE, 1968. It categorically stated that the "+2 stage is not merely a college preparatory course; but one meant for career-choice". In 1976, the NCERT prepared the document on Higher Secondary Education and its Vocationalisation. In 1977, the Govt, of India constituted a Working Group on Vocationalisation of education. It prepared a detailed scheme, along with the financial implications of implementing the scheme. The CABE. Reviewed it in 1978; and recommended it to the State Boards of Secondary Education for implementation. The joint session of Directors of Educations, Chairpersons and Secretaries of the Boards of Secondary Education accepted the recommendation of CABE of 1978. In 1985, the Govt, of India constituted "The National Working Group on Vocationalisation of Education". It examined the post-NPE, 1968 scenario relating to vocationalisation of higher secondary education and provided the guidelines for its future development.

CHALLENGE OF EDUCATION (1985)

The Challenge of Education, (1985) stated that:

i. Vocationalisation of higher secondary education was a major objective of the reformsenvisaged in the educational policy of 1968.

ii. The attempts made have not borne fruits.

iii. The enrolment in vocational higher secondary education is marginal and confined to a few states.

iv. The courses started are mostly unimaginative.

v. Radical reconstruction is an urgent imperative.

vi. The work-experience component of secondary education has remained weak.

vii. Vocationalisation of higher secondary education failed due to unimaginative andincompetent administration.

viii. It lacks professionalism.

ix. Financial constraints plague this sector.

x. It has failed to produce "skilled manpower at the middle level" as envisaged.

It reviewed the scenario relating to Vocationalization of Higher Secondary Education and observed:

"Reverting to an earlier line of reasoning regarding the place of vocational education, it is still to be decided as to whether one of the streams of vocational education would constitute an entirely independent institutional arrangement or an altogether new model should be evolved in which vocational training would be imparted in conjunction with technical institutions for higher education or production centers. This decision would have far reaching implications regarding the cost, quality and management of vocational education."

"The establishment of vocational courses of institutions will be the responsibility of the Government as well as employers in the public and private sectors. The Government will, however, take special steps to cater to the needs of women, rural and tribal students and the deprived sections of society. Appropriate programme will also be started for the handicapped."

"Graduates of vocational courses will be given opportunities, under predetermined conditions, for professional growth, career improvement and lateral entry into courses of general, technical and professional education through appropriate bridge courses."

"Tertiary level courses will be organised for the young who graduate from the higher secondary courses of the academic stream and may also require vocational courses."

"It is proposed that vocational courses cover 10 percent of higher secondary students by 1995 and 25 percent by 2000. Steps will be taken to see that a substantial majority of the products of vocational courses are employed or become self-employed. Review of the courses offered would be regularly undertaken. Government will also review its recruitment policy to encourage diversification at the secondary level."

"If only the less intelligent and academically poorer students are sent to this stream which, at least at present, offers neither a responsible chance of worthwhile employment nor any advantage in moving upwards into a professional of general programme of education. To an extent the failure of vocational stream is the result of poor linkages between it and industry or opportunities for self-employment. Both practical as well as theoretical training in vocational education are best imparted in actual work-situations."

"It has been stated by many experienced teachers that vocationalization within the secondary school system has been a casualty at the hands of educational planners who have no insight into either the opportunities of employment or the type of expertise required for vocational employment. Consequently, in planning for training of teachers, preparation of curricula, selection of courses, all initiatives have been characterized by a lack of professionalism. Naturally, therefore, adequate financial resources have neither been demanded nor provided for starting viable activities in this field. It is paradoxical that while to raising productivity and economic growth, growth of vocationalization has been stunted from the very inception of the programme."

It recommended the vocationalisation of Higher Secondary Education. It stated:

> *"The recent decision of a State Government to separate the Vocational stream of post-10th grade education from higher secondary schools has again raised the controversy as to whether or not vocational education should be regarded as an integral part of the 10+2 system. Significantly, late Prof. J. P. Naik who was the Member-Secretary of the Education Commission of 1964-66 stated in The Education Commission and After' that 'a careful examination of the recommendations of the commission will show that its proposals for vocationalization at the secondary stage are not all connected with the adoption of the new (10+2+3) pattern'. He went on to stress that the Education Commission had visualized the provision of vocational courses of 1 to 3 years duration for those who had completed the elementary state of education. He complained that, contrary to the intensions of the programme of vocationalization, secondary education was being carried on as if it was equal to the two year coursed of full-time vocational education that can be provided only outside the higher secondary schools."*

"In relation to higher secondary education, the question of objectives is of particular relevance because, if it is geared to employment, it would assume a different pattern and terminal characteristics. If, on the other hand, it is looked upon merely as a stage of general development, it would be geared more towards higher education. This raised the question of who is entitled to go in for the stream oriented to higher education and how selection should be made for vocational education. It also raised the question as to whether vocational education should be expected to provide a skill component adequate to facilitate movement from the school, straight into full employment. While vocationalization, as a concept, is favoured by economic planners, in the scale of prevalent values, it is rated lower than pre-professional and general education. If the process of branching off is determined by relative academic merit of students, with lower order of attainment being sent to the vocational stream, the dichotomy between knowledge and skill, representing higher and lower order of activities, will be perpetuated."

"It needs to be clearly stated that vocational courses are not confined to +2 stage i.e. classes XI and XII only. Depending on interest of the pupils, such courses can and should be made available even after class V (along with middle level scholastic course) or after class VIII or even after class XII of academic stream, for those who would not pursue higher education. Most of the courses would, however, be for post-10th stage. Another point about which clarity is necessary is that vocational courses are not limited to engineering and technical vocations, but include courses in agriculture, business and commerce, health and para-medical services, home science, etc. These courses are not meant to duplicate the work of such institutions as it is and Polytechnics-which train manpower primarily for the organised secondary sector. Instead, these are identified in response to the felt training needs on the basis of socio-economic survey and would mainly respond to self-employment and service sector need of the community."

"Some of the major problems of implementation of vocationalization programme arise from the paucity of trained teachers for carrying out this programme. Before going on to discuss the mechanics of vocationalization, it seems relevant to pose some of off-repeated questions about vocationalisation. The first one related to whether or not reliable models for assessment of manpower requirements are available for different patterns and rate of growth. The second question related to the extent to which vocationalisation should be attuned to employment in the organized and/or the unorganised sector and how far it can promote self-employment, especially in the rural areas. The third issue is whether vocationalisation should so organised that it would provide for vertical mobility into the streams of professional and/or general education. During 1992-93, 150 more such schools were sanctioned by Government of India and then 50 more schools during 1993-94. These institutions ostensible purported to diversity students from the general colleges and to provide them with pragmatic educational opportunities with the possibilities of employment on self-employment and, if upgraded, the employability of +2 passed candidates."

NATIONAL POLICY ON EDUCATION (1986 &1992)

The NPE, 1986 provided the detailed policy outline for implementing vocationalisation of higher secondary education. It stated,

"Introduction of systematic, well planned and rigorously implemented programme of vocational education is crucial in the proposed educational reorganisation. These elements are meant to develop a healthy attitude amongst students towards work and life, to enhance individual employability, to reduce the mis-match between the demand and supply of skilled manpower and to provide an alternative for those intending to pursue higher education without particular interest of purpose. Efforts will be made to provide children at the higher secondary level with generic vocational courses which cut across several occupational fields."

"Vocational Education will also be a distinct stream, intended to prepare students for identified occupations spanning several areas of activity. These courses will ordinarily be provided after the secondary stage, but keeping the scheme flexible, they may also be made available after class VIII."

"Health planning and health service management should optimally interlock with the education and training of appropriate categories of health manpower through health related vocational courses. Health education at the primary and middle levels will ensure the commitment of the individual to family and community health, and lead to health related vocational courses at the +2 stage of higher secondary education. Efforts will be made to devise similar vocational courses based on Agriculture, Marketing, Social Services etc. An emphasis in vocational education will also be on development of attitudes, knowledge and skills for entrepreneurship and self-employment."

"Graduates of vocational courses will be given opportunities, under predetermined conditions, for professional growth, career improvement and lateral entry into courses of general, technical and professional education through appropriate bridge courses."

"Non-formal, flexible and need based vocational programmes will also be made available to neo-literates, youth who have completed primary education, school drop-outs, persons engaged in work and unemployed or partially employed persons. Special attention in this regard will be given to women."

"Tertiary level courses will be organised for the young who graduate from the higher secondary courses of the academic stream and may also require vocational courses of the academic stream and may also require vocational courses."

"It is proposed that vocational courses cover 10 percent of higher secondary students by 1995 and 25 percent by 2000 steps will be taken to see that a substantial majority of the products of vocational courses are employed or become self-employed. Review of the courses offered would be regularly undertaken. Government will also review its recruitment policy to encourage diversification at the secondary level."

PROGRAMME OF ACTION 1986

The POA, 1986 provided the detailed guidelines for implementation of vocational education, It stated the details of vocationalisation at the higher secondary stage.

"The vocational courses at higher secondary stage are to be regarded not as a preparation for the college, but as a period of preparing an increasingly large number of school-leavers for different vocations in life. The need for vocationalisation of higher secondary education has been conceded by all, but only a small percentage of students population has been covered by vocationalisation in the past nine years (1976-85). The estimated number of students seeking admission to +2 in 1985 is of the order of 25 lakhs. Even if 10% of this population was to be diverted for vocational courses, the number should have been over 2.50 lakhs, against the present intake of 0.72 lakhs. The problem can be further appreciated, if this data is seen against the Kothari Commission's recommendation, expecting a diversion of 50% of 10+ students for vocational education."

"The country has developed over the years, a network of vocational schools, vocational institutes and polytechnics. Nearly 2% to 3% of the school-going children enter such institutes like Industrial Training Institutes (ITIs), Junior Technical Schools etc. These institutions handle essentially full time students who meet the need of organized sector. The annual intake is of the order of 5 lakhs."

"Kothari Commission has visualised that at 8+, about 20% of the students will step off the general stream and enter schools of vocational education. Similarly, a large percentage of 10+ students are to be diverted to such vocational institutions are not able to cater to this large number of students of 8+ and 10+ stage. There is, therefore, a need for expansion of the regular vocational education programmes in terms of opening more institutions and introduction of new vocational areas."

"One of the factors responsible for the slow progress of vocationalisation of secondary education is the lack of opportunities for the vocational pass-outs for their professional growth and career advancement."

"The current prejudice against vocational education will not disappear unless a reasonable chance of worthwhile employment or an advantage in moving upwards into a professional or general programme of education is provided to the students of vocational courses at the secondary level."

PROGRAMME OF ACTION, 1992

On the basis of the past experience and the intellectual inputs of the Ramamurti Committee and the Jannardana Reddy Committee, the Programme of Action, 1992 recommended the vocationalisation of secondary education at plus two level, It stated,

SCHEMATIC PATTERN AND COVERAGE

"As already mentioned, the scheme of vocationalisation of secondary education at +2 level was started in 1987-88 and taken up for implementation in 24 states and UTs. Facilities have thus been created for diversion of about 6.27 lakh students at +2 level @25 studentsper vocational section at +2 level. The NCERT undertook a quick appraisal of the implementation of the programme in seven states in 1990. The Department of Education has engaged M/S Open Main Systems to collect data on implementation of the programme. Data up to 1991 has been received for 19 states and UTs. A computerized Management Information System (MIS) has been developed so that necessary information on different aspects of the programme implementation are available at different levels from the district to the Central Government. The MIS will become operational from July 1992-93."

"A determined effort will be made to introduce the programme in Tripura, Daman & Diu, Dadra & Nagar Haveli and Lakshadweep. The main emphasis during the 8th Plan would be consolidation and quality improvement of the existing programme. By the end of the 8th Plan, it is proposed to create facilities for diversion of an additional 2.62 lakh students at +2 level, taking the cumulative coverage to 8.89 lakh students or in percentage terms, approximately 11% of the student population at +2 stage."

Revision of the Scheme

"In the light of the feedback received from the states and the experience gained in implementation, certain aspects in the scheme are being revised. These include the financial outlays for equipment, construction of work-sheds, vocational surveys, raw materials and field visits. Assistance to vocational organisations would be a separate scheme hereafter.

ESSENTIALS FOR A SUCCESSFUL VOCATIONAL PROGRAMME

- "The credibility of the programme should be established. This would depend on its quality, relevance and acceptability.
- Education-Employment linkages should be firmly established.
- Adequate infrastructure-physical and academic should be provided.
- Assured supply of funds over an extended period of 5 to 10 years.
- Training programme for teachers both pre-service and in-service.
- Training of teacher trainers.
- Effective management structures at all levels-at the Centre and in the States/UTs and reasonable tenure for their functionaries.
- Equivalence among the vocational, technical and academic courses.
- Curriculum development in consultation with employers.
- Enlisting common involvement and participation of commercial establishments and industrial houses.
- Need for active co-operation of other government Departments with the Department of Education at the Central and State level?

APPRENTICESHIP TRAINING

It has been consistently felt that students of the Vocational courses at +2 level should be provided facilities for apprenticeship training under the Apprentices Act as an important catalyst for promoting vocational education. The training would strengthen the skills of the vocational education. The training would strengthen the skills of the vocational students by placing them in real work situation in industries/farms whereby establishing their worthiness in the area of vocational training obtained. In 1986, the Apprentices Act administered by the Ministry of Labour (DGE&T) was amended to provide training to vocational students of +2 level (Technician Vocational Apprentices). This scheme is being implemented through the four Regional Boards of Apprenticeship Training (BOAT) at Mumbai, Kolkata, Chennai and Kanpur. Twenty subject fields were notified for apprenticeship training in 1988. Despite that, the actual number of students who could actually get the benefit of these facilities is very small. The Central Apprenticeship Council under the Ministry of Labour has approved the inclusion of 40 more subject fields.

The POA, 1992 recommended the setting-up of the following administrative arrangements to facilitate the effective implementation of vocational at various levels:

I. National Level

1. Joint Council of Vocational Education (JCVE)
2. Bureau of Vocational Education in the Ministry of Human Resources Development of Govt, of India.
3. Department of Vocational Education in the NCERT, Pandit Sundarlal Sharma Central Institute of Vocational Education, Bhopal, was set-up in fulfillment of this requirement.

II. Regional Level

1. Boards of Apprenticeship to provide opportunities of practical training to pass-out of +2 vocational courses.

2. Regional Institute of Education at Bhubaneswar, Bhopal, Mysore, Ajmer and Shillong under the NCERT to function as

   a. Regional Vocational Teacher Training Institute and

   b. Perform Research & Development functions.

III. State Level

1. Establish a State Council of Vocational Education (SCVE)
2. Directorate of Vocational Education to provides administrative leadership.
3. SCERTs to provide research & development support.

IV. District Level

1. District Vocational Education Committees to be set-up.

PROGRESS OF VOCATIONAL EDUCATION

The Govt, of Orissa decided to implement the Centrally-sponsored Scheme of Vocational Education in Orissa from 1988-89. The Vocational Higher Secondary Schools were envisaged to be opened in three phases:

1988-89   : 31 Schools

1990-91   : 150 Schools

1995-96   : 50 Schools

Of the total 231 Vocational Higher Secondary Schools, 60 were to be located in the Tribal areas of the State, and 171 in non-tribal areas. These schools were located in High Schools, Govt. Colleges and Aided non-Govt. Colleges. Of these 231 GHSV Schools, 51 were attached to Govt. Colleges and 180 to Govt. High Schools.

As per the report of the Director of Vocational Education, Orissa "all these 231 institutions were not functional; only 85 were functional around 2000; and by 2003 seventy one (71) GHSVs were functioning in the State.

High Schools are administered by the Department of School and Mass Education; and Colleges by the Department of Higher Education of the Govt, of Orissa. The Nabakrishna Choudhury Centre for Development Studies was requested to review this programme and it submitted the "District Vocational Survey Report". On the basis of its recommendation, all the GHSVSs were shifted in 2003-04 to the Government or Aided Colleges of the vicinity. They have been re-designated as Government Vocational Junior Colleges after shifting them from the schools.

The State Council of Vocational Education decided to streamline the management system by creating a separate Directorate of Vocational Education. But this decision got mired in legal tangles. Finally, it was brought under the State Plan with effectfrom the financial year 1995-96. The Courses of Studies are prescribed by the Council of Higher Secondary Education, Orissa which also conducts the examinations.

The progress of vocational education can be gauged from Table No.8.1, which depicts the growth of institutions, number of students enrolled, number of students appeared, passed and pass percentage.

TABLE 8.1

Enrolment & Success in Vocational Higher Secondary Education (1988-89 to 2006-07)

Year	Government Vocational Higher Secondary Schools	Admitted Admitted	Enrolled for Examination	Appeared	Passed	Percentage
1988-89	31	1174	...	...	...	...
1989-90	31	1338	997	994	679	68.30
1990-91	31	4774	1416	1397	720	51.53
1991-92	181	2376	4037	4009	2920	72.83
1992-93	181	...	1766	1766	1272	72.80
1993-94	181	1638	...	...	...	...
1994-95	181	2818	1532	1405	638	45.40
1995-96	181	2120	2637	1359	123	9.05

Year	Government Vocational Higher Secondary Schools	Admitted Admitted	Enrolled for Examination	Appeared	Passed	Percentage
1996-97	181	1580	1916	1611	556	34.51
1997-98	181	1132	1454	1370	601	43.86
1998-99	181	1187	1055	1099	345	31.39
1999-00	181	1239	1062	743	312	41.99
2000-01	231	1116	631	587	275	46.84
2001-02	231	1178	886	861	638	74.09
2002-03	231	1144	983	956	873	91.31
2003-04	231	1561	1125	1103	1045	94.74
2004-05	231	2584	1426	1402	1248	89.01
2005-06	231	2685	...	...	...	...
2006-07	231	3281	...	...	...	...

From 1988-89 to 1990-91, there were only 31 Government Higher Secondary Vocational Schools (GHSVS); whose number increased to 181 during 1991-92 and is now stationary at 231.

The Centrally-sponsored scheme of Higher Secondary Vocational Education was implemented in Orissa with effect from 1988-89. The Centre subsidized the scheme for the first five years. From 1994-95, it has become a State scheme. However, one trade of "Computer Application" continues to be a Centrally-sponsored scheme operating in the vocational higher secondary schools of Orissa.

This scheme was under the administrative control of the Department of Higher Education of Govt, of Orissa up to 31.07.2000. Its administration was with:

   i. Directorate of Higher Education acting as the nodal administrative agency controlling all the schools.

  ii. Directorate of Teacher Education and S.C.E.R.T, Orissa providing the academic support; and

iii.   The Additional Inspectors in the Inspectorates charged with the responsibilityof inspection of these schools.

Under this scheme, it continues to be part of Higher Education. The Council of Higher Secondary Education, Orissa accords recognition to the Vocation Junior Colleges, prescribes the courses and conducts the examinations and awards the certificates.

DIRECTORATE OF VOCATIONAL EDUCATION, ORISSA AND R.O.V.E.s

The Directorate of Vocational Education was created on 1st August, 2000. The administrative function of the Directorate of Higher Education, Orissa, the academic responsibilities of the Directorate of Teacher Education & SCERT, Orissa and the inspecting function of the Inspectorates were withdrawn and integrated into a single window system of a Directorate of Vocational Education, Orissa, It has a sanctioned staff strength of 39. It is under the Department of Higher Education (2007).

The Director of Vocational Education, Orissa is the administrative head. Normally, the post is held by an LA. S. officer of the rank of an Additional secretary. The Director is assisted by a Joint Director, a Deputy Director, three Consultants, one Administrative Officer, one accountant, one section officer and 24 supporting staff members.

It has three Regional Offices of Vocational Education (ROVEs) at Bhubaneswar, Berhampur and Sambalpur. These Regional offices operate from the premises of the respective Regional Directorates. Each Regional Office has a Deputy Director and three Assistant Directors, and nine supporting staff members. A number of posts were lying vacant due to financial crunch.

There is a Vocational Education Cell in the Department of Higher Education of Govt, of Orissa, with a Deputy Secretary as its branch officer. The Commissioner-cum-Secretary, Department of Higher Education is in overall charge of this programme.

FORMULATION OF VOCATIONAL COURSES

The National Council of Educational Research & Training (NCERT) through its constituent organization known as Pandit Sundarlal Sharma Central Institute of Vocational Education, Bhopal has developed detailed courses of studies for more than 100 vocational courses at the higher secondary stage.

The Govt, of Orissa has approved only 14 trades and with the inclusion of Computer Application in 2006-07, there are 15 Trades encompassing five major areas of Agriculture, Business and Commerce, Engineering, Health and Pare-Medical Services, Home Science and Humanities. In 2007-08, the number of trades offered are twenty. They are:

DIFFERENT TRADES OFFERED (2007)

During 2007-08, twenty trades are taught in GVJCs of Orissa. Two trades have been allotted to each GVJC. A student can take admission in one trade only. Presendy, teaching is imparted in the following 20 trades in different GVJCs of the State:

Agriculture Area

1. Dairying (DAI)
2. Poultry Farming (PF)
3. Horticulture (HORT)
4. Inland Fisheries (IF)
5. Crop Production (CP)
6. Sericulture (SERI)

Engineering Area

7. Computer Technique (CT)
8. Maintenance and Repair of Electrical Domestic Applications (EDA)

Commerce Area

9. Office Management (OM)
10. Tax Assistant (TA)
11. Insurance (INS)

Health and Paramedical Area

12. Medical Laboratory Technician (MLT)

Home Science Area

13. Creche and Pre-School Management (CPM)

The District Vocational Education Committee meetings of all the thirty (30) Districts of Orissa were convened separately and they have approved the following seven new trades which have already been introduced in each of the Government Vocational Junior Colleges from the academic session 2007-08.

14. Accountancy and Auditing (AA)
15. Repair and Maintenance of Power Driven Farm Machinery (PDFM)
16. Textile Designing (TD)
17. Audio Visual Technician (AVT)
18. Building Maintenance (BM)
19. Tourism and Travel Technique (TTT)
20. Catering and Restaurant Management. (CRM)

TABLE 8.2

Trade-Wise Admission Position During 2002-03 & 2003-04

Sl. No.	Name of the Trade	No. of Students admitted	
		2002-03	2003-04
1.	Horticulture (HORT)	152	212
2.	Computer Application (CA)	189	124
3.	Repair and Maintenance of Radio and T. V. Receiver (RTV)	289	278

SI. No.	Name of the Trade	No. of Students admitted	
		2002-03	2003-04
4.	Office Management (OM)	171	249
5.	Repair and Maintenance of Electrical Domestic Applications (EDA)	165	172
6.	Crop Production (CP)	23	23
7.	Farm Mechanic (FM)	16	15
8.	Poultry Farming (PF)	9	
9.	Medical Laboratory Technician (MLT)	32	58
10.	Diary Farming (DF)	76	131
11.	Inland Fishery	22	42
12.	Tax Assistant (TA)	...	11
13.	Sericulture (SERI)	...	90
14.	Insurance (INS)	....	8
15.	Creche and Pre...School Management	...	...
	Total	1144	1343

Students are admitted twice in an academic session, after publication of the Annual and Supplementary High School Certificate results. The maximum number of students to be admitted for each section in any trade shall be 24 and the minimum shall be 12 in case of Computer Application trade and 8 in case of all other trades. In other words, when one section has been allowed in a GVJC for a particular trade, the maximum number of students who may be admitted for that trade shall be 24. If, however, two sections have been allowed for a particular trade, the maximum number of students who may admitted for that trade shall be 48, i.e. 24 in each section. In case the number of students taking admission in a section in a particular trade is less than 8 (or less than 12 in case of CA/CT trade), such section of that trade shall not be allowed to be opened. For example, when two sections in a particular trade have been allotted to a particular GVJC and 30 students are found eligible for admission, only one section with 24 students will be opened and no admission will be made in the second section. Thus to open two sections, at least 32 students should be eligible for admission in case of Computer Application/Computer Technique trade and at least 36 students should be eligible for admission. To open more than one section prior permission of the Director of Vocational Education is essential.

TEACHERS OF THE PROGRAMME

Teaching is imparted by qualified teachers who are either Part Time Resource Persons (PTRPs) or deployed or contractual Full Time Resource Persons (FTRPS). One PTRP is paid remuneration of Rs. 35 per period. The contractual FTRP receives aremuneration of Rs. 3,000/- per month. The deployed FTRPs are qualified vocational instructors who receive their usual salary from their parent organizations. The educational qualification of the contractual FTRPs/PTRPs of different trades are as follows.

TABLE 8.3

Educational Qualification of the Contractual FTRPs/PTRPs on different trades

SI. No.	Name of the trade subject	Eligibility criteria
AGRICULTURE BASED		
1	Inland Fisheries (IF)	B.F.Sc. with 55% of marks
2	Horticulture (HORT)	B.Sc. (Agri) with 55% of marks
3	Crop Production (CP)	B.Sc. (Agri) with 55% of marks
4	Poultry Farming (PF)	B.V.Sc. & A. H. with 55% of marks
5	Repair and Maintenance of Power Driven Farm Machinery (PDFM)/Farm Mechanics (FM)	Degree in Agricultural Engineering
6	Dairying (DAI)/Dairy Farming (DF)	B.V.Sc. & A. H. with 55% of marks
7	Sericulture (SERI)	B.Sc. Sericulture with 55% of marks

SI. No.	Name of the trade subject	Eligibility criteria
BUSINESS AND COMMERCE AREA		
8	Office Management (OM)	M.Com. with 55% of marks
9	Insurance (INS)	M.Com. with 55% of marks
10	Accountancy and Auditing (AA)	M.Com with 55% of marks having knowledge in Computer application/M.Com with 55% of marks with DCA/BCA
11	Tax Assistant (TA)	L.L.B with 55% of marks
ENGINEERING AREA		
12	Audio Visual Technician (AVT)/ Repair and Maintenance of Radio and T V. (RTV)	B.E/B. Tech, in any branch of Electronics engineering or equivalent— (1) Instrumentation & Control Engineering, (2) Electronics & Telecom Engineering, (3) Applied Electronics & Instrumentation, (4) Electrical & Electronics, (5) Electrical Engineering, 6. Electronics Engineering
13	Repair & Maintenance of Electrical Domestic Appliances (EDA)	B.E/B. Tech. in Electrical engineering or equivalent
14	Building Maintenance (BM)	BE/B. Tech Degree in Civil Engineering or Bachelor of Technology in Construction Management (BTCM) from IGNOU

SI. No.	Name of the trade subject	Eligibility criteria
15	Computer Technique (CT)/ Computer Application (CA)	Post Graduate degree in any discipline with P. G Diploma in computer Application from any Institute recognized by DOECCA or PGDCA from any recognized University or MCA or B. Tech/ B.E. in Computer Science/ Engineering
HUMANITIES & OTHERS		
16	Textile Designing (TD)	Post Graduation in clothing and Textiles/M.Tech. in Textile Technology/+2 with five years diploma in textile designing from Govt. recognized Institute such as National Institute of Designing, Ahmedabad/National Institute of Fashion Technology/Home Science Graduate plus two years P. G Diploma in Textile Designing from any Govt, recognized Institute such as National Institute of Designing, Ahmedabad and National Institute of Fashion Technology.
17	Tourism and Travel Technique (TTT)	MTA/MTM or a Post Graduate degree with Diploma in Tourism Management from a recognized institution/MBA with Hospitality/Tourism as a subject/ Project

SI. No.	Name of the trade subject	Eligibility criteria
HEALTH AND PARAMEDICAL AREA		
18	Medical Laboratory Technician/ Technology (MLT)	M.B.B.S with 55% of marks (Preference to M.D M.B.B.S with 55% of marks (Preference to M.D in Pathology/Microbiology/Path and Bact./Biochemistry)
HOME SCIENCE		
19	Creche & Pre-School Management (CPM)	(1) MA/M.Sc. in Home Science with 55% of marks and having Child Development as a special paper,
		(2) M.A. in Education with 55% of marks having education of the Pre-School Child as special paper, (3) M.Ed, with 55% of marks with early childhood Education as special paper.
20	Catering and Restaurant Management (CRM)	Degree/Diploma (Minimum 3 years duration) in Hotel Management and Catering Technology/Hospitality and Hotel Administration from any Institute affiliated to National Council for Hotel Management and Catering Technology/State Board of Technical Education/Recognised University having minimum 50% marks in aggregate with two years of experience in Industry or Teaching/M.A or

SI. No.	Name of the trade subject	Eligibility criteria
		M.Sc in Home Science with 55% of marks (in Food and Nutrition/ Nutrition and Dietetics/ Institutional Management and deities or equivalent/B.Sc (Home Science) with one year certificate course in Food and Beverage Service/Food Production with one year experience in relevant trade.

APPRENTICESHIP TRAINING

To obtain national level competence, a vocational passout has to go for apprenticeship training for a period of one year. During this period the apprentice receives a stipend of Rs. 1090 per month; 50% of which is paid by Government of India through Board of Practical Training (BOPT), Kolkata and the rest 50% is paid by the Firm/Organisation/ Enterprise where the apprentice received the training. The list of vocational passouts is sent by the Directorate every year to BOPT, Kolkata for selection of the apprentice trainee. The Principals are to send the information to the Director of Vocational Education every year about the passouts of their institute in a prescribed proforma which contains name of the candidate, name of father/guardian, permanent address, sex, caste, year of passing, name of the trade, percentage of marks secured etc.

MANAGEMENT STRUCTURE

In order to monitor the activities at the Central level a Joint Council for Vocational Education (JCVE) was created under the Ministry of Human Resource Development and a Central Institute of Vocational Education known as Pundit Sundarlal Sharma Central Institute of

Vocational Education (PSSCIVE), Bhopal, has been established as a constituent of NCERT. It is the apex level research and development body for Vocational Education Programmes (VEP) at the National level. The PSSCIVE prepares the curriculum for different trades of the +2 Vocational Education Programme which are taken as guideline for preparing the curriculum at the CHSE (O) level. As the State level counterpart of the JCVE, a State Council for Vocational Education (SCVE) was created in Orissa along with the District Vocational Education Committee (DVEC) to facilitate the promotion and supervision of Vocational Education at the District level. The Collector of the District, in which the GVJC is located, is the Chairperson and the Deputy Director of the ROVE concerned is the convener of the DVEC.

SYLLABUS AND EXAMINATION

A student, who has passed in the High School Certificate Examination from a recognized Board or Council, is eligible to take admission in a vocational trade running in one of the GVJCs in the State. The duration of the course is two years, at the end of which the examination is conducted by the Council of Higher Secondary Education (CHSE), Orissa, which also issues certificates to the passouts. The examination consists of the following four compulsory subjects, each carrying 100 marks-English, MIL, General Foundation Course (GFC) and Basic Foundation Course (BFC). Besides these, there are three theory papers and three practical papers related to the trade subjects, each carrying 100 marks. The examination in a trade carries a total of 1000 marks. A passout of a trade becomes a holder of Higher Secondary Certificate of CHSE, Orissa, in the vocational stream in a particular trade just as there are Higher Secondary Certificate holders in Science, Humanities (Arts) and Commerce streams.

There are in total 34 working weeks in an academic session. There are two periods per week in each of the four compulsory subjects. In each of the three theory papers of a trade, there are three periods per week. In each of three practical papers of a trade, there are two practical sessions in a week, each of either in 1st year or in 2nd year, are depicted in the table below.

TABLE 8.4

Vocational Syllabus

Name of the Subject/Paper	Number of Periods per week	Number of periods per session	Total Marks
English	02	68	100
MIL (O)	02	68	100
GFC	02	68	100
BFC	02	68	100
Theory Paper-1	03	102	100
Theory Paper-2	03	102	100
Theory Paper-3	03	102	100
Practical Paper-1	03 + 03 = 06	204	100
Practical Paper-2	03 + 03 = 06	204	100
Practical Paper-3	3 + 03 = 06	204	100

The syllabus of each of these trades is prepared and approved by the CHSE, Orissa. The syllabus of the BFC is linked to the concerned trade. A student studying Maintenance & Repair of Electrical Domestic Appliances shall study part of Physics and Mathematics of the +2 level in the Basic Foundation Course (BFC). He/She shall study the techniques of fault finding, dismantling, repairing and reassembling of domestic electrical appliances such as fan, oven, mix-grinder, refrigerator, washing machine, electrical pump, electrical iron, hair drier, room heater etc. Similarly, in the BFC course of Dairy Farming trade, a student has to study part of Botany and Zoology of the +2 level.

PROPOSED REVISION (2008-09)

The following vocational +2 courses has been proposed by the Director, Vocational Education, Orissa to be introduced with effect from the academic session 2008-09. In order to provide vertical mobility, it is proposed to modify the course structure of compulsory, BFC, GFC and trade papers in the following manner because the existing syllabi do not cover topics on +2 Physics, Chemistry, Biology and Mathematics sufficiently which are generally set in the Orissa Joint Entrance Examination (OJEE).

+2 Vocational	1st Year	2nd Year
(a) Compulsory	English 100 Marks MIL 100 Marks EE 100 Marks	English 100 Marks MIL 100 Marks
(b) BFC	Paper-I 50 Marks Paper-II 50 Marks Paper-Ill 50 Marks	Paper-I 50 Marks Paper-II 50 Marks Paper-Ill 50 Marks
(c) Trade	Theory Paper-I 50 Marks Theory Paper-II 50 Marks Practical Paper-I 50 Marks Practical Paper-II 50 Marks	Theory Paper-I 50 Marks Theory Paper-II 50 Marks Practical Paper-I 100 Marks Practical Paper-II 100 Marks

The compulsory papers will consist of English, MIL, BFC-I, BFC-II & BFC-III papers total carrying 700 marks in total for the entire programme of 2 years. One of the theory papers of the trade concerned may be dropped so that total marks for the entire two year programme remains 1200.

The above pattern will be followed in all the trades. However, BFC courses will be modified on the basis of special situations. The existing GFC course may be abolished. The equivalence of trades and the detail BFC courses for different trades (8+4) trade is as follows:

a. BFC-I   Physics
    BFC-II   Chemistry

    BFC-III   Biology or Mathematics

The detailed course of the above BFC papers will be prepared by the experts on the basis of guidelines provided by the consultants/Deputy Directors who are from faculties of Physics, Chemistry, Botany & Biology.

b. In trades-AVT, EDA, BM and CT (Engineering area) the +2 Vocational passouts may appear at the OJEE for engineering branches, B.Tech. Architecture, Ag. Engineering. These trades may have the following compulsory papers.

English and MIL   Compulsory

BFC-I and II   Physics and Chemistry respectively

BFC-III   Mathematics.

The detailed course of Physics and Chemistry shall be same as those for agriculture and MLT trades. BFC-III shall contain Mathematics in lieu of Biology the syllabus of which will be prepared by experts from Mathematics.

c. In trades like OM, AA, TA and INS, a pass-out can have vertical mobility to study courses like BBA, 5 years integrated Law, B.Com or BA. The course structure for the above trades shall be as follows:

Compulsory -Englishand MIL
BFC-I   Commerce
BFC-II   Commerce
BFC-III   Economics
Trade   Theory Papers I & II
               Practical Papers I & II

d. In trades like CRM, CPM and TD, a pass-out can have vertical mobility to study the courses like BBA, 5 years integrated law, BA and B.Com. The BFC papers will contain topics on History, Political Science, Economics etc.

The course structure for the above trades shall be:

Comp.   English and MIL
BFC-I   History and Geography
BFC-II   Political Science and Sociology

BFC-III   Economics (same as in commerce trades)
                 Trade Theory Papers-I & II
                 Practical Papers-I & II

The Vocational Higher Secondary Courses have totally failed to attract the students. Only 2032 students have sought admission to these courses during the academic session 2006-07. The five most attractive trades were:

1. Repair and Maintenance of Radio & TV
2. Computer Application
3. Repair and Maintenance of Electrical Domestic Appliances
4. Office Management
5. Horticulture

PROBLEMS AND NEEDED REMEDIATION

Inadequacy of finances since the discontinuance of the Centrally Sponsored Scheme in 1995 have haunted these institutions. Non-implementation of apprenticeship Training and *on the job* Training have eroded the professional credibility of these courses. The competencies of the pass-outs wee not of an adequate standard to invite recognition of equivalence from AICTE. The inadequacy of duly qualified staff with high professional degrees has adversely affected the academic status of these schools. Lack of School-industry linkage and appropriate opportunities for vertical mobility have made these courses insular and unattractive. The Department of Higher Education of Government of Orissa is already overburdened with a gigantic educational system. These GVJCs are extra-burden on the camel's back; and are getting neglected.

The Courses should be need-based and industry-linked. The 'general' academicians should all be withdrawn from this Vocational education. The Government may also consider the question of handing over the administration of these institutions to the Directorate of Technical Education, Orissa. The credibility of this scheme is at stake. An in-depth analysis of all its short-comings should be made by competent professionals. The system is on the verge of collapse; and immediate interventionist measures are the need of the hour.

CONCLUSION

This Programme has totally failed to live up to the grand theoretical expectations. It has degenerated into a 'respectable slogan' and a conveniently confused cliche. It has failed because its administration was delegated to the Department of Higher Education which has no experience of planning and implementing vocational courses. The conservative cultural ethos inherited as a legacy of the colonial times is a constant constraint. The overpowering burgeoning general secondary education had never permitted the vocational culture to develop in the school system. Lack of opportunities for vertical academic growth in this branch; and its nebulous and doubtful vocational status has reduced its professional standing. The general perception is that it is an option for the poor and the less talented. It is a historically jinxed programme. Many consider it as an unrealizable unrealistic educational dream.

It can be rescued, revived and revitalized if the entire programme is handed over to the technocrats and experts of high standing in the field of technological education. The Directorate of Technical Education and Training: the Biju Pattnaik Universityof Technology; and professional bodies like the All India Council of Technical Education should manage every aspect of this programme. The "+2 vocational course" should be integrated with the general stream; and the present isolation should be done away with.

CHAPTER-9

SECONDARY SCHOOL CURRICULUM (1835-2007)

HIGHLIGHTS

- Instructional Autonomy, 1835-1850 and Secondary School before the establishment of the universities in 1857
- University Controlled Curricuium
- Towards Diversified Curriculum (1882 & after)
- Vernacular System, 1901
- Satyabadi School Curriculum
- Recommendations Relating to Secondary School Curriculum of:
    - Secondary Education Commission, 1952
    - Indian Education Commission, 1966
    - 10 + 2 + 3
    - NPE, 1986
    - POA, 1986
    - Curriculum Framework, 1988
    - POA, 1992
- National Curriculum Framework, 2000
- National Curriculum Framework, 2005
- Secondary School Curriculum, 2006

SECTION I

1835 TO 1947

INSTRUCTIONAL AUTONOMY

The Orientalists lost ground to the Anglicists in 1835. From 1835 onwards there was an increasing emphasis on English studies and western view of life. Indian literature and culture were either neglected or given a marginal place in the curriculum. The early missionary schools of Orissa taught the 3R's, English, History, Geography and the Gospel, mainly the New Testament.

The Anglo-vernacular School at Puri was opened in 1835. This was the first secondary school of Orissa. English, English grammar, Elementary Geography and Arithmetic were the subjects that were taught in this school. This school at Puri with its foreign curriculum did not appeal to the people. The school had a poor start, an unhappy existence and an ignonimous end. It was closed in 1840. "Puri with its long tradition of Sanskrit culture and conservatism did not easily subscribe to the first invasion of English culture..."

A Secondary School was established at Cuttack in 1841. This became a Zillah School in 1854, the Ravenshaw Collegiate School of to-day.

In 1842-43, the following was the curriculum of the School:

1st **class:**

1. Translation from English to Oriya & Vice-versa
2. Nicholl's Geography
3. Arithmetic up to Practice
4. History

IIndClass:

1. Translation from English to Oriya & Vice-versa
2. Arithmetic
3. Clift's Geography
4. History (not examinable)

IllrdClass:

1. Oral work in English and Oriya
2. Writing

IVth class:

3. Oral work in English and Oriya
4. Writing

The entire instruction was through the English medium and no Oriya text-books were used. The Local Committee had suggested in 1843-44 for the provision of Oriya books and an Oriya grammar text prepared by Pandit Biswambhar Bidyabhusanwas printed. It cost 6 annas or around 0.40 p. Mr. Sutton proposed certain terms for the translation of other text-books and those were accepted. In 1845-46, Mr. Sutton completed the 'Vernacular Class Reader' and 200 copies were taken for the use of the school. During 1846-47 the Head Pandit Biswambar Bidyabhusan translated Harle's Arithmetic, and this was used as a class-book. 500 copies of it were purchased for the use of Government.

In 1843-44, the courses of study of the Cuttack School were as follows:

1st class:

1. *Marshman's* Survey of History
2. Prose Reader No.5
3. Popular Introduction to Natural Philosophy
4. *Nicholas* Geography of Asia and Europe, with reference to maps and globes.

5. Arithmetic.
6. Translation from English to Vernacular and Vice-versa

IInd Class:

1. *Lennie's* Grammar as far as syntax.
2. *Guy's* Geography of Europe, Asia and Africa with reference to maps and globes
3. Arithmetic (up to practice).
4. Translation from English to Oriya and Viva-versa.

The studies of the junior classes were stated to be of an elementary nature.

By 1850-51, the Cuttack School was already in existence for almost a decade. The Local Committee of the School in its report for the year 1850-51, made thefollowing pertinent remarks relating to the curriculum:

The studies at these provincial government schools are, in our judgment, at the same time too high and too confined. They aimed at a standard beyond that adopted in the poorer schools at home (i.e. U.K.). While collateral European knowledge is unacquired, we cannot see why it should tend to European civilization, that an Oorya boy, the son of a poor Government employee, should know when Richard I went to the Crusades; what is the capital of Saxony; what sea the river 'Yenisee' runs into, and so on; and that he should not know who 'Sewajee' was; who fought the battle of Assaye; and what is the difference between a 'Suni' and a 'Sheah'. The result of all this is, he learns by rote what he does not understand and is not interested in and what can never be brought to bear upon the general history of his own country, its various races and its customs. The great point seems to us to be to encourage general knowledge of whatever stamp; and not to train boys merely to know obscure English history, the higher branches of arithmetic, and to write a good hand. We will venture to assert that there are not three boys in this school here with all their attainments, who can turn a sentence of Ooreah into tolerable English, such as an English boy would do in England,at the age of twelve years. We have already said, we are opposed to the teaching of theoretical agriculture. But why should they not learn the growth and manufacture of the products of their own country, the relative value of these articles in India and in Europe... the principles of book-keeping, index-making, land-surveying and journalizing ? or, in a word, that will turn to their use and profit, as they may hereafter live by trade or head better than by stating, that, we can scarcely know a single Native or Eurasian, in this Province, brought up to speak and write English as can express himself even tolerably well; or who in writing is anything more than a mere copyist."

Whoever penned the foregoing lines was definitely a first-rate educationist. He had realized where exacdy the English education was failing and what the remedies were. Even today, after the lapse of more than a century and a half, it makes very good reading. Today's curriculum cannot be said to be beyond the reproach cast in the foregoing paragraph against the early English secondary education of Orissa.

In 1854, the Cuttack School became a Zilla School. The courses of studies of the Cuttack Zilla School in 1854-55 were as follows:

First class: Studies of the First Section

1. Keighdey's History of England, Vol.1.
2. Stewart's Geography-whole.
3. Terrestrial Globe-all the problems
4. Arithmetic—the whole course.
5. Algebra—simple equations.
6. Moral Tales—the whole.
7. Geometry—the 6th and 11th books
8. Goldsmith's Essays—the whole
9. Poetical Reader No.III—80 pages.
10. Crombie's Etymology and Syntax, Parts I and II
11. Translations.

Studies of the Second Section

1. Keighdey's Elementary History of England - 116 pages
2. Stewart's Geography - Europe and Asia.
3. Arithmetic - the whole course.
4. Algebra - simple equations.
5. Geometry - 1st, 2nd and 3rd Books.
6. Grammar - Murray's Etymology and Syntax.
7. Poetical Reader No.II - 76 pages.
8. Translations.

The course of the Second Section was lighter than that of the first section. The second section was not studying the Moral Tales, Goldsmith's Essays and the Terrestrial Globe.

Second Class:

1. Marshman's Brief Survey of History—from pages 1 to 24.
2. Marshman's History of Bengal pages 132 to 207
3. Chamber's Geography - from page 5 to 50
4. Lennie's Grammar — from page 5 to 94
5. Chamier's Arithmetic - to the end of the Vulgar fractions.
6. Pinock's Catechism of Roman History — the whole.

Third Class:

1. Prose Reader No.II - the whole.
2. Clift's Geography - from page 3 to 26
3. Elements of Grammar - the whole.
4. Chamier's Arithmetic - Reduction.
5. Writing copies
6. Dictation.

Fourth Class:

1. Prose Reader No.1 - the whole
2. Arithmetic - compound addition.
3. Writing copies

Fifth Class: Studies-1ˢᵗ Section

1. Prose Reader No.1 - from page 1 to 14
2. Arithmetic - Multiplication.

Studies-IIⁿᵈ Section.

1. Spelling Book No.1 - the whole.
2. Arithmetic - Subtraction.

The Courses of Studies of the Puri School were not similar to that of the Cuttack School. The Balasore School curriculum was different. With only three secondary schools, there were three curricula. The curricula were framed keeping the capability of the students in view. Every school had freedom to frame its own curriculum. This institutional autonomy relating to curriculum.

The curriculum of the Puri School was as follows:

First class:

1. Poetical Reader No.1 as far as the 6ᵗʰ page.
2. Marshman's History of Bengal - 157 pages
3. Pinock's Catechism of the History of Rome - to the end of the 2ⁿᵈ Punic War.
4. Clift's Geography - the whole
5. Lennie's Grammar - the whole.
6. Hind's Arithmetic - Vulgar and decimal fractions
7. Algebra - division.
8. Vernacular - History of Orissa and Grammar.

Second Class:

1. Prose Reader No.II - 42 pages.
2. Elements of Grammar - 2ⁿᵈ of Etymology
3. Clift's Geography - 2ⁿᵈ, 3ʳᵈ & 4ᵗʰ Chapters
4. Arithmetic - compound Multiplication.
5. Vernacular - History of Orissa

Third Class:

1. Prose Reader No.1 - 38 pages
2. Arithmetic - Addition.
3. Vernacular-Neetikotha

Fourth Class: Section A

1. Prose Reader No.1 - 10 pages
2. Vernacular - Neetikotha.

Section B

1. Spelling Book No.1 - 25 pages
2. Neetikotha.
3. The Curriculum of the Balasore School was as follows in 1854.

First class:

1. Prose Reader No.II - to the end of the First Chapter.
2. Wollaston's Elements of Grammar - as far as interjection.
3. Geography - outline of Asia
4. Arithmetic - as far as Reduction.

Second Class:Section A

1. English Spelling Book No.1 - to page 37
2. Arithmetic - Multiplications.

Section B

1. English Spelling Book No.1 - to page 17.
2. Arithmetic - Addition

Third Class: Section I

1. Spelling Book No.1 - to page 16.
2. Arithmetic - simple subtraction.

SECTION II

Comparatively, the Cuttack School had the most ambitious curriculum; then came Puri and last was Balasore. In the Puri School, History of Orissa was taught; but in the Cuttack and Balasore Schools this was not done. In 1856-57, Zoology was introduced as a subject of study in the First Class of the Puri School. During 1858-69, Surveying was introduced in the Balasore Zilla School.

The curricula of the English Schools at Cuttack, Puri and Balasore were specifically designed to meet the needs of the colonial government. The products of the school were likely to occupy positions in, "1st. The subordinate branch of the judicial, revenue and other public departments; 2nd. The teachership of the education department, and 3rd the mere manual copying of the writer, or the unvarying routine of an accountant's life." The secondary school curriculum had been designed keeping these requirements in view. The proficiency in written and spoken English and Oriya; and the felicity in translation would greatly help the scholar to be a good clerk. The emphasis placed on Geography was with a view to orienting the students to practical geography and surveying because there was heavy demand for educated persons in the land survey operations. Arithmetic was essential to be a clerk and an accountant. History of England was the instructional medium to brainwash the Indians regarding the superiority of the English. During 1858-59, teaching according to subjects was introduced in place of class-teaching. This led to specialization amongst teachers and to better instruction. The greatest obstacle was the non-availability of slates and books and of library books and furniture.

UNIVERSITY CONTROLLED CURRICULUM

The University of Calcutta, after its inception on 24th January. 1857, had prescribed the following subjects for its Entrance Examination - English, Sanskrit, Bengali or Oriya or Hindi or Burmese, History, and Geography, Mathematics, Mechanics, and Natural History. After several modification, the course was almost the same in 1881, except for the elimination of Mechanics and Natural History and the addition of mathematical subjects like Algebra, Geometry, and Mensuration. In the curriculum,Vernacular was greatly neglected and English had received undue importance. The Courses of Studies for the Entrance Examination were prescribed by the Calcutta University. As a consequence, the institutional variations in matters of curriculum were eliminated and uniformity prevailed.

During 1857-58, 'A Committee for the Improvement of Schools" was appointed. It suggested that instead of grades, marks be awarded, that monthly examination be held, that written examinations should be substituted for oral examinations.

The three Zilla Schools were preparing candidates for the Entrance Examination from 1857 onwards. The Entrance Examination of the Calcutta University roughly corresponded to the erstwhile Junior Scholarship Examination and required, besides, a knowledge of 'Vegetable Physiology, of Mechanics and Natural Philosophy'. In the Inspector's Report for 1857-58, it was stated that the Zillah schools were aiming too high and he recommended that those schools which could not cope with the stiff requirements of the Entrance Examination with its staff be designated as 'second grade' Zillah Schools. The extraordinary stress on intellectual development adversely affected the secondary school curriculum. The secondary schools became adjuncts to the University.

The following Courses of Studies were prescribed for the Middle English Scholarship Examination - English text, English Grammar, Elementary Sanskrit, History of India, Geography, Arithmetic, Algebra, Geometry

(Euclid I), Popular Elements of Natural Philosophy, Political Economy and Preservation of Health.

For the Middle Vernacular Scholarship Examination, the following Course was prescribed: Literature, Grammar, Composition, History, Geography, Arithmetic, Geometry, Natural Philosophy, Political Economy and Preservation of Health.

The Middle English and Middle Vernacular School Courses were similar except for the instruction of English in the former. The Middle English Schools were popular and the Middle Vernacular Schools were fast losing ground. The Joint Inspector of Schools for Orissa in his report for the year 1875-76 commented: 'The Middle Vernacular Course has not much attraction for either the middle classes or the lower classes'. In 1877, the Middle English and Middle Vernacular School curricula were made similar to each other except for English. The subjects now were English language including Physical Geography, Euclid Book I, Mensuration, and Sanitary Science. One of the following subjects was to be studied in addition - Elements of Natural Philosophy, Elements of Chemistry and Elements of Botany. Such important subjects like Drawing, Music, Manual Work, Moral and Physical training were neglected.

In 1881, the following was the Course prescribed for the two top classes of the High Schools. This course was the Entrance Examination Course.

Course for the Preparatory Entrance Class

(1) English:

Lethbridge's *Easy Selection.*

Hiley's *Grammar with exercises.*

Gordon's *Exercises, Part I.*

Morrel's *Analysis and Parsing.*

(2) Sanskrit:

First Book of Sanskrit (half year course).

Second Book of Sanskrit (half year course) *Shastri's notes*

(3) Persian:

Entrance Course prepared by the Committee appointed by the Calcutta University.

Persian Grammar with notes by Moulvi.

(4) History:

Lethbridge's *History of India* (whole)

(5) Geography:

Clarke's *Geographical Reader.*

(6) Mathematics:

Euclid I, II <& Part of III with introduction to Mensuration.

Algebra (to simple equations).

Arithmetic (the whole)

Course for the Entrance Class

(1) English:

"Selections" prepared by the Committee appointed by the Calcutta University Hiley's *Grammar with exercises* Gordon's *Exercises Part II* Analysis and Parsing.

(2) Sanskrit:

Course prepared by the Committee as appointed by the Calcutta University Grammar and oral notes.

(3) Persian:

Entrance Course prepared by the Committee appointed by the Calcutta University.

Grammar and oral notes.

(4) History:

Edith Thompson's *History of England,.*

Revisal of Lethbridge's *History of India.*

(5) Geography:

Blandford's: *Physical Geography.*

Revisal of Clarke's *Geographical Reader*

(6) Mathematics.-

Euclid I to IV.

Algebra to simple equations.

Arithmetic (the whole)

In European and Eurasian Schools, Latin was studied in place of Sanskrit/Persian.

The high school curriculum was the same at Sambalpur, Balasore, Puri and Cuttack schools as all of them were affiliated to the Calcutta University.

The following Courses of Studies were followed in the Middle Schools of Sambalpur in 1881.

Fourth Class (Highest Class)

A. Language

(1) English	Reading	*Royal Reader No.III*
	Writing	Dictation & Letter-writing.
	Translation	Revision of *Stapley's Exercises*
	Grammar	Howard's *Rudimentary Grammar,* Essay &Parsing
(2) Sanskrit	Language &	*Gopal Bhandarkar's 2nd Book.*
	Grammar	First 12 Chapters. Revision of First Book
(3) Persian	Reading	*Nigari — Danish*
	Grammar	*ZAWABIT - I FARSI*
	Translation	From Urdu to Persian.
(4) Vernacular		As in fifth Class.

B. Mathematics

(1) Arithmetic		The whole.
(2) Algebra		To simple equations
(3) Geometry		33 propositions, *1st Book of Euclid.*

C. General Knowledge

(1) Geography		Revision of 1st Geography. Map drawing from Blandford's *Physical Geography*
(2) History		Lethbridge's *Introduction to the History of India* Muhammadan Period.

Third Class

A. Language

| (1) English | Reading Writing Translation Grammar | *Sequal to the Royal Reader* Pages 159 to end to be omitted. Saturday Translation. Poetry to be memorized. |

		Dictation & Letter-writing & small text in copy books. The letters written are to be original, not copies *Stapley's Exercises Part I.* Selected passages from *Illrd Vernacular Book.* Revision of *Grammar Primer* with Parsing.
(2) Sanskrit	Language & Grammar	Ramakrishna Gopal Bhandarkar's *1st Sanskrit Book.* Each boy must have a copy of the *Upakarmanika.* Students of Hindi and Marathi will study Sanskrit.
(3) Persian	Reading & Grammar Translation	Students of Urdu to Study Persian. ZAWABIT - I FARSI From Urdu to Persian.
(4) Vernacular		As in the 5th Class.

B. Mathematics

(1) Arithmetic		The whole omitting the Cube root.
(2) Algebra		The first four rules
(3) Geometry		To the 26th Proposition.

C. General Knowledge

(1) Geography		1st Book of Euclid The whole of *1st Geography* with maps of Africa and America. Map drawing.

Second Class

A. Language

I. English	Reading	*Royal Reader No.II.* Translation on Saturdays. Poems to be learnt by heart.

	Writing	Large and small hand. Copies in copy books Dictation.
	Translation	Select Passages from 2*nd* *Vernacular Book*
	Grammar	Grammatical Primer with Parsing.

B. Mathematics

(1) Arithmetic		Barnard Smith from page 1 to 137 omitting decimal coinage.

C. General Knowledge

(1) Geography		*The 1*st* Geography Book* pages 1 to 33 with maps of Europe and revision maps of Asia and India.

First Class

a. Language

(1) English	Reading	*Howard's Primer* with explanations (1/2 year course). *Royal Reader No. 1* omitting page 52.
	Writing	Copies on slates (capital letters, large and round sentences). Large and bound hand copy books
(2) Translation into English		Sentences are to be learnt at home. Easy sentences may be translated into English. The Hindi or Marathi Primer to be translated or Vernacular sentences.
(3) Vernacular		History and Geography of Vernacular Class IV.

The courses of studies were grouped into three categories—Language, lathematics, and General Knowledge. Neglect of physical education, drawing, music:c. is evident.

The schools of Ganjam district and Koraput region were under Madras residency's administration. The curriculum of the high schools of Ganjam were influenced by the developments in the Madras Presidency. The high schools were affiliated to the Madras University. The Courses of Studies of the High Schools of Ganjam district consisted of English, History, Geography, Arithmetic, Algebra, uclid, Translation, Composition and Vernacular. These courses remained unaltered up to 1882.

In 1882, the Middle School curriculum comprised of the following.

(1) Compulsory Group: Language.
Mathematics.
History.
Geography.

(2) Optional Group: Mathematics.
Science.
Physical Geography.
Botany.
Physiology.
English History.
Political Economics.
Agriculture.

TOWARDS DIVERSIFIED CURRICULA

Lord Ripon appointed the first Indian Education Commission on 3rd February, 1882 with W W Hunter, the eminent historian and Civil Servant, as its chairman. This Commission is generally known as the Hunter Commission. This Commission recommended the bifurcation of secondary education. It recommended that "in the upper classes of the High Schools there be two divisions; one leading to the Entrance Examination of the Universities, the other of a more practical character intended to fit youths for commercial or non-literary pursuits." This recommendation of the Hunter Commission to design a school course based upon pragmatic principles with a modern approach did not bear immediate results. The implementation of this programme was started in 1883 in Madras. However, the Upper Secondary Course Examination with modern and technical subjects incorporated into it did not find favour with the people. Only 210 candidates passed the test during the subsequent 20 years.

In the two decades after the Hunter Commissioner Report, there was an increasing influence of English over the high schools. By 1895-96, all attempts to make the Vernacular the medium of instruction were abandoned and English was made the medium. Even at the Middle School stage, the English schools were becoming more and more popular when the Vernacular schools were slowly and steadily losing favour with the people. Middle Vernacular education did not help a man in procuring a job and as such was considered useless.

The syllabus of 1881 continued without any change until 1900. Science and Physical Geography were introduced in 1887 at the high school stage. In 1890, Drawing became an examinable subject for the Entrance Examination. Due to the dearth of teachers, it could not be made compulsory.

By 1st January, 1901, English was the medium of instruction in the first four classes of the high schools. Sanskrit and other languages were taught as second languages. In the classes below Class IV, in all Government and Aided high schools, the Vernacular of the district was the medium of instruction, English being taught as a second language only from the 'B' Section of the VIIth Class.

In accordance with the recommendations of the Hunter Commission, the Director of Public Instruction, Bengal submitted a detailed scheme for introducing the bifurcation of studies in High Schools and for the development of education on modern lines in his letter No.3502 dated 15th May,1899. The Government of India were emphasizing the recommendations relating to the bifurcation of studies and practically nothing had been done in Bengal. Mr. T. S. Slater, Principal of the Civil

Engineering College, Sibpur had suggested the modification of the existing courses in 1898 after inspecting the different technical schools. Slater's suggestions contained a complete technical bias. The Director of Public Jnstruction, however, suggested that it should be towards almost all forms of practical, industrial and commercial pursuits, and not merely towards the engineering trades and professions as proposed by Mr. Slater. On the basis of the D.P.I's report, it was decided that the first two years of the high school course should be a core course and that opportunities would be provided in technical, commercial or general studies in the last two years.

The courses of studies of the Zilla Schools comprised of the following subjects in 1901: English, Second language (Sanskrit, Persian, Etc.), Mathematics (Arithmetic, Algebra and Geometry), History, Geography, Science Primer and Drawing. Mr. Slater proposed an alternative *'B' course* comprising of modern English, Mathematics, Drawing and Practical Geometry, Mensuration, Elementary Engineering and Surveying and Manual Training. The D.P.I, suggested a *'C course* with English, Mathematics, History, Geography and Science Primer, Drawing and Practical Geometry, Elementary Chemistry and Physics and Manual Training. "The new examinations, however, did not prove very popular and the Matriculation Examination dominated the entire field of Secondary Education. Thus 'B' and 'C course were never introduced in Orissa as there was no demand. Though the bifurcation of courses had taken place as early as 1883 in the Madras Presidency, it did not influence the Ganjam district till 1889. In 1899 an Upper Secondary Course of two years with higher sections of the Matriculation Course was instituted. It consisted of English, a second language, free hand geometrical drawing, needle work for girls, geography, singing, hygiene, history of India, British history, mensuration, agriculture, domestic economy for girls, geometry and algebra. For the Matriculation Examination, English, a second language, Mathematics, Physics and Chemistry, History and Geography and Drawing were compulsory. The Matriculation Course came into effect in 1890. The Upper Secondary Examination did not become popular in Ganjam because the examinations were very strict and there were large failures at the examinations. Secondly, this course did not lead up to a University.

During 1882-1900, practically there was no improvement in the curriculum of the Middle Schools. However, greater emphasis was laid, wherever possible on subjects like Mensuration, Physics and Hygiene. In the Post-Hunter Commission period, the Middle School curriculum of Madras underwent certain changes. Early vocational training was provided for in these schools. Language, Arithmetic, Geography and History of India were compulsory subjects and the students had to choose two subjects from among subjects like gardening, mensuration, agriculture, etc. South Orissa started on the right path while North Orissa tenaciously clung to the traditional curriculum.

The Vernacular System of Education was introduced at the Middle School stage in North Orissa in accordance with Resolution No.I dated 1st January, 1901. According to this scheme, instruction in English was to begin in Class VIIB as a second language. The courses of studies of Middle English School and Middle Vernacular School were exactly the same except for the existence of English in the one and the absence of the same from the other.

The following tabular statement compares the old Middle Vernacular School course with the 1901 course.

MIDDLE VERNACULAR EXAMINATION- PRE & POST 1901

SI. No.	Pre-1901 Course	SI. No.	Course introduced in 1901
01	Vernacular language (i) Two-text-books (163 pages) (ii) Grammar (100 pages) (iii) Composition (100 pages)	01	A. Literature book including (i) Prose (100 pages) (ii) Poetry (50 pages) (iii) Grammar & Composition (50 pages)

SI. No.	Pre-1901 Course	SI. No.	Course introduced in 1901
02	European Arithmetic & Subhankar's Rules (100 pages)	02	Arithmetic, European and Native (100 pages)
03	History of India (100 pages)	03	Historical Reader India (120 pages)
04	Geography (a) General with special reference to India & Bengal (150 pages) (b) Physical (55 pages)	04	Geographical Reader (Chiefly the British Empire) including physical Geography (60 pages)
05	Euclid Book I, including Mensuration (86 pages)	05	Euclid Book I (80 pages) or Practical Geometry and Mensuration (50 pages)
06	Science (a) Physics (100 pages (b) Hygiene (140 pages)	06	Science Reader (Standard V and VI) 132 pages)
		07	Free hand-Drawing
		08	Drill
		09	Manual Work (optional)
		10	English (optional (20 pages)
	Total course of reading 1094 pages		Total course of reading 692 or pages (±20)

The above system of Vernacular education was modified in 1912 in accordance *mth* the Resolution No. 109 T-G. dated 20th April, 1909. A revised syllabus for standard [II to VI was published. Under the Vernacular System of Education, Vernacular was:he medium of instruction in the infant stage and in all the six standards. According:o the revised syllabus instead of teaching English from Class VII B, its instruction vas to begin from class V through the Direct Method. Separate books were prescribed "or Nature Study, Hygiene, and Geography. "The new syllabus of studies for standards V to VI drew a line of demarcation between Middle English and Middle Vernacular Schools.

The Simla Conference of the D.P.Is. of India of 1901, recommended the nstitution of a School Final Examination. A Committee was appointed to examine bis issue which met on 1st September, 1908 and made its recommendations. Instead of the School Final Examination, it was contemplated to institute a School Leaving Certificate which "will contain a record not only of one single examination but of:he whole work of a boy during at least the last three years of his school career"[29] 3ut nothing tangible emerged out of this.

In 1912, Bihar and Orissa became a separate province. A Committee was ippointed to devise a course of study for the School Leaving Certificate Examination vhich submitted its report in August,! 914. An important feature was the institutionof special courses designed to prepare students for commercial or clerical courses or for further instruction in special institutions. The examination at the end of the course was to be divided into three parts, namely, a scrutiny of the record of progress in school, a public examination, and in the case of those candidates who fail in one subject only at the public examination, an examination conducted *in situ* by the Inspector, with such assistance as he might require, in order to obtain a final decision. Thus, while at the Matriculation Examination a student passed or failed on the written work done on one occasion, the new scheme while giving due weight to a written examination also envisaged taking into account the work done during the period spent in school. The scheme was to be implemented in all Government Schools and in as many aided selected school, aided or unaided at stations where there are Government High Schools as might succeed in obtaining recognition. The first S. L. C Examination was held in 1921. Only 216 students appeared at this examination in 1921; and 313 in 1922. The reason for the slow progress was the inability of the Government to provide additional finances for the teaching of the new subjects. The expenditure for the conduct of this examination was exorbitantly high in view of the small numbers that took this examination.

The Satyabadi School (1912-21) was one of the high schools of Orissa which did comply with the requirements of the Calcutta and Patna Universities. However, it was a unique institution. If curriculum is defined as the 'totality of school experiences' then it provided a different curriculum. Pandit Nilakantha Dash and the band of dedicated teachers that worked in the Satyabadi School had a noble conception of education. Their cherished goal was not just another high school, but to create a unique man-making institution of the best variety. The students of this school were to bear a stamp of distinction. They were to receive an altogether different training. It was a residential school where the teachers and students lived together as a community and had ample scope for mutual interaction. The headmaster was one among his equals. The assistant teachers were all stalwarts of eminence. Individual attention, supervised study, remedial teaching, community life, literary activities, debates, excursions were some of the salient features of the school. The teachers and students of the school considered themselves the missionaries for combating traditionalism, orthodoxy, superstitions and wanted to bring about revolutionary changes in the social set-up of Orissa. Consequent on its becoming a National High School, it lost its affiliation and later died. But it left behind a trail of glorious tradition, unforgettable in the annals of the educational history.

During 1917-22, a wide series of optional subjects were introduced in connection with the School Leaving Certificate Examination. History and Geography were made compulsory subjects for the Matriculation Examination of the Patna University. It was made compulsory for every candidate appearing at the Matriculation Examination to produce a Certificate that he has attended not less than ten lecturers on hygiene delivered by a Medical Officer of a status not lower than that of an Assistant Surgeon. The teaching of Drawing was improved by the appointment of trained teachers. Moral instruction was given in all schools for 'at least one short period' a week. The question of introducing

Vernacular as the medium of instruction in the Matriculation classes and giving more vocational teaching was engaging the attention of the Government.

A Board of Secondary Education was set up during the year 1922-23. The constitution was revised in 1925-26. The Director of Public Instruction was the ex-officio Chairman and there were 16 nominated members and five elected members. The Board took over the powers of recognizing schools from the Director of Public Instruction.

The Education Committee of 1923, recommended that Vernacular should be the medium in the Matriculation classes (i.e. the top four classes of the secondary schools). Accordingly, it was decided that from 1928 onwards, the medium of examination would be Vernacular for all subjects except English and Mathematics. Therefore, instruction in the top four classes was switched over to the Vernacular medium gradually from 1925 to begin with in History and Geography on an experimental basis. The opening of the Cuttack Training College in 1923 improved the position as regards the availability of trained graduate teachers in Orissa. It was decided during 1929-30, to continue instructing the top four classes of the high schools through the English medium for a further period of two years. The main difficulty in implementing the scheme of Vernacular as the medium of instruction was the non-availability of books in the Vernacular language. In 1933-34, it was decided to leave religious instruction in schools to the discretion of school authorities concerned. By 1934-35, a noticeable trend was that of introducing vocational courses in the Middle Schools.

On 1st April, 1936, the new State of Orissa was formed. The curricular differences between North and South Orissa became glaringly apparent because educationists found that the schools in North and South Orissa operated on different lines. Science and Manual Training were compulsory in South Orissa. During 1938-39 Oriya became the medium of instruction in all the high schools of North Orissa in accordancewith the new regulations of the Patna University. The Matriculation

Examination of 1942 was held in the Vernacular medium. Diversification of studies was provided in 20 high schools of Orissa. More and more of middle schools provided vocational education.

India became independent in 1947. This necessitated certain curricular changes. The curricular structure remained almost the same. But the text books and their content were revised in tune with the changed circumstances. The curricular changes in the post-independence period have been described hereafter.

The North Orissa syllabus was introduced in the high schools of South Orissa during 1947-48. In the same year Science was introduced in all the High Schools of Orissa. Vocational subjects like Carpentry, Agriculture and Paper-making were introduced in a few high schools. During 1949-50, teaching of Hindi was made compulsory in classes VI to XI. Agriculture was introduced as an optional subject in the high schools at Hinjlicut, G. Udaigiri, Nawarangpur, Khurda, Nayagarh, Karanjia, Champua, Sonepur, and Tihidi. Supervised study was introduced with two periods a week. General Knowledge was taught in all high schools for one period a week. Urdu became the medium of instruction and examination in the Sayed Seminary, Cuttack.

CURRICULAR CHANGES AFTER INDEPENDENCE (1947-2007)

SECONDARY EDUCATION COMMISSION REPORT (1952) AND CURRICULUM

The Multipurpose Higher Secondary Schools were started in 1957-58. There was provision for Science and Humanities streams. The technical stream was introduced during 1963.

The opening of a Senior Basic School in 1951-1952 and the post-Basic School in 1954 lent a new dimension to curricular designing. The basic school curriculum unified general studies with vocational training. By 1966, the Higher Secondary Schools had become unpopular and so many of them were converted into High Schools. The experiment of Higher Secondary totally failed in Orissa.

Teaching of Hindi was started on an experimental basis in the Middle English Schools during 1947-48. The same year, vocational training in Agriculture, Carpentry,Cane work, Tailoring and Paper-making were introduced in 26 Middle Schools. Teaching of Hindi became compulsory in the Middle Schools during 1949-50. During 1950-51, some features of the Basic Schools were introduced in M.E. Schools. During 1957-58, Craft was introduced in 60 M.E. Schools.

The New courses of studies for classes VI and VII prescribed by the Board of Secondary Education, Orissa was introduced in the Middle Schools of Orissa. The Middle School Certificate Examination was held with effect from 1964 and was discontinued in 1969. Nationalised text books were published in English for Class VI in 1964-65 and for class VII in 1965-66.

From 1969-70 onwards the curriculum of the Middle Schools was removed from the purview of the Board of Secondary Education, Orissa. The Government of Orissa in the Education Department prescribed the Courses of Studies for Class VI from 1969-70 onwards and for class VII from 1970-71 onwards.

The subjects of study were as follows:

01.	A. (i) Modern Indian Language (Oriya, Bengali, Telugu, Hindi or Urdu).	Marks 100
	(ii) Sanskrit	50
	B. (i) Hindi (for students who take Oriya as M.I. L)	
	(ii) Oriya (for students who take a language other thanOriya as M.I. L.) (No public examination for B (i) & (ii) for the present)	50
02.	English	100
03.	Mathematics (Arithmetic 75 + Geometry 25)	100
04.	History + Civics (40 +10)	50
05.	Geography	50
06.	General Science	100
07.	Drawing and Fine Arts	50
08.	Agriculture or any other Craft (Theory 25 + Practical 25)	50
09.	Physical Education (No Examination in this subject; but is a compulsory subject).	50

The Press, Preparation and Publication Committee, Cuttack was in charge of lationalized text-books for all the Classes from I to VII. Sri Birakishore Das, an

eminent poet of patriotic literature was its first Secretary. He was succeeded by the illustrious litterateur Sri Ananta Patnaik. This Committee under the able stewardship of two eminent creative writers produced quality text-books for classes I to VII.

In 1976, the responsibility of prescribing the curriculum and producing the textbook was transferred from the Press, Preparation and Publication committee to the Board of Secondary Education, Orissa. The Board started the work of preparing an integrated syllabus from grades I to X in 1976. It constituted a Syllabus Co-ordination Committee. The Syllabus of the Middle School classes was prepared on the lines of the syllabi prepared by the National Council of Educational Research and Training (NCERT), New Delhi.

On the basis of the recommendation of the Secondary Education Commission, Social Studies was introduced as a subject of study in place of History and Geography in 1961. The new syllabus for Mathematics was introduced during 1961-62. English Paper I Course was revised in 1961-62 for the High School Certificate Examination of 1964-65.

Pandit Jawaharlal Nehru's classic speech on the occasion of Mahatma Gandhi's death "The Light has gone out" was included in English prose at the request of Sri M. C. Chagla. During 1968-69, Social Studies was abandoned and History, Civics and Geography were introduced. During 1972-73, steps were taken to revise the syllabus and text-books following the ones prepared by the National Council for Educational Research and Training. Logic, Psychology, Orissi Dance, and Project Technology were introduced as Optional subjects for the Matriculation classes during 1972-73 and Dramaturgy in 1973-74. Steps were taken to introduce modern Mathematics during 1974-75.

INDIAN EDUCATION COMMISSION REPORT (1964-66) & CURRICULUM

The Indian Education Commission Report of 1966 critically assessed the schoolcurriculum. It recommended the revision of the school curriculum in the light ofexplosion of knowledge, technological advances and scientific progress. It opined:"The school curriculum is in a state of flux all over the world today. In developingcountries it is generally criticized as being inadequate and outmoded, and not properly designedto meet the needs of modern times... This widespread dissatisfaction with the curriculum isdue to many causes. In the first place, tremendous explosion of knowledge in recent yearsand the reformulation of the basic concepts in the physical, biological, and social scienceshave brought into sharp relief the inadequacies of existing school programme."

The Commission exhorted that curricular revisions had become imperative in the light of international development. It stated:

"Against background of the striking curricular developments that are taking place abroad, the school curriculum in India will be found to be very narrowly conceived and largely out of date. Education is a three-fold process of imparting knowledge, developing skills, and inculcating proper interests, attitudes and values. Our schools (and also our colleges) are mostly concerned with the first part of the process—the imparting of knowledge and carry out even this in an unsatisfactory way. The curriculum places a premium on bookish knowledge and rote learning, makes inadequate provision for practical activities and experiences, and is dominated by examinations, external and internal. Moreover, as the development of useful skills and the inculcation of right kind of interests, attitudes and values are not given sufficient emphasis, the curriculum becomes not only out of step with modern knowledge, but also out of tune with the life of the people. There is thus urgent need to raise, upgrade and improve the school curriculum."

It recommended that the school curriculum should be restructured keeping the following considerations in mind:

1. School curriculum should be upgraded through research and should be undertaken by University Department of Education, Training Colleges, State Institutes and Boards of School Education.
2. There should be a periodic revision of curriculum based upon research.

3. The preparation of textbooks and teaching-learning materials should be taken up on a large scale.

4. Orientation programme to teachers tuned to the revised curriculum should be organized.

5. Schools should be given freedom to devise and experiment with new curricula suited to their needs.

6. Ordinary and Advanced curricula should be prepared by State Boards of School Education in all subjects and introduced in a phased manner in schools which fulfill certain conditions of staff and facilities.

7. The Subject Teachers' Associations in different school subjects should be framed which would help stimulate experimentation and up-gradating curricula".

CURRICULAR REVISION, 1975

The Board revised the curriculum for the High School classes in 1975 in the light of the recommendations of the Indian Education Commission though no firm steps had been taken as regards the implementation of the uniform pattern of education (10+2+3). 'Social Science' replaced the erstwhile 'Social Studies'. The revised curriculum is depicted in Table No. 9.2.1

TABLE 9.2.1

Revision of High School Curriculum, 1975

SI. No.	Subjects	Full Marks		Weightage in percentage of the Total Course
1.	Languages: English	200	400	50.00
	M. I. L	100		
	Classical Language (Sanskrit)	100		
2.	Mathematics:		100	12.50

SI. No.	Subjects	Full Marks		Weightage in percentage of the Total Course
3.	Social Science: History	40	100	12.50
	Civics	20		
	Geography	40		
4.	General Science		100	12.50
5.	Optional subject		100	12.50
	Total		800	100

The following subjects were *compulsory* for the H. S. C. Examination of 1979-80.

1. English
2. Mother Tongue (M. I. L)
3. Sanskrit/Sanskrit 50 + Hindi 50/Oriya Lower Standard 50 + Sanskrit 50 or Hindi 50
4. Compulsory Mathematics or Domestic Science
5. General Science
6. History, Civics and Geography
7. Anyone of the following subjects may be offered as an Optional Subject

    a. English
    b. Hindi
    c. Spinning & Weaving
    d. Music
    e. Mathematics
    f. Civics
    g. Physical Education & Military Science
    h. Forestry
    i. Engineering Drawing
    j. Wood Work
    k. Radio Servicing
    l. Sanskrit

  m. Physics & Chemistry
  n. Tailoring
  o. Fine Arts
  p. Agriculture
  q. Commerce
  r. Animal Husbandry
  s. Fishery
  t. Physiology & Hygiene
  u. Manual Drawing
  v. Metal Work
  w. Mechanics
  x. Electrician's Course
  y. Psychology
  z. Surveyor's Course
  aa. Logic

The most popular optional subjects were:Mathematics, Physiology & Hygiene, Sanskrit, Physics & Chemistry. Theoretically a wide areas of optional subjects were available, but practically only three to four optionals were available in most of the schools.

10+2+3 PATTERN AND ORISSA

During 1974-75, the Board decided in principle to introduce the 10+2+3 scheme. The Board has introduced the new pattern of education from the school session 1976-77. The framework for the studies for grades 7 to 10 were prepared. The Board of Secondary Education, Orissa accepted, in principle, the introduction of vocational education in the context of 10+2+3 pattern during 1973-74. Necessary approval was obtained from Government for amendment of the Regulations for incorporating the changes in the courses of studies. It accepted the work-experience as an integral part of the new curriculum. It introduced work-experience programmes in some high schools in collaboration with the Khadi and Village Industries Board.

The acceptance of the 10+2+3 pattern necessitated curricular revisions. The 11 year school had become the 10 year school. '*Classes*' were designated as ^*Grades'*, The Board revised the High School Curriculum in 1981.

CURRICULAR REVISION (1981)

A revised secondary school curriculum came into effect from 1981 H. S. C. Examination. In this revision, the burden of the languages were reduced and the languages together had a weightage of 300 marks. The total marks of the examination were reduced to 700 marks from the earlier 800 marks.

TABLE 9.2.2

Revision of H. S. C. Course, 1981

SI. No.	Subjects	Full Marks		Weightage in percentage
1.	Languages English	100	300	42.86
	M.I.L (Oriya/Telgu/Hindi/Urdu or Bengali)	100		
	Hindi, Sanskrit, Lower Oriya (any two)	50 + 50		
2.	Mathematics		100	14.285
3.	General Science		100	14.285
4.	Social Science: History	40	100	5.714
	Civics	20		2.857
	Geography	40		5.714
5.	Optional subject		100	14.285
	Total		700	100

NATIONAL POLICY ON EDUCATION, 1986

The National Policy on Education and the accompanying detailed document called "Programme of Action,1986" advocated a national curriculum framework for primary and secondary education. The suggested salient features of the curriculum frameworkwere:

- "Emphasis on the attainment of the personal and social goals and propagation of values enshrined in the constitution."
- The development of human resources for the realization of the national goals of development.
- Broad-based general education for all learners at the primary and secondary stages.
- "Learner-centred approach rather than the teacher-centred approach" in the transaction of the curriculum
- Provision for flexibility in terms of selection of content and learning experiences which would facilitate the attainment of the expected learning outcomes.
- Applicability of the curriculum to all learners, irrespective of their modes of learning.
- "Provision of resources (physical and academic) necessary for effective transaction of the curriculum in all schools"

On the basis of the National Curriculum (1988) and National Policy on Education (1986), Nationwide Orientation Programmes of teachers were conducted thereafter. Orientation programmes were held every year during summer vacations. Efforts were afoot to bring about significant changes in the transactional curriculum of the secondary schools.

SCHOOL CURRICULUM & POA 1986

The POA, 1986 in its section dealing with *"Content and Process of School Education"*had very forcefully stated:

"In a knowledge-based society, the content and process of education has to undergo a continuous reorganization and up-gradation. A major reorganization of curriculum took place in 1975 with the introduction of the 10+2 pattern of school education...one of the major weaknesses of the attempts to bring about curricular reforms in the past has been the lack of a comprehensive plan to link curricular changes with the processes of teaching-learning, teacher training and examination reform." (POA,1986.R139).

It suggested the following modalities to translate the curricular policies implicit in NPE, 1986 into practical realities.

(a)	Content Reorientation	1. 2. 3.	National Core Curriculum Revised Work Experience Programme National curriculum frame work, syllabi and in structuralpackages
(b)	Process Reorientation	4. 5.	Reorientation of In-service Training of Teachers Special Training Programmes for In-service Teachers in: (i) Work Experience (ii) Art Education (iii) Physical Education (iv) Establishment of Educational Testing Service
(c)	Both Content & Process	6.	Strengthening of the Technical Support System (i) Existing Institutions (ii) Linkages & Networking (iii) Establishment of DIETs
(d)	Mobilisation & Motivation	7.	Communication Technology (i) Terrestrial Radio & TV (ii) Audio & Video Cassettes (iii) Electronic Notice Boards & Tele- texts.
(e)	Triggering & Monitoring	8.	Planning (i) Budgeting (ii) Coordinating & Monitoring Net-work

It indicated *"ten core curricular areas"* which needs to be incorporated into the curriculum immediately. They are:

i. History of India's Freedom Movement;

ii. Constitutional obligations;

iii. Content Essential to Nurture National Identify;

iv. India's Common Cultural Heritage;

v. Egalitarianism, Democracy & Secularism;

vi. Equality of Sexes

vii. Protection of the Environment;

viii. Removal of Social Barriers;

ix. Observance of the Small Family Norm; and

x. Inculcation of the Scientific Temper.

The curricular reforms must adhere to a pre-determined time-frame; and all activities for curricular streamlining must be completed as per schedule. Curriculum should not be viewed as a happy-go-lucky side-show of the educational process. Its centrality needs to be recognized and urgency evinced and exhibited by all connected with the process of education.

CURRICULUM FRAMEWORK, 1988

In 1988, the NCERT presented a *"National Curriculum for Elementary and Secondary Education"*. It incorporated the salient recommendation of the NPE,1986 and its accompanying POA. It viewed secondary education as the 'terminal state of general education.' According to it the secondary school curriculum should be built around the following curricular areas:

i. Languages (Mother Tongue, Hindi and English),

ii. Mathematics,

iii. Science,

iv. Social Sciences (History, Geography, Civics & Economics),

v. Work Experience,

vi. Art Education, and

vii. Health and Physical Education.

As the NPE, 1986 and POA, 1986 were subjected to review by the Ramamurti Committee, this Curriculum Framework was held back. Many State Boards of Education heavily drew upon it. It did influence the curriculum of the country.

CURRICULAR REVISION OF 1991

The Board of Secondary Education revised the curricula for Classes VIII, IX and X in 1991. This curriculum is in force in 2007. It has been depicted below:

CURRICULUM FOR CLASS VIII (1990-91 TO 2006-07)

The new Scheme of Studies and Syllabus was prescribed for Class VIII during the session 1990-91 on implementation of NPE, 1986 vide letter No.1208 (4000)/Syllabus dated 19th June,1990 of the Secretary, Board of Secondary Education, Orissa.

The subjects to be studied, number of papers, total marks and periods per week have been depicted in Table No. 9.2.3.

TABLE 9.2.3

Curriculum for Class VIII, 1990

Sl. No.	Subject	No. of Papers	Total Marks	Pass Marks	Periods per week
01.	1st Language (Mother Tongue) Oriya/Bengali/Urdu/Telugu/ Hindi/Alternative English	One	100	30	6
02.	2nd Language...English/Hindi	One	100	30	6
03.	3rd Language...Hindi/Oriya	One	50	15	3
04.	Classical Language...Sanskrit/ Persian/Higher English	One	50	15	3
05.	Mathematics	One	100	30	7
06.	Science	One	100	30	6
07.	Social Science	One	100	30	4

SI. No.	Subject	No. of Papers	Total Marks	Pass Marks	Periods per week
08.	Work Experience	One	100		4
09.	Art Education	One	50		2
10.	Health & Physical Education	One	50		4
11.	Library and Debate				1
	Total		800	180	48

The prescribed instructional time was to be at least 200 working days and each day should comprise of 6 (six) teaching hours.

- Number of periods of instruction per day   ... 8 period
- Duration of each period   ... 40 minutes

Each day the instruction time should be utilized as follows:

- Prayer and Roll Call   ... 10 minutes
- 8 periods (40 minutes each)   ... 320 minutes
- Recess   ... 30 minutes

360 minutes

= 6 hours

A working week should have six full working days with 8 periods of instruction each day. There should be 48 periods in all per week. Out of seven periods of mathematics, two periods should be kept consecutively for clearing students' doubts and class tests etc. The duration of the examination in all papers carrying 100 marks should be 2 (two) hours and that of Third Language and Classical Language carrying 50 marks should be 75 minutes. On the basis of the written tests, the Headmaster and the Subject Teacher should assess the performance of the pupils.

The following text-books have been published by the Board of Secondary Education, Orissa during 1990 and 1991. They were adopted or adapted as per the text-books developed by the NCERT, New Delhi.

1. Steps to English (New Edition,1991)
2. Stories from Far <& Near (New Edition, 1991)
3. Sahitya (New Edition,1991)
4. Galpo Ekanikika (New Edition,1991)
5. Byakaran
6. Sarala Sahitya (Lower Oriya)
7. Subodha Hindi Patha (New Edition, 1990)
8. Sanskruta Sudha (New Edition,1990)
9. Bijaganita O Prayoga (New Edition, 1990)
10. Jyamiti O Prayoga (New Edition, 1990)
11. Bhugolo
12. Itihas O Nagar Bigyan (New Edition, 1991)
13. Bigyana (New Edition, 1990)

CURRICULUM FOR HIGH SCHOOL CLASSES (CLASSES IX & X) (1990-91 TO 2000-01):

The Board of Secondary Education, Orissa thoroughly revised its Courses of Studies for Classes IX and X, which came into force from the H. S. C. Examination of 1990-91. This Course has remained almost unchanged up to 2000-01. The textbooks have been prepared in conformity with the objective of the NPE,1986. The text-books prepared by the NCERT, New Delhi have mostly been adapted keeping the local requirements in view.

(a) Subject to be Studied

Pupils enrolled in the course leading to the H. S. C. Examination must receive instruction in the following subjects in accordance with the detailed syllabi prescribed:

1. Languages
2. Mathematics
3. Science
4. Social Science
5. Work Experience

6. Art Education
7. Health and Physical Education

(1) Languages

Every pupil shall study the following languages namely,

a. First Language:
   Mother Tongue: Oriya/Bengali/Telugu/Urdu/Hindi/English.

b. SecondLanguage:
   English/Hindi:

   i. English for those who do not offer English as their FirstLanguage.
   ii. Hindi for those who offer English as their First language.

c. Third Language:
   Hindi/Oriya/Sanskrit/Persian:

   i. Hindi or Sanskrit for those who offer Oriya as their FirstLanguage
   ii. Oriya or Hindi or Sanskrit for those who offer Bengali/Telugu as their First Language
   iii. Hindi or Persian or Oriya for those who offer Urdu as their First Language
   iv. Oriya or Sanskrit for those who offer Hindi as their First Language
   v. Oriya or Sanskrit or Persian for those who offer English as their First Language
   vi. Visual Arts for deaf and dumb candidates in lieu of 3rd Language.

b) Externally and Internally Assessable Subjects

The following subjects shall be Externally Assessable.

1. First Languages
2. Second Languages

3. Third Languages
4. Mathematics
5. Science
6. Social Sciences

The following subjects shall be Internally Assessable.

7. Work Experience
8. Art Education
9. Health & Physical Education

(c) Time Allocation and Weightage for different subjects

Instructional time should be at least 200 working days and each day should comprise of 6 (six) teaching hours.

- Number of periods of instruction per day   ...   8 period
- Duration of each period   ...   40 minutes

Each day the instruction time should be utilized as follows:

- Prayer and Roll Call   ...   10 minutes
- 8 periods (40 minutes each)   ...   320 minutes
- Recess   ...   30 minutes

      360 minutes

      = 6 hours

A working week should have six full working days with eight periods of instruction each day. There should be 48 periods in all per week. There should be no half day.

The allocation of instructional periods for each subject and full marks assigned to each subject for purpose of the H. S. C. Examination or for internal assessment shall be as follows:

TABLE 9.2.4

Curricular Revision, 1991

SI. No.	Subject	No. of Papers	Total Marks	Periods per week
I. Externally Assessable Subjects				
01.	1st Language (Mother Tongue)	One	100	5
02.	2nd Language	One	100	6
03.	3rd Language	One	100	3
04.	Mathematics	Two	150	7
05.	Science	Two	150	8
06.	Social Science			
01.	Paper — I (History & Civics)	One	75	4
01.	Paper II Geography & Economics)	One	75	4
	Total	**Nine**	**750**	**37**
II. Internally Assessable Subjects				
07.	Work Experience	One	100	4
08.	Art Education	One	50	2
09.	Health & Physical Education	One	50	3
10.	Library and Debating			1
11.	School Broadcasting Programme			1
	Total	**3**	**200**	**11**
	Grand Total	**12**	**950**	**48**

Out of seven periods allocated to Mathematics, there should be two consecutive periods once a week which should be devoted to clearing pupils doubts and holding class examinations. Out of eight periods per week allocated for Science, there should be two consecutive periods once a week to facilitate practical work/experiments in the laboratory. Four periods allocated to Work Experience shall be in two consecutive periods each time twice a week. Two periods allocated to Art Education shall be taken once a week in two consecutive periods. The periods allocated to Health and Physical Education should as far as possible, be the last period of the day thrice aweek, so that the children can continue their games beyond the school hours if they so like.

(d) Evaluation and Assessment

There shall be external examination at the end of the Class-X course in the Externally Assessable Subjects namely — First Language, Second Language, Third Language, Mathematics, Science and Social Sciences. The duration of the examination in all papers carrying 100 or 75 marks will be 2.30 hours (two and a half hours). In case of Work Experience, Art Education and Health & Physical Education, the performance of the candidates shall be internally assessed by the schools and grades will be awarded as per the principles of the syllabus. These grades will be reflected in the mark sheets and the pass certificates. Although a minimum of 200 days of class room instruction is prescribed, the detailed syllabi have been drawn up on the assumption of 210 days or 35 working weeks for class - IX and 126 days or 20 working weeks for class X. The shorter instructional time assumed for class X is due to the necessity for completing the course for class X before the test examination. The allocation of teaching periods among different units of the syllabi is only indicative and not to be rigidly taken as binding on the teachers.

SECONDARY SCHOOL CURRICULUM & POA, 1992

The Programme of Action, 1992[19] made the following observations relating to secondary school curriculum.

i. Curriculum for the two stages of secondary education viz., the secondary stage (classesIX & X) and higher secondary stage (classes XI & XII)

ii. These two stages are very different

iii. Secondary Education is the concluding stage of general education

iv. Higher Secondary Education "marks the beginning of differentiation and diversification."

The secondary curriculum while revolving around subject areas attempts to provide an 'integrated whole of all the learning experiences'.

i.   Its salient recommendation relating to subject-areas were:

ii. ... The study of the second and the third language must start from the upper primary stage (classes VI,VII & VHI) and continue up to the secondary stage (classes IX & X).

iii. "The secondary stage (classes IX — X) marks a beginning for the transition from functional mathematics...to the study of mathematics as a discipline. The logical proofs of propositions, theorems, etc. is introduced at this stage. Apart from being a specific subject it should be treated as a contribution to any subject involving analysis and reasoning." 'Mathematics should be re-designed keeping the use of computers in this subject, in view'.

iv. Science is viewed as an intellectual training 'Primarily directed towards problem-solving and decision-making through the learning of key-concepts which cut across all the disciplines". "Science is a continuing human endeavour and... It is international in character." Teaching of science should promote the "spirit of inquiry, creativity, objectivity, courage to question and aesthetic sensibility." Learning of Science will be oriented to ensure that the learners discover the relationship of Science with health, agriculture, industry, and other aspects of daily life.

v.   Social Sciences include Geography, History, Civics, and Economics, "to promote an understanding of contemporary India", "develop a world perspective," and "develop a formal outlook and aversion to injustice and bigotry".

vi. Art Education aims to promote "sensitization of learners... To respond to the beauty in colour, form, movement and sound", and to augment, "knowledge and understanding of the cultural heritage".

vii. Work Education was expected to be purposive meaningful manual work, organized as an integral part of the learning process and resulting in either goods or services useful to the community". Self-reliance, co-cooperativeness, work ethics, attitudes and values related to productivity are the values that can be developed through the medium of work education.

viii. Health and Physical Education is an integral and important part of school curriculum. Personal health and hygiene; and social and preventive community health care were expected to be promoted through it. (viii) Value Education was accorded importance for combating "obscurantism, religious fanaticism, violence superstitions, fatalism, exploitation and injustice", and to inculcate positive values like 'honesty, truthfulness, courage, conviction, straight forwardness, fearlessness, tolerance, love for justice, dependability, compassion, etc. to create a 'humane society' and 'balanced individuals.

ix. Population Education is expected to act as the best contraceptive for the future generations. The six major themes of (a) Family size and family welfare; (b) Responsible parenthood; (c) Delayed marriage; (d) Population-related Beliefs and Values; and (e) Status of Women were to be taught.

NATIONAL CURRICULUM FRAMEWORK, 2000

National Policy on Education 1986 with modification of 1992 indicated the broad parameters and general direction of Indian education. But, *"... Curriculum is a device to translate national goals into educational experiences."* The NCERT constituted a curriculum group in September, 1999 to prepare the framework. It came forthwith a *"National Curriculum Framework: School Education: A. Discussion Document."* In January, 2000 it was widely circulated and sent to all the state governments/universities/eminent academicians/and other stakeholders for their considered views. For the secondary stage of education it recommended the study of:

a. Three Languages: Mother tongue/the Regional language, Modern Indian Language and English
b. Mathematics
c. Science and Technology

d. Work Education

e. Health and Physical Education (including games and sports, yoga, NCC, Scouts and Girl Guides).

Democracy survives on controversies and debates. Consensus is difficult to attain. This framework was criticized as translation of the political agenda of the rulingparty into a practical academic programme. The same criticism is now being leveledagainst the National Curriculum Framework,2005.

NATIONAL CURRICULUM FRAMEWORK: 2005

The Executive Committee of the NCERT took the decision in its meetings held on 14th and 19th July 2004 to revise the National Curriculum Framework of 2000. A National Steering Committee with Prof. Yash Pal as its Chairperson was appointed. It had 33 members. Professor M. A. Khader was the member Secretary. The Steering Committee of 35 eminent intellectuals was assisted by 21 Task Forces on various facets of school education. It is an excellent document. It is balanced and makes good reading. Prof. Yash Pal in the Forward to the document has described the framing of the curriculum as a remarkable process of serious deliberations. It has focused public attention...on *"what should be taught to our children and how"*. He hoped that,... 'this effort might start a freedom movement in education of our young away from some tyrannies in which we have enveloped ourselves.' It recommended the teaching of the following subjects.

1. *Language.*—"as a resource for the enrichment of school life;" "renewal of the three language formula" on the basis of development of linguistic skills through all the curricular areas to enable the children to construct knowledge.

2. *Mathematics.*—Was viewed as the "ability to think logically, formulate and handle abstractions" "to formulate and solve problems" and "to encourage the children" to think and reason.

It stated that "to *quality mathematics education is the right of every child*".

3. *Science.*—As a subject was viewed as "content, process and language of science", as one "that will arouse a curiosity, and creativity...". It should be organically related to the environment."

4. *Social Sciences.*—Need to focus on "Conceptual understanding rather than lining up facts". It should have inter-disciplinary orientation and approach.

5. *Work.*—"Needs tio be reconstructed to realize the pedagogic potential of work as a pedagogic medium in knowledge acquisition.."

6. *Peace Education.*—Was emphasized in view of the prevailing global scenario ridden with strifes; and the looming nuclear catastrophe.

7. *Health & Physical Education.*—Are considered essential for 'overall development' and to "handle successfully the issues of enrolment, retention and completion of school". This subject has a magnetic attraction for the young.

8. *Habitat <& Learning.*—Has environmental ideational approach with a fair-mix of practicals.

Both the curriculum frameworks of 2000 & 2005 are excellent documents. But we must wait and watch to see how it gets translated into transactional curriculum at the institutional level.

SECONDARY SCHOOL CURRICULUM OF 2001 OF ORISSA:

The Course consists of 6 examinable subjects of three Languages, Mathematics (two papers) Science (two papers) and Social Sciences (two papers) Physical Education is taught and internally assessed. The subjects of study, their weightage and the periods allocated per week have been depicted in the Table 9.2.5 below.

TABLE 9.2.5

Subjects of Study, their weightage and allocation of periods

SI. No.	Subject	Total marks	Periods per week
1.	**First Language (MIL)**	100	5
	(A) Oriya		
	(B) Hindi		
	(C) Urdu		
	(D) Alternative English		
2.	**Second Language English**	100	6
3.	**Third Language**	100	3
	(A) Sanskrit		
	(B) Hindi		
	(C) Oriya		
	(D) Persian		
4.	**Mathematics**		7
	(A) Algebra & its Application (MTA) Paper-I	75	
	(B) Geometry & its Application (MTG) Paper-II	75	
5.	**Science**		8
	(A) Physical Science (SCP) Paper-I	75	
	(B) Life Science (SCL) Paper-II	75	
6.	**Social Science**		4
	(A) History & Civics (SSH) Paper I	75	
	(B) Geography & Economics (SSG) Paper-II	75	
7.	**Physical Education**		
	Total	**750**	**37**

SECONDARY SCHOOL CURRICULUM: 2006

The Board of Secondary Education, Orissa approved a new courses of studies for classes IX & X in its Annual General Body meeting held on 13th May, 2005. The Government of Orissa in the Department of School

& Mass Education accorded its approval in its letter No.IX-SME (BSE) 01/2005/13207/SME dated the 2nd July, 2005.

The subjects prescribed for study at the secondary level are eleven; out of which eight (8) are scholastic subjects and three are non-scholastic subjects. The Scholastic subjects are:

i. First language
ii. Second language
iii. Third language
iv. Mathematics
v. Science
vi. Social Science
vii. First Optional subject
viii. Second Optional subject

The non-scholastic subjects are:

ix. Work Experience
x. Art Education
xi. Health & Physical Education

The courses of studies has prescribed the study of three languages compulsorily for every student.

1. First language: Mother Tongue:

One from among Oriya, Bengali, Telugu, Urdu, Hindi or Alternative English.

2. Second Language:

i. English for those who do not offer English as their First Language.
ii. Hindi for those who offer English as their First Language
iii. Environment & Population Education for the hearing impaired students only.

3. Third Language: (Hindi/Oriya/Sanskrit/Persian):

i. Hindi or Sanskrit for those who offer Oriya as their First Language.

ii. Oriya or Hindi or Sanskrit for those who offer Bengali/Telugu as their FirstLanguage.

iii. Hindi or Persian or Oriya for those who offer Urdu as their First Language

iv. Oriya or Sanskrit for those who offer Hindi as their First Language.

v. Oriya or Sanskrit or Persian for those who offer English as their FirstLanguage.

vi. Visual Arts for the deaf and dumb - Hearing Impaired students only.

A student with hearing impairment may on his application be allowed to offer (i) Environment and Population Education in lieu of Second Language and (ii) Visual Arts in lieu of Third language. He/She shall have to offer one language under first language. Such students offering Environment & Population Education/Visual Arts in lieu of 2ndlanguage/3rd language will not be allowed to offer the subjects as optional subjects. The syllabus of the above said "Environment & Population Education" will be same with "Environment & Population Education (Optional) under Group-B. Class X students with hearing impairment will have to apply through the Headmaster concerned well in advance to avail themselves of the above said facility.

THE SCHEME, STRUCTURE & WEIGHTAGE

The new scheme of studies for classes IX & X will contain the following internally assessable compulsory subjects with number of papers and maximum marks indicated against each.

TABLE 9.2.6

Scholastic Subjects

Sl. No.	Subjects	No. of Papers	Total Marks	No. of Periods per week
1.	1st Language	One	100	05
2.	2nd Language	One	100	06
3.	3rd Language	One	100	03
4.	Mathematics	One	100	04
5.	Science	One	100	05
6.	Social Science	One	100	06
Optional Subjects				
7.	Mathematics/Agricultures/Dairy & Pisciculture/Higher Languiages (English/Hindi/Oriya/Sanskrit/Urdu) (Any one subject from Group A to be offered)	One	100	04
Optional Subjects (Group B)				
8.	Science/Computer Education/Environment &Population Education/Basics of Commerce & HomeManagement (Any one subject from Group B to be offered)	One	100	04
Co-Scholastic Subjects				
9.	Work Experience	One	100	04
10.	Art Education	One	50	02
11.	Health & Physical Education	One	50	03
Other School Activities				
12.	Library Work and Debating			01
13.	School Broadcasting Programme			01
	Total	11	1000	48

DETAILS OF TRANSACTION

Four periods allocated to Work Education shall be in two consecutive periods each time twice a week. Two periods allocated to Art Education shall be taken once a week in two consecutive periods. The periods allocated to Health and Physical Education should as far as possible, be the last period of the day thrice a week, so that the children can continue their games beyond the school hours, if they so like.

Securing pass marks in two optional subjects will be determined by taking into account the combined marks obtained in two optional subjects. 20% marks will be allotted for Project work/Practical Work in compulsory Science and optional papers on Agriculture, Dairy & Pisciculture, Computer Education and Science in Class IX. If a student offers Computer Education as an Optional subject under group-B he/she cannot offer" Computer Education as an elective subject under Work Education and vice versa.

There will be 210 working days or 35 working weeks for class-IX and 120 working days or 20 working weeks for Class X for instruction during an academic session. The duration of school hours will be six hours as usual. There may be eight periods a day and duration of such period may be forty (40) minutes.

The instruction time in each day will be as follows:

- Prayer and Roll call — 10 minutes
- Eight (08) periods of 40 minutes each (40X8) — 320 minutes
- Leisure and recreation — 30 minutes

| | **Total** | 360 minutes |
| | | = 6 hours |

A working week will have six full working days with eight periods of instruction each day. There will be 48 periods in all per week. There will be no half day.

There will be internal examination in classes IX and external examination at the end of class-X course in the externally assessable subjects (compulsory and optional subjects). The duration of the examination in all papers carrying 100 marks will be 2ª/2hrs each. In case of internally assessable subjects Work Education, Art Education and Health & Physical Education, the performance of the candidates will be assessed internally by the schools and letter grades on a five point scale as per the existing practices will be reflected in the mark sheet as well as the certificate.

The candidates securing less than 35% marks in any subject and securing less than 264 marks in aggregate will be treated as unsuccessful candidates. The pass marks in two optional subjects will be determined taking into account the combinedmarks secured in both optional papers (60 marks in total). The divisions of the candidates will be as follows:

Candidates securing minimum of 305 marks in each compulsory subject and 30% in both the Optional subjects securing aggregates of:

a.   264 to 359 marks will be declared to have passed in the Third Division

b.   360 to 479 marks will be declared to have passed in the Second Division.

c.   480 marks and above will be declared to have passed in the First division

CONCLUSION

The courses of studies introduced with effect from the academic session 2006-07 in class IX is a highly ambitious one. It has tried to accommodate as wide a spectrum of knowledge as possible. The load of the languages is quite high. The introduction of practicals and project work is enjoyed by the students. The conservative old teachers are averse to these innovations. The operational realities of co-scholastic subjects as they are transacted and translated into action of the curricula can silently be sabotaged by the teachers. Teachers need intensive in-service orientation regarding the specific innovative features of these courses of studies.

The NCF,2005 has recommended far reaching curricular reforms. They are being critically scrutinized to give concrete shape to a detailed curriculum on the basis of the pedagogical insights and indications embedded in the framework. Working out the desired details on the basis of the framework is a challenging task of beset with many problems. The scheme of studies (syllabus/scheme of studies/intended curriculum) must broadly conform to the parameters set by NCF.2005; and must also be tuned to the regional and local needs. The logistics of operational viability of the scheme of studies need to be taken note of. Steps have to be taken for the reorientation of the academic culture of the secondary schools and the administrative ethos of secondary schools.

****

CHAPTER-10

BOARD OF SECONDARY EDUCATION, ORISSA

HIGHLIGHTS

- Background
- Legislation
- Constitution
- Powers and Functions
- Beginnings
- Administrative Structure
- Recognition
- Examinations
- H.S.C. Results
- Examination Reforms
- Curricular Reforms
- Presidents
- Secretaries

BACKGROUND

The Resolution of the Government of India on Educational Policy of 1913 had called for the Assignment of "distinct spheres of activity to the universities and high schools". It stated that, "The Universities should be relieved of the responsibility of granting recognition to high schools and they should be kept under Provincial Governments". Further, it endorses the view of the Indian Universities Commission (1902) which had stated that "The conduct of a School Final or other School Examination should be regarded as altogether outside the function of a University."[398]The Calcutta University Commission (1917) had recommended the establishment of separate High School and Intermediate Boards and to free the universities from governmental control.

In spite of these recommendations the Universities continued to conduct the Matriculation Examination and the High Schools were recognized by the Universities. The High Schools of Orissa were affiliated to the Calcutta University up to 1917. In 1917, the affiliation was transferred to the Patna University consequent on its creation. In 1944, the Utkal University came into existence and the affiliation of all the High Schools of Orissa was transferred to this University. In 1946, the Government of Orissa appointed a Committee under the Chairmanship of Pandit Godavarish Mishra to examine, among other things, the establishment of a Board of Secondary Education for Orissa.

LEGISLATION

In 1953, an Act was passed ' to provide for the establishment of a Board' * to regulate, control and develop Secondary Education in the State of Orissa.' It was the Orissa Act X of 1953. It received the assent of the Governor on the 23rd May,1953 and was first published in an extraordinary issue of the Orissa Gazette, dated the 27th May,1953.[399] In

---

398
399

this Act, Secondary Education has been defined as "such general, special and vocational education forming in itself a complete and purposive whole, which follows immediately such stages of education as has been defined as Primary or Basic Education in the Orissa Basic Education Act, (i.e. the Orissa Act XVIII of 1951) and precedes immediately the stage of education controlled by the University established by law in the State of Orissa."[400]

SECONDARY EDUCATION

The following have been included in the category of Secondary Schools by this Act.[401]

"Middle schools, Ashram Schools, High Schools, Higher Secondary Schools, Post-basic Schools, Agricultural High Schools, Technical High Schools, Trade Schools, Industrial Schools, Senior Technical Schools, Schools of Art and Craft, Schools of Music, Schools of Physical Education and such other institutions as may be recognized by the Board."

Some of the provisions relating to the composition and functioning of the Board Of Secondary Education were changed by the Orissa Secondary Education Amendment) Act, 1979. It was the Orissa Act 6 of 1979 and was assented to by the Governor on the 20th March, 1979. It was published in the Extraordinary Orissa Gazette dated March 26, 1979. This Act amended sections 3, 4,7,11,17,18,19 and 21. sections of 14A, 14B, 18A and 18B were inserted.

CONSTITUTION OF THE BOARD

The Board of Secondary Education, Orissa was constituted for the first time in accordance with the provisions of the Orissa Secondary Education Act, 1953 as per Notification No.11283.E dated 22.12.1955. This Board held its first meeting in Vpril,1956.

400
401

The Board consisted of the following members:

A. Ex-officio Members

    i.   President

    ii.   Vice-President

    iii.   Director of Public Instruction, Orissa

    iv.   Principal R. N. Training college, Cuttack

    v.   Additional D. P. I. (Women's Programme), Orissa

    vi.   All Inspectors of Schools of Orissa

    vii.   Inspector of Physical Education, Orissa

    viii.   Secretary, Board of Basic Education

    ix.   Principal, Sadasib Sanskrit College, **Puri**

B. Nominated members by the State Government

    i.   One District Inspector of Schools,

    ii.   One nominee each of the Directors of Industries, Agriculture, Health and Animal Husbandry, having special knowledge of the respective subjects,

    iii.   One member representing the Ashram Schools to be nominated by the Tribal and Rural Welfare Department,

    iv.   (a) Two Headmasters of High and Higher Secondary Schools,
(b) One Headmistress of Girls' High School or Girls' Higher Secondary School,
(c) Three registered teachers of High Schools, Higher Secondary Schools and Post-Basic Schools,

    v.   Two registered teachers of Middle Schools or Senior Basic Schools,

    vi.   Two registered teachers of Girls' Middle Schools or Senior Basic Schools and Girls' High or Higher Secondary or Post-Basic Schools,

    vii.   Two persons having special knowledge of Basic Education,

    viii.   One teacher from Orissa School of Engineering, &

    ix.   One technical expert in Arts or Crafts.

C. Elected Members

i. Three members of the Orissa Legislative Assemble to be electedfrom among themselves,

ii. Three representatives of the Utkal University, at least two of whom should be college teachers, to be elected by the Senate.

The Board might co-opt not more than three members as extra-ordinary members.

This constitution of the Board has been changed as per the Amendment of 1979. The present constitution of the Board is as follows:

A. Ex-offlcio Members

i. President

ii. Vice-President

iii. All Inspectors of Schools

B. Members to be nominated by the State Government

i. One officer of the Directorate of Public Instruction not belowthe rank of a Deputy Director,

ii. Three Principals of Training Colleges, one from each of the groups of Colleges affiliated to the Utkal, Berhampur and Sambalpur Universities,

iii. Three District Inspectors of Schools, one from each Revenue Division,

iv. Three Headmasters of recognized High Schools and oneHeadmistress of a recognized Girls' High School,

v. Five registered teachers of recognized High Schools and tworegistered lady teachers of recognized Girls' High Schools

vi. Four teachers of Middle Schools of whom one shall be a ladyteacher,

vii. Four teachers of Primary Schools of whom one shall be a ladyteachers,

viii. Oneeminent educationist who has made special contribution inhe field of Secondary Education,

ix. Not more thaneight specialists in subjects forming part ofSecondary Education of whom one shall be a women and two shallbe representing the subjects Arts, Crafts and Physical Education.

C. Elected Members

i. Three members of the Orissa Legislative Assembly to be electedamong themselves,

ii. One representative from each of the Universities in the State to be elected by the members of the respective Academic Councils from among themselves.

The Board may co-opt not more than five members as extra-ordinary members. The members other than the ex-officio and co-opted members shall hold office for a term of five years from the date of the notification.

COMMITTEES

As per Section 19 (1) of the Orissa Secondary Education Act 1953, the Board appoints the following Committees for the smooth discharge of its multifarious activities.

i. Education Committee
ii. Syllabus Committees
iii. Examination Committee
iv. Recognition and Grants Committee
v. Finance Committee
vi. Executive Committee
vii. Appeal Committee
viii. Committee for Technical Education
ix. Teacher Education Committee

And such other Committees as may be prescribed from time to time.[402]

POWERS AND FUNCTIONS OF THE BOARD

a. To prescribe courses of instruction for recognized institutions in such branches as it may think fit,

b. To take steps to co-ordinate Secondary Education with University Education on the one side and Primary or Basic Education on the other, and if necessary for this purpose, to take such steps as it deems proper for preparing syllabi and textbooks for primary and middle school classes,[403]

c. To make regulations for the purpose of prescribing and recommending any book as a textbook or a hand-book and to undertake completion and publication of such books,

d. To make regulations for imposing penalties for acts of misconduct of students, teachers, examiners, examinees, printers of text-books or question-papers and of persons connected with an examination of the Board,

e. To conduct examinations based on such courses,

f. To admit candidates to its examinations in accordance with regulations,

g. To publish the results of its examinations,

h. To grant diplomas or certificates to successful candidates,

i. To recommend to Government in respect of teachers and other employees of Secondary Schools or other institutions controlled by it, conditions of service such as appointment, promotion, punishment, appeals against orders of punishment, transfer, pay, allowances, provident fund, pension, gratuity, if any, age of superannuation etc., and to incorporate such conditions as approved by Government in the regulations,

j. To recommend scales of pay or allowances for employees of SecondarySchools,

k. To establish, control, regulate, and administer new Secondary Schools ofPost-Basic Schools subjects to approval of the State Government,

---

403

1. To bring about practical co-ordination between industrial establishments and factories and Secondary Schools for providing systematic practical training,

BEGININGS

The Board of Secondary Education was established on 22nd December,1955 as per Notification No.11283E. dated 22.12.1955 of the Government of Orissa in the Education Department. Mr. Radhanath Rath, a veteran freedom fighter and the renowned illustrious Editor of the highly popular daily "Samaj" was the Minister of Education. The Orissa Legislature did pass the Orissa Secondary Education Act 1953 and had been assented to by the Governor of Orissa on 23rd May, 1953 and was published in the Orissa Gazette (Extra-ordinary) dated the 27th May,1953. It was he who salvaged it from the cold storage. People would have forgotten it had not Mr. Radhanath Rath insisted on its immediate implementation. So, the Education Department of Government of Orissa issued the Notification on 22nd December,1955. The Board came into existence officially "only on pen and paper" from that date.

Dr. Sreenivas Sahu, M. A (Patna), Ph. D (Bonn), a faculty member of the Department of Philosophy, Ravenshaw College, Cuttack was appointed the first Secretary of the Board of Secondary Education, Orissa; and he joined the Board on 6th March,1955. Prof.(Dr.) Balabhadra Prasad was the first *ex-officio* President. Mr. Harihar Mishra, Joint D. P. I., Orissa became the first *ex-officio* Vice-President. The headquarters was at Cuttack. The bungalow of Late Mr. Samuel Das, the then Secretary to the Education Department was taken on rent to start the office of the Board. The Board had no employees of its own. Therefore, two senior assistants from the D. P. I's office (then at Cuttack) and one senior assistant from the office of the Inspector of Schools, Cuttack were deployed on deputation.

Dr. Sreenivas Sahu, Secretary of the Boards was the only officer. He drafted the original rules, regulations and bye-laws of the Board. Four acres of land in the Bajrakabati area of Cuttack was purchased to erect the permanent buildings. The massive office buildings, the quarters for some staff members and the Secondary Board High School are all located there. The Board conducted the first High School Certificate Examination from the Supplementary examination of 1956. Dr. Sreenivas Sahu is the pioneer administrator and architect of the Board of Secondary Education of Orissa. He demitted office on 17.9.1962. The Board had struck roots and was safe. Dr. Sahu had nurtured it with vision and dedication.

ADMINISTRATIVE STRUCTURE OF THE BOARD

The executive authority of the Board is vested in the President. The Director of Public Instruction, Orissa was the *Ex-officio* President of the Board from 22.12.1955 to 31.3.1968. The erstwhile Directorate of Public Instruction, Orissa was bifurcated with effect from 1.4.1968 and a separate Directorate of Public Instruction (Schools) was created. The D. P. I. (Schools) was designated as the *ex-officio* President of the Board. Professor Baidyanath Rath retired from service as D. P. I. (Schools) on 31st December, 1970. He was appointed full-time President of the Board from 01.01.1970 to 27.01.1972. He was the first whole-time *non-ex-ofjicio* President. Again, the old practice was revived and Dr. Debendra Chandra Mishra, Ph.D (Harvard) D. P. I. (Schools) became the *ex-officio* President. Thereafter, the government started appointing a full-time president for the Board and D. P. I. (Schools) was no more the President. Normally, an academician of the rank of a Professor was appointed as the President. From 26.08.1983 to 26.09.1990 i.e. for 6 years 7 months, it was administered by officers belonging to the I. A. S cadre as Presidents. Again, academicians became Presidents from 27.09.1990 to 20.09.1999. From 20.09.1999 onwards the post is manned by officers of the I. A. S cadre. From 24.06.2005 its President was an officer belonging to the Indian Foreign Service on deputation to the Government of Orissa. The Government in its supreme wisdom has started reposing confidence in the I. A. S officers' competence and almost all top posts of the Education Departments are assigned to I. A. S officers. The average tenure of the academicians was 2 years 9 months, as seven D. P. Is were Presidents for a period of 19 years 5 months 10 days. With the dawn of the "I. A. S. Age of administration", 11 I. A. S officers and one I. F. S. officer had a total tenure of 7 years 11 months or on an average 7 months. Such rapid changes disrupt continuity, and long-term planning becomes impossible. The ""*culture of ad hoc administration*" is sure to emerge. The succession list of the Presidents and Secretaries of the Board can be seen in Appendix I & II.

ZONAL OFFICES

The Board has six zonal offices. The name of the zone offices, their headquarters and the revenue districts under their respective jurisdictions have been indicated below:

1. *Central Zone, Cuttack:*
   Districts of Angul, Dhenkanal, Cuttack, Jajpur, Jagatsinghpur and Kendrapara
2. *Bhubaneswar Zone, Bhubaneswar:* Districts of Puri, Nayagarh and Khurda
3. *Balasore Zone, Balasore:*
   Districts of Balasore and Bhadrak
4. *Baripada Zone, Baripada:*
   Now it is functioning from Balasore (i.e. in October,2006) Districts of Mayurbhanj and Keonjhar
5. *Sambalpur Zone, Sambalpur:*
   Districts of Sambalpur, Jharsuguda, Deogarh, Baragarh, Bolangir, Subarnapur, Kalahandi and Nuapada
6. *Berhampur Zone, Berhampur:*
   Districts of Ganjam, Gajapati, Kandhamal, Boudh, Koraput, Nawarangpur, Malkangiri and Rayagada

It is an effort to decentralize the Board's functioning. Each Zonal office is headed by an officer of the rank of a Deputy Secretary of the Board.

The important officers of the Board are:

    i.   President,

    ii.   Vice-President

    iii.   Secretary

    iv.   Controller of Examinations

    v.   Finance Officer

    vi.   Establishment Officer

    vii.   Text Book Production Officer

    viii.   Two Joint Secretaries and two Deputy Secretaries

    ix.   Six Deputy Secretaries of the Board each in charge of a Zonal Office andSix Assistant Secretaries of the Zonal Offices

    x.   Other Officers are:

        a.   Eight Assistant Secretaries

        b.   One Accounts Officer

        c.   One Evaluation Officer

        d.   One Chief Librarian &

        e.   Subject Experts

Organogram No. I depicts the organizational structure of the Board of Secondary Education, Orissa as it exists on 31st December, 2007

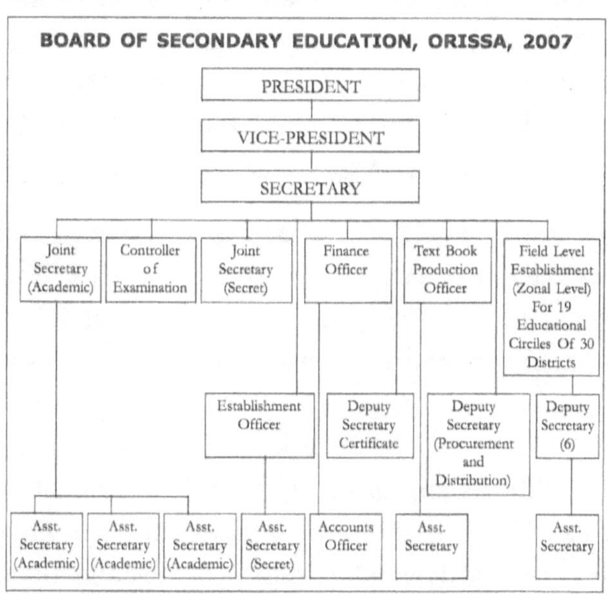

RECOGNITION OF NEW HIGH SCHOOLS

One of the most important functions of the Board is to grant recognition to High Schools of the State, so that these schools may be able to present candidates at the examinations conducted by the Board.

EXAMINATIONS CONDUCTED

The Board of Secondary Education, Orissa conducts the following examinations:

   i.   High School Certificate Examination since Supplementary Examination of 1956. It is conducted twice an year — the Annual Examination and the Supplementary Examination
   ii. Madhyama Certificate Examination since 2001
   iii. Prathama Certificate Examination since 2001
   iv. Middle School Scholarship Examination
   v.   National Rural Talent Search Examination
   vi. Half Yearly Language Test in Oriya
   vii. Certified Teachers' Examination (viii) Hindi Teachers Training Certificate Examination

The prime responsibility of the Board is to conduct the High School Certificate Examinations twice an year. The High School Certificate Examination Results from 1956 to 2007 indicating therein, the number of secondary schools that presented the candidates and the pass percentage has been shown in the Table that follows.

The Board of Secondary Education is primarily an examining body. Its workload has been increasing year by year because its responsibility in this respect has been increasing and the number of candidates appearing at these examinations is also increasing every year. In 1956, the Board conducted examination for the 3,579 candidates who appeared at the Supplementary High School Certificate[9] Examination. By 2007, the number of candidates appearing at the HSC Examination alone has gone up to 3,22,979. It is almost a 90 fold increase in the quantum of work. Besides, the Board is holding eight other examinations. Table 10.1

depicts the number of recognized high schools, number of candidates appeared, passed and percentage of results of high school.

TABLE 10.1

Total number of Candidates Appeared at the H. S. C. Examinations Conducted by the Board from 1956 to 2007

Year	No. of Schools	No. of Candidates Appeared	Pass Percentage	Year	No. of Schools	No. of Candidates Appeared	Pass Percentage
1956	234	3579	....	1982	2619	119222	42.34
1957	264	10411	...	1983	2902	230525	35.03
1958	...	7901	59.00	1984	3220	122181	33.11
1959	....	9029	59.50	1985	3454	121939	42.09
1960	283	10904	54.40	1986	3657	135227	42.39
1961	313	11447	57.61	1987	3954	143901	36.10
1962	366	12193	59.06	1988	4024	126523	46.23
1963	422	14615	60.39	1989	4074	138192	47.00
1964	530	17574	56.03	1990	4335	166733	50.25
1965	606	20282	55.00	1991	4641	147558	44.07
1966	706	23746	51.66	1992	4794	174243	56.06
1967	830	30133	50.09	1993	4899	189944	39.96
1968	973	35171	45.08	1994	5084	202945	55.23
1969	1140	31134	56.08	1995	5374	219083	56.06
1970	1332	43022	51.07	1996	5967	226578	53.29
1971	1407	47622	48.42	1997	6068	234523	62.86
1972	1411	56139	48.64	1998	6074	268456	52.14
1973	1619	54421	41.48	1999	6256	270069	54.64
1974	1706	53851	47.01	2000	6383	273745	40.04
1975	1789	63255	47.03	2001	6431	263617	38.38
1976	1885	66497	35.38	2002	6648	246803	41.01
1977	1979	65102	30.00	2003	6615	241395	50.00
1978	2035	72503	44.81	2004	6648	265083	52.54
1979	2099	37386	56.03	2005	6857	283650	55.66
1980	2271	89730	50.02	2006	7018	298982	56.40
1981	2443	108031	50.70	2007	7128	374320	56.62

EXAMINATION REFORMS

The Board has initiated some examination reforms in the wake of the Kothari Commission Report (1966).

- Central valuation of answer scripts was introduced in 1977
- The NRTS Examination is conducted through Optical Mark Reading (OMR) Method. The results are normally published within 15 days of the examination.
- All activities related prior to and after have been computerized since 1982.
- The first HSC Examination based on the 10+2 pattern at the end of Class X was held in 1983.
- The Board adheres to the Conduct of Examinations Act, 1988 enacted by the Ofissa Legislature.
- The appointment letters of all examiners are sent through the Head of the institution.
- Certificates are distributed from the district headquarters.
- The practice of training paper setters was introduced in 1991 in collaboration with the NCERT. Such workshops had been held in 1996 and 2001 also.
- Question papers are packed centre-wise and are distributed by the Board itself.
- Supervisory squads at the Zonal, Central and special levels are appointed to check malpractices.
- Secret distribution of answer papers to valuation centres initiated in 1997.
- In 1998, the Board attempted to streamline its HSC Examination on the CBSE pattern.
- Parallel and multiple sets of question papers was introduced in 1998 and 1999. Three parallel sets of question papers were set during 2000 for the HSC Examination.
- The results of the HSC Examination are published through the Internet since 2000.

CURRICULAR REFORMS

The Board is responsible for prescribing the curricula for the various examinations conducted by it. The Syllabus Committees constituted by the Board consist of eminent experienced educationists. They normally frame the curricula keeping the national rends in mind. The Board and the State Government approve the courses of studies. The Board adopted the broad curricular approach adopted by the Utkal University 7ith minor modification from time to time from 1956 to 1980.

The curriculum adhering to the academic recommendations of the NPE,1968 was followed from 1981 to 1988. The curriculum based on NPE, 1986 was prepared in 1989 and shall be in vogue up to 2007. A new curriculum based on the National Curriculum Framework, 2000 has been introduced in Class IX from 2006 and the first HSC Examination based on it shall be held in 2008. The Board is critically examining the National Curriculum Framework, 2005.

TEXT BOOKS

The Board is responsible for preparing, printing and publishing the books for the various courses it prescribes. The Editorial Boards recommended by the Syllabus Committees prepare the manuscripts. They are critically examined by senior subject teachers. Then they are approved by the Syllabus Committee, the Education Committee and the Governing Body of the Board. They are got printed and distributed. In such a massive and intricate process a few lapses are unavoidable. The press highlights these lapses and a single word of praise is never accorded to the excellent presentation of content in some books. The Board is at the receiving end of many caustic criticisms in the field of text-book production. Eternal academic vigilance and absolute academic accuracy are social expectations.

The Board undertakes in-service training programmes for teachers. It has a Central Library of its own. The Secondary Board High School, Cuttack has emerged as a pioneering pace-setting secondary school of the state. Such schools need to be established at every district headquarters.

The Board is an examining body and its primary responsibility is to conduct the various examinations that the government of Orissa in the Department of School and Mass Education directs it to. Its most important functions is to conduct the High School Certificate Examination at the end of Class X. It recognized the schools, prescribes text books, conducts in-service training programmes for teachers, administers the endowment funds and manages the Secondary Board School at Cuttack and the six zonal offices.

The Board conducted the HSC Examinations in July,1956 (the Supplementary Examination). It held the first Annual HSC Examination in 1957 for 3579 candidates of 234 recognized High Schools. In 2007, it conducted the said examination for 3,22,979 candidates of 7128 high schools. The schools have increased more than 30 times and the increase in the candidates has been more than 90 times. Managing such a mega educational enterprise requires high levels of integrity, intelligence and tact.

The Board is the target of may vitriolic criticisms, real or fancied. It must decentralize further and try to win the confidence of the people. Millions of citizens are closely watching its activities.

SUCCESSION LIST OF PRESIDENTS

SI. No.	Name	Tenure	
		From	To
1.	Prof(Dr.) Balbhadra Prasad, DPI	22.12.1955	30.04.1957
2.	Prof(Dr.) Bama Charan Das, DPI	01.05.1957	20.01.1962
3.	Prof(Dr.) Sadasiv Mishra, DPI	21.01.1962	15.02.1966
4.	Prof(Dr.) Banshidhar Samantarai, DPI	16.02.1966	29.02.1968
5.	Shri Gokul Chandra Satapathy, DPI (S)	01.03.1968	31.07.1968
6.	Prof. Baidyanath Rath, DPI(S)	01.08.1968	27.01.1972

SI. No.	Name	Tenure	
		From	To
7.	Prof(Dr.) Debendra Chandra Mishra, DPI(S)	28.01.1972	01.05.1975
8.	Prof. Brajabandhu Mishra	02.05.1975	03.03.1978
9.	Prof. Batakrushna Mohanty (I/C)	04.03.1978	31.01.1979
10.	Prof. Bibekananda Pati (I/C)	01.02.1979	03.03.1979
11.	Prof. Harekrushna Mishra	02.04.1979	22.09.1980
12.	Prof. Batakrushna Mohanty	29.09.1980	20.08.1981
13.	Shri Gopal Chandra Pattnaik (I/C)	21.09.1981	08.04.1982
14.	Prof(Dr.) Sarat Chandra Das, Addl. Charge	09.04.1982	04.081982
15.	Prof. Batakrushna Mohanty	05.08.1982	21.08.1983
16.	Shri Raimohan DAS, IAS	26.08.1983	01.02.1985
17.	Shri Sakti Prasad Mishra, IAS	02.02.1985	12.07.1987
18.	Shri Ardhendu Sekhar Sarangi, IAS	29.07.1987	26.02.1990
19.	Prof.(Dr.) Chitrananda Nanda (I/C)	27.02.1990	01.04.1990
20.	Prof.(Dr.) Chitrananda Nanda (I/C)	02.04.1990	30.09.1990
21.	Prof.(Dr) Jayanarayan Patnaik (I/C)	01.10.1990	31.10.1990
22.	Prof.(Dr) Jayanarayan Patnaik	01.11.1990	07.07.1992
23.	Shri Sivaram Patnaik	13.07.1992	05.08.1992
24.	Prof(Dr.) Phanindra Bhusan Das	07.08.1992	31.12.1993
25.	Prof. (Dr.) Pravat Kumar Mishra	31.01.1994	31.01.1995
26.	Dr. Debakanta Mishra (I/C)	01.02.1995	06.06.1995
27.	Dr. Debakanta Mishra	07.06.1995	01.11.1996
28.	Prof(Dr.) Prafulla Chandra Mahapatra	01.11.1996	28.02.1999
29.	Shri P. S. Guha, IAS, Addl. Charge	01.03.1999	09.03.1999
30.	Dr. Narendra Prasad Das, O.E.S. (I)	10.03.1999	20.09.1999
31.	Sri Digambar Mohanty, IAS, Addl. Charge	20.09.1999	25.11.1999
32.	Shri Dandanirodha Mishra, IAS	26.11.1999	05.01.2001
33.	Shri S. N. Tripathy, IAS, Addl. Charge	16.01.2001	18.01.2001
34.	Shri Niranjan Padhy, IAS	19.01.2001	17.03.2003
35.	Shri Isaac Behera, IAS, Addl. Charge	25.03.2003	24.07.2003
36.	Shri B. C. Swain, IAS, Addl. Charge	25.07.2003	22.09.2004
37.	Shri Sanjaya Rastogi, IAS, Addl. Charge	22.09.2004	28.12.2004

Sl. No.	Name	Tenure	
		From	To
38.	Dr. Subhakanta Behera, IFS, Addl. Charge	29.12.2004	01.02.2005
39.	Shri Dandanirodha Mishra, IAS, Addl Charge	02.02.2005	30.04.2005
40.	Dr. Subhakanta Behera, IFS, Addl. Charge	03.05.2005	09.06.2005
41.	Shri B. C. Swain, IAS, Addl. Charge	16.06.2005	23.06.2005
42.	Dr. Subhakanta Behera, IFS, Addl. Charge	24.06.2005	31.08.2006
43.	Dr. Subhakanta Behera, IFS,	01.09.2006	29.06.2007
44.	Shri Debendra Chandra Mishra, I. A. S *Commissioner-cum-Director of Secondary Education, Orissa (Ex-officio)*	29.06.2007	06.08.2007
45.	Sri K. K. Mohanty, OAS (S)	07.08.2007	20.08.2007
46.	Dr. Harihar Sahu, OES (I) *(Jt. Director of Schools)*	20.08.2007	27.08.2007
47.	**Sri** K. K. Mohanty, OAS (S)	27.08.2007	22.10.2007
48.	Sri Arun Kumar Samantray, I. A. S *(Principal Secretary's Grade in the I. A.. S.)*	22.10.2007	Continuing

SUCCESSION LIST OF SECRETARIES

Sl. No.	Name	Tenure	
		From	To
1.	Dr. Sreenivasa Sahoo	06.03.1955	17.09.1962
2.	Shri Debendra Nath Dutta	18.09.1962	03.02.1964
3.	Shri Prasanna Kumar Das	04.02.1964	23.07.1967
4.	Prof. Paresh Chandra Ray	24.07.1967	31.05.1973
5.	Sri Banchhanidhi Mohanty (I/C)	01.06.1973	18.09.1973
6.	Prof. Rama Krushna Kar	19.09.1973	10.12.1973
7.	Shri Gopal Chandra Pattnaik	23.12.1973	22.02.1977
3.	Capt. Radha Kanta Mishra	23.02.1977	28.02.1979
9.	Shri Ramanarayan Padhi (I/C)	01.03.1979	20.03.1979
10.	Shri Sivram Pamaik	21.03.1979	10.03.1980
11.	Maj. Dhirendra Kumar Nanda	11.03.1980	17.05.1981

SI. No.	Name	Tenure	
		From	**To**
12.	Shri Gajendra Nam Das	18.05.1981	16.05.1983
13.	Shri Sivaram Pamaik	17.05.1983	01.12.1986
14.	Shri Kanhu Charan Sahoo (I/C)	01.12.1986	03.03.1987
15.	Miss Kalyani Ghose	04.03.1987	31.07.1987
16.	Shri Trilochan Sarangi	01.08.1987	23.07.1990
17.	Dr. Debakanta Mishra	24.07.1990	20.07.1992
18.	Shri Debabrata Mishra	20.07.1992	02.12.1995
19.	Maj. Dr. Bikartan Pal	07.04.1996	25.02.1997
20.	Dr. Mihir Das	26.02.1997	31.07.2001
21.	Sri Dwijaraj Kar (I/C)	01.08.2001	13.03.2002
22.	Dr. Hemandra Narayan Das	14.03.2002	30.06.2006
23.	Dr. M. K. Pany	26.07.2006	22.08.2007
24.	Soumya Ranjan Mishra, OFS	22.08.2007	22.09.2007
25.	Sri P. K. Samal, O.A.S. (Selection Grade)	22.09.2007	Continuing

NOTES:

1. *K N. Training College, Cuttack:*

   Itwas established in 1923. It was known as Government Training College, Cuttack from 1923 to 1948. It was renamed Radhanath Training college in 1948 after Radhanath Ray, the celebrated poet and educationist of Orissa. In 1988, it became the Radhanath Institute of Advanced Study in Education, Cuttack.

2. *Additional D. P. I. (Women's Programme):*

   It was created for a short tenure. Mrs. I. L. Sinha (Khan) was the only person who held this post. The post was abolished when she left her job as she was not promoted to the rank of the D. P. I.

3. *Ashram Schools:*

The Ashram Schools are special schools for the Scheduled Tribe students mainly where Scheduled Caste students can also study. They are generally residential schools and all children get stipends. These schools are administered by the Department of S. T. &SC Development of Government of Orissa.

4. *Basic Schools:*

Schools designed on the basis of Gandhian philosophy of education and the Zakir Husain Committee Report of 1937. Post-Basic means higher secondary; Senior Basic means schools with classes up to VIII. 'Basic School' is a primary school with classes up to class V. A Junior Basic School means a school with classes I, II & III. and the Infant Class known as Pre-Basic Class.

5. *H. S. C*

- High School Certificate Examination held after 11 years of school education up to 1982.
- From 1983, the H. S. C. is the terminal examination after the Ten-year School Education.
- From 1912 to the Annual Examination of 1956 it was known as *Matriculation Examination.*
- From 1857 to 1911 it was known as the *Entrance Examination.*
- In the Madras Presidency the *Secondary School Leaving Certificate* (SSLC) used to be conducted by the Education Department itself and not the University.
- Upto the establishment of the first three universities at Calcutta, Madras and Bombay, the *"Junior Scholarship Examination"* was held on completion of the High School Education of 11 years duration.

* * * * *

CHAPTER-11

THE COUNCIL OF HIGHER SECONDARY EDUCATION, ORISSA

HIGHLIGHTS

- Inception
- Composition
- Powers and Functions
- Administrative Structure
- Curriculum for + 2 (2006-07)
- H.S.S.C. Results
- Stream-wise Enrolment
- Chairmen
- Secretaries

INCEPTION

The Council of Higher Secondary Education, Orissa was established on 7th September,1982 in pursuance of the provisions of Ordinance No.8 of 1982. This Ordinance was placed before the Orissa Legislature and it was passed and is known as "Orissa Higher Secondary Education Act, 1982". It was established, "to regulate, control and develop higher secondary education in the state of Orissa ".

COMPOSITION OF THE COUNCIL

The Council is a corporate body with succession of (a) *ex-officio* members (b) members nominated by the Government of Orissa, and (c) elected members.

a. The *ex-officio* members are ten in number. They are:

   i. Chairman,
   ii. Vice-Chairman (if appointed),
   iii. Director of Higher Education, Orissa,
   iv. Director of Secondary Education, Orissa,
   v. Director of Teacher Education and State Council of Educational Research & Training, Orissa,
   vi. Director of Technical Education and Training, Orissa,
   vii. Director, National Cadet Corps or his nominee,
   viii. President, Board of Secondary Education, Orissa,
   ix. Principal, College of Physical Education, Cuttack, and
   x. Principal, Regional Institute of Education, Bhubaneswar.

b. Members nominated by the Government of Orissa are 45 in number. They are:

   i. A representative of the Department of Higher Education not belowthe rank of a Deputy Secretary;
   ii. A representative of the Finance Department not below the rank ofa Deputy Secretary.
   iii. Ten Principals of Colleges including Junior Colleges;

    iv. Five Headmasters of Higher Secondary Schools;

    v. Ten registered teachers of -recognized colleges including juniorcolleges.;

    vi. Five registered teachers of higher secondary schools;

    vii. Three Inspectors of Schools;

    viii. Not more than ten specialists in vocational subjects prescribed for the higher secondary courses.

c. Five elected members. They are:

    i. Three members of the Orissa Legislative Assembly;

    ii. One representative of the Board of Secondary Education;

    iii. One representative from each of the Universities of the State to be elected by the members of the Academic Councils of the respective universities.

The Council consists of sixty members in all. The Secretary of the Council is the Convener.

POWERS & FUNCTIONS

Subject to the provisions of Orissa Higher Education Act, 1982, the Council shall have the following powers and functions, namely:

a. To prescribe courses of instruction for recognized institutions in such branches of higher secondary education as it may think fit,

b. To take steps to co-ordinate higher secondary education with university education on the one side and secondary education on the other,

c. To make regulations for the purpose of prescribing and recommending any book as a text-book or a hand book or to undertake compilation and publication of such books,

d. To make regulations for imposing penalties for acts of misconduct of students, teachers, examinees, printers of text-books or question papers, of persons connected with the examinations of the Council,

e. To conduct examinations based on such courses as may be prescribed,

f. To admit candidates to its examinations in accordance with the regulations,

g. To publish the results of its examinations,

h. To grant diplomas and certificates to successful candidates,

i. To establish, control, regulate or administer any junior college or any highersecondary schools subject to the approval of the Government

j. To bring about practical co-ordination between state-owned industrial institutes, factories or workshops or vocational institute, agricultural farms, animal husbandry centers or pisciculture institutes and the higher secondary schools or junior colleges providing for vocational courses by way of providing adequate and systematic practical training which will be complementary to the theoretical instruction at the schools or colleges.

k. To call for reports from the Directorate of Public Instruction on the conditions of the institutions, applying for recognition and to direct inspection of such institutions, (1) To recognize institutions for the purpose of admitting them to the privileges of the Council including examinations conducted by it,

l. To lay down the qualifications of teachers required to teach the subjects included in the courses of study in different branches of higher secondary education, the work load of such teachers and the number of working day in an academic year and other matters incidental thereto,

m. To adopt measures to promote the intellectual, physical moral and social welfare of the students of the recognized institutions and to supervise and control the conditions of their residence, health and discipline,

n. To institute and award scholarships, medals and prizes according to a scheme framed by the Council,

o. To demand receipt of such fees as may be prescribed,

p. To administer funds placed at its disposal for the purposes for which they are intended or generally for the purposes of the Council,

q. To submit annual accounts and balance sheet together with the annual report of the Council to the Government and to publish the audited accounts and balance sheet in the Orissa Gazette,

r. To submit to Government its views on any matter with which it-is concerned,

s. To take measures to provide para-military education, opportunities to organized social services and such other activities as the Council considers necessary to inculcate in the minds of the students enrolled in recognized institutions a high sense of citizenship and to train and prepare them to discharge their civic obligations effectively,

t. To furnish to Government such reports and returns and statements as may be prescribed by regulations and such other information relating to any matter under the control of the Council as the Government may require,

u. To maintain a library of its own,

v. To have an Information Cell for dissemination of information about the activities of the Council, employment opportunities of different vocations and fields in higher general and professional studies,

w. To acquire, hold and dispose off property, both movable and immovable, for the purposes of the Council and enter into agreements there for,

x. To maintain register of teachers and register of students admitted to the Higher Secondary Course."

The affairs of the Council are managed through the following committees:

i. Executive Committee; and its three sub-committees viz,:

   a. Tenders sub-committee

  b. Purchase sub-committee

  c. Printing Material Requirement sub-committee

 ii. Examination Committee

 iii. Recognition Committee

 iv. Academic Committee

 v. Finance Committee

 vi. Syllabus Committee

 vii. Other Committees & Sub-Committees

The Council has an N. S. S. Bureau and a Library.

ZONAL OFFICES

The Council has three zonal offices at Baripada, Berhampur and Sambalpur. Each zone office is headed by a Deputy Secretary of the Council. It is an attempt to decentralize the administration.

ADMINISTRATIVE STRUCTURE & OFFICERS

The important officers of the Council are:

 i. Chairman,

 ii. Vice-Chairman,

 iii. Secretary,

 iv. Controller of Examination,

 v. Finance Officer,

 vi. Administrative Officer,

 vii. Deputy Secretary of the Head Office,

 viii. Three Deputy Secretaries heading the Zonal Offices,

 ix. Two Deputy Controllers of Examination,

 x. Asst. Controller,

 xi. Accounts Officer,

 xii. Audit Superintendent,

 xiii. Asst. Secretary and

 xiv. Programme Officer, NSS.

The Organogram depicts the administrative structure and hierarchy of the Council.

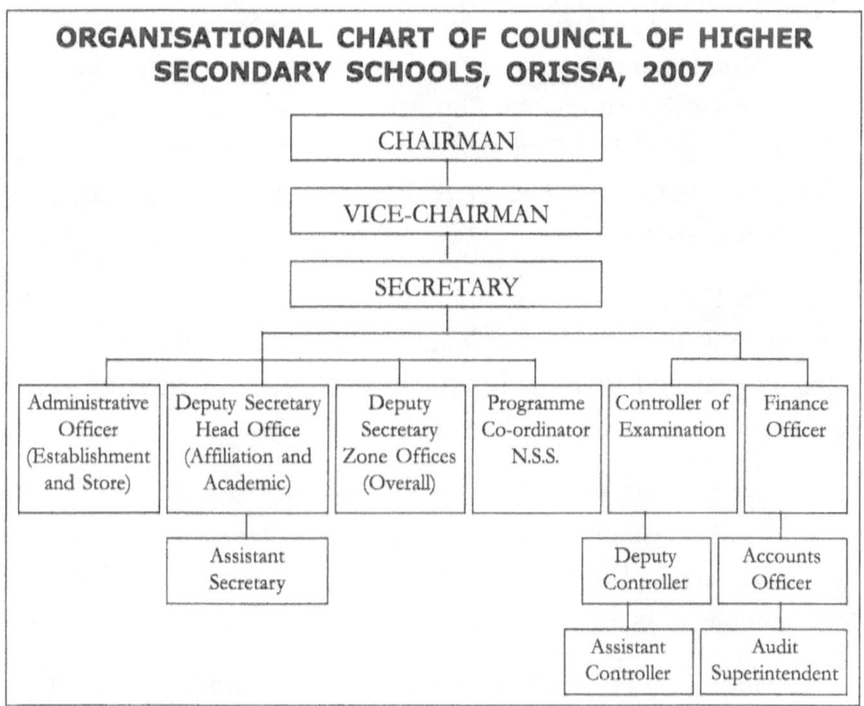

The succession list of Chairmen and Secretaries of the Council from 1982 to 2007 has been provided in Appendix I & II, respectively.

CURRICULUM FOR HIGHER SECONDARY (+2) COURSES, ORISSA (2006-07)

The Academic Committee of the Council had approved the new curriculum prepared by the Syllabus Committee to be implemented from the academic session 2006-07. This has also been concurred to by Government of Orissa in the Department of Higher Education.

According to the new course structure there shall be one examination to be conducted by the Junior College/Higher Secondary School at the end of the 1st year based on the curriculum meant for the year; and one examination at the end of 2nd year to be conducted by the Council based on the curriculum meant for that year alone. Pass certificates will be awarded to successful candidates on the basis of the performance in the Council examination to be held at the end of 2nd year only.

The examination at the end of 1st year shall be for 700 marks (including 200 marks for Environmental Education); and the examination at the end of 2nd year shall be of 600 marks. Marks secured in the examination to be conducted at the end of the 1st year shall be considered for promotion of students to the 2nd year class.

Besides English and MIL, Environmental Education (EE) shall also be a compulsory subject. But Environmental Education will be taught only in the 1st year and examination for Environmental Education will be conducted by the college at the end of the 1st year.

Restriction on selection of optional (henceforth called as *elective)* subjects will be the main feature in the new course structure. There shall be no extra optional subject. Instead each student has to offer four elective subjects as detailed below.

1. **Subjects of Higher Secondary Education:** Besides the compulsory subjects (i) English, MIL and (ii) Environmental Education, a candidates shall offer any four elective subjects from any of the grouping under (iii) A or B or C.

2. **Duration of Course:** The syllabus for 2 years course of each subject shall be divided into two parts, namely 1st year and 2nd year carrying 100 marks each. The college will conduct one examination at the end of the 1st year class of +2 course and the Council will conduct the examination at the end of the 2nd year class of +2 course. The result of a candidate will be determined only on the performance of the candidate in the Council Examination to be held at the end of the 2nd year course.

3. **Pass Criteria:** The pass criteria for the Examination shall be as follows:

a. Subjects with Practical: 30% of the total marks shall be diverted for practical examinations and the remaining 70% thereof for theory. A candidate has to pass separately in theory and practical examinations. Pass marks in Biology shall be calculated taking together the marks secured in both Botany and Zoology (adding the marks of Botany and Zoology).

b. Pass marks shall be 30% of the total marks in theory paper and 40% of the total marks in practical paper, in each subject with 35% of the total marks in the aggregate.

4. **Course Structure and Subjects of Examination:** The course structure and subjects for the Higher Secondary Examination and the maximum marks in each subject shall be as follows:

Compulsory

Subject	Marks	1st Year	2nd Year
(i) English	200	100	100
(ii) MIL (One of the following) Oriya/Hindi/ Bengal/Telugu/Urdu	200	100	100

Provided that the Council may in special circumstances permit a candidate to offer alternative papers in English of a higher standard than required in (i) above in lieu of MIL paper stating reasons.

Provided further that a candidate may be permitted to take up for the Higher Secondary Examination one of the subjects as MIL under (ii) above without attendance at Lecture in the subject if the institution in which he is admitted is not affiliated in the subject.

II. Environmental Education (EE)

Notes: The above subject will be assessed at the college level for 100 marks (70 marks for theory and 30 marks for project work) at the end of 1st year of +2 course and the grades (A,B,C, or D in order of merit) are to be awarded by the College and the same shall be recorded in the body of the pass certificate given by the Council subsequently. The grade secured in the Environmental Education (EE) will not affect the result of the candidate.

Marks	Grade
Above 70%	A+
Above 60%	A
Above 50%	B
Above 35%	C
Below 35%	C

Elective

III. A. Subjects of Examination of Arts stream:

Out of the following six groups of subjects, a student shall have to offer only four elective subjects each carrying a maximum of 200 marks — i.e. 100 marks for 1st year and 100 marks for 2nd year.

1. Political Science
2. History/Mathematics
3. Logic/Sociology
4. Economics/RPM
5. Education/Psychology/Home Science/Indian Music/Statistics/Information Technology/Anthropology/Geography.
6. Oriya/Sanskrit/Persian/Hindi/Urdu/Bengali/Telugu

III. B. Subjects of Examination for Science stream

Each elective subject shall carry a maximum of 200 marks i.e. 100 marks for 1st year and 100 marks for 2nd year.

1. Physics
2. Chemistry

Either Group A' or Group 'B' for third and fourth elective subjects:

Group 'A'	**Group 'B'**
(3) Mathematics	(3) Biology
(4) Biology/Electronics Statistics/Geology/ Geography/Information	(4) Mathematics/ Bio-Technology/ Statistics/Geology Information Technology

III. C. Subjects of Examination for Commerce Stream:

Each elective subject carrying a maximum of 200 marks i.e. 100 marks for 1st year and 100 marks for 2nd year.

1. Accountancy
2. Business Studies & Management
3. Business Mathematics & Statistics
4. Any one of the following Group

	1st year	2nd year
Group-I	Commercial Banking &	Insurance
Group-II	Fundamentals of Entrepreneurship &	Cost Accountancy
Group-III	Salesmanship &	Business Economics
Group-IV	Fundamentals of Company Accounts &	Fundamentals of Management Accounting
Group-V	Commercial Geography &	Rural Development
Group-VI	Computer Application-I &	Computer Application-II
Group-VII	Information Technology-I	Information Technology-II

FACULTY DEVELOPMENT

During the academic session 2005-06, the Council had organized Teachers Orientation Programme in Chemistry, Mathematics, Sanskrit and Logic in Khallikote Autonomous College, Berhampur; F. M Autonomous College, Balasore; G. M. Autonomous College, Sambalpur; Ravenshaw Junior College, Cuttack; and Kamala Nehru Women's College, Bhubaneswar. Around 500 college teachers joined this programme.

{Source: Reports of the Council of Higher Secondary Education, Orissa from 2001-02 to 2004-05)

EXAMINATIONS

The Council conducts the Higher Secondary Certificate Examination in the following streams.

i. Arts
ii. Science
iii. Commerce
iv. Vocational since 1988

The number of candidates who had appeared and passed at the Higher Secondary Certificate Examination from 1985 to 2006 has been provided in Table No. 11.1.

TABLE NO. 11.1

Higher Secondary Certificate Examination Results, 1985 to 2006

Year	Appeared	Passed	Pass percentage
1985	41,213	16,422	39.8
1986	92,932	34,420	37.0
1987	1,45,754	37,111	25.5
1988	1,56,665	45,121	28.8
1989	1,56,610	50,500	32.3

Year	Appeared	Passed	Pass percentage
1990	1,58,007	61,611	39.0
1991	1,66,792	60,861	36.5
1992	2,18,825	75,886	34.7
1993	2,39,415	80,807	33.8
1994	2,58,775	94,512	36.5
1995	2,80,038	1,04,112	37.2
1996	2,92,884	98,615	33.7
1997	2,76,347	1,02,699	37.2
1998	2,03,406	1,18,923	58.4
1999	N. A	N. A	N. A
2000	N. A	N. A	N. A
2001	2,14,516	70,535	32.8
2002	1,89,904	1,00,920	53.1
2003	1,53,727	89,741	58.4
2004	1,55,978	1,22,389	78.4
2005	1,57,725	112162	71.1
2006	1,63,263	1,04,812	64.2

ENROLMENT

The enrolment at the +2 (Higher Secondary) stage is steadily increasing. But it is not dloping like secondary school enrolment. There is a discernible disillusion with the higher secondary course. So the great rush is abating.

Arts stream is the most popular one and has the maximum enrolment. Science is favourite stream, but facilities for it are not adequately available. Students and parents are yet to wake up to realize the potential of the Commerce stream. Table No. 2 resents the stream-wise enrolment appeared, passed and its percentage.

TABLE NO. 2

Stream-wise Analysis of Higher Secondary Education (2001-2006)

SCIENCE STREAM

	2001	2002	2003	2004	2005	2006
Enrolled	53,078	54,024	46,423	44,151	42,988	46,507
Appeared	52,136	52,565	45,389	43,388	42,322	45,561
Passed	20,013	27,106	27,036	33,189	30,199	31,389
Pass %	38.4	51.6	59.6	76.5	71.2	70.37

COMMERCE STREAM

	2001	2002	2003	2004	2005	2006
Enrolled	14,702	13,464	11,883	12,695	12,208	12,245
Appeared	14,412	13,134	11,655	12,500	12,083	12,102
Passed	6,469	7,771	7,128	9,803	9,055	9,143
Pass %	44.9	59.2	61.2	78.4	74.9	76.65

ARTS STREAM

	2001	2002	2003	2004	2005	2006
Enrolled	1,52,218	1,29,567	1,01,096	1,03,613	1,07,745	1,09,237
Appeared	1,47,968	1,24,205	96,683	1,00,090	1,03,320	1,05,600
Passed	44,053	66M043	55,577	79,393	72,988	64,280
Pass %	29.8	53.2	57.5	79.3	70.6	60.87

VOCATIONAL STREAM

	2001	2002	2003	2004	2005	2006
Enrolled	631	886	983	1,125	NA	2,210
Appeared	587	861	956	1,103	NA	2,174
Passed	275	638	873	1,045	1248	2,060
Pass %	46.8	74.1	91.3	94.7	NA	94.76

The Vocational stream was the least popular. It has no regular full-time teachers. It is managed by Part-time Resource Persons (PTRPs) and Full

Time Resource Person (FTRPs) who get beggarly remunerations. But the greatest wonder that astonishes one is the extremely high success rate unequalled by any other stream. The needle of suspicion turns towards massive manipulation and possible corrupt practices. It is high time the Government appoints a high level committee to conduct an in-depth investigation of this Vocational stream and its credibility.

The total enrolment in the Commerce Stream is hovering around the 12,000 mark. Non-availability of access to this stream is a major deterrent. Further students and their parents have not yet realized the job potentials after "+2 Commerce".

The enrolment in the Science stream in 2006 was only 46,507. The unbridled growth of the Engineering Colleges in the State seem to have sprouted to cater to the needs of the clientele of the other States. Science holds the key to the future. The Government and the Council must streamline and update this stream so that more students of Orissa enroll in these Engineering Colleges.

The enrolment in the Arts stream is the highest. But a distinct downward trend in enrolment in this stream is discernible.

Perhaps the time has come to think of an integrated higher secondary education. A student may choose Physics, Book-keeping, Music and Horticulture as subjects and still have his/her higher secondary education completed. There is need for specialization in a subject, but compartamenlisation of streams may be an emphatic "No'.

The Council prescribes the courses of studies for the Trades approved by the Government which are taught in Government Vocational Junior Colleges affiliated to it. There are 20 Trades for which courses of studies are prepared and examinations are conducted by the Council.

OFFICE

From 7th September 1982 to 1st January. 1996, the Council was functioning from a rented building. The Council office building had been completed by December, 1995, and it functions from its own office at C-2, Samantapur, Bhubaneswar. The campus is known as "Pragnya Pitha".

The Council has a Bureau of National Service Scheme. Many activities for the students of the higher secondary stage are organized by it.

The fragmentation of secondary education into two parts — the high schools dealing with classes IX and X and junior colleges/ higher secondary schools exclusively dealing with classes XI and XII has totally defeated the purpose of secondary education. The high schools and junior colleges are "nano educational institutions". Consolidation of secondary education by amalgamating high schools and junior colleges is an urgent imperative. Vocational higher secondary education is one glaring example of transforming a serious academic experiment with far reaching socioeconomic repercussions into a farcical standing joke. It should be augmented andacademic rigour must be enforced, or else it may be abandoned. Vocational higher secondary education is not serious, has no status or standing, has no expert technical support and is a totally enfeebled appendage to the higher secondary system of education. It should be suitably upgraded or it should be totally uprooted. We have failed to translate the beautiful possible dream into a reality, and have transformed it into a nightmare for the academically sub-standard students. It is the academic choice of the last resort.

The Board of Secondary Education, Orissa and the Council of Higher Secondary Education, Orissa can be amalgamated into one unit with zonal offices in every district. Rationalization of secondary education is an unavoidable urgent necessity.

INCUMBENCY CHART OF CHAIRMEN, COUNCIL OF HIGHER SECONDARY EDUCATION, ORISSA, BHUBANESWAR (1982 TO 2007)

SI. No.	Name of the Chairman	Period	
		From	To
1.	Dr. Tapas Kabi	17.11.1982	01.08.1983
2.	Maj. Bata Krushna Mohanty	04.08.1983	31.12.1983
3.	Shri Rajendra Prasad Das (I/C)	01.01.1984	05.07.1984
4.	Dr. Naba Krishna Mohapatra	06.07.1984	31.01.1986
5.	Dr. Giridhari Prasad Guru	03.02.1986	05.06.1988
6.	Dr. (Nrs.) Girish Bala Mohanty	06.06.1988	04.06.1990
7.	Dr. Phani Bhusan Das	11.06.1990	31.07.1991
8.	Md. Fakiruddin (I/C)	01.08.1991	25.02.1992
9.	Prof. Chandra Sekhar Sarangi	26.02.1992	31.10.1994
10.	Shri Deepak Kumar Sarangi	10.11.1994	27.04.1996
11.	Dr. Gunanidhi Sahu	01.05.1996	16.02.1998
12.	Shri H. C. Pattnaik *(L/C)*	16.02.1998	28.02.1998
13.	Dr. Basanta Kumar Mohapatra	02.03.1998	31.03.1999
14.	Shri M. K. Mohapatra (I/C)	31.03.1999	10.05.1999
15.	Dr. A. K. Das	17.05.1999	30.06.2000
16.	Shri D. Mishra (I/C)	30.06.2000	13.07.2000
17.	Dr.(Mrs.) K. B. Pattnaik	14.07.2000	20.01.2003
18.	Dr. D. K. Panda	20.01.2003	31.05.2003
19.	Shri D. Satapathy (I/C)	01.06.2003	24.09.2003
20.	Shri A. K. Nayak(I/C)	24.09.2003	12.12.2003
21.	Dr. Jatindranath Mohanty (I/C)	12.12.2003	31.11.2004
22.	Dr. N. K. Sen (I/C)	30.11.2004	31.07.2006
23.	Prof. (Dr.) Umakanta Subuddhi	04.08.2006	Continuing

INCUMBENCY CHART OF SECRETARIES, COUNCIL OF HIGHER SECONDARY EDUCATION, ORISSA, BHUBANESWAR (1982 TO 2007)

SI. No.	Name of the Secretary	Period	
		From	To
1	Dr. Praffula Kumar Mohanty	01.11.1982	01.10.1985
2	Sri Nilakantha Mohanty	01.10.1985	07.12.1986
3	Dr. Rajendra Prasad Mohanty	08.12.1986	18.02.1988
4	Shri Bijay Kishore Bal	19.02.1988	28.07.1992
5	Shri Durga Prasanna Das	28.07.1992	31.01.1994
6	Shri Nikunja Kishore Das	19.03.1994	21.05.1999
7	Shri Debabrata Mishra	21.05.1999	24.07.2000
8	Dr. Bijaya Chandra Rath	26.07.2000	17.07.2003
9	Shri Braja Kishore Dhir	17.01.2003	09.07.2004
10	Shri Baidhar Pradhan	09.07.2004	31.10.2007

Notes:

1. *Ex-officio:* "Because of one's position". The Director of Secondary Education, Orissa is the ex-officio member of the Council of Higher Secondary Education, Orissa. The membership of the Council depends upon the post held and is not by name.

2. MIL: Modern Indian Language

3. Grade: A range of marks (i.e. numerical representation) are represented with alphabets and signs. Any candidate who gets more than 70% marks gets the Grade "A+".

4. CHSE: Council of Higher Secondary Education.

CHAPTER-12

FINANCING EDUCATION

HIGHLIGHTS

- Introduction
- Grant-in-Aid as a System of Financing Education (1854 to 2007)
- Priorities of Five Year Plan
- Financial Administration of Education
- Sources of Finance
- Expenditure on Secondary Education

Dr. Atmananda Mishra apty remarked that the history of educational finance "mirrors the history of the evolving concept of State and its educational aims."[404]The total history of educational finance is a fascinating and interesting challenge. However, the major obstacle to the portrayal of a continuous connected and comprehensive picture of educational finance is the lack of sector-wise firm data base. The grant-in-aid rules dating back to 1855 provide an insight into the increasing involvement of the public in improving instructional facilities. The financial importance accorded to secondary education has been portrayed, albeit sketchily.

In 1813, the Charter Act provided that "   a sum of not less than one lakhof rupees in each year shall be set apart and applied to the revival and improvement of literature and the encouragement of the learned natives of India and for the introduction and promotion of knowledge of the sciences amongst the inhabitantsof the British territories in India; "[405] This was the first legislative commitmentof the British rulers relating to education. This 'one lakh of rupees' became a bone of contention between the Anglicists and the Orientalists. Finally in 1835, it was decided to utilize this sum for the furtherance of Western education. Lord Hardinge's Resolution of 1844 placed a definite premium on the Western education. In the subsequent years Western education had a steady growth and the indigenous educational system had a gradual decline. The Government helped to establish English schools. There was no definite educational policy, much less a policy relating to educational finance up to 1854.

Wood's Despatch of 1854 is a landmark in the history of Indian education. It recognized "the impossibility of Government alone doing all that must be done" and in consequence resolved ' to adopt in India

---

404 Atmananda Mishra, (Dr.): The Financing of Indian Education, Asia Publishing House, BombaymPreface
405 East India Company: charter Act, 1813. Clause 43. Quoted by Dr. Atmananda Mishra

the system of grant-in-aid'[406]This, for the first time, was a definite statement of policy relating to the financing of education. Grant-in-aid was introduced in Orissa in 1857.

The Report of the Indian Education Commission 1882, (Hunter Commission Report) reviewed the previous policies and laid down guiding principles for the future. The Commission recommended that the Government might maintain one school in a district and it should withdraw from direct enterprise in this field and that the private schools should be run on the grant-in-aid basis.

In 1902, Lord Curzon reversed the policy of state withdrawal in the field of education and a period of rigorous quality-control began. From 1919 onwards education became increasingly a State subject and the Act of 1935 made education State subject completely. This position was maintained in the Constitution of free India. In 1976, it was included in the "Concurrent List" of the Indian Constitution.

Secondary education is the responsibility of the States of India. India accepted planned economy and the First Five-Year Plan. Had the Directive Principle of State policy of the Indian Constitution relating to the introduction of free compulsory education up to the age of 14 been properly implemented, the lower secondary education, (classes VI,VII, & VIII) in particular, and secondary education, in general, 3uld have greatly expanded. The pious wishes of the founding fathers of our Institution had been blissfully neglected, and in consequence, primary education is not become either universal or compulsory: and the progress of secondary education has been hindered thereby.

Financing of education in Orissa, *both* in private and public sectors, has been a taunting recurrent problem since independence. The, available resources for limitative expansion and qualitative development of education are quite inadequate. The State Government have consistently tried to mobilize resources to finance Aviation since the

---

406 Selections from Educational Records, Vol. II p. 378, Items 51 and 52

First Five Year Plan. Still it has not yet been able to cater to the ends of the people. The unpredicted phenomenal growth of population is partly responsible for perpetuating poverty and backwardness. This has been further celebrated by frequent natural calamities like floods and droughts. During all these are if there were any exigencies that had to be met, the axe fell on education. The minimum need of different stages of education remained unattended to.

GRANT-IN-AID AS A METHOD OF EDUCATION FINANCE, (1854-1901)

In accordance with the recommendations of the Wood's Despatch of 1854, grant-in-aid became the principal method of educational financing. The Government participated that " by thus drawing support from local resources in addition to contributions from the State, a far more rapid progress of education than would How a mere increase of expenditure by the Government; while it possesses the additional advantage of fostering a spirit or reliance upon local exertions and combination for local purposes, which is of itself of no mean importance to the ill-being of a nation."[407] Further it looked forward to a day "when any general systemof education entirely provided by the Governmentmay be discontinued, with the gradual advance of the system of grant-in-aid."[408] But aid was to be granted subject to the fulfillment of certain conditions such as:

1. The school getting such subsistence must abstain from imparting any religious instruction.
2. Such a school must be under 'adequate local management'.
3. The manager of such a school must 'consent that it would be subject to Government inspection and agree to any condition which may be laid down for the regulation of such grants and

---

407 J. A. Richey (Ed): Selections from Educational Records. Vol. II. P. 378-379
408 Ibid, para 62. p. 381

that grant-in-aid shall be made to only such schools as require some fee, however small, from their scholars'.[409]

In 1855, Government of Bengal outlined the detailed grant-in-aid rules for the development of secondary education. Secondary and Vernacular schools were eligible to get the aid. The aid was to be given in form of money, books or otherwise, to any school in which a good secular education was given. The amount of aid was to be based on the number of teachers, salaries, subjects taught and books prescribed. Aided schools were to be open to inspection and examination. There was to be no interference in the actual management of aided schools. In case of unsatisfactory management, the aid was to be withdrawn. Perfect religious neutrality was to be a condition of the grant and some kind of fee was to be charged from the scholars.[410]The Government struck a note of caution relating to the grant of aid to missionaries.[411] The Director of Public Instruction, Bengal was sceptic relating to the impact of these rules on the progress of education in a poor country like India which was not yet conscious as to the benefits of education.

There was evident enthusiasm for English education in large towns like Cuttack, Puri and Balasore. However, the rural population had not been awakened to the benefits of English education. The total expenditure on account of grant-in-aid during 1860-61 was only Rs. 552 per month.[412] Orissa was educationally backward and institutions were very few. The grant-in-aid rules were amended from time to time and every amendment made the rules more and more stringent.

The wealthy Zamindars and rulers of the Native States did not come forward to promote the cause of education. By 1874-75, the Inspector of Schools, Orissa Divisionremarked that in comparison with other parts of Bengal, Orissa had not its 'fair play' in possessing educational

---

409 Ibid, para 53. p. 379
410 Report of die Progress of Education, Bengal, 1855. p. 10
411 Report of die Progress of Education, Bengal, 1857-58, p. 32
412 Report of the Progress of Education, Bengal, 1860-61. p. 123

institutions through Government effort. In view of these circumstances, Orissa could not benefit from the grant-in-aid rules.

Campbell's Scheme of 1873, put a premium on the school results. Payment-by-results system proved a scourge for the grant-in-aid system. Schools that fared badly n the examinations had their aid forfeited. The development of the aided schools was slow due to the Campbell's scheme.

The Hunter Commission Report of 1882 made an overall review of educational policies. Its major concern relating to secondary education was, firstly, the removal of the defects in the prevailing system; and secondly, devising the ways and means "or the expansion of secondary education. It recommended that, "Secondary education should, as far as possible, be provided on the grant-in-aid basis and the government should withdraw, as early as possible, from the direct management of government Schools for secondary instruction." But this transfer was to be made without lowering the standard "of schools and when permanency and efficiency were ichieved."[413]The payment-by-results principles were shelved. The grant-in-aid principle vas used as a safety valve for receiving and neutralizing the shocks received from he public as well as the Government in matters of education. The Hunter Commission exhorted the provincial governments to revise the grant-in-aid rules. The broad principles of grant-in-aid as enunciated by the Indian Education Commission, 1882 were; (i) *locality* — the larger grants being given to schools in backward districts; and (ii) *the class of institution* — girls' schools, schools for lower castes and backward classes were to be given preference. Grants were forbidden to ;elf-supporting institutions and the total grants to an institution was, in no case, to exceed one half of the total expenditure. The recommendations of the Indian education Commission, 1882 accelerated the development of secondary education and private bodies took the initiative in this field.

---

413 Indian Education Commission Report, 1882, p. 596

GRANT-IN-AID SYSTEM IN NORTH ORISSA

Payment-by-results and *net-grant* were the two modes followed in North Orissa up to 873. The net grant provided for subsidies from provincial revenues which together with the fee receipts and other local contributions catered to the needs of the smooth management of the school. If there was a surplus it could be spent on additional establishments or unforeseen expenditure of the following year. In 1893, it was decided that, "all aided schools in Bengal, should receive grants dependent upon the average attendance of scholars, instead of upon examination results."[414] The old payment-by-results system was bid good-bye. The *needs and means* of the school became the criteria for the determination of the grant.

In 1895, the [1]*net-grant* was replaced by the *'gross-grant'* system in which all aspects of the school income and expenditure were taken into consideration while fixing the grant. All these changes facilitated the easy flow of grants to private aided schools. The principle of liberality was adhered to enkindle incentive for private effort. This continued until 1902, when the grant-in-aid rules were again revised. There was a definite expansion of secondary education, but it was markedly perceptible in the expansion of Middle English Schools. The number of high schools did not appreciably increase during this period and the impact of the revised grant-in-aid rules in the post -1902 years had very little or no effect upon high school education.

Immediately after the publication of the Report of 1882, many private schools were started with the hope of getting aid. However, the Inspectors demanded efficiency in which respect these newly-started schools were not well off and so failed to reach the standard of getting the grant. In 1881-82, all types of schools (Primary and Secondary) in Bengal were 7,771[415]and in 1983-84 this number jumped up to

---

414 Indian Education Commission Report, 1893-94, p. 19
415 Indian Education Commission Report, 1881-82, p. 64

9,001.[416]But in 1892-93, this number decreased to 5,749[417] The private initiative was disillusioned. The debate of 'quality versus quantity' began during this period. The Government was after quality, the people clamored for more and more schools.

GRANT-IN-AID SYSTEM IN NORTH ORISSA FROM 1901-1915

The rules for grant-n-aid to schools in Bengal payable from provincial revenue were revised in 1903. The grants were distributed by the Director of Public Instruction on the recommendation of the Divisional Inspector to Schools which were certified to be eligible under the rules, reference being made to the requirements of each locality as compared with others, and to the funds at disposal. The schools receiving aid were subject to inspection and the Inspecting Officers were to "interfere as little as possible with the local management of schools," but were employed to see thathe instruction was sufficient.[418] Grants were to be given, as before, on strict religious neutrality. Grants were to be given only to such schools which "required some fee, however small, from all their scholars". No grant was to be given to a high school *unless provision was made for instruction in drawing and drill, and unless the medium of instruction n the classes below the fourth was in the Vernacular,* as required under the Scheme of Vernacular Education sanctioned by Government Resolution No.l dated 1ˢᵗ anuary,1901". Every school had to satisfy the condition of having a Secretary and he information pertaining to the pecuniary resources, proposed monthly expenditure, average number of pupils to be instructed, the persons to form the Managing Committee, the class of school and course of instruction, the number and salaries of teachers, the fees to be charged in each class, the amount of aid sought, etc. had to be supplied as a precondition for the grant.

---

416 Indian Education Commission Report, 1883-84, p. 62
417 Progress of Education in Bengal, 1892-93, p. 50
418 Rules and Orders of the Bengal Education Department, 1903, p. 149

The scheme envisaged two types of *gtants-annual grants* and *special grants*. Annual rants of High School were to equal to two-third of the income guaranteed from private sources. This was a special concession to Orissa, as the general districts were 3 get only half the amount. For Middle Schools of Orissa, the grant was to be equal 3 the income guaranteed from private sources, provided the expenditure was more than Rs. 40 per month. Grants were to be sanctioned once in every three years.

The revised rules made provision for *special grants* which were meant to be give or—

a.   erecting, enlarging or furnishing of school-buildings;
b.   executing extensive repairs; and
c.   in special cases, for paying off debts incurred in erecting or enlarging school-buildings.

A sum of Rs. 10,000 was fixed as ordinarily the maximum grant for any project. Grants were also channelised through the District Boards for Middle English and Middle Vernacular Schools.[419] The special grants enabled the schools to undertake repairs for the schools and improve them properly.

GRANT-IN-AID SYSTEM (1915-1925)

During this period, the Bihar and Orissa Education Code laid down the standard staff of High Schools and Middle Schools and the payment of grant-in-aid wassubject to the appointment of the prescribed standard staff.[420] Further, the Headmasters were authorized to spend the allotment for prizes, library books and contingencies without reference to the Secretary.[421] The *minimum maintenance grant* for a High School was Rs. 75 and for a Middle English School it was Rs. 30 per month.

---

419 Ibid. pp. 149-154
420 The Bihar & Orissa Education Code, 1920, Article 317 and 318, pp. 159-160
421 Ibid Article 316 (25). p. 158

Maintenance grants were calculated to supplement the local resources. The prescribed standard was:

a. Rupees 535 in High Schools in which *the number of boys was 150 or over.*

b. Rupees 485 in High Schools in which *the number of boys was under 150.*

c. For High Schools using more than one Vernacular as a medium of instruction Rs. 45 in addition to the above rates for each extra Vernacular taught.

d. Rupees 160 for Middle English Schools.

e. Rupees 40 for Middle English Schools using more than one Vernacular as the medium of instruction Rs. 40 for each extra Vernacular.[422]

The grant receiving schools were to use the prescribed books.

GRANT-IN-AID SYSTEM IN SOUTH ORISSA UP TO 1936

In South Orissa, which was part of the Madras Presidency, the grant-in-aid principle was implemented with certain modification. In 1859, the grants were increased for "the augmentation of salaries of school masters and mistresses; provision of stipends for pupil-teachers, provision of school-books, maps etc; the establishments and maintenance of school libraries; erection, purchase and enlargement of school-building and the provision of school-furniture."[423]

In 1864, there were only two private Middle Schools and one Zilah School at Berhampur. But in 1880-81, the number of secondary institutions stood at 12, out of which 3 were aided institutions. Within the duration of three decades, only three private institutions sprang up and the rest were all Government institutions.

---

422 Selections from Educational Records, Madras, 1858-59
423 Selections from Educational Records, Madras, 1858-59

In strict conformity with the letter and spirit of the Hunter Commission Report of 1882, all the schools of Ganjam district were handed over to either private management or the management of the local boards. The Berhampur Zillah School became the private aided Khallikote High School. By 1891, all the High Schools passed into the hands of Local Boards.

High Schools of South Orissa received *salary grants*. The Lower. Secondary Schools n the temporary list received *grants under the payment-by-results* system.

During 1888-89, the average cost per pupil in a Board School was Rs. 46.00 and i aided School it was Rs. 47.99 per year; of which fees met Rs. 37.00 and Rs. 28.00 respectively. The Government aid was Rs. 9.00 per pupil for the Board School and 5. 19.00 per pupil for the other aided schools.[424] Thus, the incidence of expenditure as lessened for the Government. However, due to the stringent rules of recognition, le expansion of secondary education was checked in the Madras Presidency, in General and the Ganjam district, Ganjam Agency and the Vizagpatam Agency or Koraput region, in particular.

GRANT-IN-AID SYSTEM (1925-1947)

The *monthly grant* to an aided High School was limited to the difference between the standard cost and the fee income. The minimum grant was to be Rs. 75 per month, id the maximum grant half of the standard cost. The standard cost of a High School was made up of the following items.

(A) A lump sum for the cost of the teaching staff calculated as follows: For a School with:

(1) 00	Less than 9 teachers @	Rs. 52.50 p.m. per teacher
(b)	Less than 10 teachers @	Rs. 526.00 p.m.
(c)	Less than 11 teachers @	Rs. 565.00 p.m.

424

(d)	Less than 12 teachers @	Rs. 590.00 p.m.
(e)	Less than 13 teachers @	Rs. 630.00 p.m.
(0	Less than 14 teachers @	Rs. 655.00 p.m.
(g)	Less than 15 teachers @	Rs. 690.00 p.m.
(h)	Less than 16 teachers @	Rs. 740.00 p.m.
(2)	For a clerk	Rs.30.00 p.m
(3)	For repairs to buildings	Rs. 50.00 p.m.
(4)	For Taxes	The actual sum payable
(5)	For Provident Fund	1/32 of salaries
(6)	For contingencies	Rs. 45.00 p.m.

Report on Public Instruction, Madras, 1888-89, p. 55

The minimum grant for the Middle English School was reduced to Rs. 30 a month. The monthly grant to an aided Middle English School was limited to the difference between the standard cost and the income derived from local sources such as fees and subscriptions. The standard cost of a Middle English School was calculated as follows;

a.	Salaries of Headmaster and 4 Teachers	Rs. 135.00 (Per month)
b.	Repair to buildings	Rs. 10.00 (Per month)
c.	Contribution to Provident Fund	Rs. 14.50 (Per month)
d.	Contingencies	Rs. 15.00 (Per month)
	Total	Rs. 174.00 (Per month)

The grant-in-aid rules for the Middle Vernacular Schools were the same. The standard cost was calculated as follows.[425]

a.	Pay of 5 Teachers	Rs. 134.00 (Per month)
b.	Allowance to Head Teacher	Rs. 5.00 (Per month)
c.	Provident Fund Contribution	Rs. 4.00 (Per month)
d.	Prizes, Library and Contingencies	Rs. 15.00 (Per month)
	Total	Rs. 158.00 (Per month)

GRANT-IN-AID SYSTEM (1947 TO 1974)

The private schools of Orissa were given grant-in-aid by the Government. Grants to these schools were calculated on the basis of admissible expenditure. The admissible expenditure includes the salary of the staff, contingent expenses, and expenditure on items like rent, taxes and provident fund. Two principles were followed in sanctioning grant — *"the proportional grant system'* and *'the deficit grant system'.* According to the proportional grant system, a certain proportion of the total expenditure incurred is made available to the institution. According to the 'deficit-grant system', a certain percentage of the difference between the approved annual expenditure and income from tuition fees calculated at standard rates is sanctioned. The deficit-grant is based upon the difference between the total approved expenditure minus the total resources of the institution. Grants are also classified as *recurring and non-recurring grants.* A brief discussion of these two types of grants is given below has been provided.

Recurring Grants

In the case of boys' schools in ex-state areas (i.e. the erstwhile Feudatory States of Orissa which were amalgamated with Orissa in 1948 and 1949) recurring grant-in-aid 2/3rds of the deficit was paid from the beginning as soon as Class VI was cognized in respect of Middle English Schools and Class VIII was recognized in respect of the High Schools. This facility was also extended to educationally backward eas of non-ex-state area. The Boy's Middle English Schools and High Schools in her areas received minimum grant-in-aid @ Rs. 30 and Rs. 75 per month respectively Dm the academic year immediately following the year of presentation of candidates for the final Certificate Examination. After enjoying the minimum grant for 3 years, the school was eligible to receive grant at 2/3rds of the net deficit.

The Girls' High Schools all over the State received recurring grant-in-aid as full deficit from the inception of the schools and the Girls' Middle English Schools received recurring grant-in-aid at full net deficit one year after recognition.

The scales of the pay of teachers were revised in 1961. Additional grant-in-aid is paid at $3/4^{th}$s of the additional expenditure incurred in the case of teachers of boys' High and Middle English Schools. In case of Girls' High and Middle English Schools the entire additional expenditure was borne by the Government. This ant-in-aid was admissible while the schools were in receipt of the minimum ant-in-aid also. Dearness allowances was paid at $2/3^{rd}$s rate both to Boys' and Girls' Schools. The schools were eligible for this grant also while on the minimum grant.

Non-recurring Grant

In case of Boys' schools, non-recurring grant was paid at 50% of the total estimated best on account of buildings, equipment, furniture, library, laboratory etc. The otherwas to be met by the management. Preference was given in approving non-recurring grant to Boys' High Schools which showed pass results of 65% and above of the roll strength in the highest class in the annual examination in the following year. In the case of Girls' School, non-recurring grant was given at 66.6%schools in ex-State areas and educationally backward areas; and 60% in other on account of school-building, furniture, and equipment. But for the instruction of hostel buildings and teachers' quarters, 100% grant was paid to Girls' High Schools and Middle English Schools all over the State.

It is evident from the foregoing grant-policy that Girls' schools had been favouredpromote female education which was relatively undeveloped in the State.

GRANT-IN-AID RULES 1974 TO 1988

These grant-in-aid rules were amended and revised principles have been introduced in 1974.

Principles for High Schools (Boys' and Girls'):

  i.   Contingent expenditure @ Rs. 75.00 per month.
  ii. Loss of fee income.

  iii. 35% of pay of the employees admissible under rules and additional D. A admissible after 1st January,1974

Principles for High Schools (Boys' and Girls'):

  i. Contingent expenditure @ Rs. 30 per month.
  ii. Loss of fee income.
  iii. 40% of the pay of the employees admissible under rules
  iv. 80% of dearness Allowance and additional dearness allowances admissible after 1st January. 1974.

The Government introduced '''*direct payment of salaries to teachers* ' of aided schools with effect from 1st April,1974.

SYSTEM OF GRANT-IN-AID FROM 1988-1989

The State Government had a grant-in-aid policy for non-government upper primary schools, high schools and higher secondary institutions. Though the policies for different types of institutions were different, yet a common procedure of paying two-thirds of the net deficit of the expenditures of the institutions was followed. In the year 1974, the direct payment system was introduced which contemplated that the full salary cost of teaching and non-teaching staff would be paid along with a fixed amount of contingent and building repair cost after the institution was admitted to direct-payment system. Prior to the direct-payment system, an institution had to remain under a minimum grant-in-aid period for three years during which 40 percent of pay and 80 percent of DA to the staff was being paid. All this has been subsequently modified to 60 percent of the total salary cost (Pay plus DA).

The rate of minimum grant-in-aid for non-government Middle English schools covered 60 percent of the total emolument, that is, pay/DA as sanctioned by the State Government from time to time in respect of eligible employees, and contingent expenditure at Rs. 30 per month.

These regulations were effective from 1988. After successful completion of 33 months, an upper primary school was treated as "fully grant-in-aid institution". With the commencement of academic year, immediately following the presentation of candidates for the final certificate examination, the upper primary school was eligible to get minimum grant-in-aid.

A recognized high school was eligible for minimum grants of 60 percent when three batches of students are presented in the High School Certificate Examination. the institution will become *fully aided* after the completion of seven years. But in case of low literacy areas (with literacy percentage less than the State average) and in order areas (within two kilometers of the State border) and un-served areas having to high schools within five kilometers, grant-in-aid is provided in the next year after le presentation of the candidates for high school examination.

In case of girls' school, after the first year of presentation of candidates, the institution is eligible for 60 percent of the aids, and after two years, it becomes fully ided. In case of low literacy area and schools situated in border areas the institutions/ill be become full aided after three years; but girls' high schools will be eligible for receipt of minimum grant-in-aid at par with the co-educational non-government high school with effect from 1st April, 1989. The rate of grant during the direct payment period shall be full pay and DA of teaching and non-teaching staff to be paid directly to the employees and recurring grant of Rs. 2100 per annum for contingencies.

In Orissa, higher secondary classes are mostly integrated with the degree colleges. As a result, only the institutions established before 1983-84 are getting grant-in-aid. The rules contain that colleges can receive in advance one-third of the deficit as rant-in-aid after five years from the date of Government concurrence, two-thirds after seven years and full deficit after nine years. In case of backward areas, it will be agreed, five and seven years respectively. But after 1987, none of higher secondary institutions have received any grant-in-aid as grant-in-aid rules for higher secondary schools/junior colleges are being formulated.

EDUCATIONAL PRIORITIES OF FIVE-YEAR PLANS

India became independent on 15th August 1947. It became a Republic ion 26th January 1950. The Constitution of India came into effect from 26th January 1950. The Constitutional promises had to be kept. The country must march ahead. India accepted the Russian model of planning. India embarked on the road of planned development witheffect from 1951, when the first five-year plan commenced.

TABLE 12.1

India's Five Year Plans

Plan	Period		Duration of Plan Holiday
	From	**To**	
Ist Plan	1.4.1951	31.3.1956	
IInd Plan	1.4.1956	31.3.1961	
IIIrd Plan	1.4.1961	31.3.1966	
Plan Holiday	1.4.1966	31.3.1969	
IVth Plan	1.4.1969	31.3.1974	
Vth Plan	1.4.1974	31.3.1979	
Plan Holiday	1.4.1979	31.3.1980	One year
VIth Plan	1.4.1980	31.3.1985	
VIIth Plan	1.4.1985	31.3.1990	
Plan Holiday	1.4.1990	31.3.1992	Two years
VIIIth Plan	1.4.1992	31.3.1997	
IXth Plan	1.4.1997	31.3.2002	
Xth Plan	1.4.2002	31.3.2007	
XIth Plan	1.4.2007	31.3.2012	

The educational objectives, emphasis and priorities of the first eight plan have been briefly presented. The objectives of the Five Year Plans practically provided the thrust to the priorities and programmes of the State Government.

1. First Five Year Plan (1951-52 to 1955-56)

The quantitative targets of the first Five Year Plan were the provision of educational facilities for 60 percent of the children of the age group 6-11. It also emphasized the need to bring children up to the age of 14 to schools. It hoped that 15 percent of the relevant age-group shall enter the secondary school. It aimed to bring 30 percent of the people of the age-group 14-40 within the purview of social education. For girls, the respective targets were 40 percent, 10 percent and 10 percent.

2. Second Five-Year Plan (1956-57 to 1960-61)

The main emphases of the Second Five Year Plan were:

- Increased importance to basic education.
- Expansion of elementary education.
- Diversification of secondary education as recommended by the Secondary Education Commission.
- Improvement of the standards of Colleges and Universities.
- Expansion of technical and vocational education.
- Implementation of Social education.

3. Third Five Year Plan (1961-62 to 1965-66)

The major thrusts of the 3rd Five Year Plan were:

- Provision of universal access to primary education for the age group 6 to 11.
- Improvement of Science Education at the secondary and university stages
- Training of teachers at all stages of education.
- Expansion of technical education.

4. Fourth Five Year Plan (1969-70 to 1973-74)

"Priority will be given to the expansion of elementary education and the emphasis will be on the provision of facilities for backward areas and communities and for girls. Other programmes of importance will be: improvement of teacher education; expansion and improvement of science education; raising standards of post-graduate Education and research; development of Indian languages and book production, especially text-books; and the consolidation of technical education including reorganization of polytechnic education and its closer linking with the needs of industry and its orientation towards self-employment."

5. Fifth Five Year Plan (1974-75 to 1978-79)

The Fifth Five Year Plan emphasized:

i. ensuring equality of educational opportunities
ii. establishing closer links between the pattern of education, on the one hand, and the needs of development and the employment market on the other;
iii. Improvement of the quality of education and
iv. Involvement of the academic community including students in the tasks of social and economic development.

6. Sixth Five Year Plan (1979-80 to 1984-85)

The Sixth Five Year Plan had the following priorities:

i. Programmes of adult education for eradication of adult illiteracy;
ii. Universalization of elementary education; and
iii. Vocationalisation of education.

Other programmes of importance were: Improvement of Teacher Education; Expansion and improvement of Science Education; raising standards of Post-Graduate Education and Research; development of Indian Languages and Book Production, especially text books; and the consolidation of technical education including reorganization of polytechnic education and its closer linking with the industry.

7. Seventh Five Year Plan (1985-86 to 1989-90)

The Seventh plan stated: " Education has to develop basic life skills and competencies to foster a value system conducive to and supportive of, national development goals, both long-term and immediate. The task of education is the diffusion of new knowledge and, at the same time, in the preservation and promotion of what is basic to India's culture and ethos."

8. Eighth Five Year Plan (1992-93 to 1996-97)

The major priorities relating to Education in the Eighth Plan were:

- "Achievement of Universal Elementary Education;
- Eradication of illiteracy in the age-group 15-35 years;
- Vocationalisation and skill training;
- Up-gradation of standards and modernization of all stages of education;
- Provision of facilities for education of excellence in every district of the country; and
- Removal of obsolescence and modernization of technical education."

FINANCIAL ADMINISTRATION OF EDUCATION

Every budget must foresee the sources of income and prescribe the time frame during which the stipulated programmes and projects are to be completed. The resources available for education are scarce in relation to the demands. A good budget envisages post-effective expenditure. The budget clearly earmarks the allocations for item-wise expenditure. Appropriations and re-appropriations of the allotments are possible only after following certain established norms and procedures. A budget is an effective instrument to discipline and control public expenditure.

Educational planning is one of the major components of the over-all planning process of the State. It is regulated by the guidelines laid down by the Department: Planning and Co-ordination of Government of

Orissa. The State Planning Board jaded by the Chief Minister oversees the priorities, plans and fund allocation to each of the sectors; and the plan as a whole. The State Planning Board consists of embers drawn from various government departments so that the needed balance is maintained. Experts from diverse fields with expertise are associated as non-official embers of the Planning Board.

Educational planning has to conform to the broad guidelines and parameters id down by the Planning and Coordination Department and the Department of nance, from time to time. The instructions and advice of the Ministry of Human resource Development greatly influence the major emphases of the educational. The Planning Commission of India scrutinizes the State plan and accords its approval.

At the Directorate level, each of the Directorates has a Planning Cell to prepare Plan and to monitor its implementation. In the Directorates of Secondary education, and Teacher Education, a Deputy Director oversees the planning process.

The 30 districts of Orissa have a District Planning and Development Board instituted by the Government. It is headed by a Minister designated by the government. The District Planning and Development Officer is the Member-Secretary this Board. This Board is responsible for the formulation of the District Plan and monitoring its implementation. The Inspector of Schools and the District Inspectors Schools are the ex-officio members of the District Planning Board, and provide to necessary inputs relating to education.

The over-all responsibility for formulating the Plan for the School Education evolves on the Commissioner-cum-Secretary to the Government of Orissa, department of School and Mass Education. The State Advisory Committee on education and the Consultative Committee on Education (both under the Chairmanship of the Minister-in-charge of School and Mass Education) advise the Government. Higher Secondary Education is being looked after by the Department. of Higher Education; but is likely to be transferred to the Department of School and Mass Education. The planning relating to all Teacher Training Institutions (Schools and Colleges) is looked after by the School and Mass Education Department. There is a Planning Cell in the Department which is looked after by a Deputy Secretary.

In Orissa, preparation of the budget for Secondary Education is the responsibility of the Directorates of Secondary Education. At the initial stage detailed instructions including the procedure to be adopted in the preparation of budget estimates are issued to all heads of secondary schools and subordinate offices by the Directorate of Secondary Education. A convenient date is fixed for submission of the estimates. Since the number of institutions is very large and they are scattered throughout the State, responsibility for collecting budget proposals, in time, is vested with the Circle Inspectors of Schools. Every officer immediately subordinate to the Director is required to submit his budget proposals to the Director not later than 15th July of the year. The Inspector's proposals are to include provision for requirements of the staff of his own offices and the other subordinate Inspecting Officers working under his administrative control and to be accompanied by detailed estimates prepared by the Headmasters of Government High Schools and Secondary Training Schools.

The budget is then coordinated in the Directorates of Secondary Education. One copy of it is submitted to the Finance Department, one to the Education Department and another to the Accountant-General, not latter than 1st September, every year. The budget proposals are also to be accompanied by a list of new schemes included in it giving details of the sanction orders, nature of the schemes, ultimate cost (recurring and non-recurring) and the estimated cost during the budget year. Plan outlays and plan schemes already approved by the Planning Commission are also taken into consideration before finalizing the proposals.

In the Directorate of Elementary Education there is a whole-time Deputy Director with supporting staff who is in charge of educational planning, budget and statistics of all the Directorates of Education. Soon after the plan ceiling for a particular year is fixed, the plan proposals are prepared by the Directorates according to the guidelines received, and these proposals are sent to the Secretariat for final processing and approval in consultation with the Planning and Coordination Department and the Finance Department. The main responsibility for preparation of educational budget rests with the Department of School & Mass Education. Thereafter the same is presented to the Finance Department. The latter Department examines the budgetof the financial point of view including the pattern of central assistance available under various schemes. The Planning and Coordination Department indicates the location of plan outlay sufficiently early to formulate plan schemes and with its approval the schemes are retained in the budget. The plan and non-plan schemes are classified according to instructions of the Finance Department issued each year in August. For example, plan schemes of the State sector; plan schemes of the Central sector and non-plan schemes on the committed side are some of the classifications.

After the proposals and schemes are approved and budget provisions made by the Legislature, the Department of School & Mass Education initiates action or sanction of the schemes and proposals. In case of doubt or lack of detailed formation, reference is made to the Directorate for clarification. After obtaining e clarifications and detailed information, the proposals and schemes are processed and Government sanction is issued to the Director with the concurrence of the Finance Department. In case of non-plan expenditure, the sanction order is issued with the concurrence of the Financial Adviser who is attached to the Department of school & Mass Education. He is an officer of the Orissa Finance Service (Class-I).

STRUCTURE AND PROCEDURE OF FINANCING EDUCATION

The Financing of Education in Orissa has three major aspects; the structure or the administrative set up, financial requirements and the analysis of funds provided. The entire budget is thus analysed on the basis of programmes and activities; on e objective-wise items on which expenditure is to be incurred. The budget estimates of a particular year (say 2007-08) are based on the expenditure of the preceding the revised budget estimates (2005-06); revised budget estimates of e preceding year (2006-07); and budget estimates of the current year (i.e. 1907-08). In other words, the annual budget indicates the allocations that could be on various specified items so that the expenditure can be controlled judiciously. The expenditure is classified as 'Plan' or 'Non-Plan' according to the programmes and schemes on which they are supposed to be expended. The allotments made or meeting the expenditure for implementing various schemes such as, opening of fewschools to enroll more children, introduction of computer education programmes, orientation programmes for teachers, opening of new departments in the colleges and universities, extension of library facilities to community members c. included in the Five Year Plans constitute the *'Plan head'*. All other items of expenditure and receipt of funds needed to maintain the level of developmentreached in the previous plan constitute *Non-plan* budget. The expenditure in respect of activities connected with the construction of buildings, non-consumable stores etc. which are of non-recurring nature belong to *capital budget* while the rest belong to the *recurring budget*. The budget proposals along with a list of new schemes giving details of sanction orders, nature of schemes, ultimate expenditure, recurring and non-recurring; and the estimated expenditure during the budget year are prepared by the Director of Secondary Education and sent to Government in the Department of School and Mass Education.

SOURCES OF FINANCE

Up to 1857, it was the East India Company that financed education. The Company considered its educational activities as incidental and its educational expenditure was marginal. From 1835-1853, there was only one secondary school at Cuttack. The total expenditure on account of this school was Rs. 3,048.00, out of the total allotment of Rs. 3,996.00 for this school during 1840-41.

As early as 1843, the people of Cuttack subscribed Rs. 3,310.00 towards the construction of the school-building; the Government grant for the purpose was only Rs. 1,000.00 i.e. 23.20%. By 1854, the expenditure on account of secondary education went upto Rs. 5,918.00

Orissa did not get its due share and was at a disadvantage. In the Report for 1860-61, the Inspector of Schools of South-West Division remarked. "It is to be regretted that no new educational operation can be carried out, for Orissa is at a great disadvantage, compared with other districts. For the whole of Orissa with an area of 52.925 sq.miles and a population of 45,34,813 souls less is expended than for the small district of Howrah with an area of 800 square miles and a population of 7,50,000 souls."[426]

The decentralization of administration in 1871 devolved the responsibility of educational expenditure in the provinces. The Central Government which used to provide educational grants to the provincial governments from 1857 to 1870, stopped them. The Government of Bengal was responsible for the educational expenditure from 1871 to 1912. From 1912 to March,1936, Orissa was part of Bihar and Orissa and so the finance came from the revenues of this province. Orissa became a separate province on 1st April 1936 and separate statistics for the State are available from that date.

In 1882, the local bodies were recognized and strengthened. The Hunter admission's Report (1882) recommended that the local bodies should be associated developing education. The District Boards of Cuttack, Puri and Balasore were urged with the responsibility of managing primary and middle school education. South Orissa, District Boards were given the responsibility of managing High schools, Middle Schools and Primary Schools. The local-self government institutions began to

---

426 General Report on Public Instruction in Bengal, 1860-61, p. 123

play an effective role in the field of education. After independence, the panchayat system of local-self government was introduced and the District Boards e abolished. The Panchayat Samitis were mainly responsible for primary education. Therefore, there has been a steady decline in the role of the local-self government institutions in the field of secondary education. However, certain municipalities have n managing high and middle schools up to 2006. In 2007, the Government of Orissa had taken over these schools.

An average monthly fee collection of the Cuttack School in November, 1854 ; Rs. 68.50, in January 1854 it was Rs. 90.00; and in the Puri School the total fee section amounted to Rs. 14.56 per month. In 1854, the school fees contributed to 5% of the total expenditure. In 1856, the charging of fees was made compulsory as per the grant-in-aid rules. Fees have been one of the main source of educational financing. In the years after independence, scheduled caste and scheduled tribe dents, girls and economically backward students have been granted fee-concessions. a result, there has been a steady decline in this respect.

Bengal did not levy any local rates. Therefore, there were no local rates in North Orissa for education. In 1871, Madras Presidency levied a local rate at one sixteenth the value of the land revenue and house-tax. This was collected in South Orissathe development of education. Right from the early days of secondary education in Orissa, subscription frompublic has been an important source of educational finance. As early as 1843,public subscription for constructing the school-building at Cuttack was 76.8% the total expenditure. The public subscriptions and donations increased with the growth of aided schools in Orissa.

Tables No. 12.2 and 12.3 indicate the comparative situation relating to the various sources of educational finance relating to the secondary section in 1936-37, 1946-47, 1 1959-60.[427]

---

427 Progress of Education in Orissa for the years 1936-37, 1946-47, and 1959-60

TABLE 12.2

Sources of Finance (Middle School)

SI. No.	Source	1936-37		1946-47		1959-60	
		Amount	Percent	Amount	Percent	Amount	Percent
01	Central Government	—	—	—	—	90881.00	1.97
02.	State Government	131387.57	30.08	291074.51	36.16	2326753.00	50.40
03.	Local Fund	118076.80	27.03	164985.16	20.50	76799.00	1.66
04.	Fees	136525.28	31.26	261928.73	32.54	978466.00	21.20
05.	Other Source including endowments	50803.35	11.63	86976.60	10.80	1143683.00	24.77
	Total	436793.00	100	804965.00	100	4616582.00	100

TABLE 12.3

Sources of Finance (High School)

SI. No.	Source	1936-37		1946-47		1959-60	
		Amount	Percent	Amount	Percent	Amount	Percent
01	Central Government	—	—	—	—	203144.00	2.61
02.	State Government	216802.76	36.98	363661.82	29.55	4011825.00	51.55
03.	Local Fund	59310.49	10.12	128496.01	10.44	40966.00	0.53
04.	Fees	275167.65	46.92	659299.01	53.57	2604394.00	33.47
05.	Other Source including endowments	35076.10	5.98	79333.37	6.44	921616.00	11.84
	Total	586357.00	100	1230791.00	100	7781945.00	100

According to the Government of India Act, 1935, 'education' became a provincial subject. The constitutional position was not changed in the Constitution of free India up to 1976. The Government of India played absolutely no part in the field of secondary education in 1936-37 or 1946-47. The Government of India was constrained to open Sainik Schools and so there was some expenditure on this account. The other expense was that of the Railway Schools and Central Schools. There has been a steady increase in the expenditure of the State Government both for High Schools and Middle Schools. Expenditure on account of Middle Schools rose from 30.08% to 50.4% and that of High Schools from 36.98% to 51.55% during 1936-37 1959-60. The responsibility of die local self-government institutions has sharply declined during 1936-37 to 1959-60. The fee income registered an upward trend up 1946-47. in the post-independence period, girl students and students belonging to scheduled castes, scheduled tribes, and weaker sections of the society were exempted from fees; and as a result, a steady downward trend in fee income is evident. The other sources, mainly public contribution went up from 11.63% to 26.5% in respect of Middle Schools; and from 5.78% to 13.34% in respect of High Schools during) 36-37 to 1959-60.

TABLE 12.4

Sources of Educational Finance of Orissa

SI. No.	Year	Govt. Funds	Local Bodies Funds	Fees	Endowments & Others	Total
1.	1946-47	73.6	3.3	16.5	6.6	100.00
2.	1947-48	72.9	3.7	15.4	8.0	100.00
3.	1948-49	72.4	2.5	11.3	13.8	100.00
4.	1949-50	72.7	5.2	14.3	7.8	100.00
5.	1950-51	70.1	4.6	12.2	13.1	100.00
6.	1951-52	71.3	3.2	13.6	11.9	100.00
7.	1952-53	73.7	2.8	13.2	10.3	100.00
8.	1953-54	75.9	2.2	12.8	9.1	100.00
9.	1954-55	76.6	1.3	12.4	9.7	100.00
10.	1955-56	81.0	1.6	9.0	8.4	100.00
11.	1956-57	78.2	1.6	7.1	13.1	100.00
12.	1957-58	80.5	1.0	8.4	10.1	100.00
13.	1958-59	80.5	0.9	9.2	9.4	100.00
14.	1959-60	74.9	5.3	10.0	9.8	100.00
15.	1960-61	76.3	2.4	9.7	11.6	100.00
16.	1961-62	78.7	0.5	10.6	10.2	100.00

SI. No.	Year	Govt. Funds	Local Bodies Funds	Fees	Endowments & Others	Total
17.	1962-63	80.1	1.0	8.7	10.2	100.00
18.	1963-64	77.9	1.4	8.3	12.4	100.00
19.	1964-65	77.2	2.7	9.1	11.0	100.00
20.	1965-66	76.8	1.9	9.7	11.6	100.00
21.	1966-67	70.7	2.3	17.0	10.0	100.00
22.	1967-68	80.0	2.3	7.7	10.0	100.00
23.	1968-69	79.6	2.0	7.2	10.1	100.00
24.	1969-70	79.7	2.0	7.2	11.2	100.00
25.	1970-71	79.7	2.0	7.2	11.1	100.00
26.	1971-72	81.3	1.8	7.8	9.1	100.00
27.	1972-73	80.1	1.9	8.5	9.5	100.00
28.	1973-74	79.7	1.9	8.2	10.2	100.00
29.	1974-75	77.2	2.0	10.8	10.0	100.00
30.	1975-76	78.6	1.3	11.2	8.9	100.00
31.	1976-77	84.4	0.9	11.2	7.5	100.00
32.	1977-78	79.7	0.9	11.6	7.8	100.00

Source: Statistical abstract of Indian (various years) & Education in India (various years)

Education is free for all children up to secondary level in the State. No tuition fee is collected from the students except the annual fees for games, magazine, library, Red Cross etc. In addition to the government funds, contributions of the community on school development programmes are the major source of educational finance. There are many institutions which have their own source of income from orchards, farms, house rents and sales of the materials. The main source of finance is the government grant which accounts for the major part of resources. Some sources of indirect benefit to education are from development funds for construction of buildings, *kendu* leaf grants, mining cess and unutilized funds of the district authorities.

EXPENDITURE ON SECONDARY EDUCATION (1936-37 TO 1946-47)

The quantum of governmental expenditure on secondary education — High Schools for Boys', High Schools for Girls', Middle Schools for Boys and Middle Schools for Girls along with the total educational expenditure for the year and expenditure on secondary education as a percentage of total expenditure,[428] has been depicted in Table No. 12.5.

TABLE 12.5
Expenditure on Secondary Education (1936-37 to 1946-47)

Sl. No.	Year	Total education expenditure	Total expenditure on Secondary Education	Percentage
01.	1936-37	18,53,651.20	5,59,458.94	30.18
02.	1937-38	19,83,985.10	3,78,460.76	19.07
03.	1938-39	26,43,878.90	4,44,962.06	16.82
04.	1939-40	26,81,640.30	4,43,211.12	16.52
05.	1940-41	26,59,746.90	4,65,264.86	17.49
06.	1941-42	26,62,708.00	4,70,261.00	17.66
07.	1942-43	27,66,663.00	4,59,533.00	16.60
38.	1943-44	28,58,374.00	4,86,292.00	17.00
39.	1944-45	32,01,897.00	5,11,757.00	15.98
10	1945-46	3,86,49,89.00	6,13,014.00	15.86
11	1946-47	6,66,46,22.30	6,54,720.87	9.82

There was a decrease of expenditure in 1937-38 and again in 1943-44. But on the hole, there has been a steady increase in the expenditure on secondary education. Due to the increased emphasis placed upon primary education after 1936, the percentage of expenditure on secondary education registered a sharp decline in 1937-38. The secondary education remained more or less static when primary and basic education expanded. In 1945-46 and 1946-47, there was marginal

---

428 Progress of Education in Orissa for the respective years

increase in educational expenditure due to the Post-War Reconstruction Development Programme id it did not accelerate secondary education very much. The expansion of primary id higher education and the inception of the Utkal University overshadowed secondary education.

EXPENDITURE ON SECONDARY EDUCATION (1947-48 TO 1963-64)

The expenditure on all educational activities and secondary education during 1947-48 to 1963-64.[429] has been shown in Table No. 12.6.

TABLE 12.6

Expenditure on Secondary Education (1947-48 to 1963-64)

SI. No.	Year	Total education expenditure	Total expenditure on Secondary Education	Percentage of expenditure on Secondary Education to total expenditure on Education
01.	1947-48	1,28,63,879.00	24,88,475.00	19.34
02.	1948-49	1,17,20,506.00	35,06,578.00	29.91
03.	1949-50	1,39,82,922.00	41,85,714.00	29.93
04.	1950-51	1,69,06,809.00	53,38,267.00	31.57
05.	1951-52	1,64,99,149.00	54,74,850.00	33.18
06.	1952-53	1,98,84,223.00	64,04,795.00	32.21
07.	1953-54	2,12,36,510.00	70,70,831.00	33.00
08.	1954-55	3,12,77,509.00	76,10,995.00	24.33
09.	1955-56	2,57,54,071.00	81,30,258.00	31.56
10	1956-57	4,53,81,691.00	88,70,827.00	19.54
11	1957-58	5,34,40,178.00	98,40,971.00	18.41
12.	1958-59	5,77,16,364.00	1,09,17,806.00	18.91
13.	1959-60	5,30,48,712.00	1,23,98,527.00	23.37
14.	1960-61	67,02,08,000.00	138,83,287.00	20.71
15.	1963-64	78,48,00,000.00	1,72,25,818.00	21.90

---

429 Progress of Education in Orissa for the respective years.

The expenditure on secondary education went up by 6.9 times from 1947-48 to 1963-64. The expenditure on secondary education was 19.34% of the total educational expenditure during 1947-48. There was a steady rise up to 1953-54 and then the proportion of expenditure decreased to around 18.9% by 1958-59. It registered an increase from 1959-60 onwards.

EXPENDITURE ON SECONDARY EDUCATION (1971-72 TO 1975-76)

The expenditure on account of secondary education during 1971-72 to 1975-76.[430]has been shown in Table No. 12.7.

TABLE 12.7

Expenditure on Secondary Education (1971-72 to 1975-76)

Sl. No.	Year	Total education expenditure (Rs. in Crores)	Total expenditure on Secondary Education (Rs. in Crores)	Percentage
1.	1971-72	27.35	8.43	30.82
2.	1972-73	30.11	10.38	34.47
3.	1973-74	34.75	12.89	37.09
4.	1974-75	46.78	16.87	36.06
5.	1975-76	58.80	21.39	36.38

With the phenomenal growth in the field of secondary education, the expenditure on secondary education had gone up almost by three time from 1971-72 to 1975-76.

From 1936-37 to 1977-78, there has been a steady increase in expenditure relating to secondary education. The expenditure went up from Rs. 0.05 crores in 1936-37 to 0.06 in 1946-47. The expenditure went up from Rs. 0.24 crores in 1947-48 to Rs. 21.39 crores in 1975-76. The grant-in-aid rules have constantly been revised to promote education, especially women's education. The governmental expenditure had increased with

---

430 Report of the Third Educational Survey, Orissa, 1978, p. 257

the efflux of years; so has the people's contribution. However, the le of the local self-government bodies in the field of secondary education has come insignificant during this period.

Between the years 1950-51 and 1977-78 the State expenditure on education has been depicted in Table 12.8.[431]

TABLE 12.8

Sector-wise Educational Expenditure (1950-51 to 1977-78)

Sl. No.	Stage of General Education	1950-51 (In lakhs of Rupees)	1977-78 (In lakhs of Rupees)
1	Primary Education	24.37	2,811.04
2	Middle School Education	18.08	1,586.18
3	Secondary Education	12.06	1,007.00
4	Higher Education	12.03	1,028.00

TABLE 12.7

Expenditure on Secondary Education (1971-72 to 1975-76)

Sl. No	Year	Total education expenditure (Rs. in Crores)	Total expenditure on Secondary Education (Rs. in Crores)	Percentage
1.	1971-72	27.35	8.43	30.82
2.	1972-73	30.11	10.38	34.47
3.	1973-74	34.75	12.89	37.09
4.	1974-75	46.78	16.87	36.06
5.	1975-76	58.80	21.39	36.38

With the phenomenal growth in the field of secondary education, the expenditure on secondary education had gone up almost by three time from 1971-72 to 1975-76.

From 1936-37 to 1977-78, there has been a steady increase in expenditure relating secondary education. The expenditure went up from Rs. 0.05 crores in 1936-37 to Rs. 0.06 in 1946-47. The expenditure went up from

---

431 D. P. I., Orissa: Education in Orissa, 1978, Bhubaneswar, 1978.

Rs. 0.24 crores in 1947-48 to Rs. 21.39 crores in 1975-76. The grant-in-aid rules have constantly been revised to promote education, specially women's education. The governmental expenditure had increased with the efflux of years; so has the people's contribution. However, the role of the local self-government bodies in the field of secondary education has come insignificant during this period.

Between the years 1950-51 and 1977-78 the State expenditure on education has been depicted in Table 12.8.[28]

TABLE 12.8

Sector-wise Educational Expenditure (1950-51 to 1977-78)

Sl. No.	Stage of General Education	1950-51 (In lakhs of Rupees)	1977-78 (In lakhs of Rupees)
1	Primary Education	24.37	2,811.04
2	Middle School Education	18.08	1,586.18
3	Secondary Education	12.06	1,007.00
4.	Higher Education	12.03	1,028.00

[29]D. P. I., Orissa: Education in Orissa, 1978, Bhubaneswar, 1978.

EXPENDITURE ON SECONDARY EDUCATION PLAN-WISE

The total Plan Plan outlay on Secondary Education and the percentage of the Plan outlay on Secondary Education to total Plan outlay on General Education had been shown in Table No. 12.9.

TABLE 12.9

Break up of Expenditure on Secondary Education (Plan and Non-Plan)

PLAN

SI. No.	Item	1st Plan	IInd Plan	IIIrd Plan	Inter-Plan year	IVth Plan	Vth Plan (4 years)
1	Total Plan outlay on Secondary Education	25.34	114.48	388.137		282.94	254.00
2	Percentage of the Plan outlay on Secondary Education to total Plan outlay on General Education	15	20	28		20	10

NON-PLAN

SI. No.	Item	1950-51	1955-56	1960-61	1965-66	1968-69	1969-70	1973-74	1977-78
1	Outlay	12.06	18.34	22.532	61.833	166.60	236.97	450.30	876.93
2	Percentage to total Educational outlay	8.0	8.4	8.8	9.8	10.7	12.8	15.9	14.1

Source: Education in Orissa, 1978, p. 31

The total Plan outlay on Secondary Education in Orissa was Rs. 25.34 lakhs in the first Plan which was only 15 percent of the total plan outlay on general education. This Plan outlay went on increasing in the Second and Third Plans (Rs. 114.48 lakhs in the 2nd plan and Rs. 388.13 lakhs in the 3rd plan). Then plan outlay registered a decline. It was 282.94 lakhs in the Fourth Plan and Rs. 254.00 lakhs in the Fifth Plan. Thus the percentage of Plan outlay on Secondary Education to total outlay on general education varied from 10 to 28 in the plans under study.

The total Non-Plan outlay on Secondary Education from 1950-51 to 1973-74 registered a steady increase. Itwas 8 percent in 1950-51, 8.4 percent in 1955-56, 8.8 percent in 1960-61, 9.8 percent in1965-66, 10.7 percent in 1968-69, 12.8 percent in 1969-70 and 15.9 percent in 973-74. But the year 1977-78 registered slight decline in the Non-plan outlay on Secondary Education. It was 14.1 percent as against 15.9 percent The percentage of direct expenditure' on Secondary Education varied from 23.2 to 40.4 during 1951-52 to1977-78. The percentage of 'direct expenditure' on Primary education varied from 6.4 to 57.1 during 1951-52 to 177-78.

Primary education received greater attention during the year 1951-52 to 1977-78 and more funds were allocated to it. This was because the Government of Orissa took measures to fulfill the constitutional directive (Art.45) to enroll each and every child of the age group 6-14 in schools. Hence,-massive amounts were spent on primary education during First, Second, Third, Fourth and Fifth Five Year Plans periods.

ITEM-WISE DIRECT EXPENDITURE ON SECONDARY EDUCATION

TABLE 12.10

Item-wise Direct Expenditure on Secondary Education

SI. No	Year	Govt. Secondary Schools		Direct grants to non-Govt. Secondary Schools		Grants to local bodies for Secondary Education		Total	
		Amount	%	Amount	%	Amount	%	Amount	%
01.	1951-52	1988362	70.3	496967	17.7	339833	12.0	2825171	100
02.	1952-53	2193026	62.6	786326	22.4	522435	15.0	3501787	100
03.	1953-54	2377953	60.6	1030376	26.2	520059	13.2	3928388	100
04.	1954-55	2401312	56.8	1108728	26.2	719081	17.0	4229121	100
05.	1955-56	2404708	53.0	1164098	25.7	966814	21.3	4535630	100
06.	1956-57	2932154	53.8	1550067	28.4	971302	17.8	5453523	100
37.	1957-58	3351861	52.1	2086579	32.5	990483	15.4	6428923	100

SI. No	Year	Govt. Secondary Schools		Direct grants to non-Govt. Secondary Schools		Grants to local bodies for Secondary Education		Total	
		Amount	%	Amount	%	Amount	%	Amount	%
38.	1958-59	3464655	47.3	2889526	39.5	969308	13.2	7323489	100
09.	1959-60	3756239	45.8	3341825	40.8	1094497	13.4	8192561	100
10.	1960-61	3786455	42.7	4611531	52.0	466316	5.3	8864302	100
11.	1961-62	4719793	35.3	8608722	64.5	25754	0.2	12254269	100
12.	1962-63	5428980	31.0	11972092	68.4	100225	0.6	17501297	100
13.	1963-64	5646505	33.5	11011030	65.3	204881	1.2	16862416	100
14.	1964-65	7206780	33.8	13910864	65.2	201150	1.0	21318794	100
15.	1965-66	9416660	37.8	16325961	61.4	202850	0.8	25945471	100
16.	1966-67	11078969	39.2	17009899	60.2	170200	0.6	28259058	100
17.	1967-68	14309810	34.5	26910359	65.0	213400	0.5	41433569	100
18.	1968-69	16403634	32.6	33673095	66.9	243468	0.5	50320197	100
19.	1969-70	25343469	40.9	36415676	58.7	235024	0.4	61924169	100
20.	1970-71	30647145	41.2	43347115	58.3	362634	0.5	74356894	100
21.	1971-72	33384657	39.6	504540618	59.9	409584	0.5	84258302	100
22.	1972-73	35316777	38.7	55840233	60.8	468037	0.5	91839947	100
23.	1973-74	38688731	35.0	71524777	64.7	285500	0.3	10499008	100

Source: Government of Orissa, Finance Department Finance Accounts (Various years)

TABLE 12.11

Item-wise Direct Expenditure on Secondary Education (1973-74 to 1977-78)

SI. No.	Year	1974-75		1975-76		1976-77		1977-78	
		Amount	%	Amount	%	Amount	%	Amount	%
01.	Govt. Secondary Schools	46488408	27.5	55173038	25.8	63139739	25.8	63881246	23.3
02.	Direct grants to Non-Govt. Secondary Schools	106499820	63.1	140041104	64.69	1573807716	64.28	180157816	65.7
03.	Grants to local Bodies	69064	0.04	8530	0.003	8360	0.02		

SI. No.	Year	1974-75		1975-76		1976-77		1977-78	
		Amount	%	Amount	%	Amount	%	Amount	%
04.	Scholarships	1815174	1.1	2314555	1.9	4369631	1.8	3676655	1.3
05.	Teachers' Training	6348929	3.8	7194136	3.3	10607060	4.3	8635231	3.2
06.	Textbooks	7490671	4.4	8942641	4.2	8570561	3.5	9514366	3.5
07.	Tribal area Sub-Plan	...	....	....	....	....	....	7538264	2.8
08.	Other Expenditure	30000	0.01	299650	0.1	648000	0.3	522196	0.2
	Total	168742066	100	213973654	100	244724117	100	173925774	100

Source: Government of Orissa, Finance Department Finance Accounts (various years)

Table No. 12.11 depicts the item-wise 'direct expenditure' on Secondary Education. Direct expenditure on Secondary Education from 1951-52 to 1973-74 comprised of (i) Grants to Government Secondary Schools, (ii) Grants to Non-Government Secondary Schools, and (iii) Grants to Local Bodies. The percentage of grants received by the Government Secondary Schools varied from 27.53 to 27.3, the percentage of grants received by Non-Government Secondary Schools varied from 63.8 to 65.7, and the percentage of grants received by Local Bodies varied from 0.2 to 21.3 during the period 1951-52 to 1973-74. The Non-Government Secondary Schools received more grants and the Local Bodies received less grants from the Government during the period 1951-52 to 1973-74.

Right from the first year of the Fifth Five Year Plan (1974-75), five more items, viz., Scholarships, Teachers' Training, Textbooks, Tribal Area Sub-Plan and other expenditure were added to the existing three items (Government Secondary Schools, Non-Government Secondary Schools, and Local Bodies).

Of all these eight items from 1974-75 to 1977-78, the percentage of grants to Government Secondary Schools varied from 23.3 to 27.5, the percentage of grants to Non-Government Secondary Schools varied from 63.1 to 65.7, the percentage of grants to scholarships varied from

1.1 to 1.9, the percentage of grants to Teachers' Training varied from 3.2 to 4.3, the percentage of grants to Textbooks varied from 3.5 to 4.4 and the percentage of grants on other expenditure varied from 0.01 to 0.3. Local Bodies received grants only for the year 1974-75, 1975-76 and 1976-77. They did not receive grants during 1977-78. It is the Govt. High Schools that get the lion's share.

EXPENDITURE PATTERN

The percentage of sector-wise budget allocation (plan and non-plan) relating to School and Mass Education Department during 1989-90 and 1989-99 is shown in Table No. 12.12.

TABLE 12.12

Allocation of Funds for 1989-90 and 1988-99

SI. No.	Year Sector	Total outlay (Rupees in Lakhs)			
		1989-90		1998-99	
01.	Elementary Education	22508.68	(69.9)	93407.23	(67.02)
02.	TE&SCERT	90.22	(0.30)	2086.30	(1.50)
03.	Mass Education	210.34	(0.70)	199.39	(0.14)
04.	**Secondary Education**	9261.85	(28.76)	43277.31	(31.05)
05.	Secretariat	125.07	(0.40)	404.47	(0.29)
	Total	32195.86	(100)	139374.70	(100)

Source: School and Mass Education Department.

Note: Figures in parenthesis denote sector-wise percentage to total allocation

Source: Directorate of Elementary Education, Orissa.

It is evident that the elementary education has received the utmost priority compared to other sectors of education. There is a growth in teacher education sector due to shifting the budget of training schools and training colleges from Directorate of Higher Education and Secondary Education to the control of directorate of TE and SCERT; the up-gradation of training colleges to the status of IASE, CTE, opening of 13 DIETs; and establishment of new training colleges and implementation of revised UGC scale for teaching staff of the Teacher Training Colleges.

The allocation of funds in favour of education had increased significantly during the decade 1989-90 to 1998-99. The per capita expenditure on education (current prices) had also increased from Rs. 130.38 in 1989-90 to Rs. 336.40 during 1997-98 with an increase of 158.00 percent. More than 95 percent of the funds were exclusively meant to meet the salary cost of the teaching and non-teaching staff. Only a small amount was left for development and enhancement of quality of education.

PLAN AND NON-PLAN EXPENDITURE ON EDUCATION

Plan and Non-plan expenditure from 1947-48 to 1977-78 has been depicted in Table No.12.13. The total expenditure on secondary education has increased from Rs. 0.78 crores in 1947-48 to Rs. 72.97 crores in 1977-78

TABLE No. 12.13

Expenditure on Education in Orissa (From 1947-48 to 1975-77)

Sl. No	Year	Non-Plan	Plan	Total Rs.	Total State Plan& Non-plan Rs.	Percentage of total expenditure on education to State total
01	Pre-Plan Period					
	1947-48	0.78	...	0.78	5.84	13.30
	1948-49	0.91	...	0.91	7.58	12.00
	1949-50	1.33	...	1.33	11.71	11.30
	1950-51	1.37	...	1.37	12.01	11.40
02	First Plan					
	1951-52	1.12	...	1.25	10.86	11.50
	1952-53	1.48	...	1.48	11.52	12.80

Sl. No	Year	Non-Plan	Plan	Total Rs.	Total State Plan& Non-plan Rs.	Percentage of total expenditure on education to State total
	1953-54	1.74	...	1.74	13.21	13.10
	1954-55	1.90	....	1.90	15.48	12.20
	1955-56	2.51	....	2.51	23.91	10.00
03	Second Plan					
	1956-57	2.80	....	2.80	22.74	12.30
	1957-58	3.12	...	3.12	23.40	12.20
	1958-59	3.35	...	3.35	25.87	12.90
	1959-60	2.41	1.60	4.01	28.72	14.10
	1960-61	2.56	1.77	1.33	35.55	12.10
04	Third Plan					
	1961-62	5.64	1.08	6.72	52.36	12.80
	1962-63	5.47	2.21	7.68	65.99	11.60
	1963-64	5.63	2.47	8.10	72.00	10.90
	1964-65	6.04	3.60	9.64	79.29	12.10
	1965-66	6.46	4.06	10.52	91.31	11.50
05.	Annual Plan					
	1966-67	11.53	1.09	12.62	104.42	12.00
	1967-68	13.76	2.22	15.98	113.20	14.10
	1968-69	16.36	2.43	18.79	131.77	14.20
06.	Fourth Plan					
	1969-70	19.49	0.90	20.39	131.00	15.50
	1970-71	21.92	1.82	23.64	139.88	16.90
	1971-72	23.97	3.30	27.27	174.08	15.60
	1972-73	25.68	4.48	30.56	192.78	15.80
	1973-74	28.65	4.48	33.53	212.47	16.30
07.	Fifth Plan					
	1974-75	44.41	2.26+0.12	46.79	223.50	20.00
	1975-76	53.90	4.40+0.50	58.80	226.10	21.00

Sl. No	Year	Non-Plan	Plan	Total Rs.	Total State Plan& Non-plan Rs.	Percentage of total expenditure on education to State total
	1976-77	55.70	6.16+1.09	62.96	316.53	20.00
	1977-78	63.23	8.66+1.08	72.97	351.11	20.00

* Centrally Sponsored.

Note: Expenditure up to 1958-59 have not been separated on Non-Plan and Plan heads.

Source: Report of the Third Education Survey, Orissa 1978. pp. 249-250

The foregoing table reveals a rising trend of the total actual expenditure of the State (Plan and Non-Plan) from 1947-48 to 1975-76 and revised budget estimate for the year 1976-77 and the budget estimate for the year 1977-78 was Rs. 8.88 crores during First Five Year Plan; Rs. 17.61 crores during Second Five Year Plan; Rs. 42.66 crores during Third Five Year Plan; Rs. 135.39 crores during Fourth Five Year Plan; and Rs. 242.52 crores during Fifth Five Year Plan.

The percentage of total expenditure on education to State total reveals an increasing trend from 13.30% in 1947-48 to 20.00% in 1977-78 with an exception to the rise of percentage of 21.00% in 1975-76. But there was constant fluctuations in the percentage of expenditure on education to the total expenditure of the State. A definite trend was not discernible.

NON-PLAN EXPENDITURE ON SECONDARY EDUCATION

Apart from the Plan allocation, the non-plan outlay is an important component of educational expenditure. The trend of the non-plan expenditure on secondary education is indicated in Table No. 12.14.

TABLE 12.14

Non-Plan Expenditure (1950-51 to 1977-78)

Sl. No.	Year	Total non-plan Outlay (Rs. in lakhs)	Percentage to total General Education Outlay
1	1950-51	12.06	8.0
2	1955-56	18.34	8.4
3	1960-61	22.53	8.8
4	1965-66	61.83	9.8
5	1968-69	166.60	10.7
6	1969-70	236.97	12.8
7	1973-74	450.30	15.9
8	1977-78	876.93	14.1

The non-plan expenditure had registered a steady increase during 1950-51 to 1977-78.

DIRECT AND INDIRECT EXPENDITURE ON EDUCATION

The total amount of expenditure on education is broadly divided into two categories viz., (i) expenditure on recognized institutions, and (ii) expenditure on unrecognized institutions. The expenditure on the latter category is met totally from private funds and the government has no financial responsibility for such institutions. Expenditure of government and aided institution is met both from public and private funds. The expenditure on recognized institutions is also divided into two types, viz., (a) Direct, id (b) Indirect. *'Director charges'* comprise of expenditure on salary of the staff, allowances, contingencies, etc. 'Indirect' charges comprise of expenditure on direction, inspection, hostels, scholarships, stipends, buildings, etc.

TABLE 12.15

Direct and Indirect Expenditure on education in Orissa

(1950-51 to 1977-78)

SI. No.	Year	Total Educational Expenditure (Rs.)	Direct charges		Indirect Charge	
			Amount Rs.	%	Amount Rs.	%
1.	1951-52	12544521	7634043	60.8	4910478	39.2
2.	1952-53	14763476	9122610	61.8	5840866	38.2
3.	1953-54	17362369	10675730	61.5	6686639	38.5
4.	1954-55	19037401	12652532	66.5	6384869	33.5
5.	1955-56	25089200	17492460	69.7	7596740	30.3
6.	1956-57	27981492	22363240	80.0	5618252	20.0
7.	1957-58	31178737	25426988	81.4	5751769	18.4
8.	1958-59	33550257	27758957	82.7	5791300	17.3
9.	1959-60	40725733	31215289	76.6	9510444	23.4
10.	1960-61	43292744	33914807	78.3	9377937	21.7
11.	1961-62	67250893	57564579	85.6	9686314	14.4
12.	1962-63	76815942	65645627	85.5	11170315	14.5
13.	1963-64	78964082	66380347	84.1	12583735	15.9
14.	1964-65	96502281	82992316	86.0	13509965	14.0
15.	1965-66	105173563	89551035	85.2	12664071	14.8
16.	1966-67	115313009	10264898	88.0	17418982	12.0
17.	1967-68	159844240	142425258	89.2	16507243	10.8
18.	1968-69	187872638	171365395	91.2	17108676	8.8
19.	1969-70	203839429	186730753	91.6	19279373	8.4
20.	1970-71	236413125	217133752	91.8	22440003	8.2
21.	1971-72	273612333	251172330	91.8	25019994	8.2
22.	1972-73	305613654	280593710	91.8	26658494	8.2
23.	1973-74	335262824	308604330	92.1	15183280	709
24.	1974-75	467940742	452757462	96.7	25183280	3.3
25.	1975-76	588435146	563255960	95.7	25176240	4.3
26.	1976-77	649886301	613029872	94.3	36856492	5.7
27.	1977-78	718565354	676886077	94.3	40679277	5.7

SI. No.	Year	Total Educational Expenditure (Rs.)	Direct charges		Indirect Charge	
			Amount Rs.	%	Amount Rs.	%
REVENUE EXPENDITURE ON GENERAL EDUCATION						
28.	1984-85	193.86	NA	...	NA	....
29.	1987-88	274.50	NA	...	NA	....
30.	1988-89	323.50	NA	...	NA	....
31.	1989-90	398.10	NA	...	NA	....
32.	1990-91	424.90	NA	...	NA	....
33.	1991-92	518.80	NA	....	NA	...
34.	1992-93	588.30	NA	....	NA	....
35.	1993-94	(RE) 745.80	NA	....	NA	....
36.	1994-95	(BE) 770.10	NA	...	NA	...
37.	2000-01	1683.67	NA	....	NA	...

Source: (1) Government of Orissa, finance Department, Finance Accounts (various years)

(2) Economic Survey, 1944-95, Government of Orissa, June, 1995

Table No. 12.15 depicts the total educational expenditure (Direct and Indirect incurred during the years 1951-52 to 1977-78 (First Five Year Plan to Fifty Five Year in). From this table it is evident that the 'Director charges' were high compared to 'Indirect charges' from 1951-52 to 1977-78. During these years the 'Direct charge' were high compared to Indirect charges' from 1951-52 to 1977-78. During these years the 'Direct charge' varied from 60.8% to 96.7% whereas the 'Indirect charges' varied from 3.3% to 39%. Consequently, the qualitative improvement of education is adversely affected. The Third Educational Survey stated.

"In the field of Secondary Education, most of the schools could not be provided with adequate physical facilities to try with the new curriculum. Massive Orientation of Teachers could not be made possible due to want of resources".

STAGE-WISE DIRECT EXPENDITURE ON EDUCATION

The stage-wise expenditure on Education provides the relative importance accorded the different stages of education.

TABLE 12. 16

Stage-wise Direct Expenditure on Education

SI. No.	Year	Secondary Education		Primary Education		Special Education	
		Amount Rs.	%	Amount Rs.	%	Amount Rs.	%
01.	1951-52	2825171	37.0	2947850	38.6	558768	7.4
02.	1952-53	3501787	30.4	3317011	36.4	636075	7.0
03.	1953-54	3928388	36.8	4081973	38.2	742180	7.0
04.	1954-55	4229121	33.4	5532926	43.7	708340	5.0
05.	1955-56	4535620	26.0	9705726	55.5	792837	4.5
06.	1956-57	5453523	24.4	11938121	53.4	1150150	5.2
07.	1957-58	6428923	25.0	13443182	53.0	1507840	6.0
08.	1958-59	7323489	26.4	14211435	51.2	1706609	6.1
09.	1959-60	8192561	26.2	15454965	49.5	2309229	7.4
10.	1960-61	8864302	26.1	17608269	52.0	2480310	7.3
11.	1961-62	13354269	23.2	30669771	53.3	3202883	5.5
12.	1962-63	17501297	26.6	34555810	52.7	3540880	5.4
13.	1963-64	16862416	25.4	37535550	56.5	3760732	5.7
14.	1964-65	921318794	25.7	39682384	47.9	4430098	5.3
15.	1965-66	25945471	27.9	41943547	45.9	4660001	5.2
16.	1966-67	28259058	27.6	53579427	52.2	4871276	4.7
17.	1967-68	41433569	29.1	69178747	48.6	5656182	4.0
18.	1968-69	50320197	29.4	82141309	47.9	4982801	2.9
19.	1969-70	61994169	33.2	84556103	45.3	5242935	2.8
20.	1970-71	74356894	34.2	95040780	43.8	5781905	2.7
21.	1971-72	84258302	33.5	115402558	46.0	6660973	2.6
22.	1972-73	91839947	32.7	131583810	46.8	6294329	2.2
23.	1973-74	110499008	35.8	136129261	4.1	6884239	2.2
24.	1974-75	118742006	26.2	258284337	57.1	4261358	0.9

SI. No.	Year	Secondary Education		Primary Education		Special Education	
		Amount Rs.	%	Amount Rs.	%	Amount Rs.	%
25.	1975-76	213973654	38.0	250889050	44.5	4366703	0.8
26.	1976-77	244724117	40.0	265848439	43.4	4149503	0.7
27.	1977-78	273925774	40.4	280455489	41.4	8581069	1.2

Source: Government of Orissa, Finance Department Finance Accounts (Various years)

Table No. 12.16 presents the sector-wise Direct expenditure on education from 1951-52 to 1977-78. I it seen that there had been a marked increase in the 'direct expenditure' on education in all the sectors of education in all the sectors of education from the First Five Year Plan to the fifth Five Year Plan.

In the field of Secondary Education, the expenditure increased from Rs. 28,25,171 to 1951-52 to Rs, 27,39,25,774 in 1977-78, i.e. and an increase of 9695 percent. Expenditure on Primary Education registered on increase of 9513 percent. Expenditure on special education increased by 1535 percent.

COST PER SCHOLAR

In 1936-37, the cost per scholar in a Boys' High School was Rs. 52.49, in a Girls' High School it was Rs. 106.60; in a Boys' Middle School it was Rs. 21.24 and in a Girls' Middle School it was Rs. 25.49, and by 1946-47 these costs went up to Rs. 49.86, Rs. 82.46, Rs. 27.57, and Rs. 35.33 respectively. The per capita cost for every pupil ʷas Rs. 86.90 in both Boys' and Girls' High Schools and Rs. 52.30 in both Boys' and Girls' Middle School in 1960-61.

PER-CAPITA EXPENDITURE ON EDUCATION

Per-capita expenditure on education is a single index of the quantitative and qualitative aspects of education provided by the State.

Prior to 1951, the per capita expenditure on education in Orissa was the lowest among all the provinces of India. The per capita expenditure on education in Orissa 3 consistently on the rise as is evident from Table No. 12.17.

TABLE 12.17

Per-capita Expenditure on Education in Orissa

SI. No.	Year	Per-capita expenditure in Rupees
01.	1984-85	67.28
02.	1986-87	88.30
03.	1987-88	93.23
04.	1988-89	107.87
05.	1989-90	130.35
06.	1990-91	130.35
07.	1991-92	136.58
08.	1992-93	161.19
09.	1993-94	224.45
10.	1994-95	228.22
11.	2000-01	458.80

CHAPTER-13

EDUCATIONAL ADMINISTRATION (1823 TO 2007)

HIGHLIGHTS

- Evolution of Educational Administration
- General Committee of Public Instruction 1823-42
- Council of Education, 1842-55
- Inspector of Colleges and Schools, 1844-55
- Directorate of Public Instruction, 1855
- Inspectorates
- D.P.I., Bihar and Orissa, 1912-1936
- Departments of Education, Government of Orissa
- Department of Higher Education
- Department of School and Mass Education
- Directorate of Education
- Inspectorates:
  - Evolution
  - Duties
  - Development
  - Present States

EDUCATIONAL ADMINISTRATION: 1823 TO 1936

English schools were slowly and steadily spreading with a distinctive schooling stamp that was totally different from what was prevailing for ages in India. Isolated individual institutions with total autonomy were trying to spread western education, but they were not a group of related institutions working together subscribing to an ordered set of ideas, methods, or ways of working based on a common plan of action. There was no co-ordination, control and co-operation amongst these new institutions purportedly working to promote the cause of English education. Educational administrative system was absent.

GENERAL COMMITTEE OF PUBLIC INSTRUCTION (1823-1842)

John Adam was the Acting Governor-General for a brief period during 1823. He was the cousin of Mount Stuart Elphinstone (1779-1859), civilian, educationist and Governor of Bombay Presidency. He was a staunch supporter of indigenous education. He influenced his cousin John Adam on matters educational. Sir John Adam constituted the General Committee of Public Instruction in 1823 in consultation with his friend Sir Thomas Munro, who was an ardent advocate of education of the influential elite. It was to strive to serve "the ultimate aim of education to fit Indians to take a large and responsible share in the administration of their own country" [432]The Committee was set up "to take over the whole management of state education, including the expenditure of public funds."[433] It had ten members and all were seasoned high-level administrative officers of the East India Company and 'enthusiastic members of the Asiatic Society'[434] This Committee was strongly in favour of oriental learning as best suited to Indians and did not favour English education. Right from its inception it tried to allay 'any suspicion of proselytism.[435] It wanted to spread education among the masses and win the confidence of the elite. But the funds available at its disposal were too meager to fulfill such grandiose ambitions. "The committee of Public Instruction were reluctant to take any action which would giveimpression that a foreign system of education was being forced on an unwilling people or that any attempt was being made to interfere with the deep-rooted religious convictions."[436] The Committee was cautious and conservative. All educational institutions managed or aided by the government were under its control. It had a strong secular outlook and was committed to the promotion of Indian culture and languages. The missionaries strongly opposed it, as it was wholly committed to a philosophy of religious neutrality and staunch secularism. This Committee of Public Instruction was superseded in 1842 by the Council of Education and it gave place to the Directorate of Public Instruction which came into existence on 26th January, 1855.

The Select Committee on Education and Science (1967-68) had succinctly stated the inception of the H. M. Inspectorate of U. K. in these words: "In 1833, Parliament voted £20,000 towards the erection of school buildings for the education of the poor and in

---

432 Report from the Select Committee on Education and Science, 1967-68, U. K, H. M. S. O, 1968,p. v.

433 T. R. Bone, School Inspection in Scotland, 1840-1968, p. 14.

434 Ibid. p. 15

435 A. G. Maclain, An Evaluation of the System of School Inspection in Australian State Schools

436 Report of the General Committee of Public Instruction in Bengal, 1937-38, Item X of Adam's Report

1838 a committee of the Privy Council on Education was created to administer the grants. This was the start of H. M. Inspectorate, a watch-dog to ensure the proper spending of public money."[437] In Europe, "state inspection of schools was accepted in practice. In France, Switzerland, Prussia, and Holland, inspectors played an essential part in the organization of education, and thanks to Victor Cousin's books, these foreign systems attracted British attention in the 1930's". "In Ireland, inspectors had to be employed to ensure that Government grants, which had been awarded since 1815, were used to support the undenominational teaching that was a condition of state aid." When the Australian Colonial Government started setting up national or 'government' schools over a century ago, inspectors were appointed, primarily to ensure that public moneys were being used to good effect". Effective control on expenditure of public money in the field of education necessitated the establishment of the Inspectorate in England, Scotland, Ireland, Australia and in the various countries of Europe. And it was the case in India too.

In 1838, Lord William Bentinck appointed Mr. Adams to enquire into the state of indigenous education of Bengal and South Bihar. Mr. Adams, after careful enquiry in the districts of Burdwan, Murshidabad, Tirhoot, and South Bihar recommended in his report of 1838, among other things, a scheme, "(X) to appoint an Inspector for five districts." The General Committee of Public Instruction of Bengal did notconcur with Mr. Adam's proposals, "in consequence of the complicated details, which would involve much more expense and difficulty."[438]

COUNCIL OF EDUCATION (1842-1855)

In 1842, the Council of Education superseded the General Committee of Public Instruction and became the main agency of the Government for the administration of the schools and colleges in Bengal. In its

---

437 Ibid.
438 Report of the Public Instruction in Bengal, 1841-42, p. 34

report for the year 1841-42, the Council made the following remarks regarding visitation and inspection of Government institutions:

"We have fully noticed this subject above and we would only remark in this place, that we perceive from the Minutes of the Committee of the Privy Council on Education in England, and from the Report of the Ceylon School Commission that the place for periodical and occasional local inspection and visitation is looked upon by these authorities as one of the most important means for the success of their general measures for the promotion of public instruction, and it is obvious from the circumstances of this country, and of our institutions, that the same precautions are required here, quite as much as in Ceylon, and a great deal more than England."[439]

From the foregoing extract, it is clearly evident that inspection was considered a desirable precautionary measure and the Council had made up its mind as to its necessity, in theoretical terms. In 1843-44, the several members of the Council of Education took unto themselves the onerous task of inspecting the various schools under the Council's charge.[440] However, it seems, the scheme could not be worked out; and so Mr. Bushby's* proposal of 1840 to associate the various Principals of Colleges in inspecting the Zillah Schools was tried. In 1843-44, "The Principals of the several Colleges were directed to inspect and report upon some of the Zillah Schools."[441] Mr. Seddon, Principal of the Nizamut College; Mr. Ireland of the Dacca College; Mr. Sutherland of the Hooghly College; and Mr. Kerr of the Hindoo College inspected eight schools and submitted their reports. The other institutions, by reason of their great distance, could not be conveniendy inspected. The Cuttack School was left uninspected.

---

439 Report of the Public Instruction in Bengal, 1842-43 p. 7
440 Report of the Public Instruction in Bengal, 1843-44, p.
Mr. Bushby was the under Secretary to Govt, of India and Govt, of Bengal at
     that time.
441 Ibid

The Midnapur School, which was then under the Orissa Division, was inspected by Mr. Sutherland.[442]

INSPECTOR OF COLLEGES & SCHOOLS (1844-1855)

In 1844-45, an Inspector of Colleges and Schools was appointed. The Supreme Government sanctioned the appointment of an Inspector of Colleges and Schools in the Lower Regulation Provinces on 15th June, 1844, "The necessity of this arrangement had been repeatedly and strongly urged by the Council of Education and the experience of the past years had left no room to doubt without regular, strict and systematic supervision by a responsible and highly qualified officer, having his attention directed to no other object, the means appropriated for education of the people could not be applied with a prospect of adequate success."[443] Mr. J. Ireland, Principal of the Dacca College was appointed the first Inspector of Colleges and schools in letter No. 434 dated the 20th June 1844. He had inspected a few Zillah schools the previous year. In Circular No. 16 dated the 25th July,1844 the Local Committees were informed of their changed roles in view of the appointment of an Inspector for Bengal, Bihar and Orissa. The Inspector became an *ex-officio* memberthe Local Committees of all schools. The Inspector controlled the institutions of Dacca, Commillah, Sylhet, Chittangong, Burrisal, Jessor (all now in Bangladesh), Medinapore (now in West Bengal, then in Orissa), Cuttack (Orissa), and Baulia, Bhagalpur, and Patna (all in Bihar). In August 1844, Mr. Ireland died and Mr. E. Lodge, Principal of the Agra College succeeded him as Inspector on 27th November,1844.

The growth and development of the Inspectorate in India was influenced by the developments in the United Kingdom. The setting up of the H. M. Inspectorate in 1839 hastened the setting up of an independent inspectorate in 1844 in the Presidency of Bengal. The necessities of

---

442 Report of the Public Instruction in Bengal, 1844-45
443 Report of the Public Instruction in Bengal, 1843-44

an expanding educational structure compelled, as the developments in the U. K. impelled the colonial authorities to realize that independent administrative machinery is inevitable as it was invaluable.

DIRECTORATE OF PUBLIC INSTRUCTION OF THE BENGAL RESIDENCY (1855-1912)

As per the provisions of the Wood's Despatch (1854), the Directorate of Public instruction was established in January, 1855. On 26th January 1855, Mr. William Gordon Young assumed office as the first Director of Public Instruction of the Bengal Presidency. The Council was dissolved. The Inspectorate also came intoexistence simultaneously. The secondary schools of Orissa Divisionwere under the administrative control of the D. P. I. of the Bengal Presidency from 26th January,1855 to 23rd December,1912 (the day on which Bihar & Orissa as a separate Province came into existence).

INSPECTORATE

Orissa Division formed part of the South West Bengal for which a separate Divisional Inspectorate was appointed in 1855. There were three Deputy Inspectors at Cuttack, Balasore and Puri. In 1859, the post of the Deputy Inspector of Schools, Balasore was abolished. Under the reorganization, Cuttack and Balasore had one Deputy Inspector with headquarters at Cuttack. The other Deputy Inspector was stationed at Puri who was responsible for Puri and Angul.[444]

As there were very few schools in North Orissa; and as South Orissa formed part of the Madras Presidency; and as the rest of Orissa was ruled by Feudatory Chiefs, Orissa could not receive the due attention in matters of education and was treated as an appendage to the South Western Division. The Oriya people were dissatisfied with this state of affairs. In deference to the wishes of the people and as a measure of administrative rationalization, a separate Inspectorate was decided to

---

444 Utkal Dipika Vol. VII, No. 12 dated 23. 3. 1872

be set up in 1872 for Orissa. The jurisdiction of the Inspector was to be coterminous with that of the Commissioner of Orissa.[445] In 1874, Prof. Robert Perry of the Hooghly College was appointed the first Inspector of Schools of the Orissa Division. As there were only 60 schools under the charge of the Inspector of Schools, Orissa Division, *"Utkal Dipika"*, the mouth piece of Oriya public opinion of those times, advocated that all the schools in Oriya speaking areas viz., Ganjam, Sambalpur and the feudatory states be placed under his charge. This proposal remained unheeded.[446]

The post of the Inspector of Schools for the Orissa Division was abolished in 1875, ostensibly on the grounds that a competent Oriya gentlemen was not available for the job; instead Baboo Nanda Kishore Das, a Deputy Collector, was appointed as the Joint Inspector of Schools. This was a bitter set-back for the people of Orissa.[447]In 1877, Babu Radhanath Ray, the celebrated Oriya poet, who was then working as Deputy Inspector of Schools, Balasore was promoted as Joint Inspector. He was the first Orissan educationalist to occupy this august position.[448]

The appointment of Oriyas as Deputy Inspector of Schools, Puri in 1869,[449]of Sambalpur in 1875,[450] and of Babu Nandakishore Das[451] and later of Babu Radhanath Ray,[452] as Joint Inspector of Schools is of special significance. As sonsof the soil, they brought a sense of commitment and zeal, which could not be expected of others.

By 1878, a Sub-Inspector of Schools was appointed for the Angul Estate and Dhenkanal state and another for the states of Mayurbhanj and Keonjhar. The management of education in the feudatory states was the

---

445 Utkal Dipika Vol. VIII, No. 7 dated 16. 11. 1874
446 Utkal Dipika Vol. X, No. 4 dated 23. 1. 1875
447 Utkal Dipika Vol. XII, No. 46 dated 24. 11. 1877
448 Utkal Dipika Vol. IV No. 14 dated 09. 10. 1869
449 Utkal Dipika Vol. IX No. 12 dated 23. 3. 1872
450 Utkal Dipika Vol. XII, op. cit
451 on cit
452 Utkal Dipika Vol. XIII, dated 9. 11. 1878

responsibility of the native rulers. The appointment of Sub-Inspectors of Schools denotes a marked shift in the policy of the Government. The Government thought it worthwhile to have an overall supervisory responsibility even for these areas.[453]

The Report of the Indian Education Commission of 1882, had recommended therationalization of the Inspectorate and their working procedure. During 1904-05, there were in the Orissa Division one Inspector of Schools, three Deputy InspectorsSchools each in charge of a district, 24 Sub-Inspectors of Schools, 17 Assistant Sub-Inspectors of Schools and 67 Inspecting Pundits. The Inspector of Schools, Orissa Division, was in overall charge of the educational administration of the four districts of Cuttack, Puri, Balasore and Angul. He was also responsible for education in the Feudatory State of Orissa. The Agency Inspector of Schools, Raipur was responsible for education in the Eastern States Agency (States of Kalahandi, Sonepur, Patna, Rairakhol and Bamra) up to 1905. The Inspector of Schools, Chotnagpur Circle superintended the educational institutions of Bonai state and Gangpur state up to 1905. From 1905 onwards, the Inspector of Schools, Orissa Division was responsible for education in all the 24 Feudatory States of Orissa. The Deputy Inspectors were primarily responsible for the inspection of the middle schools, primary schoolsand Elementary Training Schools within their jurisdiction.

An Assistant Inspector of Schools was appointed in 1907-08 for the Angul and Sambalpur districts. It was upgraded in 1914 to the rank of an Additional Inspectorof Schools. He was also the *ex-officio* Agency Inspector of Schools and in this capacity was responsible for the supervision of all the schools in the 24 Feudatory States of Orissa. He was stationed at Angul up to 1917 and thereafter at Sambalpur. The 24 Feudatory States were divided into three circles and these were placed under two Deputy Inspectors of Schools. During 1911-12, there was an Agency Inspector of Schools, 2 Deputy Inspectors, 13 Sub-Inspectors, 3

---

453 Progress of Education in Orissa, 1936-37, Chapter II

Assistant Sub-Inspectors, and 19 Inspecting Pundits for the Feudatory States of Orissa.

DIRECTORATE OF PUBLIC INSTRUCTION OF BIHAR & ORISSA

Bihar and Orissa was constituted as a separate province on 23rd December, 1912. But this did not in any way alter the educational administrative structure of Orissa. Orissa Division came under the control of the Director of Public Instruction, Bihar and Orissa. During 1914-15, an Inspectress of Schools was appointed to remain in charge of the Chotnagpur and Orissa Divisions.

In South Orissa, the Circle Inspector was the chief executive officer of the Education Department and was responsible for the overall supervision and management of all types of schools within his jurisdiction. There was an Assistant Inspector who assisted the Circle Inspector in administration and supervision. The Sub-Assistant Inspectors and Supervisors were in charge of primary education. In 1922, the Inspectorate was reorganized in the Madras Presidency. As per the reorganization the District Education Officer replaced the erstwhile Circle Inspector and Assistant Inspector of Schools. The Sub-Assistant Inspectors and Supervisors of Schools were replaced by Deputy Inspector of Schools. During 1926, new cadres of Junior Deputy Inspectors were appointed. The post of the Assistant Inspector of Schools, in charge of the Ganjam Agency was redesignated Agency Education Officer. This post was abolished during 1929 and the District Education Officer, Ganjam had to look after the schools in Ganjam Agency after 1929.

The District Education Officer, 6 Senior Deputy Inspectors, 16 Junior Deputy Inspectors and 1 Sub-Assistant Inspector of Schools were transferred from the Madras Presidency to the new Province of Orissa in 1936.

On the eve of the formation of the Orissa Province in 1936, there was one Inspector of Schools and a District Inspector of Schools in each of the districts of North Orissa. Ganjam Agency was under the superintendence of the District Education Officer, Ganjam. Koraput Agency was under the control of the District Education Officer, Vizagpatam up to 31st March, 1936.

The secondary schools of Orissa were under the administrative control of the General Committee of Public Instruction (GC PI) from 1823 to 1842. It was assistedLocal Committees of Public Instruction (LCPI). Pooree Free Academy (1835 to 10) was under the GCPI, Calcutta and the LCPI, Pooree. The Cuttack School was under the GCPI, Calcutta and LCPI, Cuttack from 1841 to 1842; and under the Council of Education, Calcutta up to 1857.

The Director of Public Instruction, Bengal Presidency controlled the secondary schoolsof Orissa from 26th January, 1855 to 22nd December,1912; and the D. P. I. of Bihar and Orissa Province from 23rd December,1912 to 31st March,1936. The D. P. of the Madras Presidency controlled the secondary schools in the Ganjam district, Ganjam Agency and Vizagpatam Agency (i.e. modern districts of Koraput, Rayagada, iwarangpur and Malkangiri of Orissa).

The high schools of north Orissa were affiliated to the Calcutta University from 24thJanuary, 1857 to 30th September,1917; to Patna University from 1st October,1917 31st December, 1944. The secondary schools of south Orissa were affiliated to the Madras University. In 1890, the Government of Madras started conducting the Secondary School Leaving Certificate Examination, and so the secondary schools were recognized by the Government and not the University. From 1st January,1943 to 31st December,1944 all the secondary schools of north and south Orissa were affiliated to the Patna University. The high schools of Orissa were affiliated to the Utkal University from 1944-45 to 1956. The high schools of Orissa were affiliated to the Board of Secondary Education from 1956 onwards.

The Madras University used to conduct the Matriculation examination. It was replaced by the SSLC in 1890s in south Orissa. In north Orissa, the Calcutta University used to conduct the Entrance examination from 1858 to 1911. The Matriculation Examination was conducted from 1912 onwards by the Calcutta University up to 1916, the Patna University from 1917 to 1943; and Utkal University from 1994 to 1956. The Board of Secondary Education, Orissa conducts the High School Certificate examination from 1956 to date.

There was an Inspector of Schools for the Orissa Division of Bihar & Orissa Province and a District Education Officers for Ganjam district and Ganjam Agency. The secondary schools of undivided Koraput district were under the administrative control of the D E. O. Vizagpatnam and Special Sub-Agent to the Governor of Madras Presidency at Koraput up to 31st March, 1936.

DEPARTMENTS OF EDUCATION OF GOVERNMENT OF ORISSA (1936 TO 2007)

The Government of Orissa started functioning with effect from 1st April,1936. Department of Education was one of the Departments of the Provincial government of Orissa. This Department was reorganized in December, 1992; and was split into two.

"Education in India is essentially a State subject," writes Mr. Veda Prakashand continues, "this means that each of the States is free to develop aneducational system of its own".[454] Since 1921, education has been a State subjectunder the direct control of an elected Education Minister responsible to the Statelegislature. Sometimes he has a State or Deputy Minister to assist him.

The responsibility of the State Government in respect of education has clearlybeen described in entries 11 and 12 of the State List of the Indian Constitution. Inall, it consists of sixty-six subjects. The State Governments share concurrentresponsibility in respect of Vocational and Technical Education with the CentralGovernment. But this constitutional situation changed with the 46th Amendment ofthe Indian Constitution of 1976 whereby "Education" has been shifted to the"Concurrent List". The Central Government and the several State Governments canact in the field of education. The Government of

---

454 Progress of Education in Orissa, 1942-43, p. 8-9

India's role is not simply advisory. It has a bonafide constitution role to play.

The Governor of Orissa is the Head of the State and all actions are taken in this name, the Governor's assent is necessary for all bills to become Acts. The Governor is also the *ex-officio* Chancellor of the State Universities of Orissa. The Chief Minister wields the real power. All the educational policies require his endorsement, explicit or implicit, because if he does not approve of the policies of the Education Minister, he may drop him or may transfer him to some other department. Chief Ministers like Dr. H. K. Mahatab, Sri Nabakrishna Choudhury, and Mrs. Nandini Satpathy chose to keep the education port-folio with themselves.

The Minister of Education, who is answerable to the legislature, is the Head of the Department of Education. He is the policy-maker and the pilot of all educational affairs.

The Secretary to the Government in the Education Department is the administrative head and is responsible for the formulation of educational policies the over-all management of the Education Department. Normally, an I. A. S. Officer of the rank of a Commissioner or Principal Secretary holds this post.

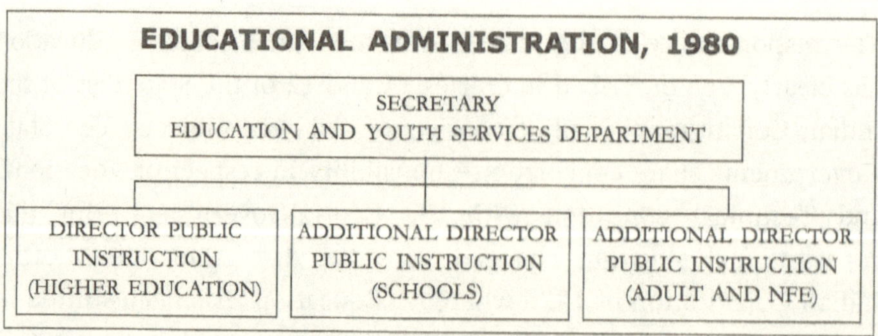

From 1st April, 1936 to 1st January, 1991 the secondary schools were under the overall control of the Department of Education & Youth Services. From 2nd January,1991 to 30th November, 1992 they were under the Department of Education. From 1st December, 1992 to date (July, 2007) they are under the administrative charge the Department of School and Mass Education of the Government of Orissa.

 In December 1992, the erstwhile Department of Education and Youth Services was reorganized into the:

i. Department of Higher Education and
ii. Department of School & Mass Education.

Its Youth Services' component was transferred to the Department of Sports &Youth Services.

TABLE 13.2.1

List of Honourable Minister for Education from
01.04.1937 to 04.01.1993

No.	Name	Rank	From	To
1.	Gorachand Patnaik	Cabinet	01.04.1937	19.07.1937
2.	Biswanath Das	Cabinet	19.07.1937	06.11.1939
3.	Godavaris Mishra	Cabinet	24.11.1941	30.06.1944
4.	Lingaraj Mishra	Cabinet	23.04.1946	12.05.1950
5.	Radhanath Rath	Cabinet	07.04.1952	19.10.1956
6.	Harekrishna Mahatab	Cabinet	19.10.1956	06.04.1957
7.	Lingaraj Panigrahi	Cabinet	06.04.1957	22.05.1959
8.	Harekrishna Mahatab	Cabinet	22.05.1959	25.02.1961
9.	Pabitra Mohan Pradhan	Cabinet	23.06.1961	02.10.1963
10.	Satyapriya Mohanty	Cabinet	02.101963	21.02.1965
1.	Smt. Saraswati Pradhan	Deputy	02.101963	21.02.1965
11.	Satyapriya Mohanty	Cabinet	21.2.1965	08.03.1967
1.	Smt. Saraswati Pradhan	Deputy	21.2.1965	08.03.1967
12.	Banamali Patnaik	Cabinet	08.03.1967	09.01.1971
13.	Sarat Kumar Kar	Cabinet	03.04.1971	14.06.1972
14.	Shriballav Panigrahi	Cabinet	14.06.1972	03.03.1973

TABLE 13.2.2

List of Honourable Minister for Education and Youth Services from 06.03.1974 to 04.01.1993

Sl. No.	Name	Rank	From	To
1.	Jadunath Das Mohapatra	Cabinet	06.03.1974	16.12.1976
	Jagannath Patnaik	Deputy	06.03.1974	16.12.1976
2.	Shriballav Panigrahi	Cabinet	29.12.1976	30.04.1977
	Sk. Mutlub Ali	State	29.12.1976	30.04.1977
3.	Pradipta Kishore Das	Cabinet	26.06.1977	25.10.1979
4.	Pratap Chandra Mohanty	Cabinet	25.10.1979	17.02.1980
	Kalindi Behera	State	25.10.1979	17.02.1980
5.	Gangadhar Mohapatra	Cabinet	09..6.1980	09.03.1985
6.	Jugal Kishore Pattnaik	Cabinet	10.03.1985	30.05.1985
7.	Jadunath Das Mohapatra	Cabinet	30.05.1985	.7.12.1989
8.	Sk. Madub Ali	Cabinet	07.12.1989	03.03.1990
	Frida Topno	State	07.12.1989	03.03.1990
9.	Chaitanya Prasad Majhi	Cabinet	24.07.1990	02.01.1991
10.	Smt. (Dr.) Kamala Das	Cabinet	24.07.1991	04.01.1993

DEPARTMENT OF HIGHER EDUCATION

The Minister of Higher Education looks after this Department. The overalladministrative responsibility for the smooth functioning of the Department vestswith the Secretary to the government of Orissa in the Department of HigherEducation who belongs either to the grade of a Commissioner or a Principal Secretary of the I. A. S. cadre. He is assisted by two Additional Secretaries, two Joint Secretaries, four Deputy Secretaries, one Liaison Officer-cum-Deputy Secretary and one Financial Adviser-cum-Joint Secretary, two Under Secretaries and a number of ministerial officers of various grades. The two assisting Directorates of this Department are:

i. Directorate of Higher Education; and
ii. Directorate of Vocational Education established in 2000.

The Directorate of Higher Education is concerned with the day to day management of general colleges. The Directorate of Vocational Education administersVocational Higher Secondary Schools and/or Government Vocational Junior College.

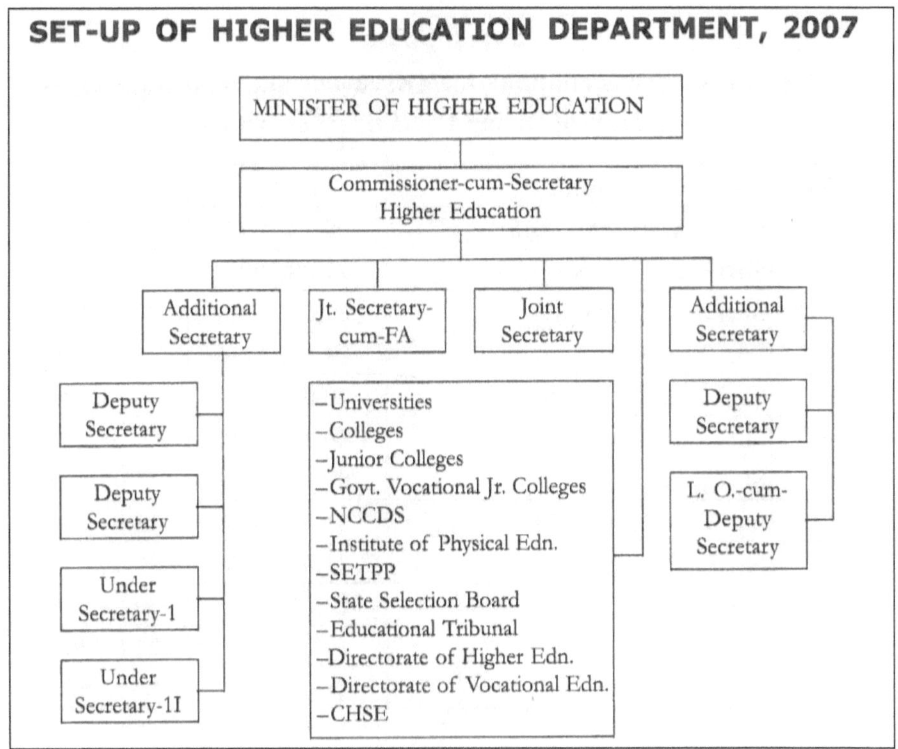

TABLE 13.2.3

List of Honourable Ministers of Higher Education,

21.03.1995 to 30.09.2007

SI. No.	Name	Rank	From	To
1.	Bhagabat Prasad Mohanty	Cabinet	21.03.1995	17.02.1999
2.	Bhagabat Prasad Mohanty	Cabinet	22.02.1999	06.12.1999
3.	Sheik Madub AH	Cabinet	10.12.1999	05.03.2000
1.	Ganeswar Behera	State	10.12.1999	05.03.2000
4.	Prasanta Nanda	State(IC)	06.12.1999	05.03.2000

SI. No.	Name	Rank	From	To
5.	Naveen Patnaik	Cabinet & Chief Minister	09.07.2001	.6.08.2002
6.	Bimbadhar Kuanr	State (IC)	06.08.2002	16.05.2004
7.	Sameer Dey	Cabinet	18.05.2004	Continuing

TABLE 13.2.4

List of Principal Secretaries/Commissioner-cum-Secretaries/ Secretaries of Higher Education Department

SI. No.	Name	From	To
1.	Shri S. M. Patnaik, IAS	08.12.1992	21.08.1996
2.	Shri P. K. Mohanty, IAS	21.08.1996	21.07.1997
3.	Shri S. P. Nanda, IAS	21.07.1997	30.06.1998
4.	Shri A. K. SamantarayJAS	01.07.1998	10.03.1999
5.	Shri S. C. Hota, IAS	10.03.1999	30.11.1999
6.	Shri R. L. Jamuda,IAS	30.11.1999	09.01.2002
7.	Shri P. C. Mishra, IAS	09.12.2002	31.05.2003
8.	Shri R. C. Behera, IAS	31.05.2003	15.01.2005
9.	Shri N. Sanyal, IAS	31.01.2005	09.06.2005
10.	Shri S. Baya, IAS	27.06.2005	30.06.2006
11.	Shri A. K. Tripathy, IAS	19.07.2006	21.08.2007
12.	Shri R. B. Naya, IAS	21.08.2007	Continuing

DEPARTMENT OF SCHOOL & MASS EDUCATION

The Department of School and Mass Education of the Government of Orissa came into existence as a separate Department in December,1992. The phenomenal expansion of every stage of education during the period 1951 to 1992 had generatedmost unbearable pressure of work. The system was becoming almost unmanageable id was virtually on the verge of collapse. Streamlining the administration of the mega educational system was overdue. It was an unavoidable administrative necessity and the bifurcation of the Department was definitely a welcome step. Time seems to have come to transfer the management of higher secondary education to the school stem and create a Department of Secondary

Education for this stage of education. Neglect of elementary education in the past has generated the present problems of adult education. The adult education of India is simply compensatory delayed primary education for those who missed the bus in their childhood due to lack of access. Therefore, adult education should be viewed as alternative elementary education for e deprived and ought to be an integral part of elementary education.

A Minister of the Council of Ministers-either of Cabinet rank or of the rank of a State Minister - is in overall charge of the Department and is answerable to the state legislature for all matters pertaining to school education and adult education. The list of Ministers who were in charge of this Department has been shown in Appendix-I. The administrative head of the Department is the Secretary who belongs the rank of the Commissioner or Principal Secretary of the Indian Administrative Service. He is assisted by two Additional Secretaries, one(or two) Joint Secretaries, a Financial Adviser-cum-Joint Secretary of the Orissa Finance Service (Senior Branch) and three (or four) Deputy Secretaries. The various Directorates related to this Department function under its. The Organogram of the Department of Schools &Mass Education graphically depicts the administrative structure (as in 2007).

ADMINISTRATIVE STRUCTURE OF THE DEPARTMENT OF SCHOOL & MASS EDUCATION (31ST DEC. 2007)

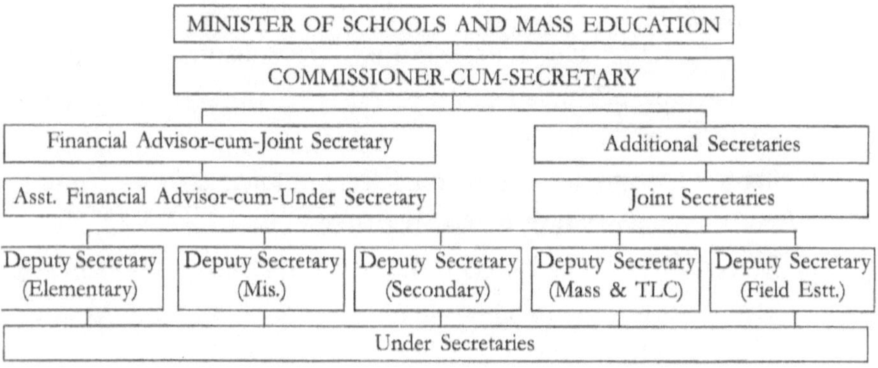

The major responsibilities of the Department of School & Mass Education are the proper administration of the following areas of school education and other related areas:

    i.   Secondary Education
   ii.   Elementary Education
  iii.   Mass (or Adult) Education
  iv.   Teacher Education

The assisting administrative Directorates under this Department are:

    i.   Directorate of Secondary Education, Orissa
   ii.   Directorate of Elementary Education, Orissa
  iii.   Directorate of Mass Education, Orissa and
  iv.   Directorate of Teacher Education & State Council of Educational Research& Training, Orissa

The other organizations operating under this Department to augment the access to and quality of school educational programmes are:

    v.   Orissa Primary Education Programme Authority promotes the quality ofprimary education;
   vi.   Education for All Cell augments access to primary education
  vii.   State Resource Centre for Adult Education, Orissa provides academic supportto Mass Education
 viii.   Odiya Bhasha Pratisthan, Orissa furthers all facets of the Oriya language
  ix.   English Language Teaching Institute subsumes the quality of learning ofEnglish as a second language across the school curriculum.
    x.   State Institute of Educational Technology, Orissa promotes multimedia learning.
  xi.   Directorate of Text-Book Production & Marketing, Bhubaneswar prints, publishes and markets nationalized textbooks for school education from class I to VII.

The Board of Secondary Education, Orissa recognizes high schools; lays shown the courses of studies; prepares and publishes textbooks prescribed by it; awards certificates; conducts other examinations as per Government direction.

In so far as secondary education in Orissa is concerned, the Directorate of Secondary Education, Orissa is the nodal apex administrative Directorate. Board of Secondary Education, Orissa plays a pivotal role in all matters pertaining to academic control and improvement. The Directorate of Teacher Education and SCERT, the State Institute of Educational Technology, English Language Teaching Institute, and the Odiya Bhasha Pratisthan play a critical role in capacity building and providing academic support to the secondary school system.

TABLE 13.2.5

List of Honourable Ministers for School & Mass Education from 04.01.1993 to 01.10.2006

No.	Name	Rank	From	To
1.	Prafulla Chandra Ghadai	Cabinet	04.01.1993	15.03.1995
2.	Ulka Rama Chandra	Cabinet	21.03.1995	14.01.1996
3.	Jayadev Jena	State (IC)	14.01.1996	17.02.1999
4.	Sheikh. Matlub Ali	Cabinet	22.02.1999	06.12.1999
1.	Ripunath Seth	State	22.02.1999	06.12.1999
5.	Nabin Chandra Narayan Das	State(IC)	10.12.1999	05.03.2000
6.	Bhagabat Behera	Cabinet	06.03.2000	03.06.2002
7.	Surendra Nam Naik	Cabinet	06.08.2002	16.05.2004
8.	Nagendra Kumar Pradhan	State (IC)	18.05.2004	16.05.2006
9.	Bishnu Charan Das	Cabinet	17.05.2006	22.08.2007
10.	(a) Shri Naveen Pamaik (b) Shri Sanjeev Sahu	Chief Minister Minister State	22.08.2007 05.02.2008	Continuing Continuing

TABLE 13.2.6

**List of Principal Secretaries/Commissioner-cum Secretaries/
Secretaries of Department of School & Mass Education**

No.	Name	From	To
1.	Shri Tarun Kanti Mishra, IAS	04.08.1992	27.09.1993
2.	Shri Dhirendra Nath Padhi, IAS	04.10.1993	02.05.1996
3.	Shri Madan Mohan Mohanty, IAS	03.05.1996	24.04.1998
4.	Shri Jogendra Patra, IAS	24.04.1998	10.02.1999
5.	Shri Cinmaya Basu, IAS	10.02.1999	10.03.1999
6.	Shri Sreenivas Rath, IAS	10.03.1999	07.05.1999
7.	Shri S. Nautiyual, IAS	07.05.1999	08.07.1999
8.	Smt. Bandana K. Jena, IAS	10.07.1999	19.07.1999
9.	Shri Ashok Kumar Tripathy, IAS	02.08.1999	02.01.2002
10.	Dr. Hrushikesh Panda, IAS	02.01.2002	17.05.2002
11.	Shri Jagadananda Panda, IAS	20.05.2002	21.09.2004
12.	Shri Gagan Kumar Dhal, IAS	28.09.2004	30.06.2006
13.	Shri Bhaskar Chatterjee, IAS	03.06.2006	28.09.2006
14.	Shri Suresh Chandra Patnaik, IAS	28.09.2006	Continuing

DIRECTORATES OF EDUCATION (1936-2007)

DIRECTORATE OF PUBLIC INSTRUCTION, ORISSA (1936-1968)

A separate Directorate of Public Instruction was set up for Orissa in 1936 consequent on the formation of the new provice.[455] "The Director of Public Instruction is the administrative head of the Department and Adviser to Government on all educational matters. He has to carry out the policies laid down by Government and is immediately responsible to Government with regard to the administration of the Department. He has also to perform the duties of an Inspector of European Schools, as there is no separate Inspector for them, their number being meager. He is competent to inspect recognized public institutions for collegiate education and any other general or commercial public institution in the province. The administration and control of government colleges and sanction of grants to aided colleges rest with him subject to the orders of the Government."[456]

The D P. I., Orissa was the chief executive officer of all educational affairs and was responsible for assisting the Government in the formulation of educational policies and their implementation; preparation of budget and control of expenditure and human resources development. He was respected as the top-most powerful administrator of the

---

455 Report of the Third Educational survey, Orissa, 1978, p. 286-287
456 Progress of Education in Orissa, 1942-43 p. 14-15

Education Department. The DPI's office was located in the Kathajodi Hostel opposite R. N. Training College, Cuttack. It was shifted to Bhubaneswar in 1967.

The first three D. P. Is. of Orissa were officers belonged to the Indian Education Service. They were:

1. Mr. H. Dippie, I. E. S.   1936 to 1938
2. Mr. Syama Charan Tripathy,I E. S.   1938 to 1948
3. Mr. Sachi Ray, I. E. S.   1948 to 1949

Mr. H. Dippie, Chief Education Officer of the Eastern States Agency was the first Director of Public Instruction, Orissa; and had his set of firm educational priorities. The black clouds of economic depression and the gathering storm of the Second World War loomed large on the horizon. The feudatory states were out of his administrative jurisdiction. He wielded power over the schools in the British-administered districts of Cuttack, Puri, Balasore, Ganjam, Koraput and Sambalpur.

There were only 36 high schools and 193 middle schools by 1937-38. So, he decided improve primary education. He wrote a number of pertinent monographs relating to different aspects of primary education and the translated versions were widely dated. He personally visited primary schools in the far flung Kondhamal and Koraput areas. He closely interacted with the teachers. He is perhaps the first and also the last Director who understood the principles and practice of educational extension. The Primary School Teachers' Association published his biography in 2002. He has left a lasting imprint on the educational system, in general; and primary education, in particular. He developed deep differences with the then Prime Minister of Orissa Mr. Biswanath Dash who wanted to introduce the concept of GandhianBasic Education in one go in Orissa. Mr. Dippie advised him to take a small step, a

slow step and a steady step; and then to expand rapidly, if the experiment succeeded. These details were conveyed to the author by late Professor

Satrughna Nath, M. A. London) who gready adored Mr. Dippie and had penned his biography.

Mr. Syama Charan Tripathy's tenure from 1938 to 1948 was a period of

catastrophes and unprecedented upheavals. The Second World War from 1939 to 1945 dampened all educational activities. Immediately, after the war, India attained independence. In the Administrative Report of the Education Department for the year 1947-48, there is no mention at all about this momentous transfer of power. Mr. Tripathy could not achieve anything tangible in the field of school education during his long tenure of a decade. But the number of colleges increased and the Utkal University was established during his tenure. During his time the Basic Training Schools and the *'Campari Areas of Basic Schools'* were established. The Government Training College, Cuttack was renamed Radhanath Training College, Cuttack in 1948 afterthe celebrated poet and first Inspector of Schools of Orissa late Mr. Radhanath Rai.

Mr. Sachi Ray was the last D. P. I of Orissa of the I. E. S cadre. He had spent almost his entire career as an Inspecting Officer and his term as DPI was too short accomplish anything tangible. The era of IES Officers came to a close with the retirement of Mr. S. Ray in 1948. The Government had to choose an academician of towering status to man this post. The Principal, Ravenshaw College, Cuttack was always enjoying the Senior Administrative Cadre in the Education Department and s next in status only to the DPI. Therefore, it became a convention to appoint the Principal of Ravenshaw College, Cuttack as the Directors of Public Instruction, Orissa. This tradition continued up to 31.03.1968. Five Principals of Ravenshaw College, Cuttack were appointed as DPIs of Orissa after the retirement of the last IES Officer from 1949 to1968.

Professor Mahesh Chandra Pradhan, M. A, (Patna) B. T. (London) was an eminent Professor of Mathematics. He was the Principal of Radhanath Training College, Cuttack for more than a decade (1936 to 1948) and had thorough pedagogic knowledge. He had translated the text-book on geometry by Stanley & Hall into Oriya; and it was a basic text for decades together Prof. Balabhadra Prasad was a physicist and had earned both Ph.D & D. Sc degrees.[457] He greaedy loved research and had temporarily foregone his promotion to the rank of DPI. He encouraged the younger generation of lecturers to engage themselves in doctoral research. He was the DPI with a very strong research orientation and high research credentials. Later, he was the Vice-Chancellor of Patna and Allahabad Universities. Prof. Bama Charan Das, the illustrious mathematician, succeeded him. Prof. (Dr.) Sadasiv Mishra, M. A (Patna), Ph.D (London) was an eminent economist and a very forceful speaker and succeeded Prof. B. C. Das. He had a charismatic personality. He is remembered for his erudition, forceful oratory and able administration. Prof. Bansidhar Samantray, an eminent Professor of Science Education and a prolific researcher, succeeded him. He had to grapple with the outfall of the Report Indian Education Commission, 1964-66 and the emerging educational exertion of the National Council of Educational Research and Training. The eminent Prof, of Mathematics Mr. Ramanath Mohanty succeeded him and worked as DPI, Orissa up to 31.03.1968. On 1st April,1968 the unified Directorate of Public Instruction was split into two-the DPI (Higher Education) and the DPI(Schools), Orissa.

DIRECTORATE

Up to 1945-46, the only gazetted officer of the Directorate was the Personal Assistant to the Director of Public Instruction. He was also the ex-officio Registrar of School Examinations Board. In 1945-46, a Deputy Director was appointed. Consequent on the merger of the Feudatory State with Orissa, an additional post of Deputy Director was created, with effect from 1st April, 1949. It was abolished with effect from 20th February,!950 as a measure of economy. In 1955-56, the post of the DDPI (Primary and Basic) was created. The post of the Joint DPI was created with effect from 14th February,1959, "to implement successfully the scheme of Secondary Education under the changed

---

457 Progress of Education in Orissa, 1947-48, p. 10

pattern."[458] In 1979, there were 9 Deputy D. P. Is. There were seven Assistant Directors of Public Instruction and 27 Section Officers in the Directorate.

By 1957-58, there were three Deputy Directors of Public Instruction (General, Planning, Primary & Basic). There were 4 Class-II Officers in the Directorate viz., Personal Assistant to D. P. I, Publicity Officer, Organizer of Basic Education, and Special Officer for Educational Survey.

BIFURCATION OF THE DIRECTORATE (1968)

After independence there was unprecedented expansion in all sectors and stages of education, the growth of primary and secondary education was propelled due to the implementation of the Five-year Plans. The administrative pressure was steadily increasing. To cope with the increased administrative work-load, the monolithic Directorate of Public Instruction, Orissa was split into two Directorates on 1st April,1968; viz.

    i.   Directorate of Public Instruction (Higher Education)
    ii. Directorate of Public Instruction (Schools)

The Directorate of Higher Education was assigned the responsibility of managing higher education of Orissa — Universities and all types of colleges. The Directorate Public Instruction (Schools) was in charge of the administration of the total school cation including adult, social, and non-formal education.

---

458 Progress of Education in Orissa, 1958-59, p. 10

TABLE 13.3.1

Directors of Public Instruction, Orissa

(1.4.1936 to 31.3.1968: Total 32 years)

Sl. No.	Name of the D.P.I.	Period	
		From	**To**
1.	Mr. H. Dippie, I. E. S.	01.04.1936	1938
2.	Mr. Syama Charan Tripathy, I. E. S.	1938	1948
3.	Mr. Sachi Ray, I. E. S.	1948	1949
4.	Pro. Mahesh Chandra Pradhan	1949	1952
5.	Prof. Balabhadra Prasad, D. Sc. (London)	1952	30.04.1957
6.	Porf. Bama Charan Das	01.05.1957	20.01.1962
7.	Prof. Sadasiv Mishra, Ph.D. (London)	21.01.1962	15.02.1966
8.	Prof. (Dr.) Bansidhar Samantray	16.02.1966	09.02.1968
9.	Prof.(Dr.) Ramanadi Mohanty	09.02.1968	29.02.1968
10.	Sri Gokul Chandra Satapathy, I/C	29.02.1968	31.03.1968

DIRECTORATE OF HIGHER EDUCATION

There was one monolithic Directorate of Public Instruction, Orissa to oversee the total education of the state. The Directors were all either I. E. S. Officers or outstanding senior professors. In 1968, it was divided into two Directorates. The Directorate of Public Instruction (Higher Education) was later redesignated as Directorate of High Education. The Directorate of Higher Education functions under the Department of Higher Education, Government of Orissa. The Director is either a senior Professor or the Principal of a Lead College. This Directorate recognizes, inspects and administers the Junior Colleges and Higher Secondary Schools. A DDPI is in charge of higher secondary education. The list of DPIs (Higher Education) and Directors of Higher Education with their tenures is given below:

TABLE 13.3.2

List of Directors of Public Instruction (Higher Education) & Directors of Higher Education, Orissa

SI. No.	Name	Period	
		From	To
1.	Prof. Bidhubhusan Das	1968	1975
2.	Prof. Debendra Chandra Mishra, A.M., Ph.D. Haryana	1975	1976
3.	Prof. Mahendra Kumar Rout	19.11.1976	18.12.1977
4.	Prof. Bidhubhusan Das	19.12.1977	30.04.1980
5.	Prof. Mahendra Kumar Rout	01.05.1980	31.03.1983
6.	Prof. Khetramohan Patnaik	01.04.1983	31.05.1986
7.	Prof(Dr.) Dinabandhu Mishra	31.05.1986	13.07.1987
8.	Prof(Dr.) Ghanashyam Das	13.07.1987	31.10.1990
9.	Prof(Dr.) Laxmikanta Das	31.10.1990	30.06.1992
10.	Prof (Dr.) (Mrs.) Girishbala Mohanty	01.07.1992	04.07.1994
11.	Prof(Dr.) Pradipta Kumar Jeshthi (I/C)	05.07.1994	18.08.1994
12.	Major Prafulla Kumar Patra	19.08.1994	30.11.1995
13.	Prof(Dr.) Gorachand Patnaik (I/C)	04.12.1995	31.07.1996
14.	Prof(Dr.) Pradipta Kumar Jeshthi	01.08.1996	30.04.1997
15.	Dr. Prakash Kumar Mohapatra (I/C)	01.05.1997	16.02.1998
16.	Prof(Dr.) Gunanidhi Sahu	16.02.1998	30.04.1999
17	Prof(Dr.) Trilochan Dash (I/C)	04.05.1999	30.01.2000
18	Prof(Dr.) Trilochan Dash	31.01.2000	31.01.2000
19	Prof. Parth Sarathi Singh,(I/C)	02.02.2000	31.07.2001
20	Dr. (Mrs.) Sashikala Patnaik	31.07.2001	31.12.2001
21	Dr. Tarun Kumar Sinha	31.12.2001	31.05.2002
22	Prf. Prafulla Kumar Mishra	31.05.2002	31.05.2003
23	Dr. (Mrs.) Arati Swain (I/C)	05.04.2003	31.07.2003
24	Dr. Haridas Dutta (I/C)	31.07.2003	30.11.2003
25	Dr. Kalpana Manjari Das (I/C)	30.11.2003	08.08.2004
26	Dr. Sashikanta Mishra (I/C)	09.08.2004	30.09.2004
27	Dr. Kalpana Manjari Das (I/C)	01.10.2004	31.12.2004
28	Prof. Saroj Kumar Singh (I/Q	01.01.2005	30.04.2005

SI. No.	Name	Period	
		From	To
29	Dr. Biraja Prasanna Das (I/C)	31.04.2005	30.06.2006
30	Dr. Nirmala Kanti Sen (I/C)	05.07.2006	31.07.2006
31	Dr. Parbati Charan Pati (I/C)	01.08.2006	31.05.2007
32	Dr. P. K. Rath, (I/C)	01.06.2007	31.07.2007
33	Dr. Aditya Mohanty, (I/C)	01.08.2007	Continuing

The Directorate of Higher Education, Orissa is still headed by an academician and not an I. A. S. officers like other Directorates. He/she is assisted by three Regional Directors, one Additional Director (the post is not always filled up): three Deputy Directors in the three Regional Director; five Deputy Directors at the Headquarter; three Assistant Directors; one Accounts Officer, one Establishment Officer and an Assistant Engineer. The section officers and ministerial officers assist in the administration.

The organogram of Directorate of High Education, Orissa briefly provides the pen-picture of its organization and structure.

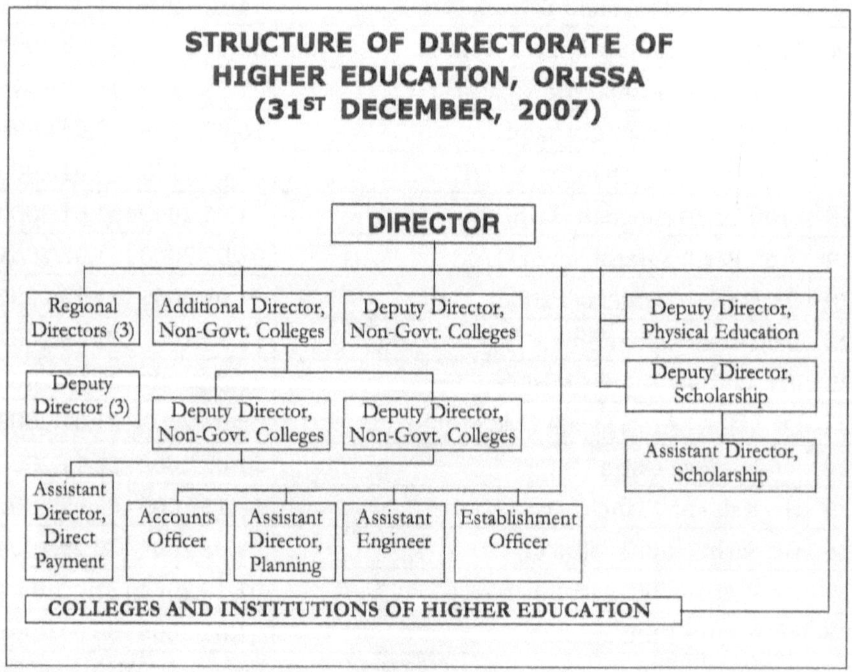

This Directorate is already overburdened by the work pressure of the Universities and Colleges. In the fitness of things the administration of higher secondary education should be transferred to the Department of School and Mass Education. A new Directorate of Higher Secondary Education needs to be created to administer 1084 institutions imparting higher secondary education(by September, 2007).

DIRECTORATE OF PUBLIC INSTRUCTION (SCHOOLS) (1968 TO 1983)

This Directorate was in overall charge of high school education along with other assigned responsibilities pertaining to other stages and phases of school education. Mr. Gokul Chandra Satpathy, B. A. (London) who was already working as the Joint DPI became the first DPI (Schools). He worked from 1.4.1968 to 31.7.1968; and was succeeded by Professor Baidyanath Rath, M. A (Patna), D. Ed. (Patna), M. A. (London) who was the Principal, Radhanath Training College, Cuttack. The post was sometimes downgraded to the level of an Additional or Joint DPI of Schools.

Prof. Baidyanath Rath, M. A (Patna), D. Ed.(Patna), M. A. (London) was the DPI Schools), Orissa from 1st August, 1968 to 31st July, 1968. Prior to his appointment as DPI (Schools), he was the Principal (1948 to 1955) and Prof.-cum-Principal (1958 to 68) of the Radhanath Training College, Cuttack. While working as the DPI (Schools), Orissa. The author of this book was his student and Ph.D scholar. Most of the material from 1882 to 1966 incorporated in this book are part of the doctoral thesis conducted under his scholarly guidance entitled "Development of Secondary Education in Orissa 1882 to 1966." Mr. Dinabandhu Panigrahi, M. Ed.(Patna) M. A. (Leeds), a veteran Inspector of Schools remained in charge of this Directorate from 1.1.1971 to 31.1.1971. Again he was kept in full charge with full power of the Director; but wasdesigned Joint D P. I. (Schools) from 1.1.1975 to 21.02.1977.

From 1.2.1971 to 31.12.1974, Prof. Debendra Chadra Mishra, M. A (Patna), A. M, PhD (Harvard) was the D P. I. (Schools). Later, he became the Vice Chancellor of the Sambalpur University. Dr. Mishra was an eminent economist and an erudite scholar. Above all, his humane and informal approach and absolute simplicity make him memorable. He was also the D. P. I. (Higher Education). Prof. (Dr.) Brajabandhu Mishra, an eminent Professor of Mathematics succeeded Dr. Mishra. Prof. Mishra retiredon 4.3.1978; and the then Director of Higher Education Professor Bidhubhushan Das remained in additional charge of this directorate from 5.3.1978 to 18.6.1978. On 19.6.1978, Prof. Gadadhar Mishra, Prof, of Botany, and Principal Gangadhar Meher College took over the charge of the Directorate with the designation of Additional Director and continued up to 13.9.1980. Prof. Harekrushna Mishra succeeded him as Director from 22.9.1980 to 31.7.1981. Prof. (Dr.) Ghanasyama Samal, an eminent Professor of Mathematics was the D. P. I. (Schools) from 1.8.1981.3.1983.

From 1st April,1968 to 31st March,1983, it is the Director (Additional or Joint) Director of Public Instruction of Schools who controlled the secondary schools. From1983 to the present day i.e. 31st December, 2007, the Director of Secondary Education, Orissa controls the high schools of Orissa.

The Directorate (by whatever name it may be called) was always headed by a director. The Directors from 1936 to 1996 were all eminent academicians of repute. During 1996, officers of the Indian Administrative Services began to occupy all the posts of the Directors in the Education Department. The Directorates of Higher Education and Teacher Education are the two exceptions where the remnants of educationists still become Directors. The Government of Orissa in its wisdom has reposed its faith in the capability of the generalist administrators for the last onedecade. It has not appointed academicians of outstanding caliber with excellent academic credentials and reputation as researchers to the post of directors during the last ten years. The reasons seem to be mysterious and elude logic. The healthy tradition of appointing outstanding educational administrators as directors of all directorates; and other academic bodies like the Board of Secondary Education and the Council of Higher Secondary Education needs to be restored.

Without prejudice, malice, ill-well or disrespect to the claims of the IAS incumbents of the various directorates, it can safely be stated that they:

i.   Lack hands-on experience of teaching, guiding research and administration of eitherschools or colleges;
ii. Lack of the specialist academic orientation; and
iii. Are more bureaucratic and less academic in their administrative style of functioning.

The Directorate of Secondary Education, Orissa has four Deputy Directors in class I of OES (School Branch); and one Senior Establishment Officer in class-I (Gazetted Service). There are seven class II posts out of which two are Assistant Directors, one for *directpayment* and the other for Physical Education. There are two Special Officers-one for Muhammadan Education and the other for Arts & Crafts. There is a Superintendent of Sanskrit Studies; one Accounts Officers and an Establishment Officer. There are three Regional Directors heading the three Regional Directorates at Bhubaneswar, Berhampur and Sambalpur.

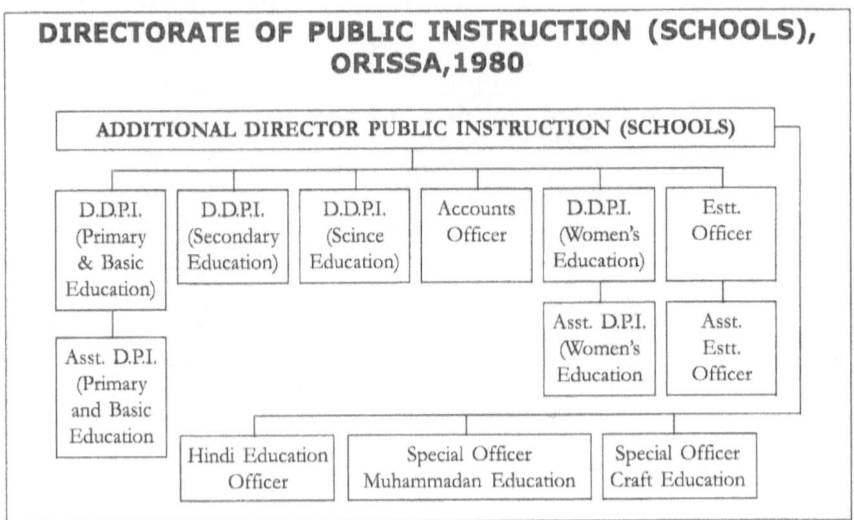

The Additional Director of Public Instruction (Adult and Non-formal Education) was in overall charge of adult and non-formal education of the State. He was assisted by aDeputy Director and two Assistant Directors.

The State Council of Educational Research and Training, Bhubaneswar with a Professor of Education as its Director acts as a permanent centre of in-service training, extension, research and professional publications The State Bureau of Educational and Vocational Guidance and the Educational Technology Cell are attached to it.

The organizational chart briefly and clearly depicts the regional level administration of Secondary schools in December, 2007.

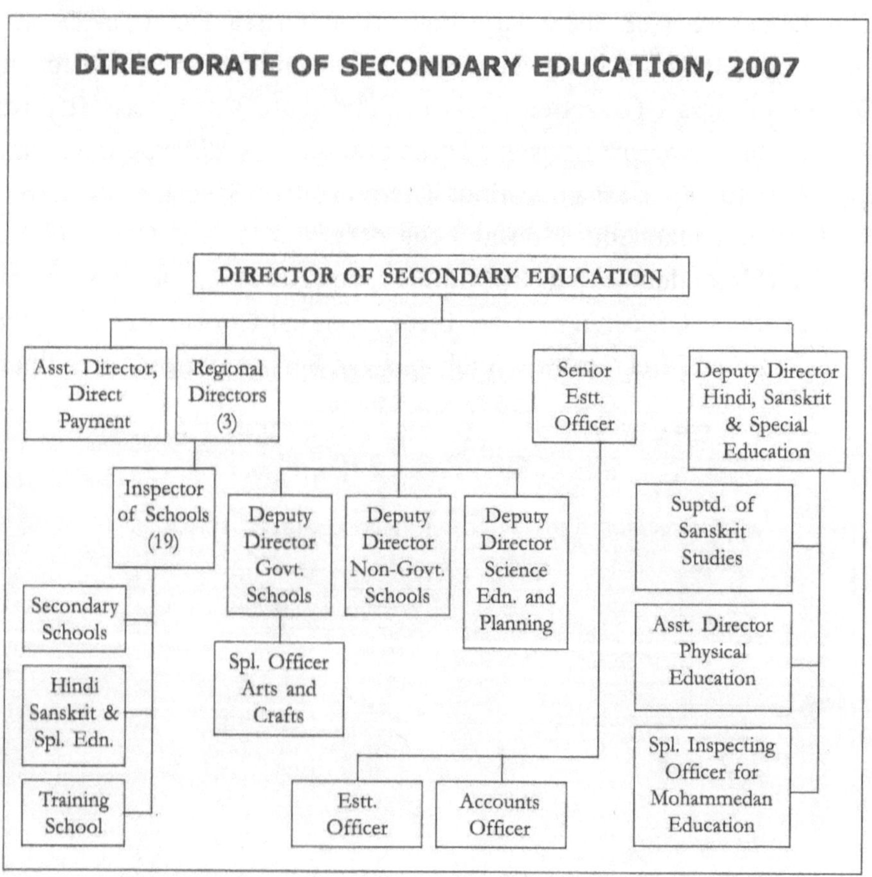

TABLE 13.3.3

Director Public Instruction (Schools), Orissa (In full charge of Secondary/ Primary, Adult Education of Orissa

SI. No.	Name of the Director of Secondary Education, Orissa	Period	
		From	To
1.	Mr. Gokul Chandra Satpathy, B. A. (London)	01.04.1968	31.07.1968
2.	Prof. Baidyanath Rath, M. A. (London), M. A. (Patna) D. Ed. (Patnal	01.08.1968	31.02.1970
3.	Sri Dinabandhu Panigrahi, I/C	01.01.1971	31.01.1971
4.	Prof. Debendra Chandra Mishra,M. A. (Patna), A. M. PhD. (Haravard)	01.02.1971	31.12.1974
5.	Sri Dinabandhu Panigrahi, Jt. DPI	01.01.1975	21.02.1977
6.	Prof. (Dr.) Braja Bandhu Mishra, Addl. DPI	21.02.1977	04.03.1978
7.	Prof. B. Das, Addl. Charge	05.03.1978	18.06.1978
8.	Prof. (Dr.) Gadadhar Mishra, Addl. D. P. I.	19.06.1978	13.09.1980
9.	Prof. Harekrushna Mishra	22.09.1980	21.07.1981
10.	Prof. (Dr.) Ghanasyam Samal	01.08.1981	31.03.1983

DIRECTORATE OF SECONDARY EDUCATION (1983)

With effect from 1st April, 1983 the Directorate of Public Instruction (Schools) was split into two parts — Directorate of Secondary Education and Directorate of Elementary & Adult Education, Orissa.

Professor (Dr.) Ghanasyam Samal, D P. I. (Schools) became the first Director of the newly created Directorate of Secondary Education, Orissa. He was the Director, Secondary Education, Orissa from 1.4.1983 to 31.7.1985. Up to 1996, the post was held by officers of the rank of Professor.

From 7.9.1996 onwards the post is held by officers of the I. A. S. cadre of the rank of an Additional Secretary to Government of Orissa. On 1st September, 2006, the Director Mr. Debendra Chandra Mishra, I. A. S. was promoted to the rank of a Commissioner and was allowed to continue as the Director of Secondary Education, Orissa. It is a significant departure from the tradition. May be it is a temporary administrative arrangement or alternatively in the years to come Commissioners may take over charge of the different Directorates of Education Dr. Subhakanta Behera, Ph.D. (Oxford) an Indian Foreign Service Officer of the rank of a Special Secretary had also been posted as full time President of the Board of Secondary Education,Orissa. The logic of educational administration is not very clear and seems to be puzzling and enigmatic. Succession list of Director of Public Instructions, Director of public Instructions (Schools) & Directors of Secondary Education, Orissa who were in full charge of Secondary Education, Orissa from 1.4.1983 to 31.7.2007 has been furnished below.

TABLE 13.3.4

Director of Secondary Education, Orissa 1.4.1983 to 31. 12. 2007

SL No.	Nameof the Director of Secondary Education, Orissa	Period	
		From	To
1	Prof. (Dr.) Ghanasyam Samal	01.04.1983	31.07.1985
2	Prof. (Dr. Tapas Kabi	01.08.1985	08.10.1985
3	Prof.(Dr.) Dinabandhu Mishra	09.10.1985	15.07.1986
4	Prof. (Dr.) Tapas Kabi	16.07.1986	06.08.1986
5	Dr. C. C. Dash	07.08.1986	10.11.1987
6	Prof.(Dr.) Umakanta Mohapatra	11.11.1987	31.12.1987
7	Prof(Dr.) M. K. Chakravarti	01.01.1988	26.9.1988
8	Prof.(Dr.) Umakanta Mohapatra	27.09.1988	30.11.1989
9	Prof. (Dr.) Ghanasyam Das	01.12.1989	05.01.1990
10	Prof.(Dr.) Lakshmikant Dash	06.01.1990	31.10.1990
11	Prof. (Dr.) Giridhari Prasad Guru	01.11.1990	31.07.1991
12	Prof. (Dr.) Phani Bhusan Das	01.08.1991	04.08.1992
13	Sri Gopal Chandra Patnaik	05.08.1992	31.07.1991
14	Dr. S. C. Jena, I/C	01.08.1996	07.09.1996
15	Sri Monoranjan Saran, I. A. S.	07.09.1996	05.08.1997
16	Sri Niranjan Jali, I. A. S.	16.08.1997	18.11.1998
17	Sri P. S. Guha, I. A. S.	19.11.1998	01.06.1999
18	Sri Digambar Mohanty, I. A. S.	10.07.2001	07.07.2000

SL No.	Nameof the Director of Secondary Education, Orissa	Period	
		From	To
19	Sri Satyendra Narayan, I. A. S.	07.07.2000	01.06.2001
20	Sri Lokanath Tripathy, I. A. S.	01.06.2001	03.10.2001
21	Mr. Isaace Behera, I. A. S.	03.10.2001	25.07.2003
22	Sri Pranta Charan Swain, I. A. S.	25.07.2003	22.09.2004
23	Sri Sanjaya Rastogi, I. A. S.	22.09.2004	10.03.2005
24	Dr. S. L. Jena, I/C	11.03.2005	24.08.2005
25	Sri Debendra Chandra Mishra, I. A. S. Commissioner-cum-Director	25.09.2005	30.09.2007
26	Sri K. K. MohantyA A. S. (S)	01.10.2007	Continuing

FURTHER REORGANISATION

The Directorate of Public Instruction, Orissa was divided into the Directorate of Higher Education, Orissa and the Directorate of Public Instruction (Schools) with effect from 1st April, 1968. On 1st April, 1983 later Directorate was divided into the Directorates of Secondary Education and the Directorate of Elementary, Adult and Non-formal Education and in September,1988 it was again reorganized into the Directorates of Elementary Education and Directorate of Mass Education. In 1990, the Directorate of Teacher Education & SCERT, Orissa was created as the successor to the State Council of Educational Research and Training (formerly State Institute of Education). The other Directorates created during the period were: The Directorate of Text Book Production and Marketing Orissa; Primary Education Programme Authority headed by a Director each. The Board of Secondary Education, Orissa which was functioning since 1955 was the apex body conducting examination at the end of the secondary and higher secondary courses. On 7th September, 1982, the Council of Higher Secondary Education was established to oversee all academic and examination aspects of Higher Secondary Education of Orissa. The State Institute of Educational Technology, English Language Teaching Institute, Odiya Bhasha Pratisthan and the State Resource Centre for

Adult Education are supportive academic institutions and their heads are designated as Directors. The Directorate of Vocational Education came into existence on 1ˢᵗ August,2000. The State Bureau of Text Book Preparation & Production, Orissa, Bhubaneswar prepares the textbooks for higher secondary education courses.

DIRECTORATE OF TEACHER EDUCATION & SCERT, ORISSA

Teacher Education is traditionally viewed as the quality assurance, quality control and quality up-gradation sub-system of the education system. All the teacher training colleges of Orissa are controlled and managed by the Directorate of Teacher Education and State Council of Educational Research and Training, Orissa. There are three Institutes of Advanced Study in Education at Cuttack, Sambalpur and Berhampur which provide B. Ed., M. Ed. and M. Phil Courses. There are nine Government Colleges of Teacher Education at Angul, Bhubaneswar (only for Women), Bolangir, Balasore, Baripada, Bhawanipatna, Bhanjanagar, Koraput and Rourkella. There is a Government Training College at Anandpur. These institutions serve the pre-service and in-service training needs of the State.

This Directorate contains in itself the State Bureau of Educational & Vocational Guidance. It is headed by a Director who is normally the senior most Professor of Education of the State. The present Director is Prof. (Dr.) Sebak Tripathy. This Directorate is under the Department of School and Mass Education. It also controls the secondary training schools (52 Govt, and one private) and 24 Govt. District Institutes of Education and Training and 6 District Resource Centres. The organogram of the Directorate is provided below.

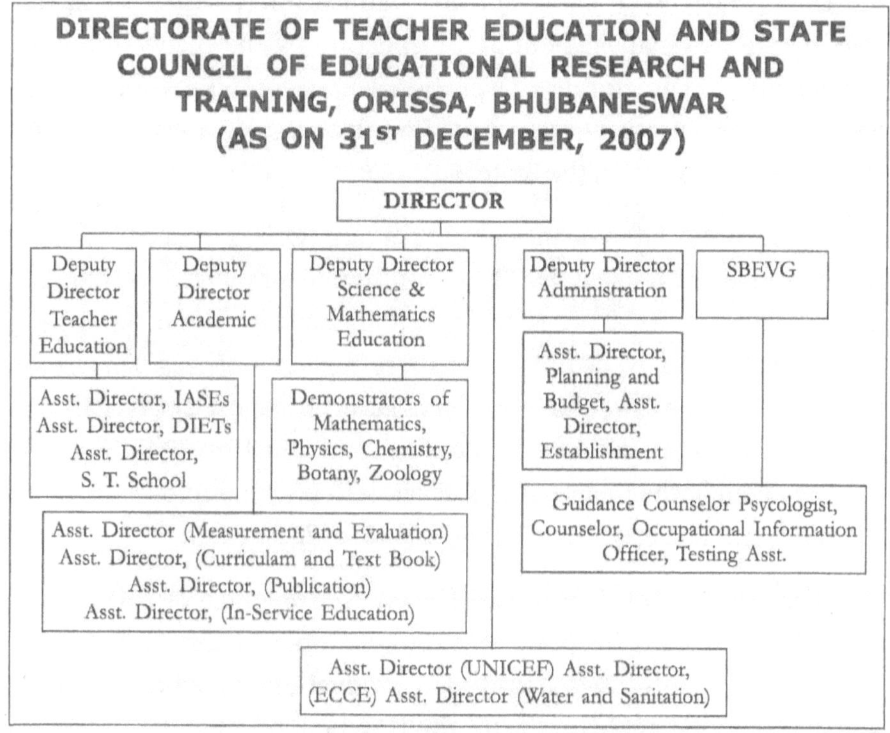

DIRECTORATE OF VOCATIONAL EDUCATION, ORISSA

The Indian Education Commission (1964-66) had recommended the vocationalization of higher secondary education in 1966. It was adopted in the National Policy on Education, 1968. The National Policy on Education of 1986 and its modification of reiterated the critical importance of vocationalisation of higher secondary education. The Centrally Sponsored Scheme of Vocationalisation of Secondary

Education commenced with effect from the academic session 1988-89 and continued as a centrally sponsored scheme up to 1994-95. Since 1995-96, it has become the state's responsibility.

The Directorate of Vocational Education was created as a separate Directorate with effect from 1st August,2000. The erstwhile three tier administrative structure of administration, recognition and control by Directorate of Higher Education; academic support by the Directorate of Teacher Education and SCERT, Orissa ; and field level day-to-day management and inspection by the Inspectorate was abolished. The Directorate of Vocational Education, Orissa is a single window administrative organization in full charge of vocational higher secondary education in the State.

The Directorate of Vocational Education, Orissa is headed by a Director. He is assisted by 33 sub-ordinate employees. There are three Regional offices at Berhampur, Bhubaneswar and Sambalpur. There are 13 employees in each of these Regional offices. Directorate comprises of one Director, one Joint Director, one Deputy Director, three Consultants, one Accounts Officer and 26 Class III and Class IV officers. Each of the Regional offices has a Deputy Director, 3 Assistant Directors and eleven class III and Class IV officers each.

The Government of Orissa sanctioned the opening of 231 Higher Secondary Vocational Schools. By 2003-04, only 71 were functioning. The academic control regulation and examination of Higher Secondary Vocational Courses belongs to the Council of Higher Secondary Education.

The administrative structure of the Directorate of Vocational Education, Orissa as on 31st December, 2007 has been depicted in the organogram below.

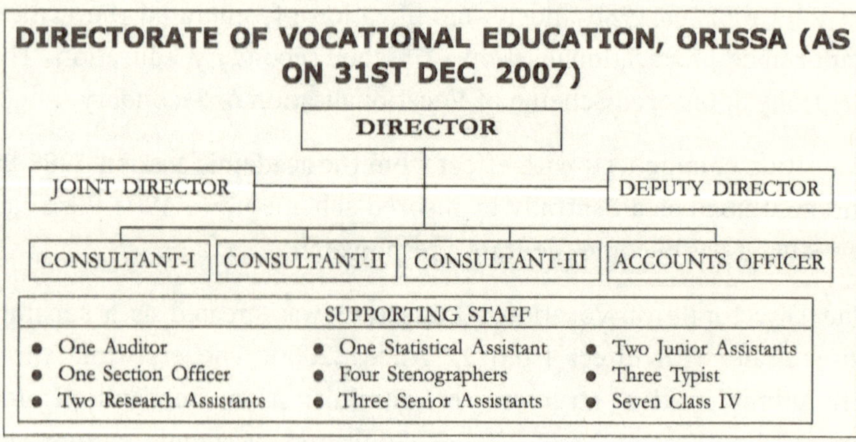

The following posts were vacant on 31st December, 2007—one Consultant and Accounts Officer.

The three Regional Offices of Vocational Education are headed by academicians of Class I rank and are assisted by three Asst. Directors who belongs to Class-II. Each regional office has eleven supporting staff members.

ECTORATE OF VOCATIONAL EDUCATION ORISSA, BHUBAESWAR ESST.-01.08.2000

TABLE NO. 13.3.5

Incumbency Chart of Directors

SL No.	Name of the Director	Period	
		From	To
1	Dr. Lalit Narayan Pattnaik	01.12.2002	30.11.2002
2	Dr. Arati Swain, I/C	30.11.2002	10.03.2003
3	Dr, Kanchanbala Patnik	10.03.2003	30.04.2003
4	Dr. Arati Swain. I./C	30.04.2003	02.06.2003
5	Dr. Sofia Khanum	02.06.2003	31.07.2003
6	Dr. Haridas Dutta, I/C	29.08.2003	30.11.2003
7	Dr. Kalpana Majari Das, I/C	30.11.2003	08.08.2004
8	Dr. Sashikanta Mishra	18.08.2004	30.09.2004
9	Dr. Kalpana Majari Das, I/C	01.10.2004	31.12.2004
10	Sri Saroj Kumar Singh, I/C	07.01.2005	30.04.2005
11	Sri Biraja Prasanna Das, I/C	06.05.2005	30.06.2006
12	Sri Rabindranath Dash, IAS Commissioner-cum — Director	28.07.2006	Continuing

REGIONAL DIRECTORATES (2007)

The Government of Orissa has established three composite unified single-window Regional Directorates at Bhubaneswar, Berhampur and Sambalpur. The territorialjurisdiction of each of the Regional directorate is co-terminus with that of the general Universities of

Utkal, Berhampur and Sambalpur as it existed before the creation of universities at Balasore and Baripada. It is a bold step towards decentralization of administration. The organogram provided below depicts the composition and structure of the Regional Directorates.

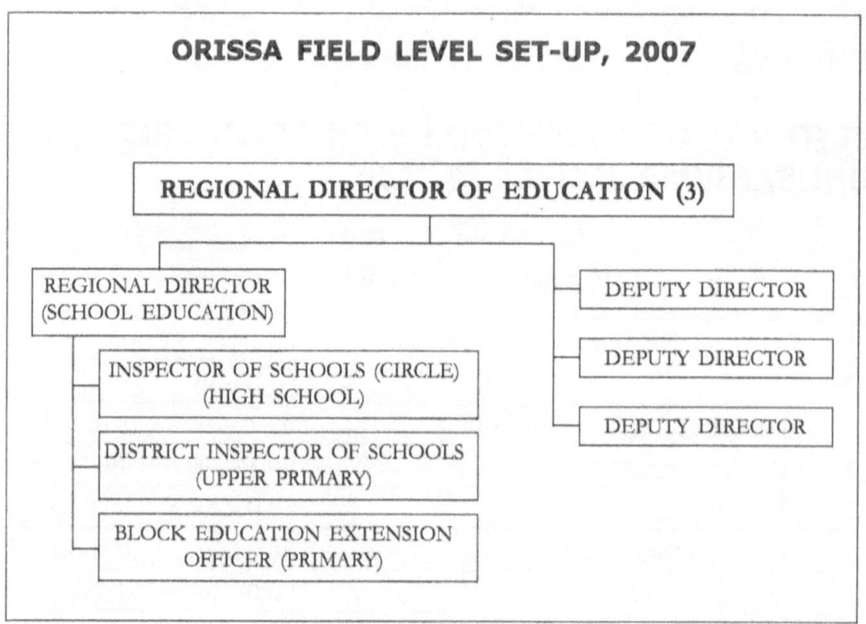

The Regional Directorate is headed by a Regional Director. He/She is assisted by one Regional Joint Director of School Education and three Deputy Directors. The Inspectors, District Inspectors and Block Educational Extension Officer (S. I. of Schools) report to the Regional director through the Regional Joint Directors of School Education. Teacher Education, Vocational Education and Mass Education sectors have not been amalgamated in the Regional Directorates.

The Regional Directorates are responsible for all administrative matters pertaining to degree colleges, junior colleges, higher secondary schools, high schools, upper primary schools (the erstwhile middle schools) and primary schools of their respective territorial jurisdiction. Administrative and financial powers have been delegated to these Regional Directorates.

INSPECTORATES OF EDUCATION

The Inspector of Schools is the pivot of educational administration. He plays a role in shaping the educational policies by providing the pragmatic academiac insights on the basis of the experience he has gained by supervising different types of schools functioning in various styles subscribing to different philosophis of education.

The Inspector is the least discussed officer though he occupies a strategic position in the network of educational administration. The Director is too highly placed in the hierarchy and is far away from 'the realities of the field. He is engrossed in assisting the Government in hammering out policy decisions and is enmeshed in a variety bureaucratic and academia tingles. The teacher is entirely enveloped in engaging educational activities and is caught in the whirlpool of class-room activities. The headmaster is intensely involved in institutional management. It is the Inspector who occupies a position of vantage. He is nearer to the Director, the policy shaper; and has a hot-line with the school-system which actualizes the theoretical education policies into practical pedagogic possibilities.

He is the most powerful and influential person; and strangely enough he is the most neglected person in the field of all educational discussions. He is like the director of a drama who is responsible for its successful presentation. The author gets applause for writing it; the actors are accorded accolades for their talented portrayal; but the director remains unseen, unknown and unnoticed. So is the case of the Inspector. The teacher is always a hero; however poor he be, of the educational drama. The education drama is of the children, by the children and for the children. They occupy the centre-stage. The Inspector receives a word or two, in the passing at the handseminent professional educationists. The Inspector descends upon the school like a lightning with great sound and fury; but vanishes not with a bang, but a whimper.

The word 'Inspector' is derived from 'inspieere' meaning, 'to look in'. There is particularly nothing wrong with the word from the etymological point of view. However, it has attained historical notoriety due to the high-handed and brash behaviour of a few black-sheep in the Inspectorate. He is not an invetigator of crimeswiththe psychology of suspicion. The earlier style of inspection was mainly of a policing nature; and this attitude is out of tune with the present democratic ethos. he Secondary Education Commission (1953) suggested and the Indian EducationCommission (1966) too approved the term, 'Educational Adviser'. 'Education Officer' is also an acceptable alternative. They are the officers who can give constructive advice and encouragement to the teachers.

NATURE OF DUTIES OF THE INSPECTORS

"The Memoranda for Inspectors"[459] published in the General Report on Public Instruction in Bengal for the year 1842-43 was the first text which outlined the nature of duties of the Inspectors. In all there were twenty-nine items of instruction in the Memoranda. The Inspector was expected to report as to how far the schools were adhering to rules; whether there were any deviations. He was also to report whether any of the rules were adversely affecting the educational institutions and in that case he was expected to substantiate his contention. The Inspection Report was to contain "the general character of the town, its conditions, the occupation of the people-agricultural, commercial or manufacturing."[460] The Inspector's Report was to contain, "an examination of state and progress of each boy, or as many as possible,

459 Progress of Education in Orissa, 1960-61, p. 51-52
460 Report on the Public Instruction in Bengal, 1842-43, p. 7

and to state the numbers present at the Examination in the respective classes."[461] He should record "the appearance of the boys, whether listless or indolent" and also of "impressions formed of the masters, their energy and general intelligence, tact or indifference and state of health"[462] and "whether the Head ever takes the classes of the lower masters."[463] He was to take cognizance of the state of the school-building, furniture, library, school-registers etc., He should see as to how far the Local Committee was evincing interest in matters of education and as to how many times it was inspecting the school.[464] After 165 years, today in 2007 it is to be noted that the 'Memoranda' is still highly relevant and useful.

According to Article 31 of the Orissa Education Code, "The functions of an Inspector are two fold; (1) Inspection and (2) Administration."[465]

"The Inspector is responsible for the efficient inspection of ail recognized educationalinstitutions in the area entrusted to his charge He is required to inspect every recognizedHigh School under his Inspectorate at least once in every calendar year and to send thereports of these inspections to the Board of Secondary Education. Each report should contain i definite recommendation as to whether or not the school should continue to be permitted to present candidate at the Matriculation Examination. He is required to inspect annually a certain number of Middle and Primary Schools in order to test the work of his sub-ordinate inspecting officers."[466]

The Inspector is responsible for ensuring that the departmental rules are adhered to and that the curricula are strictly followed.[467] He is the agent for the administration of grants to recognized schools, under

---

461 Ibid
462 Report on the Public Instruction in Bengal, 1842-43, p. 7
463 Ibid
464 Ibid
465 Government of Orissa, Orissa Education code, Article 31, p. 14
466 Ibid
467 Ibid, Article 33, page 15

private management.[468] When inspecting an aided school he is required to see that the conditions attached to the grant are fully carried out, that the accounts are correctly kept, departmental regulations are strictly followed and discipline properly maintained. He is empowered to recommend to the school authorities the dismissal or removal of any teacher with whose work he is dissatisfied or whose presence in the staff he considers undesirable, and to make such other recommendations with regard to the staff of the school, the constitution of the Managing Committee, the provision of suitable buildings, equipment etc. as may seem to him necessary. It the Inspector finds any infringement of the conditions of the grant, or if there is any unwillingness or unwarrantable delay on the part of the school authorities in giving effect to his recommendations he is empowered to suspend the payment of the grant. The Inspector has powers, even to withdraw the grants.[469] Even in case of aided schools he should require a "certain minimum of efficiency" and can recommend withdrawal of recognition.[470]

In addition, the Inspector has to maintain liaison with the District Magistrate and Revenue Divisional Commissioner. He is expected to fully cooperate and to participate in the activities of the Board of Secondary Education, Orissa of which he is an ex-officio member.

The powers of the Inspectors are too sweeping and very often of a delicate nature. The Inspectors could afford to be 'dictators' when the teachers were meek and mild and the teaching profession was not well organized. With the emergence of a conscious professional teaching corps and increasingly politically-oriented Managing Committees of the private schools, the Inspector finds himself in a veritable predicament. There are 7128 full fledged recognized High Schools as on 31.03.2007 in the State of Orissa to be inspected by 19 Inspectors of Schools. This

---

468 Ibid, Article 34, Page 15

469 Ibid

470 Narendra Deva Committee (Report of the Primary and Secondary Education committee, Government of United Provinces) 1939

means each Inspector has to look after more than 375 high schools on an average. What wonder "if the office swallows up the man!"[471]

Even Dr. S. N. Mukherjee writes that, "the first and foremost responsibilities of an Inspector are his executive functions and that secondly he is a professional leader."[472]The Study Group on Inspection and Supervision pointed out that "the deadwood of non-academic and para-academic work was corroding the efficiency of the Inspector".[473]

EVOLUTION OF THE INSPECTORATES OF SCHOOLS OF ORISSA

By 1936-37, there was an Inspector of Schools for North Orissa and a District Education Officer for South Orissa. There were District Inspectors for the districts of Cuttack, Puri, Balasore and Sambalpur. There were 6 Deputy Inspectors of Schools, 50 Sub-Inspectors of Schools in North Orissa and 9 Sub-Inspectors of Schools and 16 Junior-grade Sub-Inspectors in South Orissa. There was an Inspectress of Schools, Orissa in Class I of Orissa Education Service; a District Inspectress of Schools North Orissa, and Deputy Inspectress of Schools for Ganjam and Koraput districts. The Special Inspecting Officer were — Inspector of Sanskrit Schools, special Inspecting Officer for Muhammadan Education, Inspector of Student Residence, Inspecting Moulvi, Senior Special Inspecting Officer for Depressed Classes for North Orissa, Junior Special Inspecting Officer for Depressed Classes, South Orissa,[474]

Consequent on the merger of the Feudatory States with Orissa, the post of an Inspector of Schools, Western Circle was created in 1947-48. The post of the Organizer of Basic Education was created for the development of Basic Education in Orissa. The number of the

---

471 S. N. Mukherjee, Secondary School Administration, 1959, p. 52

472 NCERT, Report of the Study Group on Supervision and Inspection, p. 6

473 Progress of Education in Orissa, 1942-43 p.14-15

474 Progress of Education in Orissa,1 947-48, p. 10

posts of District Inspectors increased to 7 and the number of Deputy Inspectressess of Schools increased to 3 by 1947-48.[475] The post of Adult (Social) Education Officer in Class I of the Orissa Education Service was created with effect from the 1st July, 1949 to organize the Adult (Social) Education Scheme in Orissa. The number of District Inspector of Schools increased to 13 and a District Inspector was appointed for every district by 1949-50.[476]

In 1951-52, there were 3 Inspectors of Schools, one Organizer of Basic Education, one Adult (Social) Education Officers, 13 District Inspectors of Schools, 24 Deputy Inspectors and 185 Sub-Inspectors of Schools in the Men's Branch. There was oneInspectress of Schools, one District Inspectress of Schools, 2 Deputy Inspectresses Schools and one Inspectress of Physical Education in Women's branch of the Inspectorate. The Special Inspecting Officers were-Superintendent of Sanskrit Studies (one) Assistant Superintendent of Sanskrit Studies (one); Special Inspecting Officer for Mahomedan Education (one); Auditor of Accounts (four); Chief Inspector of physical Education (one); District Organizers of Adult (Social) Education (six); Audio Visual Education Officers (three); Inspecting Moulvi (one).[477] By 1955-56, there was a District Social Education Organizer in each of the 13 districts.[478]

By 1957-58, there were 4 Inspectors of Schools, one Inspectress of Schools and one Adult (Social) Education Officer, in Class-I of the Orissa Education Service. The State was divided into 4 areas for the purpose of educational administration, each being designated as a Circle under the charge of an Inspector of Schools, who was assisted by an Assistant Inspector of Schools. The Inspector inspected all high schoolsfor boys except those attached to Government Colleges

---

475 Progress of Education in Orissa, 1949-50, p. 6
476 Progress of Education in Orissa,1951-52,p.12
477 Progress of Education in Orissa, 1955-56,p.7-8
478 Progress of Education in Orissa,1957-58,p.17

and supervised the work of the District Inspectors of Schools. There were 13 District Inspectors, one in each of the Districts. There were 3 District Inspectresses of Schools. There were 26 Deputy Inspectors of Schools, 30 trained graduate Sub-Inspectors of Schools, 45 trained Intermediate Sub-Inspector of Schools, and 142 trained Matriculate Sub-Inspectors, 9 trained Matriculate Assistant Sub-Inspectors, and 70 Elementary trained Assistant Sub-Inspectors of Schools in Orissa during 1957-58.[479]

Due to the increase in the number of secondary and primary schools, the State was divided into 7 Circles in 1960-61. The Sambalpur-Sundergarh Circle had its headquarters at Sundergarh. The Dhenkanal-Keonjhar Circle had its headquarters at Dhenkanal. Balasore was the headquarters of the Balasore-Mayurbhanj Circle. Cuttack district was a Circle by itself. Puri and Phulbani formed one Circle with headquarters at Puri. Ganjam Circle had its headquarters at Berhampur. The three districts of Koraput, Kalahandi and Bolangir formed one Circle with headquarters at Bolangir.[480]

By 1980, the State was divided into 15 Educational Circles. Every revenue district was a Circle. The Cuttack District was divided into three Circles. There were 56 District Inspectors, one in each of the subdivisions of the State except Jharsuguda. Every sub-division was an Education district (except Jharsuguda which continued to be part of the Sambalpur Educational district). There were 36 Deputy Inspectors, 5Deputy Inspectresses and 632 Sub-Inspectors of Schools in the State of Orissa. Table 1 depicts the position of the Inspectorate in Orissa in 1980.

---

479 Progress of Education in Orissa,!958-59,p.l0
480 Progress of Education in Orissa, 1958-59,p.l0

TABLE 13.4.1

Inspectorate of Orissa at a Glance, 1980

SI. No.	Revenue Dist.	Number of Inspectors	Number of District Inspector of School	Number of Deputy Inspectors of Schools	Number of Deputy Inspectresses of Schools	Number of Sub-Inspectors of Schools
1.	Cuttack	3	7	6	...	105
2.	Puri	1	5	4	....	55
3.	Balasore	1	4	5	...	47
4.	Sambalpur	1	6	4	...	54
5.	Ganjam	1	4	3	...	63
6.	Bolangir	1	4	1	...	36
7.	Keonjhar	1	3	1	...	27
8.	Sundergarh	1	3	2	...	29
9.	Dhenkanal	1	4	5	1	40
10.	Kalahandi	1	3	1	1	34
11.	Koraput	1	6	1	1	62
12.	Mayurbhanj	1	4	1	1	48
13.	Phulbani	1	3	2	1	32
	Orissa	15	56	36	5	632

Note: Out of the 56 District Inspectors, 5 posts were reserved for women.

There are 19 Inspectors of Schools in the State of Orissa (2007). The State is divided into 19 Educational Circle and each circle is headed by an Inspector of Schools who belongs to class I of the Orissa Education Service (School Branch). The administrative jurisdiction of each of the 19 Inspectors has been depicted in table No.13.2.4

TABLE NO. 13.4.2
Administration Jurisdiction of the Inspectors of Schools of Orissa
(December, 2007)

Sl. No	Name of the Educational Circle	Headquarters	Jurisdiction	Area Sq. Kms.	Population (2001) Population	No. of High Schools (2005)
1	Jeypore	Jeypore, Distt. Koraput	(a) Jeypore sub-division of the Koraput District (b) Nabarangpur District (c) Malkangiri District	13,741	21,00,000+	160
2	Koraput	Koraput,	(a) Koraput subdivision of Koraput District (b) Rayagada District	13,521	14,21,000+	97
3	Ganjam	Berhampur Dist. Ganjam	(a) Ganjam District (b) Gajapati District	12,531	36,79,472	552
4	Phulbani	Phulbani Dist. Kandhamal	(a) Kandhomal District (b) Boudh District	1,119	10,21,573	142
5	Kalahandi	Bhawanipatna Dist.Kalahandi	(a) Kalahandi District (b) Nuapada District	11,772	18,79,029	358
6	Bolangir	Bolangir	(a) Bolangir District (b) Sonepur District	8,912	18,79,584	352
7	Sambalpur	Sambalpur	(a) Sambalpur District (b) Bargarh District (c) Jharsuguda District (d) Deogarh District	17,515	30,65,900	545
8	Sundargarh	Sundargarh	(a) Sundargarh District	9,712	18,30,673	310
9	Mayurbhanj	Baripada, Dist. Mayurbhanj	(a) Mayurbhanj District	10,418	22,23,456	475
10	Keonjhar	Keonjhar.,	(a) Keonjhar District	8,303	15,61,990	441
11	Dhenkanal	Dhenkanal,	(a) Dhenkanal District (b) Angul District	10,827	22,06,881	464
12	Balasore	Balasore,	(a) Balasore District	3,806	2,24,508	471
13	Bhadrak	Bhadrak,	(a) Bhadrak District	2,505	13,33,749	325
14	Jajpur	Jajpur	(a) Jajpur District	2,899	16,24,341	392
15.	Jagatsinghpur	Jagatsinghpur,	(a) Jagatsinghpur District	1,688	10,37,629	258
16.	Kendrapara	Kendrapara,	(a) Kendrapara District	2,644	13,02,005	326

Sl. No	Name of the Educational Circle	Headquarters	Jurisdiction	Area Sq. Kms.	Population (2001) Population	No. of High Schools (2005)
17.	Cuttack	Cuttack,	(a) Cuttack District	3,932	23,41,094	448
18.	Khurda	Khurda,	(a) Khurda District (b) Nayagarh District	6,603	17,41,991	440
19.	Puri	Puri, Dist. Puri	(a) Puri District	3,479	15,02,682	264
19.	Circles		30 Revenue Districts	1,55,707	3,68,04,682	6820

Area-wise the Sambalpur Educational Circle which comprises of the revenue districts of Bargarh, Deogarh, Jharsuguda and Sambalpur with an area of 17,515 sq.Km. is the largest circle. The educational circles of Jeypore (13,741 sq. kms.), Koraput (13,521 sq. kms.) Ganjam (12,531 sq. kms.), Kalahandi (11,772 sq. kms.), Dhenkanal (10,827 sq kms.) and Mayurbhanj (10,418 sq kms.) are mega circle. The logistics of administration in these districts are daunting.

The Education Circles of Ganjam with 552 high schools and Sambalpur with 545 high schools are almost unmanageable. It is not possible to inspect a high school once in every two years in the educational circles of Ganjam, Sambalpur, Balasore (471), Dhenkanal (464), Mayurbhanj (475), Cuttack (448), Keonjhar (411) and Khurda (440).

The special Inspecting Officer for Muhammadan Studies and the Superintendent of Sanskrit Studies who are located in the Directorate of Secondary Education, Orissa, Bhubaneswar inspect schools belonging to their assigned areas i.e. Madrasas, Maktabs and Sanskrit tolls.

There are four (4) Inspectors of Schools under the Scheduled Caste and Scheduled Tribes Development Department with offices at Koraput, Berhampur, Cuttack and Sambalpur who inspect the special secondary schools i.e. Government high schools under the S. C. & S. T. Development Department.

The subject experts of the Board of Secondary Education, Orissa visit the schools and render pedagogic assistance.

The Organogram of an Inspectorate of Schools (2007) is provided below.

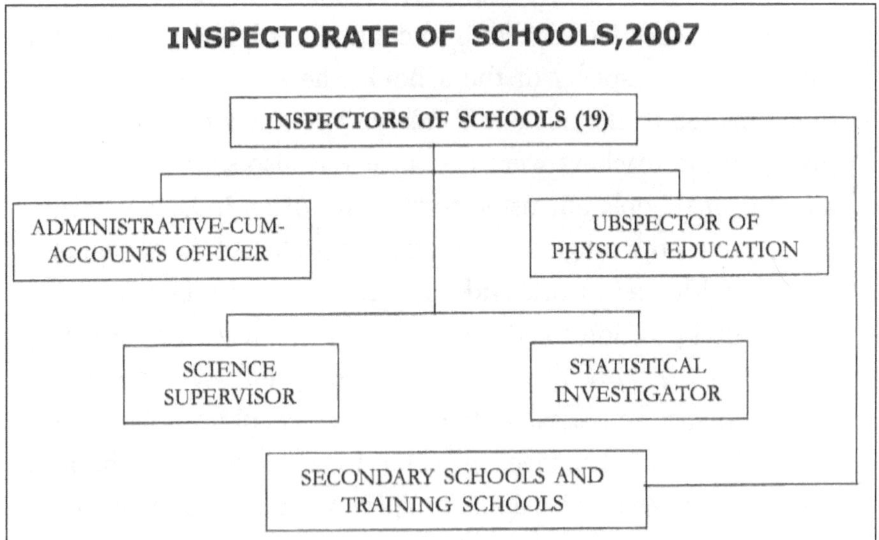

The Inspectorate is breaking down under the pressure of the secondary schools. Anurgent reorganization of the inspectorates is unavoidable. But the Directors of Education and the Government remains blissfully happy as long as there are no major problems. The absolute lack of academic vision is clearly evident from the near collapse situation of the Inspectorates. Further, the total separation of the elementary School Inspectorate from that of the secondary system is a short sighted step. Inspectorate for the "*7 to XII schools' needs* to be conceptualized and implemented.

CONCLUSION

Criticisms against the Inspectorates of Schools are as old as the Inspectorate itself. It is permanently under-staffed and has never been able to keep pace with the rapid expansion of education. Two serious drawbacks to its smooth functioning are its pre-occupation with file work and the incessantly increasing number of meetings that he is expected to attend. The Secondary Education Commission (1953) described *e* defects in these words:

"It was pointed out that inspections were perfunctory, that the time spent by the Inspector at any particular place was insufficient, that the greatest part of this time was taken up by routine work like checking accounts and looking into the administrative aspects of the school. There was not enough time devoted to the academic side and contacts between the Inspectorand teachers were casual. It was also stated that the number of schools entrusted to the care of an Inspector was too large and the range too wide for him to be able to acquaint himself with their work and appreciate their problems; nor was he in a position to advise and guide the teaching staff in improving the work of the school. It occasionally happened that the Inspector instead of being, the friend, philosopher and guide of the school behaves in such critical and unsympathetic way that his visit was looked upon with some degree of apprehension if not resentment" (P. 149)

After the lapse of more than half a century from the date of publication of this report, the remarks resoundingly seem to be too true even to-day in 2007. The duties of the Inspector need to be redefined. The job-chart needs to be critically scrutinized. The work relating to accounts and legal matters may be delegated to designated specialists of the fields. It should be adequately strengthened to do justice to the job assigned to it. Compulsory rota of inspection may be abandoned and the system adopted by the Office for Standards in Education (OFSTED) of U. K. may be followed. They should assist in the cross-fertilization of educational ideas and in conducting inservice training programmes. They should be encouraged to bring out departmental publications and production of professional literature. The operational procedures need to be urgendy overhauled and streamlined. As it is the quality-control sub-system of the education system; and can be neglected at the cost of grave dangers. A good inspectorate is essential to ensure the efficient and effective functioning of the schools.

CHAPTER-14

NATIONAL EDUCATIONAL POLICY 2020 AND SECONDARY EDUCATION

Macalay's Minutes of 1835 approved by Willium Bentinck totally changed the idea of what is education and what is not only English education was given extraordinary importance and indigenous education conducted through the various local languages of India; and the classical Sanskrit knowledge was devalued. English education provided the passport to all the governmental jobs to Indians with the security provided. Secondary education also provided the possibility of transiting from the primary school to higher education. Secondary education not only provided clerical jobs but also opened the doors of higher education.

In 2014, the Bharatiya Janata Party got a thumping majority of seats in parliament, and was in a firm position to implement education of its own choice. Nationalism, cleanliness and skill development were the most important features of the educational system the party desired. The congress party was ruling India from 1947 to 2014. Mr. Narendra Damodardas Modi emerged as the tallest figure with a clear vision. The minority religious groups were blackmailing the previous government and had their say in every aspect of education.

There were certain fundamental administrative reorganisation viz...

- The Directorate of Higher Secondary Education to oversee all the Higher Secondary Schools or Junior college.
- The Higher Secondary Education was transferred from the department of High Education, Odisha to the school and Mass Education Department in the year 2016.

The Teacher Training Institute providing B. Ed, M. Ed were transferred from School and Mass Education Department to the Higher Education Department because they were providing post graduate professional education affiliated to the universities. In 2016, the Directorate of Higher Secondary Education was created to oversee the higher secondary sector of education.

The organogram below depicts the state level administrative structure of the Department of School and Mass Education of Govt. of Odisha.

ORGANOGRAM OF DEPARTMENT OF SCHOOL AND MASS EDUCATION

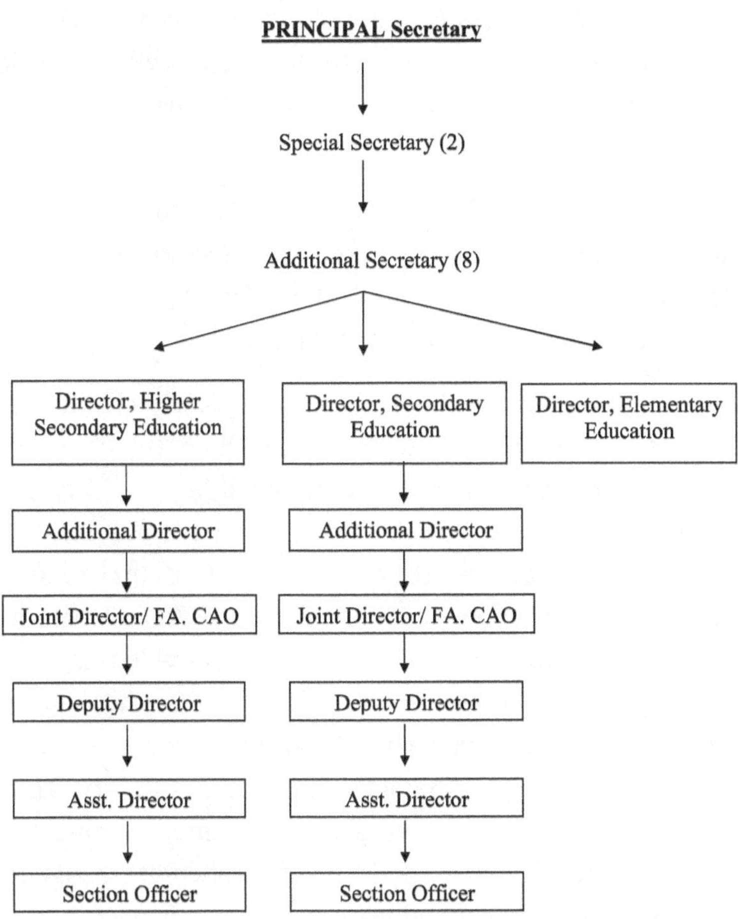

The above organgram depicts the administrative struction of the School and Mass Education which controls all types of secondary and higher secondary schools of Odisha. Right from the days of the establishment of the Directorate of Public Instruction of the Bengal Presidency in 1855 of which north Orissa was a part (the 24 feudatory states excepted), the secondary schools of South Orissa, i.e. districts of Ganjam, Gajapati, Koraput, Nabarangpur, Raygada amd Malkangiri were under the administrative control of the Madras Presidency. North Orissa at that time consisted of Balasore, Bhadrak, Cuttack, Kendrapara, Jagatsinghpur, Jajpur, Puri, Khordha, Angul, Kandhamal districts.

There was only one Director of Public Instruction in Orissa who was looking after the higher education, secondary education and primary education. As time progressed, due to the heavy workload, this directorate was bifurcated into two; Director of Higher Education and Directorate school education in the year 1968.

This system was going on till 1983, when the Directorate of Elementary and Adult Education was created. In the year 1988, the Adult Education nomenclature was eliminated and the Directorate of Elementary Education was created which continues till today.

The different stages of education were very clearly elucidated in the Hadow Report of 1926 prior to which no clear cut concept of the different stages of education was absent. The Report of the consultative Committee of the Board of Education called the Education of the Adolescent greatly influenced the secondary school curriculum and the future education of the adolescent in England and Wales? (International Dictionary of Education-page 157). This report provided clarity relating to the different stages of education- primary, secondary and tertiary. He went on to describe primary education as necessity; secondary education as a comfort; and higher education as a luxury. The Hunta Commission (1882) stated that the government should provide primary education only and the entire governmental expenditure on education will be limited to this stage of education.

If the Indian people want to have secondary and higher education, it is they who should fund it.

After India attained independence in 1947 the constitution was formulated in which it clearly, stated that the government is bound to provide free compulsory education upto the age 14; i.e. class VIII.

The Kastrirangam Committee Report of 2020 stated that the state must provide preschool education of three years; and two years of education of literacy and numercy only for children of classes I & II, further this report stated that under the Right to Education form the age of three to eighteen years by the state. This committee suggested the curricular and pedagogical structure should be 5+3+3+4.

To administer the fifteen years of school education i.e. three years of pre-school education + two years of fundamental literacy and numercy + three years of primary education + three years of elementary education + four years of secondary education, the district level structure in Odisha is fully equipped. The District Level structural changes in school education were made in the year 2016 for proper implementation of the NEP 2020. The following organogram depict the clear structure at the district level.

ORGANOGRAM

District/Block Level Administrative structure of Odisha

DISTRICT EDUCATION OFFICER(DEO)

↓

Additional District Education Office/District Project Co-ordinator(ADEO)

↓

Block Education Officer (BEO)

↓

Asst. Block Education Officer/Block Cluster Resource Centre Co-ordinator

↓

Cluster Resource Centre Co-ordinator

The above organogram depicting the district level responsibilities has delegated accountability up to the lowest level of educational administration. The inspection of the total school system, right from the higher secondary level to the lowest level of school education is being shared by different levels of officers. Educational administration is being properly streamlined.

The NEP 2020 envisages a paradigm shift in the entire education system in India. The most important points have been high listed which will the system of education in the school level, more so at the four years of secondary stage.

(Source: National Education Policy 2020; Ministry of Human Resources Development, Government of India, P.P-11-17)

Paedagogic changes suggested in NEP – 2020:

Major reforms have been suggested by the National Education Policy 2020 which are elaborated briefly in the following discussion.

- "The secondary stage will comprise of four years of multidisciplinary study, building on the subject oriented pedagogical and curricular style of the middle stage, but with greater depth, greater critical thinking, and greater attention of life aspirations and greater flexibility and student choice of subjects. In particular students would continue to have option of exiting after Grade 10 and re-entering the next phase to pursue vocational or any other courses available in Grades 11-12, including at a more specialised school, if so desired."

- "Curriculum content will be reduced in each subject to its core essentials, to make space for critical thinking and more holistic, inquiry based, discussion based and analysis based bearing. The mendated content will focus on key concepts ideas, applications and problem solving. Teaching and learning will be conducted in a more interactive manner, questions will be encouraged and classroom sessions will regularly contain more fun, creative, collaborative and exploratory activities for students for deeper and more experiential learning,"

- "Art – integration is a cross-curricular pedagogical approach that utilizes various aspects and forms of art and culture as the basis of learning of concepts across subjects. As a part of the thrust on experiential learning, art-integrated education will be in classroom transactions not only for creating joyful classrooms but also for imbibing the Indian ethos through integration in Indian art and culture in the teaching and learning process at every level. This art-integrated approach will strengthen the linkages between education and culture."

- "Sports- integration is another cross curricular pedagogical approach that utilizes physical activities including indigenous sports in pedagogical practices to help in developing skills such as collaboration, self-initiative, self-direction, self discipline, teamwork, responsibility, citizenship etc. Sports integrated learning will be undertaken in classroom transactions to help students adopt fitness as a lifelong attitude and to achieve the related life skills along with the levels of fitness as envisaged in the fit India movement. The need to integrate sports in education is well recognised as it serves to foster holistic development by promoting physical and psychological well being while also enhancing cognitive abilities."

- "Students will be given increased flexibility and choice of subjects to study, particularly in secondary school including subjects in physical education, the arts and crafts and vocational skills. So that they can design their own paths of study and life plans. Holistic development and a wide choice of subjects and courses year to year will be new distinguishing feature of secondary school education."

- "All efforts will be made in preparing high quality bilingual textbooks and teaching –learning materials for science and mathematics. So that students are enabled to think and speak about the two subjects both in their home language/mother tongue and English."

- "Concerted curricular and pedagogical initiatives including the introduction of contemporary subjects such as Artificial Intelligence, Design Thinking, Holistic Health, Organic Living, Environmental Education, Global Citizenship Education (GCED) etc at relevant stages will be undertaken to develop these various important skills in students at all levels."

- "It is recognized that mathematics and mathematical thinking will be very important for India's future and India's leadership role in the numerous upcoming fields and professions that will involve artificial intelligence, machine learning and data sciences etc. Thus, mathematics and computational thinking will be given increased emphasis throughout the school years, starting with the fundamental stage, through a variety of innovative methods including the regular use of puzzles and games that make mathematical thinking more enjoyable and engaging. Activities involving coding will be introduced in middle stage.

- "Students will be taught at a young age the importance of "doing what's right" and will be give a logical framework for making ethical decisions. In later years this would then be expanded along themes of cheating, violence, plagiarism, littering, tolerance, equality, empathy etc; with a view to enabling children to embrace moral/ethical issues from multiple perspectives and use ethical practices in all work......."

- Concerted efforts, through suitable changes in curriculum and pedagogy, will be made by NCERT, SCERTs. Schools and educators to significantly reduce the weight of school bags and textbooks.

CHAPTER-15

QUEST FOR QUALITY IN SECONDARY EDUCATION

HIGHLIGHTS

- Introduction to Quality of Secondary Education
- Instructional Effectiveness
- Teacher's Role
- Insights from Canada
- Inspiration from Cuba
- Finland's Fineness Strategies
- Korea's Futuristic Approach
- What India should do?

Quality, it is alleged, is going down due to unprecedented quantitative expansion of secondary education. There is general dissatisfaction and the common man feels that he is given a raw deal. Elite secondary schools have sprung up in urban areas, mostly. The urban-rural divide is glaringly evident. Even in case of government secondary schools those in the urban are well-staffed and well equipped; and those in the rural areas are under-nourished neglected ones. The quality of the secondary schools under the management of the Department of Scheduled Castes and Scheduled Tribes Development is in no way better. Good education for the urbanites and poor-quality education for the rural masses is a politically expedient option as the urban people are highly vocal and the rural people are the mute millions. Quality secondary education is the right of every adolescent irrespective of caste, creed, colour, gender and place of residence.

In 1973, the UNESCO Institute for Education, Hamburg after a critical scrutiny of secondary education scenario in the various countries of the world remarked — "Criteria for various qualities in education, e.g. more or less creative, are far fromsatisfactory beyond a limited context...."

The search for quality has continued to haunt educationists. The 'Total Quality Management' movement is already yielding high dividends in the industrial sector. Service sectors including education were frantically designing various approaches to augment quality. The EFA Global Monitoring Report 2005 focuses its attention on "The Quality Imperatives". It greatly helps us to have a conceptual framework relating to quality parameters of education.

Quality of education has not attracted focused attention. Specific mention and needed elaboration are absent in most of the policy documents relating to education. The POA,1986 is virtually silent regarding this aspect and failed to provide a detailed roadmap to achieve quality in secondary education. The quality of the impersonal institution i.e. the secondary school is sometimes alluded to. The quality aspects of the students, teachers, heads, supervisors and policy-makers are silently skipped. The magnetic attraction of quality alone would arouse the stakeholders (parents, community, the managers etc.) to evince increased interest towards high schools. Policy-makers, bureaucrats and Inspecting Officers are satisfied with the stupor of statistical satisfaction. It is tangible, concrete and definite. They are not prepared to either address the quality issue or to promote it. Top educationists are at the stage of 'concrete thinking', and have not yet attained the maturity to handle abstraction like quality.

'Learning To Be', (the UNESCO document), stated emphatically that:

> "Improving the quality of education would require systems in which the principles of scientific development and modernization could be learned in ways that respected learners' socio-cultural contexts."

"Learning: The Treasure within" reiterated it through "The Four Pillars of Learning." Quality must provide the basic information and the needed feedback for improvement. The main elements of quality regarding which there is a lot of consensus are:

- Learners' characteristics
- Context of education
- Enabling Inputs
- Outcomes

Quality of secondary education on the basis of research findings is advocated to be important because; there is a high correlation between good secondary education and future learning. It accelerates societal development. It augments a better cultural life. The following conclusions relating to "Quality" are based on research findings:

- Achievement studies really do not reflect the quality.
- The improvement in achievement over a period of time remains unexplained as the causative factors are not well documented for inter-tempered comparisons.

Quality education is closely interlinked to instructional effectiveness, which depends upon:

- Aptitude: If the students love a subject they learn it better.
- Opportunity to learn depends upon the availability of time for learning.
- Perseverance or willingness to learn.
- Quality of Instruction: Sub-standard teaching demands more time to learn.
- Ability to understand depends upon linguistic competence.
- Teachers who aspire for better results do obtain them.

Determinants of Effective Teaching are:

- *Relevance:* It is congruence between teaching, learning and evaluation.
- *Time utilisation* in major curricular areas.
- *Structured teaching.*
- *Task-oriented* classroom *climate.*
- Thorough *content-knowledge* of the teachers.

Fundamental rethinking of the role of secondary education as an indispensable link in the total spectrum of education and its centrality in re-engineering the entire educational system needs to be reali2ed. The cascading effect of universalisation ofelementary education is generating the demand for universal secondary education. It is the education of the adolescents who have a critical role in a society that is fast changing. According to the World Education Forum of Dakar, "Secondary education is the fastest growing sector of formal education'. Attrition attends expansion; and is an index of systemic failure. Access must be assured and equity must be ensured for all.

It is the teacher who is the key player in the quality game. Maclean had aptly averred:

"Countries believe that teachers are the corner-stone of educational development and that (as the Delor's Report put

it) 'good schools require good teachers'. Teachers are at the forefront of the process of educational reforms, since the quality and effectiveness of any educational system ultimately depends on the quality and nature of the interaction that occurs between learners and their teachers. A major problem that exists in many countries concerns attracting the most suitable, talented people into secondary school teaching, since those who have the qualifications and qualities to become good secondary school teachers are precisely the ones who are most in demand by other industries, as they are likely to be university graduates or to have other post-secondary qualifications. To enable the quantitative expansion and qualitative improvement of secondary education to occur, there is a demand for greater numbers of high quality recruits to the teaching profession. Much more needs to be done to provide incentives to attract (and keep) suitable individuals in secondary school teaching."
(Prospects, XXXI,2001 p.41)

In India, *contract-teachers* on a paltry consolidated pay without any security of service and practically zero chances of promotions can hardly be expected to provide quality secondary education. Quality of secondary education has improved significantly in many countries due to their sustained systematic efforts over long periods of time. Quality cannot be achieved overnight through quick-fix approaches, academic slogans and administrative gimmicks.

Canada is a big country to the north of the USA. It is the only country which has provided each and every primary school with computers and internet-connectivity. It has consistency been trying to improve its secondary education system by closely monitoring excellence and under-performance of every student, every school, every district and every province. Its strategies of tracking and monitoring performance are worth emulating. Appropriate remedial action is initiated wherever under-performance is detected. Excellence is recognized and rewarded. A well developed 'support system' operates. Pro-active

''*School Development Teams'* consisting of specialists are at work. There is evident great respect for teachers; and they are not under estimated or slighted as in India.

Cuba is an island country. It has succeeded in providing quality secondary education though it is not a highly rich country. It has taken up quality upgradation as a necessary requirement of the post-war expansion programme. It accorded high recognition to such co-scholastic areas like sports, health education, personality development and artistic development, and needless to say, these features have a magnetic attraction for the adolescents. Once the students fall in love with the school, achievement automatically takes place. Quality quietly pervades the school-climate. Competitions of self-improvement further accelerate this process. Indian academic culture has always kept the co-scholastic activities at the periphery; and at no point of time have they been accorded rightful respect and recognition. Respect for teachers is another important factor augmenting quality of secondary education.

Finland is one of the cold Scandinavian countries of north Europe. It believes that quality education is not really expensive. The money invested in improving the quality of the secondary schools is received back as dividends of better tertiary education and higher levels of productivity. It is conscious that it cannot spend lavishly likeher neighbours Sweden and Norway. So, it has adopted a policy of continuous and consistent expenditure. "One thing at a time and that done well" is its guiding motto. Combination of high performance and moderate expenditure single out Finland as an acceptable role-model for the developing countries. It has wonderfully succeeded in ensuring high academic performance through moderate expenditure. It ensures the minimization of disparities in achievements among students. All students have the capability to perform well if the requisite congenial academic environment can be provided. Gross disparities need to be eliminated. Uniform academic progress of a huge cohort is the best index of quality education.

South Korea is a leaping industrial tiger of Asia. Compared to its size and population its bold presence is really enviable. The secret of the success of South Korea lies in its excellent secondary and higher education system. To finance education, it introduced an *'Education TcdS.* It shifted its priority from higher enrolment figures to quality performance parameters. Students are constantly reminded of their own future and their future role in building their country. This futuristic awareness makes the Korean students serious and scholarly. The skill standards of the teachers are constantly and continuously upgraded through prolonged pre and in-service teacher training. Distance education is utilized as an effective mode to upgrade the knowledge of the teachers and students. ICT is a vibrant reality. Korean Educational Development institute (KEDI) is a unique institute that is ably and efficiently providing robust leadership and guidance to the school system of South Korea.

CONCLUSION

Indian secondary education is facing an unprecedented crisis. Its quality is unable to satisfy the clients. It is generating client's depression and despondency instead of delight. Urgent action to augment quality is an unavoidable imperative. Suggestions for improvement are:

- The viability of secondary education should be achieved by consolidating 'secondary' and 'higher secondary' education into one unit. Together they must form one unity and their isolation from one another should be broken. A comprehensive common curriculum should be envisaged and implemented to develop knowledge, skills and personality.
- Revitalization of secondary education should be undertaken on a war-footing. The existing dichotomy of 'general' and 'vocational' streams should be done away with. An 'Integrated Flexible Comprehensive Secondary Education Programmes' needs to be designed and implemented.

- A hierarchically well-articulated support system for secondary education from the district to the national level needs to be created. The NCERT can be the national level agency, the SCERTs as the State-level agencies and district-level support agencies may be located in well-established and reputed training colleges or quality secondary schools.

- School Development Teams need to be constituted at the national, state, district and local levels with eminent educationist as members. Most of them may be retired persons with good track record. The appointments must be viewed more as honorary and less as remunerative. Voluntarism of pedagogic vision, action and monitoring for the particular level must be their mission.

- Excellence and under-performance needs to be carefully and closely monitored as in Canada.

- Continuous, consistent expenditure on quality upgradation of secondary education must be commitment of the Central and State Governments and Zilla Parishads.

- Secondary school teachers must be respected and associated in every activity relating to quality improvement. Para-teachers can never deliver quality.

- State Bureaus of Educational and Vocational Guidance needs to be revived.

- Most importantly, a massive Total Quality Management Movement for Secondary Education needs to be launched. It should spread like wildfire. TQM Movement ultimately holds the master-key to Quality in Secondary Education.

Let us hope Secondary Education would not degenerate into second-rate education. It should be second to none in quality. Its centrality in the total scheme of education needs to be reemphasized. A massive TQM movement would surely infuse quality into it.

Glaring regional imbalances are clearly evident. These regional imbalances need to be corrected, and failure to correct the developmental distances would generate socio-cultural tensions. Secondary education is the right of every child as it is the royal road to higher education, upward mobility and social transformation.

Too much attention had been accorded to quantitative growth to the detriment of qualitative development. The pragmatic recommendations of the Secondary education (Mudaliar) Commission (1952) were not taken seriously. The recommendations of the Indian Education (Kothari) Commission (1966) were grudgingly implemented. Reorganization of secondary education still remains an unfinished agenda. It is time to turn to qualitative development. Secondary education requires a new deal. Vigorous steps to improve its quality need to be undertaken.

National Education Policy – 2020 was formulated under the Chairmanship of Krishnaswamy Kasturirangan, Former Chairman, ISRO. After 34 years the Government of India revisited the Education system of the country. The Prime Minister Shri Narendra Modi, after long deliberation with different stake holders to develop a purely nationalistic Educational System to provide joyful and realistic education to the children of India in 21st century. He appointed a Commision under the Chairmanship of Dr. Krishnaswamy Kasturirangan. It was accepted after two years and was implemented in all the instutions directly under the control of the Government of India. The erstwhile Minstry of Human Resouces reverted back to its original name Ministry of Education. This Commission included pre-school education provided in Anganwadies etc. in the fold of regular Educational System. It is time to turn to qualitative development of School Education. It requires collective effort of all concerned. Vigorours steps to improve its qulity need to be undertaken.

CHRONOLOGY

1757	Lord Clive wins Battle of Plassey and the foundations of the British Empire in India were laid.
1781	Calcutta Madrissa established by Lord Warren Hastings.
1792	Sanskrit College established at Benaras by Jonathan Duncan.
1813	India Bill passed by the British Parliament renewing the Charter of the East India Company for a further period of 20 years with the stipulation that the company should spend 10,000 pounds per annum to promote the native learning of India.
1815	Lord Moira proposes the introduction of Western Education in India.
1816	Hindoo College, Calcutta established. The first window of India to Western Education.
1821	Poona College established by the Peshwa at the instance of Mr. Chaplin, the Resident.
1823	General Committee of Public Instruction constituted by Lord Adam Acting Governor General to oversee all the Government Schools and Colleges.
1835	Macaulay's Minutes on Education advocating English education for Indians approved by Lord William Bentinck, Governor General of India.
1842	Council of Education replaces GCPI.
1844	Inspector of Colleges and Schools appointed.

1854	Wood's Despatch from the Court of Directors of the East India Company clearly outlined the future educational policy to be pursued in India.
1855	Directors of Public Instruction appointed for the Presidencies of Calcutta, Madras and Bombay.
1857	Universities established at Calcutta, Madras and Bombay.
1858	Crown takes over the administration of India from the East India Company after the first uprising for freedom. The Governor General also becomes the Viceroy of India.
1859	Stanley's Despatch reaffirms the policies outlined in the Wood's Despatch of 1854.
1882	Indian Education Commission appointed with Mr. WW. Hunter as its Chairman.
1901	Vernacular System of Education introduced.
1902	Indian Universities Commission appointed.
1904	Indian Policy on Education announced.
1905	Partition of Bengal. Swadeshi Movement. National System of Education visualised.
1911	Partition of Bengal undone.
1912	Capital of India shifted from Calcutta to Delhi. Bihar and Orissa province created on 23 December.
1913	Indian Policy on Education announced.
1914-18	World War I
1917	Calcutta University Commission appointed with Sir Michael E. Sadler as its Chairman.
1919	Montague - Chelmisford Reforms. Education transferred to provincial control.
1919-21	Non-Cooperation Movement launched. National Schools and Azad Schools started as alternatives to English Schools.

1928   Hartog Committee appointed.

1935   India Act, 1935. Education becomes a provincial subject.

1936   Provinces of Orissa and Sind created.

Burma gets separated from India and becomes a separate country.

1937   Zakir Husain Committee outlined the Scheme of Basic Education in accordance with the Gandhian Nationalistic approach to education.

1939   Outbreak of the Second World War.

1942   Quit India Movement.

1944   Post — War Reconstruction Programme (Sargent Report) announced.

1945   Second World War comes to an end.

1947   India attains Independence. Partition takes place.

1948   University Education Commission appointed under the Chairmanship of Dr. S. Radhakrishnan.

1950   India becomes a Republic. Constitution comes into force. Education is included in the 'State List'.

1951   First Five Year Plan launched.

1952   Secondary Education Commission appointed with Dr. Lakshmanswamy Mudaliar as its Chairman.

Community Development Projects inaugurated.

1953   Mudaliar Commission Report published.

1958   First Educational Survey conducted.

1962   NCERT established.

1964   Indian Education Commission appointed with Dr. D.S. Kothari as its Chairman.

1966   Kothari Commission Report published.

1968   National Policy on Education, 1968 announced endorsing almost all the recommendations of the Indian Education Commissions (1964-1966) Report.

1976	EDUCATION shifted from the 'State List' to the 'Concurrent List' through the 42nd Amendment to the Constitution.

1976   EDUCATION shifted from the 'State List' to the 'Concurrent List' through the 42nd Amendment to the Constitution.

1985   Task force appointed by Government of India submits its report entitled *Challenge of Education.*

1986   *National Policy on Education,* 1986 and its accompanying *Programme of Action,* 1986 announced.

1990   Acharya Ramamurti Review Committee submits its report.

1991   Janardhan Reddy Committee reviewed the Ramamurti Review Committee report; and its recommendations were endorsed by the Central Advisory Board of Education.

1992   National Policy on Education, 1986 and POA, 1986 reformulated.

2000   National Curriculum Framework published.

2002   Sixth Educational Survey conducted.

2005   National Curriculum Framework: 2005.

2006   Universalization of Secondary Education suggested by Hon'ble Minister Human Resources Development, Government of India in the Indian Parliament.

2020   NEP 2020 was formulated under the Chairmanship of Krishnaswamiy Kasturirangan, former Chairman, ISRO.

ABBREVIATIONS AND ACRONYMS

A.LCT.E.	All India Council of Technical Education
Asst.	Assistant
B.T.	Bachelor of Teaching alsoBasic Training
B.S.E.	Board of Secondary Education
B.C.T.M.	Bachelor of Construction Technology Management
B.F.Sc.	Bachelor of Fisheries Science
B.F.C.	Basic Foundation Course
B.O.P.T.	Board of Practical Training
B.O.A.T.	Board of Apprentice Training
B.V.SC. & A.H.	Bachelor of Veterinary Science and Animal Husbandry
C.A.B.E.	Control Advisory Board of Education
C.T.	Certified Teacher
C.H.S.E.	Council of Higher Secondary Education
C.L.A.S.S.	Computer Literary and Studies in School
C.T.E.	College of Teacher Education
C.S.	Covenanted Servant (of the East India Company)
D.Ed.	Diploma in Education
D.A.	Dearness Allowance
D.E.O.	District Education Officer
D.I.S.	District Inspector of Schools
D.D.P.I.	Deputy Director of Public Instruction
D.D.	Deputy Director
D.H.E.	Director of Higher Education
D.S.E.	Director of Secondary Education

D.E.E.	Director of Elementary Education
D.T.E.	Director of Teacher Education
D.I.E.T.	District Institute of Education and Training
D.R.C.	District Reserve Centre
D.V.E.C.	District Vocational Education Committee
E.C.CE.	Early Childhood Care and Education
Edn.	Education
Esst.	Establishment
E.EA.	Education for All
F.A.	First Arts
G.H.S.V.S.	Government Higher Secondary Vocational Schools
G.J.V.C.	Government Junior Vocational College
G.C.P.I.	General Committee of Public Instruction
Govt.	Government
I.A.	Intermediate of Arts
I. Sc.	Intermediate of Science
I. Com	Intermediate of Commerce
I.A.S.E	Institute of Advanced Study in Education
I.C.S.	Indian Civil Service
I.A.S.	Indian Administrative Service
I.E.S.	Indian Education Service
I.F.S.	Indian Foreign Service
I.G.N.O.U	Indira Gandhi National Open University
J.C.V.E.	Joint Council of Vocational Education
J.D.	Joint Director
H.S.C.	High School Certificate
H.S.S.C	Higher Secondary School Certificate
L.D.	Lower Division
L.T.	Licentiate in Teaching
L.C.	Liaison Officer
L.P.	Lower Primary
L.S.E.S	Lower Subordinate Education Service

L.C.P.I	Local Committee of Public Instruction
M.E. School	Middle English School
M.V. School	Middle Vernacular School
M.C.A.	Master of Computer Applications
M.B.A.	Master of Business Administration
M.T.A.	Master of Travel Administration
M.T.M.	Master of Travel Management
M.I.L.	Modern Indian Language
M.H.R.D.	Ministry of Human Resource Development
M.D.	Doctor of Medicine
N.A.	Not Available
N.P.E.	National Policy on Education
N.C.E.R.T.	National Council of Educational Reserch and Training
N.I.E.P.A	National Institute of Educational Planning and Administration
N.R.T.S.	National Rural Talent Search
N.C.F.	National Curriculum Framework
N.C.T.E.	National Council of Teacher Education
O.A.S.	Orissa Administrative Service
O.E.S.	Orissa Education Service
O.J.E.E.	Orissa Joint Entrance Examination
O.M.R.	Optical Mark Reading
P.P.C.	Pre-Professional Course
P.V.C.	Pre-University Course
P.O.P.	Programme of Action
P.G.D.C.A.	Post Graduate Diploma in Computer Applications
P.S.S.CI.V.E.	Pandit Sundarlal Sharma Control Institute of Vocational
	Education
R.D.	Regional Director
R.O.V.E.	Regional Office of Vocational Education

R.O.S.L.A.	Raising of School Leaving Age
S.L.C.	School Leaving Certificate
S.S.L.C.	Secondary School Leaving Certificate
S.I.	Sub-Inspector
S.O.	Special Officer
S.E.S.	Subordinate Education Service
s.c.	Scheduled Caste
S.T.	Scheduled Tribe
Spl.	Special
S.B.E.V.G.	State Bureau of Educational and Vocational Guidance
S.T. School	Secondary Training School
S.C.E.R.T.	State Council of Educational Research and Training
S.C.O.P.E.	School Computer Programme Everywhere
U.T.	Union Teritory
U.G.C.	University Grants Commission
U.N.I.CE.F.	United Nations International Children's Emergency Fund
UP.	Upper Primary
U.D.	Upper Division
V.E.P.	Vocational Education Programme
N.E.P.	National Education Policy

NATIONAL EDUCATION POLICY 2020

Major Transformational Reforms in Education Sector

Evolution of Education Policy

- University Education Commission (1948-49)
- Secondary Education Commission (1952-53)
- Education Commission (1964-66) under Dr. D.S. Kothari
- National Policy on Education, 1968
- 42nd Constitutional Admendment, 1976-Education in Concurrent List
- National Policy on Education (NPE) (Programme of Action, 1992)
- T.S.R. Subramaniam Committee Report (27th May, 2016)
- Dr. K. Kasturirangan Committee Report (31st May, 2019).

NEP 2020: Consultation Process

- Online: www.mygov.in (26.01.2015 – 31.10.2015)
- Nearly 2.5 lakhs Gram Panchayats, 6600 Blocks, 6000 ULBs, 676 Districts (May-Oct, 2015)
- Draft NEP, 2019 Summary in 22 languages/Audio Book
- Education Dialogue with MPs (AP, Kerala, Telengana, TN, Puducherry, Karnataka & Odisha).
- Special Meeting of CABE (21.09.2019)
- Parliamentary Standing Committee on HRD on07.11.2019

Major Reforms: Higher Education

- 50% Gross Enrolment Ration by 2035
- Holistic and Multidiciplinary Education – Flexibility of Subjects
    - Multiple Entry/Exit
    - UP Programme – 3 or 4 year
    - PG Programe – 1 or 2 year
    - Integrated 5 year Bachelor's/Master's
    - M.Phil to be discontinued
- Credit Transfer and Academic Bank of Credits
- HEIs: Research Intensive/Teaching Intensive Universities and Autonomous Degree Granting Colleges.
- Model Multidisciplinary Education and Research University (MERU) (in or near every District)

Major Reforms: Higher Education

- Graded Autonomy: Academic, Administrative & Financial
- Phasing out Affiliation System in 15 years.
- National Mission on Mentoring
- Independent Board of Governors (Bog)
- Single Regulator for Higher Education (excluding Legal and Medical)
- On-line Self Disclosure based Transparent System for Approval in place of 'Inspections".
- Common Norms for public and private HEIs
    - Private Philanthropic Partnership
    - Fee Fixation within Board Regulatory Framework
- Public Investing in Education Sector to reach 6% of GDP at the earliest

Major Reforms: Higher Education

- National Research Foundation (NRF)
- Internationalisation of Education
- Integration of Vocational, Teacher and Professional Education

- Setting up of New Quality HEIs has been made Easier
- Standalone HRI and Professional Education Institutions will evolve into Multidiciplinary
- Special Education Zone for Disadvantaged Regions
- National Institute for Pali, Persian and Prakrit
- National Educational Technology Forum (NETF)
- MHRD to be renamed as M/o Education

Indian Knowledge Systems, Languages, Culture and Values

- Focus on Literature & Scientific Vocabulary of Indian Languages
- Language Faculty
- Research on languages
- Strengthening National Institutes for promotion of Classical Languages & Literature
- Indian Institute of Translation and Interpretation (IITI)
- Cultural Awareness of our Indian Knowledge Systems
- Promoting Traditional Arts/Lok Vidya
- HEI/School or School Complex to have Artist(s)-in-Residence

Use of Technology

- Use of Technology in
  - Education Planning
  - Teaching, Learning & Assessment
  - Administration & Management
  - Regulation – Self Disclosure & Minimum Human Interface
- Increasing Access for Disadvantaged Groups
- Divyang Friendly Education Software
- e-Content in Regional Languages
- Virtual Labs
- National Education Technology Forum (NETF)
- Digitally Equipping Schools, Teachers and Students

Major Reforms: Schools Education

- Universalization of Early Childhood Care Education (ECCE).
- National Mission on Foundational Literacy and Numeracy
- 5+3+3+4 Curricular and Pedagogical Structure
- Curriculum to integrate 21st Century Skills, Mathematical Thinking and Scientific temper
- No Rigid separation between Arts & Sciences, between Curricular and Extra-Curricular activities, between Vocaional and Academic streams
- Education of Gifted Children
- Gender Inclusion Fund
- KGBVs upto Grade 12
- Reduction in Curriculum to Core Concepts
- Vocational Integration from class 6 onwards.

Major Reforms: School Education

- New National Curriculum Framework for ECE, School, Teachers and Adult Education
- Board Examination will be Low Stakes, Based on knowledge Application.
- Medium of instruction till at least Grade 5, and preferably till Grade 8 and beyond in Home Language/Mother tongue/ Regional Language
- 360 degree Holistic Progress Card of Child
- Tracking Student progress for Achieving Learning Outcomes
- National Assessment Center – PARAKH
- NTS to offer Common Entrance Exam for Admission to HEIs
- National Promotion Policy and Digital Libraries
- Transparent online self disclosure for public oversight and accountability

Outcomes of NEP 2020

- Universalization from ECCE to Secondary Education by 2030, aligning with SDG4
- Attaining Foundation Learning and Numeracy Skills through National Mission by 2025
- 100% GER in Pre-School to Secondary Level by 2030.
- Bring Back 2 CR out of School Children
- Teachers to be prepared for assessment reforms by 2023
- Inclusive & Equitable Education System by 2030
- Board Exams to test core concepts and application of knowledge
- Every child will come out of School adopt in at least one skill
- Common standards of Learning in public & private schools

National Institute for Pali, Persian and Prakrit

National Education Technology Forum (NETF)

MHRD to be renamed as M/s Ecuation

Focus on Literature and Scientific Vocabulay of Indian Languages